*On Keynesian Economics
and the Economics of Keynes*

On Keynesian Economics and the Economics of Keynes

A STUDY IN MONETARY THEORY

· AXEL LEIJONHUFVUD

New York

OXFORD UNIVERSITY PRESS

London 1968 Toronto

Copyright © 1966, 1968 by Oxford University Press, Inc.
Library of Congress Catalogue Card Number: 68-29721
Printed in the United States of America

TO MY PARENTS
ERIK G. AND HELENE LEIJONHUFVUD

ACKNOWLEDGMENTS

The greatest debt should be put foremost. Mine is to my wife, Märta, for her encouragement and patience over the years and particularly the four years during which this study has been undertaken. Our children, Carl and Gabriella, helped many times to dispel the black moods of an author whose work often failed to be "in progress"—and I am grateful to them also.

The responsibility for what follows rests with the author. But my intellectual debts are many and, unfortunately, larger than they appear, being more closely related to input than output. In deciding to concentrate my graduate studies in the field of monetary theory, I was first influenced by Professor James G. Witte, Jr., then of the University of Pittsburgh. Professor Franco Modigliani's courses at Northwestern University gave me the definitive impetus in this direction. I owe a great debt, both personal and intellectual, to Professor Meyer L. Burstein for countless long and stimulating sessions on a wide variety of monetary topics. Since I learned so much of his work by word-of-mouth, the footnote references in the text give a most inadequate reflection of his influence. Later correspondence with Professors Burstein and Robert Clower has aided me greatly. I have benefited from conversations with many friends and colleagues who have given freely of their time. In addition to those already named, I would like to mention Drs. Walter S. Salant and Sam B. Chase at Brookings, and Professors Armen Alchian, Jack Hirshleifer, and Earl Thompson at UCLA. An earlier version of this study was my doctoral dissertation at Northwestern. My dissertation committee, of which Professors Clower and Robert H. Strotz remained the permanent members over the years, was both patient and helpful in tolerating the various permutations of subject matter which the thesis underwent.

Through the generosity of Professor Werner Z. Hirsch, as Director of the UCLA Institute of Government and Public Affairs, I was given the opportunity to circulate the thesis in mimeographed form. In editing and rewriting the manuscript for publication, I have benefited from the encouragement and comments of several readers of the thesis. I am especially grateful to Professors Alchian and Milton Friedman, both of whom made margin notes in the earlier version that have been most helpful in preparing this one. A series of letters from Meyer Burstein saved me from a major error of judgment. In trying to pay heed to a great many comments, unfortunately, I have failed on the point on which the advice was most unanimous—to make this a shorter book.

Since coming to the United States in 1960, I have received financial help towards my graduate studies from the University of Pittsburgh, Northwestern University, and Riddarhusets Löfvenskjöldska fond (Sweden). The work on this study was begun during a year as a Brookings Research Fellow. I am especially grateful to the Brookings Institution, and particularly Dr. Joseph A. Pechman, for letting me freely pursue a "roundabout" program of study not designed to lead to a specified final product by a prescheduled date. The support of the Relm Foundation during the summers of 1967 and 1968 enabled me to rewrite the manuscript and to edit the final version. I also acknowledge financial aid from the Lilly Endowment, Inc., research grant to UCLA for the study of property right and behavior. Miss Margaret Calvo and Miss Muffet Bailey have cheerfully borne the drudgery of typing. Without the help of Michael Carney and Richard Sweeney the Indexes would never have been completed.

A prefatory note: It is well known (we are told by John Masters) that the function of cavalry in battle is to add tone to what would otherwise be an unseemly brawl. The same may be said for the use of mathematics in economic theoretical controversy. This book, unfortunately, will be lamentably pedestrian, so I cannot very well invoke Keynes' apology and ask forgiveness if my controversy is "too keen." I do wish to apologize, however, if the mopping-up operations here essayed appear "unseemly" to the discriminating taste. I have picked my quarrels with those from whom I have learned the most— and often on points that are of only minor significance in their original context. It is only fitting, therefore, that I acknowledge my great debt to those distinguished economists whom I have here quoted only to dispute. I am grateful to the following for their consent to my use of excerpts from their works: Kenneth J. Arrow, Martin J. Bailey, Robert W. Clower, Robert Eisner, William J. Fellner, Milton Friedman, Gottfried Haberler, Alvin H. Hansen, Roy Harrod, Friedrich A. von Hayek, H. Robert Heller, John R. Hicks, William Jaffé, Harry G. Johnson, Reuben A. Kessel, Lawrence R. Klein, Frank H. Knight, Robert E. Kuenne,

Thomas S. Kuhn, Kelvin J. Lancaster, Edmond Malinvaud, David Meiselman, Franco Modigliani, Arthur M. Okun, Don Patinkin, G. B. Richardson, Joan Robinson, Paul A. Samuelson, Robert M. Solow, James Tobin, Jacob Viner, and Leland B. Yeager. I also wish to thank Dr. Mordecai Ezekiel for permission to quote a letter from Keynes to him previously quoted by Professor Klein.

I am particularly indebted to Lord Kahn and Sir Geoffrey Keynes, the executors of Lord Keynes' estate, for permission to quote extensively from Keynes' writings and to Harcourt, Brace and World for permission to use the very large number of excerpts from *A Treatise on Money* and *The General Theory of Employment, Interest and Money.*

Appreciation is expressed to the publishers and/or copyright owners of the following works for permission to use quotes appearing in this book:

Bailey, M. J., *National Income and the Price Level.* New York: McGraw-Hill Book Co., 1962.

Hansen, A. H., *A Guide to Keynes.* New York: McGraw-Hill Book Co., 1953.

Harris, S. E., ed., *The New Economics.* New York: Alfred A. Knopf, Inc., 1950.

Harrod, Roy, *The Life of John Maynard Keynes.* London: Macmillan and Co., Ltd., 1951.

Kessel, R. A., *The Cyclical Behavior of the Term Structure of Interest Rates.* New York: National Bureau of Economic Research, 1965.

Ketchum, M. D. and Kendall, L. T., eds., *Readings in Financial Institutions.* Boston: Houghton Mifflin Co., 1965. By permission of the U.S. Savings and Loan League and the publishers.

Patinkin, Don, *Money, Interest, and Prices,* 2nd ed. New York: Harper & Row, 1965.

Pigou, A. C., *Theory of Unemployment.* London: Macmillan and Co., Ltd., 1933.

Robinson, Joan, *Economic Philosophy.* London and Chicago: C. A. Watts and Co., Ltd., and Aldine Publishing Co., 1963.

Samuelson, Paul A., *Foundations of Economic Analysis.* Cambridge, Mass.: Harvard University Press. Copyright © 1947 by the President and Fellows of Harvard College.

Schumpeter, J. A., *History of Economic Analysis.* New York: George Allen and Unwin, Ltd., 1954.

Walras, Leon, *Elements of Pure Economics,* trans. by William Jaffé. Homewood, Ill.: Richard D. Irwin, Inc., 1954.

Wiener, Norbert, *The Human Use of Human Beings*. Boston: Houghton Mifflin Co., 1950.

Excerpts from articles originally published in the *American Economic Review* are reprinted by permission of the American Economic Association. Sir Roy Harrod's "Are We Really All Keynesians Now?" has been quoted by permission of *Encounter* magazine. Excerpts from the *Economic Journal* are reprinted by permission of the Royal Economic Society and from *Econometrica* by permission of the Econometric Society. Acknowledgment is also due to the editors of the *Quarterly Journal of Economics*, published by Harvard University Press, the *Review of Economics and Statistics*, and the *Review of Economic Studies*. The International Economic Association and the publisher have given permission to quote from the following:

Hahn, F. H. and Brechling, F. P. R., eds., *The Theory of Interest Rates*. London: Macmillan and Co., Ltd., 1965.

Lutz, F. A. and Hague, D. C., eds., *The Theory of Capital*. London: Macmillan and Co., Ltd., 1961.

The "Resolution on Permissions" of the Association of American University Presses—for which many academic authors must feel truly grateful—has been relied on in quoting from articles appearing in the *Journal of Political Economy* and from the following books:

Abramowitz, *et al.*, *The Allocation of Economic Resources: Essays in Honor of Bernard Francis Haley*. Stanford, California: Stanford University Press, 1959.

Fellner, W. J., *Monetary Policies and Full Employment*. Berkeley and Los Angeles: University of California Press, 1946.

Friedman, M., *A Theory of the Consumption Function*. Princeton, N.J.: Princeton University Press, 1957.

Green, H. A. J., *Aggregation in Economic Analysis*. Princeton, N.J.: Princeton University Press, 1964.

Kuenne, R. E., *The Theory of General Economic Equilibrium*. Princeton, N.J.: Princeton University Press, 1963.

Kuhn, T. S., *The Structure of Scientific Revolutions*. Chicago: University of Chicago Press, 1962.

Simons, H., *Personal Income Taxation*. Chicago: University of Chicago Press, 1938.

In many instances the requests for these permissions went out very late. I want to apologize to the recipients in question and to thank them especially for their prompt and courteous responses.

Los Angeles, California   Axel Leijonhufvud
September 1968

CONTENTS

On Keynesian Economics
and the Economics of Keynes

I·INTRODUCTION

I:1 The New Economics Reconsidered

John Maynard Keynes' *The General Theory of Employment, Interest and Money* [1] signaled a revolution in economic theory and the beginning of "modern" macrotheory. No other economic work in this century has been the subject of anything even approaching the vast outpouring of commentary and criticism that the *General Theory* has received. But in the last five or ten years, theoretical and exegetical interest in the *General Theory* has declined markedly. The long "Keynes and the Classics" debate, devoted to the appraisal of the precise nature and significance of Keynes' innovations, has at last almost petered out. The label "post-Keynesian" attached to much recent theoretical research is symptomatic of the widespread view that the book on the *General Theory* is closed, that the "Keynesian Revolution" is over, and that what was worthwhile in it has been digested and the rest discarded. The *General Theory* has itself become a classic—a work which the active theorist need not consult but in which historians of economic doctrines will have a continuing interest.

---

1. London, 1936. Hereafter referred to as *General Theory*.

Although most economists would probably resist, and many resent, being labeled "Keynesians," almost all would agree that there does exist today a recognizable majority view on the theory of income determination and that the term can reasonably be used to refer to the main outlines of this view. Keynesian economics, in this popular sense, is far from being a homogeneous doctrine. The common denominator, which lends some justification to the identification of a majority school, is the class of models generally used. These short-run, simultaneous equation models have their prototype in the famous, early "Keynes and the Classics" paper by Hicks.[2] The basic analytical framework, which these models have in common, one finds conventionally summarized in most textbooks in the familiar Hicks-Hansen IS-LM apparatus. This framework will hereafter be (not altogether adequately) referred to as "the Income-Expenditure model."

For the majority of economists, this standard income-expenditure model has reached the same position of established orthodoxy as that occupied in the interwar period by the Marshallian economics from which Keynes had to wage such a hard "struggle to escape." The measure of its acceptance has been indicated by Professor Solow:

. . . I think that most economists feel that short-run macroeconomic theory is pretty well in hand. . . . The basic outlines of the dominant theory have not changed in years. All that is left is the trivial job of filling in the empty boxes, and that will not take more than 50 years of concentrated effort at a maximum. . . .[3]

---

2. J. R. Hicks, "Mr. Keynes and the 'Classics': A Suggested Interpretation," *Econometrica*, April, 1937. One should recall that Hicks warned against the uncritical use of his "skeleton apparatus": " . . . it remains a terribly rough and ready sort of affair . . . the concept of 'Income' is worked monstrously hard. . . . Indeed, what [our curves] express is something like a relation between the price-system and the system of interest rates; and you cannot get that into a curve." During the editing of this study I have had the opportunity of reading Professor Hicks' *Critical Essays in Monetary Theory* in page proof. I have been much encouraged by finding myself in substantial agreement with the appraisal of Keynes' contribution contained in that work. (This does not mean, of course, that I can claim Professor Hicks' *approbatur* for the position taken in this study.)

3. R. M. Solow, "Economic Growth and Residential Housing," in M. D. Ketchum and L. T. Kendall, eds., *Readings in Financial Institutions*, New York, 1965, p. 146.

In any scientific field, the most important form of activity must normally be the hard, day-to-day task of "filling the empty boxes" with empirical content. For the effective conduct of this enterprise it is quite impossible to treat all the fundamental theoretical propositions of the field as up in the air, as open issues that remain to be settled. To some extent, an orthodoxy must be present to serve both as a guide to the questions that ought to be asked and as a framework for the development of hypotheses specific enough for the purposes of empirical testing. Yet in any scientific field there is an obvious, potential danger in letting the current orthodoxy go unquestioned for any considerable length of time. For it also determines the questions that will *not* be asked. It embodies a particular view of what the world is like "in the large" even while it points out to the investigator the questions that need be answered about its nature "in the small."

As time goes on, either of two things may happen: (1) Ongoing research leads to the accumulation of anomalous findings that make it increasingly difficult to maintain the orthodox Vision—to use Schumpeter's term—of how the world functions.[4] The sharper the cutting edge of the empirical tools available in the field, the more likely this is to happen. (2) As the empty boxes are filled, new generations of researchers are inculcated with an orthodox Vision elaborated with more and more concrete details. The increasing amount of empirical findings accumulated and organized within the given conceptual framework requires an increased effort on the part of the individual who would learn the "state" of the field. It also creates more questions than it settles and tends, therefore, to lead to increasing specialization.[5] When this happens, it becomes more and more difficult

---

4. Readers acquainted with the work of Kuhn will recognize this statement as paraphrasing his description of how "normal science" prepares the way for "scientific revolutions." Cf. T. S. Kuhn, *The Structure of Scientific Revolutions*, Chicago, 1963.

5. In the days of Keynes and Pigou, a "monetary economist" was still someone who took the entire economic system as his study object. Today, of course, the label is more likely to designate an economist known for his research on the demand for money, for example. The consumption function and the investment function of the standard model have in the same way developed into specialized fields of study.

for the individual to avoid scientific myopia, and to keep his subject in perspective and maintain a dispassionate overview of the entire field. In particular, it becomes difficult to keep in mind that alternative, latent Visions, capable of organizing the same collections of "facts," must always exist—or to imagine what these alternatives would be. To appraise the state and prospects of the field comes to require a "struggle to escape."

Surely this second type of process resembles the development of the majority school in macroeconomics more than does the first. It is certainly a situation of this type that Solow's quoted statement describes.

Purpose   The *main objective* of this study is to contribute towards a reappraisal of the conceptual framework which has crystallized out of the debates triggered by the *General Theory*. Implicit in this is the need for an "outside" frame of reference, an alternative Vision of what the world is like, to juxtapose against the orthodoxy being reconsidered. The present author cannot make any pretense of providing, as it were, a Copernican theory with which to lambast the Ptolemaic edifice of the income-expenditure model (nor would he wish to be on record as arguing that the latter is a fair analogy to describe the current majority school). In fact, I will not attempt to present a complete, fully specified, alternative model. Rather, the "outside" frame of reference I have chosen is the Economics of Keynes, to which latter-day "Keynesian" Economics will be compared.

Theme   The *theme* of this book, consequently, is "Keynes and the Keynesians" rather than "Keynes and the Classics." But, although in aim this study differs from most writings on Keynes, in execution much of the same ground must nonetheless be covered. In order to understand the development of the Keynesian tradition, we must first see how subsequent writers came to regard Keynes' contribution to economic theory (as distinct from his influence on "practical" matters of economic policy). In order to gain perspective on the question of to what extent the "Keynesian Revolution" has represented the realization and refinement of Keynes' theoretical aims, it is also necessary to consider the departures from "Classical" doctrine that he made or attempted. Thus, the issues of the "Keynes and the Classics" debate must form one of our major concerns.

By linking our definition of the "Keynesian tradition" to the use of the standard simultaneous equation model the term has been given very broad coverage. Within the majority school, so conceived, at least two major factions live in recently peaceful but nonetheless uneasy coexistence. One, which we may label the "Revolutionary Orthodoxy" for short, comprises economists who still feel emotionally committed to the Keynesian Revolution and still embrace the main tenets associated with that phase of the development of the New Economics. The other, aptly described by Professor Eisner as the "Neoclassical Resurgence," [6] is quite critical of many of these same tenets. Both, however, employ the standard model, although with different specifications of the various elasticities and adjustment velocities. In the more extreme revolutionary version, the model is supplied with rigid wages, liquidity trap, and constant capital-output ratio, and manifests a more or less universal "elasticity pessimism," particularly with regard to the interest-elasticities of "real" variables. The Revolutionary Orthodoxy tends traditionally to slight monetary in favor of fiscal stabilization policies. For present purposes, negating these statements sufficiently characterizes the position of the Neoclassical faction.

The terms of the truce between the two factions comprise two broad propositions: (1) the model which Keynes had the gall to call his "general theory" is but a special case of the Classical theory, obtained by imposing certain restrictive assumptions on the latter; and (2) the Keynesian "special case," while theoretically trivial, is nonetheless important because it so happens that it is a better guide in the real world than is the general (equilibrium) theory. Together the two propositions make a compromise that both parties can accept, since one of them has been more interested in having the policy-relevance of its views recognized, and the other in carrying off the theoretical honors. And the compromise permits a decent burial of the major issues that

---

6. R. Eisner, "On Growth Models and the Neo-Classical Resurgence," *Economic Journal*, Dec. 1958.

almost everyone on both sides has grown tired of debating—
namely, the roles of relative values and of money (and, between
the two, the role of the interest rate) in the "Keynesian system."
Keynes thought he had made a major contribution towards a
synthesis of the theory of money and "our fundamental theory of
value." [7] But, ironically, the truce between the orthodox Keynesians and the Neoclassicists is based on the common understanding that his system was *sui generis*—a theory in which neither
relative values nor monetary phenomena were "important."

The first proposition gives a thumbnail description of the so-
called "Neoclassical Synthesis." It embodies a conception of the
state of the arts which is better described, in Professor Clower's
term, as "the Keynesian Counterrevolution," [8] for it represents the
final rejection of Keynes' every claim to being a major theoretical
innovator. This has been the outcome of the long "Keynes and
the Classics" debate. But this outcome, I will argue, should not
be accepted as final and this study attempts to reopen the case.

Thesis   Our objective and our theme have thus been outlined.
Somewhat surreptitiously, the main thesis has also been let out
of the bag. *The main thesis is that Keynes' theory is quite distinct from the "Keynesian" income-expenditure theory.* In the
following chapters, it will be shown that it is possible to describe, at least in rough outline, a model (or class of models),
with a substantially different structure from that of the income-
expenditure model, that is *more consistent with the textual evidence of Keynes' two major works—and with pre-Keynesian,
"Classical" theories.*

The development of the Keynesian tradition, especially in the
United States, has to a considerable extent and for a long time
meant elaboration on the basic income-expenditure model. This
process, we will see, has not been one of expanding, clarifying,
and improving on Keynes. Rather than building upon Keynes'

---

7. *General Theory*, pp. vi-vii.

8. R. W. Clower, "The Keynesian Counterrevolution: A Theoretical Appraisal," in
F. H. Hahn and F. P. R. Brechling, eds., *The Theory of Interest Rates*, London,
1965.

achievement, it appears that the income-expenditure theory has gradually abandoned several of its chief elements.

The crucial step in this process of departure from Keynes' theory lies in the adoption of the standard model, in one or another of its many versions, as the formal framework within which to interpret and organize his ideas. The usual simultaneous equation model imposes a comparative static frame of reference of minimal value-theoretical content and shoves the operation of financial markets into the background of the picture. A framework of this sort contains its own imperatives for development, and the process of tidying up the income-expenditure theory, to give it the intellectually satisfying coherence that befits a reigning orthodoxy, has led to further modifications that have increased the distance between it and Keynes' theory.[9] But these later modifications are of relatively minor importance compared with the establishment of the standard model as the formal representation of the "Keynesian system."

Limitations Since this study is quite critical of the usual interpretation of Keynes, it follows that it will be necessary to deal at length with the question of "what Keynes really said." This exegetical concern implies that one of my objectives is doctrine-historical. To pre-empt otherwise warranted and inevitable criticism, I would emphasize strongly from the outset that this doctrine-historical objective is strictly secondary. A full-scale study of the development of Keynes' ideas on monetary theory and policy, adhering to customary standards of exegetical scholarship, would require an effort of an entirely different magnitude from that essayed here.[10] The primary objective remains as

---

9. Keynes, as an illustration, laid heavy emphasis on his Speculative Demand for Money. In time, this element of his thought was seen to have an unsatisfactory "fit" to other tenets associated with the income-expenditure theory. Since a substantial degree of interest-elasticity of the demand for money is crucial to any Keynesian model, the more recent "Keynesian" literature has come to depend upon the inventory theory of the demand for transactions balances to provide this vital property. This is discussed below in Chapter V.

10. The present study relies primarily upon the *General Theory* and the *Treatise on Money* (Vols. I and II, London, 1930; hereafter referred to as *Treatise*). An

stated above, namely, to provide a fresh perspective from which the income-expenditure theory may be reconsidered.

For that purpose, it is Keynes' *Gestalt*-conception of how a modern capitalist economy works, and not "what he really said," that we ultimately want to grasp. There is an obvious difference between the two: the task of distilling a logically consistent model from a coherent "Vision" [11] is an extremely difficult one. To communicate such a vision, with the help of a model, in both an accurate and convincing manner is perhaps even more difficult. Several comments need to be made on this point:

(1) Keynes was not entirely successful in the two tasks just mentioned. His model was not logically watertight and, that apart, the *General Theory* was in several respects, as has frequently been said, "a badly written book." The defects of organization and presentation were disappointing in view of Keynes' prior literary reputation for elegance and clarity, but if this had been the only difficulty, few problems of interpretation would remain now, after the vast exegetical efforts that have been spent on this work. It is the defects of the model that are serious.[12] When a model contains logical errors, later interpreters are given

---

adequate treatment would require close scrutiny not only of Keynes' total published output, but also of his correspondence which, surprisingly enough, has not yet been assembled and published. To deal exhaustively also with the subsequent development of the Keynesian tradition in relation to the Economics of Keynes is a task which would seem entirely beyond the capacity of any individual. It is also a quite fascinating task and should keep future generations of doctrine-historians, as well as specialists in the sociology of knowledge, fully employed for a long time. The more one becomes acquainted with the Keynesian literature, the more one is impressed with the seeming impossibility of explaining the vagaries of this development merely in terms of some inherent logic of the scientific process.

11. ". . . [A]nalytic effort is of necessity preceded by a pre-analytic cognitive act that supplies the raw material for the analytic effort. . . . [T]his pre-analytic cognitive act will be called Vision." In illustrating his famous thesis, Schumpeter chose Keynes as the "outstanding example from our own field and time. . . . [Keynes' Vision] antedated all the analytic efforts which Keynes and others bestowed on it." Cf. J. A. Schumpeter, *History of Economic Analysis*, New York, 1954, pp. 41–42.

12. Since the whole effort here is to argue that we still have much to learn from Keynes, it will be obvious to the reader that the author is partial to Keynes. But it is *not* part of the purpose of this study to argue that Keynes was always "right" or to defend him at all costs against the usual charges of errors in the argument.

considerable freedom in deciding where "repairs" should be undertaken. It is in the nature of all major theoretical innovations that the visions of the innovator and his audience are at variance. A flawed model is therefore likely to be "corrected" so as to correspond to the interpreter's view of the world rather than the originator's. This, it appears, is what happened to Keynes.

(2) There is room, then, for differing interpretations of Keynes. Any attempt to get behind the flawed model to the *Gestalt* of the underlying theoretical conception must necessarily be somewhat speculative in character. Keynes' views are by now buried under such a mound of exegetical and critical literature that, were it possible to ask "the real Keynes to please stand up," the man himself might not be easily recognized. If this study, therefore, is seen to be somewhat speculative, this is something that it shares with all other guides to the Economics of Keynes. But we will endeavor to show that the interpretation advanced here has a much firmer foundation in Keynes' writings than can be claimed for the interpretation that—with some variations from writer to writer, to be sure—is the most widely accepted today.

(3) Given our main objective, furthermore, it will be desirable on some issues to try to go somewhat beyond Keynes. I would not maintain for example, that everything in Chapters II and IV is actually to "be found in Keynes." Just as the early versions of the income-expenditure theory contained a number of weak points that required considerable work to clear up, so Keynes' presentation of his system relied on more or less intuitive shortcuts and was analytically very sketchy on several important points. In a purely doctrine-historical study, attempts at extending the argument on these points would not be permissible. But we are interested in getting a feel for the kind of questions that are likely to be missed by someone who looks at the world through the glasses of the income-expenditure theory. While these questions cannot be answered here, it is still desirable to make a preliminary investigation of some of the analytical issues which Keynes' theory (as interpreted in this study) suggests but does little to solve.

(4) A balanced treatment of the development of Keynesian economics would allot space to the different topics on the basis either of their substantive importance or of the extent to which they have aroused controversy in the literature to date.[13] Our primary aim is to get an empathic grasp of Keynes' vision. To serve this purpose, some topics will be treated at disproportionate length. Others will be relatively neglected. Not much will be said, for example, on the relationship of Keynes' theory, as it evolved over time, to those of D. H. Robertson and the Swedes— Wicksell, Lindahl, Myrdal, Ohlin, and Lundberg.[14] This may admittedly result in giving the false impression of Keynes as the lone pioneer on the frontiers of monetary theory in his time. But to put his analytical achievements in proper historical perspective is not a major concern of this study.

Another omission may be more glaring to most readers: The aspect of Keynes' theory which has created the most trouble for later interpreters, Keynesians and anti-Keynesians alike, is his theory of interest—which is rather a theory of short-run interest *movements*. Even more to the point is Keynes' own obvious dissatisfaction with this aspect of the *General Theory*. His repeated efforts at repairing this vital part of his theoretical structure were not only unsuccessful—they produced new contradictions and compounded the confusion.[15] The role of the rate of interest in Keynes' theory will indeed be a major topic of later chapters. But no systematic, critical examination will be made of either the Hicks-Hansen "reconciliation" of Keynes and the Classics on the determinants of the interest rate, or the long-smoldering Liquidity Preference versus Loanable Funds controversy, despite

---

13. The staggering volume of writings on the Pigou-effect, for example, would indicate that these two criteria are not synonymous.

14. On the other hand, Keynes' affinity for some of Cassel's ideas will be discussed at some length, this being a subject which has not previously received the attention it deserves.

15. Cf., e.g., J. M. Keynes, "The Theory of the Rate of Interest," in *The Lessons of Monetary Experience; Essays in Honor of Irving Fisher*, New York, 1937; "Alternative Theories of the Rate of Interest," *Economic Journal*, June, 1937; "The 'Ex-Ante' Theory of the Rate of Interest," *Economic Journal*, Dec. 1937.

the importance of these two closely interrelated topics in the development of Keynesian economics.[16]

I:2   Problems in Keynesian Exegesis

The income-expenditure model has long provided the basic framework for the exposition of Keynes' system, and for comparing Keynesian with Classical theory as well as the *General Theory* with later versions of Keynesian doctrine. While the numerous interpretations of Keynes in the last thirty years are not identical, the great majority are cast in this mold. Within this framework there is, admittedly, ample room for differences of emphasis in the various interpretations of Keynes, room that has been well utilized—"Nature abhors a Vacuum." But the basic mold is there. Yet the warning signals against accepting the income-expenditure tradition as a faithful development of Keynes' ideas have been in plain view all the time.

The role of money   The major mystery that the development of Keynesianism poses is "why a theory in which money is important should have turned into the theory that money is unimportant." [1] Interest in monetary aspects of macrotheory reached its nadir in the mid-1940's—the period of the Keynesian Revolution's "Anti-Monetary Terror"—and has been in the ascendance ever since. But despite this increasing interest in monetary theory and growing faith in the efficacy of monetary policy, the analysis of the interaction of "real and monetary phenomena" remains basically the same as twenty years ago. One element— the real balance effect—has been added. But the great theoretical debate which has centered on the Pigou-effect has been conducted on the common understanding that its empirical relevance is nil, at least in the short run.

---

16. A discussion of these two topics had at one time been planned and in part prepared, but this was subsequently made redundant by G. Horwich's valuable critical study, *Money, Capital, and Prices,* Homewood, Ill., 1964.

1. H. G. Johnson, "The *General Theory* after Twenty-five Years," *American Economic Review,* May 1961, p. 15.

The role of the rate of interest The corollary of the "unimportance of money" has been the "unimportance of interest." There has been a type of "vulgar Keynesianism" in which the investment-multiplier was the only piece of theoretical equipment. This type of mechanical model need not concern us here. To a degree, however, the "unimportance of money and interest" is true also of the complete income-expenditure model, i.e., when it is complemented with the usual assumptions of low interest-elasticity of investment, etc.

In matters of aggregative economic policy, reliance on fiscal policy has been the hallmark of the Keynesian tradition. Recently, in appraising the economic policies of the Johnson administration, several newspapers and magazines took note of the political influence the New Economics has achieved. *Time* magazine was not alone in daring the generalization that all academic economists were now Keynesians. Quite apart from the disregard for academic minority views, this characterization of the majority contrasts strangely with the appraisal of one distinguished Keynesian. Only a few years ago, Sir Roy Harrod wrote a short article for *Encounter* magazine entitled "Are We Really All Keynesians Now?" The question was answered in the negative: ". . . quite apart from Keynes' more radical themes, his central doctrines have not been so thoroughly assimilated as might first appear." It is of particular interest to note that, among the items which Harrod listed to document his assertion that the current orthodoxy is un-Keynesian, the "unimportance of interest" ranked first:

Keynes always attached the utmost importance to low interest rates; he never ceased to preach them. . . . They [members of the Establishment] are being completely anti-Keynesian in regard to the matter that he held to be of the *greatest importance of all.*[2]

There is abundant evidence in Keynes' writings of the paramount importance that he attached to low interest rates. This

---

2. Cf. Roy Harrod, "Are We Really All Keynesians Now?" *Encounter,* Jan. 1964, pp. 46–50 (italics added). While the paper was intended more as a contribution to the British economic policy debate than to the academic debate on theory—*vide* the address to "The members of the Establishment"—there can be little doubt that Harrod's judgment of textbook Keynesianism would be much the same.

implies a judgment of the way in which the economic system works, which is hardly understandable in terms of the standard income-expenditure model. On this point Keynes' vision of the world is quite at variance with the vision commonly taught as the Keynesian system. While Harrod justly insists on the significance of this discrepancy, he does not provide a theoretical explanation of it. It will be a major objective of the following chapters to provide this explanation.

It will be argued here that not only the interest rate, but *relative prices generally, play a more important role* in Keynes' thought than they have usually been accorded. The price-theoretical content of the *General Theory* appears to have been generally underestimated. The corollary of this is the exaggeration of the divergence between Keynes and other prominent monetary theorists of the interwar period and, in particular, between the Keynes of the *General Theory* and the Keynes of the *Treatise*.

The Keynes of exegetical legend The literature devoted to the *General Theory* frequently bears certain peculiar characteristics worth keeping in mind. It is hardly an exaggeration to say that customary standards of interpretation have been less consistently employed in the analysis of Keynes' contribution than in assessing the accomplishment of any other major economist.

The usual approach to the analysis of a man's life-work, whether it belongs to the arts or to science, rests on the assumption that his thought will show a consistency and continuity of development which, once grasped, make it possible to view his work as a coherent whole. Consistency, in this context, need not be understood in the restrictive sense of logical consistency, e.g., of a mathematical structure, but more loosely as the intellectual compatibility of the various beliefs and tenets attributed to the man. Nor is continuity to be understood as implying no changes in basic views, or merely a process of gradually more detailed elaboration of these views. The premise is simply that it should be possible to explain the development of a man's views in terms of the intellectual influences and important events he is known to have been exposed to. The main accomplishments of a genius are still likely to escape such deterministic explanation and appear as "emergent properties" of the scientific process even long afterwards.[3]

This is the approach which doctrine-historians take towards the classic works in economics. But it hardly describes the treatment of Keynes in the "Keynes and the Classics" debate. Instead, there has sprung up a legend about Keynes, to which many have contributed.

This legend puts a smokescreen over the *General Theory* that is quite difficult for the student who is new to the subject to penetrate. It tends even to discourage the effort, for part of the legend is that what is worthwhile in Keynes' thought can be better learned elsewhere. The smoke has not been generated altogether without fire. As an economic theorist, Keynes was not without faults; he was not proof against logical inconsistencies and, errors apart, he had certain irritating habits of analysis and presentation that have not been at all helpful to later students. These are facts which cannot be denied. Still, the problem is to keep his faults in the right perspective. In the view of Keynes that seems to be increasingly more widespread, these faults are blown up out of all proportion, distorting both the magnitude of his accomplishments, and more importantly the substantive content of his theory.

Three aspects of this legend tend to distort our view of the *General Theory:* (a) the tendency to underestimate the analytical quality of the work, (b) the tendency to underestimate the continuity in Keynes' intellectual development and, in particular, to exaggerate the *General Theory*'s departures from the theory of

---

3. In economics, Schumpeter is the main proponent of this exegetical approach. His term "Vision" refers precisely to this consistent *Gestalt* which the doctrine-historian postulates and uses as an organizing frame within which he attempts to put aspects of the subject's work in an understandable relation to each other. Similarly, Schumpeter always took pains to paint the intellectual and historical environment of the subject's analytic contribution. If anything, Schumpeter overstressed the continuity aspect—or at least one would like to think so. His well-known thesis that a scholar's main ideas are *all* arrived at before thirty years of age—that his Vision is complete by then—and that his work beyond that point consists solely in refining these ideas, is somewhat depressing.

the *Treatise*, and (c) the tendency to overemphasize the extent to which Keynes was intellectually independent of other monetary theorists both of his own and earlier generations.

Belief in the legend reflects a patronizing attitude towards Keynes. Not a patronizing attitude towards the man and his work as a whole—few people have attained an eminence which would permit them to adopt such a stance—but towards Keynes as a theoretical economist, as an academic professional. Strangely enough, this notion of Keynes as a brilliant man and a great man, but a great man dabbling in economics, seems to be most prevalent among professed "Keynesians." The danger in all three elements of the legend is that they give so much leeway in the interpretation of Keynes' writings: These presumptions do not require that one's analysis of Keynes' work yield a very coherent picture.

We have an illustration of this in the view which states that a few chapters of the *General Theory* contain the meat and that the others are basically redundant and may be ignored. The "redundant" chapters are, of course, those whose content is not needed for the explanation and presentation of the standard income-expenditure model. Professor Hansen, for instance, argues that "not much would have been lost" if Chapter 16 and the difficult Chapter 17 "had never been written." [4] Thus one meets two propositions in the standard interpretation of Keynes that are hard to reconcile: (a) the logic of the work is "sloppy" because Keynes was anxious to reach his audience as soon as possible, and (b) large parts of the work are irrelevant to the message and need never have been written.

This view of the *General Theory* as a work of only loosely integrated parts provides a good deal of latitude for the interpreter's own judgment in selecting the parts he wants to emphasize. The same selective approach has prevailed with respect to Keynes' theoretical output as a whole. Keynesian exegesis has focused overwhelmingly on the *General Theory* and the handful of articles in which Keynes sought to summarize or to clarify certain aspects of the *General Theory* in the years immediately

---

4. Cf. A. H. Hansen, *A Guide to Keynes*, New York, 1953, pp. 155–59.

following its appearance. The degree to which this part of his work can properly be regarded as independent of what went before and came after it has been much exaggerated.

At the time when the popular "Keynesian" conviction on the lack of importance of money and financial markets was at its peak, a view of Keynes' work as almost completely lacking in continuity was necessary in order to make the *General Theory* "fit" the then-current doctrine. Before the *General Theory* Keynes had consistently approached macrotheoretical problems from the "monetary" side, and in subsequent years he resumed, and concentrated almost exclusively on his work with monetary problems. In the mythology of the New Economics, the *General Theory* made a clean break with Keynes' own previous major contributions, while his later efforts show a regrettable tendency to "relapse" into modes of thought that the *General Theory*—i.e., the income-expenditure version of it—had made outmoded. This theme in Keynesian exegesis provides some of its most curious passages. The tendency to read contemporary income-expenditure dogma into the *General Theory* is exemplified, for example, by Klein, who notes statements made by Keynes both before and after the *General Theory* expressing the conviction that aggregate investment is very responsive to low rates of interest. In Klein's version, the Keynes of the *General Theory* sees the income-expenditure "Truth" of the matter and draws the appropriate conclusion, i.e., that monetary policy cannot be relied upon, thus departing from his previous views. Later, the validity of the assumption of low interest-elasticity of investment escapes him and he relapses into a preoccupation with monetary matters.[5]

Still, Keynes more than once showed a "lack of patriotism for his own past ideas."[6] He had the courage to change his mind on occasion. The risk which the interpreter runs is to exaggerate this pragmatic trait and then to use the resulting caricature to gain excessive "degrees of freedom" in his interpretation of

5. Cf. L. R. Klein, *The Keynesian Revolution*, New York, 1960 edn., pp. 66–67. Compare the discussion in Chapter III: 3, below.

6. J. Robinson, *Economic Philosophy*, Chicago, 1962, p. 86.

Keynes' work. Schumpeter expresses a view at the opposite
extreme:

So far as this line of endeavor of a man of many interests was concerned, the whole period between 1919 and 1936 was then spent in
attempts, first unsuccessful, then increasingly successful, at imple-
menting the particular vision of the economic process of our time that
was fixed in Keynes's mind by 1919 at latest.[7]

This may also be a caricature, but as a general presumption on
which to base the exegetical effort, it is sounder than the opposite approach.

The points at which this issue of continuity versus "change of
mind" must be considered are numerous in Keynes' work. Two
things, at least, must therefore be kept clear.

First, one must not give undue significance to changes in
terminology, in the definitions of variables, etc. For instance, the
fact that realized savings and realized investment are unequal
when income is changing in the *Treatise,* while realized savings
and investment are always equal in the *General Theory,* does not
per se indicate a change in Keynes' basic views. Most often, such
changes as these merely reflect Keynes' continuous struggle to
achieve a clearer and more powerful analytical formulation of
his theories.

Second, the political objectives and the political context of
Keynes' writings must be remembered. He was forever preoccupied with immediately pressing practical problems. In trying to
find policy solutions for these problems through the application
of general theoretical principles, he was led to a series of
theoretical innovations. In presenting his results, however, his
sole objective was not to communicate these innovations to the
academic community; rather, the more important objective was
to press for the adoption of the policy proposals he had arrived
at. It appears that Keynes' judgments of what was politically

---

7. Schumpeter, *op. cit.,* p. 42. There is very strong support for Schumpeter's view
in Harrod's *Life of John Maynard Keynes* (London, 1951; hereafter, Harrod's
Life), p. 350: "[It is interesting to reflect on] . . . how early (1924) Keynes had
completed the outline of the public policy which has since been specifically associated with his name. . . . The main framework was there in 1924."

feasible at the time has colored his writings to an extent that more academically oriented economists have not always fully appreciated. Consideration of this is particularly important in developing the right perspective on the policy views that Keynes expressed in the *General Theory,* particularly his preference for fiscal policy measures in combating a depression, and his pessimistic views on the efficacy of monetary policies.

In the *Treatise,* Keynes had already arrived at the conviction that, *if a contraction were once allowed to gather momentum,* the type of monetary policy measures conventionally used by the Bank of England up to that time would be inadequate to correct the situation rapidly enough. A belated Central Bank action, he urged, must take the form of "open-market operations to the point of saturation" or a "monetary policy *à outrance*" as he termed it. He was careful to point out that such a policy would mean that the Central Bank would incur losses on its open market operations over time. This type of monetary policy already borders on the fiscal policy measures advocated in the *General Theory.* The suggestion that the Old Lady of Threadneedle Street should run her affairs in this manner was—if possible—received with even more horror in 1930 than the "unsound" Keynesian fiscal policy recommendations in later years.[8] Keynes' experiences with the Bank of England representatives, when he was a member of the Macmillan Committee, demonstrated quite clearly the uselessness of investing his influence and energy in pressing for this type of monetary policy. If the Central Bank could not be made to take losses for the general welfare, the government must. In reading the *General Theory,* Keynes' "political" experiences from 1930 on must be remembered.[9]

The relationship between the "Treatise" and the "General Theory"   A "classic" is often defined as "a book which no one

---

8. Keynes' broad hints that he regarded these losses as quite appropriate punishment for being late are not likely to have made his prescriptions more palatable. Cf. *Treatise,* Vol. II, esp. pp. 369-74. The theoretical issue involved is discussed in greater detail in Chapter V, below.

9. Cf. Harrod's *Life,* Chs. X–XI, esp. pp. 413 ff. Harrod's eloquent and well-balanced testimony to the consistency of conception underlying the changes in Keynes' position in response to unfolding events is found on pp. 467–73.

reads." The *General Theory* may now be in danger of falling irrevocably into this category. The *Treatise* has not been widely read for a long time. This is hardly because it has attained the status of a classic—rather, because of the belief that the *General Theory* made it superfluous to study the *Treatise*. Keynes' insistence that the *General Theory* built on the *Treatise* has not been heeded; later developments have verified his statement that "the relation between this book and my *Treatise on Money* . . . is probably clearer to myself than it will be to others; and what in my own mind is a natural evolution in a line of thought which I have been pursuing for several years, may sometimes strike the reader as a confusing change of view." It is well known that Keynes invested a tremendous amount of time and effort in the *Treatise* and that his hopes about its reception were not fulfilled. It was not hailed as a "great contribution," but merely as a worthwhile book marred by certain errors of analysis.

The contrasts between the two works are dramatized by the switch from the "Fundamental Equations" of the *Treatise* to the investment-multiplier of the *General Theory* as the expository device whereby Keynes sought to compress a complicated and sophisticated theory in a nutshell. The switch is theoretically significant, yet it must not be misinterpreted. The multiplier does, indeed, summarize the *two* major changes in his model, i.e., (1) the idea that the system responds to disturbances by quantity adjustments and not simply by price-level adjustments (while remaining at full employment), and (2) the idea that initial disturbances are amplified through the consumption-income relation.

In another respect, however, this switch of expository devices can very easily be misleading. The Fundamental Equations were recognizable descendants of the traditional Equation of Exchange.[10] In the *Treatise*, the Quantity Theory lineage is still very evident—the various factors affecting income are still analyzed in terms of their impact on the excess demands for the assets and liabilities of the banking system.[11] The multiplier-

---

10. Cf. *Treatise*, Vol. I, Ch. 10: iv and Ch. 14.

11. Cf. *Treatise*, Vol. I, pp. 142–44, 182–84. These passages will be discussed below in Chapter V.

analysis, in contrast, focuses directly on the demand for and supply of commodities. This switch in the immediate focus of the analysis from the excess demand (supply) of "money" to the excess supply (demand) of commodities has probably contributed heavily to the widespread impression that the *General Theory* represents a clean break with Keynes' "monetary" past and an attempt to approach macroeconomics practically from scratch—and then from the "real" side. What is involved, however, is merely a translation, from one language to another, of the terms used to discuss the maladjustments forcing a change in the level of money income. The "code-key" is simply the budget-identity for the system as a whole—Walras' Law, if you will [12]— which, under the dynamic assumptions used by Keynes, dictates that the excess supply of commodities should be equal in value to the excess demand for money. There is no evidence that this translation reflects any basic change in Keynes' views of the processes generating changes in money income and of the role of financial markets in such processes. In particular, it does not reflect some new-found conviction that "money is unimportant."

The development in Keynes' views that is relevant here did not take place between the *Treatise* and the *General Theory* but between the *Tract on Monetary Reform* [13] and the *Treatise*. To appreciate properly the relevance of the *Treatise* to the *General Theory,* it is exceedingly important to be clear on this point. By and large the *Tract* still respected the traditional boundary between monetary theory and value theory, whereby the former dealt with the demand for output in general and the value of money, and the latter with relative prices. In the interval between the two works, Keynes—very much under the influence of D. H. Robertson—had come to the conviction that it was necessary to relinquish this traditional compartmentalization in order to explain the disequilibrium processes producing changes in money income and price levels and, in particular, to explain the *modus operandi* of monetary policy. *The analysis of these dis-*

---

12. Use of the term "Walras' Law" here risks some misunderstanding. The problems involved must, however, wait to Chapter II where, following Clower, we will prefer the term "Say's Principle" as less likely to invoke irrelevant connotations.

13. London, 1924.

equilibrium processes—the "short run"—was always his chosen subject. The disaggregation of total output into consumer goods and investment goods was a *sine qua non* of the process-analysis presented in the *Treatise,* since it invoked systematic changes in the *relative price* of the two (and in their relative rates of output) in explaining how money income moves from one short-run "equilibrium" level to another.[14] In the *Treatise,* however, Keynes did not succeed in distilling a logically consistent model from this vision of how income changes are generated. The trouble was that the Fundamental Equations still incorporated a variable purporting to represent the total physical volume of output, in the way of the traditional Equation of Exchange, and thus they were inconsistent with the verbal explanation of the processes studied.[15]

---

14. The basic contention here is that a monetary injection (for example) will not impinge with the same force on all markets and all prices. Consequently, an understanding of the *modus operandi* of monetary policy requires an analysis which descends at least one step from the ultimate level of aggregation of both the Cambridge-equation and the Equation of Exchange. (This idea was later all but buried in the avalanche of static, one-commodity models produced first by the Keynesian Revolution and then by the Neoclassical Resurgence.) When all is serene once more, of course, only the new level of nominal values remains as a ghostly, "unreal" monument to past Central Bank efforts. Keynes' repeated acknowledgments of the validity of the Quantity Theory in the long run show that he understood quite clearly that this traditional tool was sufficient in order to obtain comparative static results. Similarly, his criticisms of Quantity Theory formulations reveal his understanding of what witnesses to the later "Neutrality" debate known only too well, namely, that comparative static analysis can tell us nothing about the "real" powers of Central Banks or of how they should be used in different circumstances.

15. For the purposes of the following discussion, the *coup de grâce* to the unhappily baptized "Fundamental Equations" was dealt by F. A. von Hayek, "Reflections on the Pure Theory of Money of Mr. J. M. Keynes, Part I" *Economica,* Aug. 1931, section VII, esp. p. 287. Cf. also, A. H. Hansen, "A Fundamental Error in Keynes's 'Treatise on Money,'" *American Economic Review,* Sept. 1932; and A. G. Hart, "An Examination of Mr. Keynes's Price-Level Concepts," *Journal of Political Economy,* Oct. 1933. D. H. Robertson's review article "Mr. Keynes' Theory of Money," *Economic Journal,* Sept. 1931, is also important.

That, when handled with some circumspection, the "Fundamental Equations" can still be used to heuristic advantage in elucidating Keynes' conception is amply demonstrated by M. L. Burstein, *Money,* Cambridge, Mass., 1963, Chapter XII, App. A; and also by J. R. Hicks in Chapter 11, *Critical Essays in Monetary Theory.*

In the *General Theory,* the Fundamental Equations (and mathematical ambitions generally) were given up. Quite ironically, Keynes' successors immediately reverted to an algebraic model devoid of relative prices and with only a single commodity aggregate—a model which showed no trace of the analytical problem that Keynes had wrestled with for a decade.

Relative prices and the importance of money The main innovation—and virtually the only major innovation—attempted in the *General Theory* was the effort to provide a systematic analysis of the behavior of a system that reacts to disturbances through *quantity adjustments,* rather than through price-level or wage-rate adjustments.[16] The explanation of sustained and substantial unemployment is, of course, the main theme of the Keynesian Revolution and must, therefore, be our main subject in later chapters. This revolution we will interpret as an attack upon the foundations of the received Theory of Markets as a tool for the analysis of short-run problems. But there was also another revolution, almost equally important to Keynes, which we should consider here. It had been attempted earlier but remained, as just described, unfinished business, since the flawed weapons with which it had been launched in the *Treatise* had not carried the day. This was the attack on the received Theory of Money as a tool for the analysis of short-run problems.[17] When one strips Keynes' work of the great efforts at economic-

---

16. Cf. *General Theory,* pp. vi–vii: " . . . what now seems to me to be the outstanding fault of the theoretical part of [the *Treatise* is] that I failed to deal thoroughly with the effects of *changes* in the level of output." Note especially that Keynes here says the *effects,* not the *causes,* of changes in output. Apart from Chapter II, this study will concentrate on the initial causes of changes in output and employment. This requires that we deal with Keynes' "instantaneous picture taken on the assumption of a given output," which he cited as the focal point of the *Treatise,* and therefore rely heavily upon that earlier work.

17. This was the revolution to which D. H. Robertson had the greater claim and it remained the more important to him. When its issues became first confounded and then lost in the later theoretical upheaval, Robertson—being at the same time much sounder than Keynes on the crucial interest-theoretical issues and much more firmly wedded than Keynes to the Marshallian Theory of Markets—opted out of the "Keynesian" revolution.

political persuasion, these stand out as his two main themes as an economic theoretician.

The older theme was almost entirely submerged in the fervor caused by the newer. In its burial, down went most of the price-theoretical and monetary content of Keynes' theory and into the light came strange new doctrines of the "unimportance of money" and the "ineffectiveness of monetary policy." This led also, as we shall argue in Chapter II, to a distorted view of Keynes' new theme. It is in this unbalanced view of Keynes' theoretical aims that one finds the roots of the biases against price theory and against monetary theory which came to characterize the New Economics.

That Keynes was still preoccupied with the older theme when writing the *General Theory* there can be no doubt. The issue is very clearly stated in the Preface:

When I began to write my *Treatise on Money* I was still moving along the traditional lines of regarding the influence of money as something so to speak separate from the general theory of supply and demand.

And towards the close of the body of the book:

The division of Economics between the Theory of Value and Distribution on the one hand and the Theory of Money on the other is, I think, a false division.[18]

Again, the Preface promises that the theory of a monetary economy will be:

. . . linked up with our fundamental theory of value. We are thus led to a more general theory, which includes the classical theory with which we are familiar, as a special case.

And towards the end (with unwarranted satisfaction, as it turns out):

18. *General Theory*, p. 293.

One of the objects of the foregoing chapters has been to escape from this double life and to bring the theory of prices as a whole back to close contact with the theory of value.[19]

Three observations are pertinent:

(1) The *Treatise* remains the better guide to Keynes' views on the old theme. Keynes did not feel obliged to repeat in the *General Theory* all the Money and Banking material developed at length in the earlier work. Unfortunately, the *General Theory* is frequently so sketchy as to make references unnecessarily obscure and cryptic:

> . . . whilst it is found that money enters into the economic scheme in an essential and peculiar manner, technical monetary detail falls into the background.[20]

This states the intention, but in execution "technical monetary detail" too often fell right out of the picture to the extent that it has proved difficult for many later Keynesians to convince themselves that "money enters into the economic scheme" not just in a peculiar but also in an essential manner. Although the number of pages devoted to Liquidity Preference, interest rate movements, the operation of securities markets, etc., is quite large in the *General Theory*, it has nonetheless been quite easy to underestimate the significance Keynes attached to the financial side of "real" processes. But with a comprehensive treatise on money and finance behind him, it was only natural for Keynes to concentrate on Employment and give only a condensed treatment of Interest and Money—the other two-thirds of his title. But "the appearance of the *General Theory* greatly militated against the reading of the *Treatise*." [21]

---

19. *Loc. cit.*

20. *General Theory*, p. vii.

21. Harrod's *Life*, p. 404. Harrod's judgment (p. 403) is again worth quoting: "There is, however, something to be said for the view that the student of the future, if he had to choose among Keynes' works, would get the best picture of his total contribution to economics in the *Treatise*. It is not his last word on his central theme, but it supports that theme by a whole host of characteristic views about all the details of the complex subject of money which are only to be found in this volume."

(2) If Keynes had not been so convinced that relative prices were an essential part of the way in which "the causal process actually operates during a period of change," [22] and that they therefore could not be thrown out in the construction of a macromodel, the *General Theory* would presumably have followed in the traces of the *Tract* and the *Treatise* and Keynes' novel ideas would have been presented as a "new twist" on the Cambridge-equation. His followers could not then have avoided regarding him as the latest in the long line of great British monetary economists rather than as the man who ruled monetary theories of fluctuations out of contention.

The distinguishing feature of Quantity Theories is simply the idea that the most convenient method of analyzing income movements is to define a collection of assets, called "money," and to organize the determinants of money income in terms of their effects on the supply of and the demand for money. One cannot require that a Quantity Theory should postulate either pure price-level adjustment or continuous constancy of velocity over time—if these criteria were imposed on the short-run analysis we might well find that history is devoid of "pure" Quantity theorists. Keynes could not accept the assumption that aggregate real output can be unambiguously defined. An excess demand for money, for example, would in general not be accompanied by an excess supply evenly distributed over the components of that output. Relative prices do not stay constant as "the" price level adjusts. Had Keynes not insisted on the distinction between the output of investment goods and consumption goods, there would have been little, if anything, to prevent him from taking the traditional monetary approach: (a) by incorporating the prospective yield on commodities into the money-demand function, one of the desired properties of his system would be taken care of—a decline in the marginal efficiency of capital would cause a decline in aggregate demand (velocity); (b) by postulating less than perfect price-flexibility, he would still obtain the short-run quantity adjustments to explain reductions in output and employment (as the New Quantity theorists do today); and (c) by

---

22. *Treatise,* Vol. I, p. 133.

assuming the money-demand function (or the supply function) recursive in income, he could even have introduced the type of amplification of initial disturbances that the multiplier embodies.

In a mechanical way, at least, such a procedure would have taken care of the most prominent features of his model, i.e., those features that the income-expenditure theorists adopted and elaborated. We will have to probe much deeper into Keynes' views vis-à-vis received value theory to get a grasp of the ideas that would not be adequately represented by a model of the type just sketched.

(3) The price-theoretical content of Keynes' theory was inextricably intertwined with his views about the connection between what Keynesians have come to call the "real sector" and the "monetary sector." The early income-expenditure literature entirely missed the price-theoretical content and, much for that reason, came unduly to neglect the monetary side of "real" processes.[23]

What went wrong? I believe that Keynes' incredibly tortuous formulation of his interest theory, and the interminable conundrums this caused, is principally to blame. It is curious that, while he has been much criticized for error on this account, he has also been highly praised for having supplied a simple, powerful, and durable apparatus for the analysis of the determination of income and interest.[24] It seems fair to ask whether that accolade is really deserved. The apparatus is still in use, it is true, but it contains a semantic trap or two which makes it less than simple to handle correctly. The main trouble, I suspect, lies simply in Keynes' taking over the definition of "saving" as "non-consumption" from the "pure" theories of interest, which he

---

23. The literature contains, for example, an abundance of short-run fiscal policy models and recursive growth and/or cycle models which postulate only some simple relationships among Income Account (flow) variables and say nothing at all about the Capital Accounts. Thus, we have had analyses of fiscal measures which suggest that the effects are invariant to the means of financing government expenditures (borrowing or money creation), and cycle models which exclude not only relative values but money supply and money demand relationships, and therefore the price level, as well.

24. D. H. Robertson, who saw most clearly what was wrong, did tie his criticism of Keynes' interest theory to a critique of the conceptual apparatus.

wanted to criticize. These theories dealt with barter systems in which context the definition is quite appropriate. Keynes' "*ex ante* saving" variable makes no clear distinction between the two components of this flow—the demand for non-money assets and the demand for money.[25]

The propositions about the determination of the interest rate in the short run that Keynes wanted to build into his model are quite simple: Only in the very long run need long-term interest rates conform to the underlying physical transformation possibilities and intertemporal preferences of households. In the "short run," speculation in securities markets will make them diverge from the levels that would obtain under conditions of full information about transformation possibilities and "tastes." Hoarding or dishoarding is the concomitant of this speculative activity which stabilizes yields at levels that do not permit perfect coordination of saving and investment plans.

In trying to communicate these ideas, Keynes chose to hammer away at two related statements: (a) saving and investment determine income, and not the interest rate; and (b) liquidity preference (and the supply of money) determines the interest rate, and not money income. Both statements were aimed to dramatize his departures from received doctrine and both turned out to be quite misleading. For they put stress on the differences in language between Keynes and the "Classics" at the expense of the underlying correspondence on matters of substance. What is involved is simply the "translation" previously mentioned. The traditional statement was that the supply and demand for money determined money income, e.g., that an excess of *ex ante* demand for money over the supply must necessarily lead to an all-around reduction in expenditures and incomes. An excess of *ex ante* saving over investment, in Keynes' model, says exactly the same thing: In the aggregate, attempts to hoard must be self-defeating if the money supply is constant.[26] *Ex ante* saving minus *ex ante*

---

25. Cf. Horwich, *Money, Capital, and Prices, op. cit., passim.*

26. Keynes was not unaware of this. While many Keynesians saw great significance in his so-called "Paradox of Thrift" as pointing out a danger which Classical theory had failed to reveal (thus not recognizing it as a translation of the most ancient proposition of monetary theory), Keynes concluded his discussion of

investment equals *ex ante* hoarding—*ex post,* both sides of the equation must be zero.

The frequent confusion of the role of money in the determination of money income found in the early income-expenditure literature must be associated with its disregard for general price-theoretical principles. Keynes' followers were greatly perplexed by his apparent denial of any role to Thrift and Productivity in the determination of the interest rate, even while they accepted his dictum on saving and investment determining income unquestioningly (and without a clear grasp of its implications with regard to the excess demand for money). This led to curious results, exemplified by Professor Hansen's "integration" of Classical and Keynesian interest theory—an analysis which is still well entrenched in the textbook literature. Hansen's demonstration of the role of saving and investment in the determination of the interest rate involved the description of certain processes, of which the following is an illustration: (1) an increase in "Thrift" is interpreted as an upward shift of the saving schedule; (2) with investment "autonomous," this leads to a reduction in income; (3) the money stock being given, the reduction in income is seen to create an excess supply of money, which (4) spills over into demand for bonds and drives down the interest rate.

The reasoning is false. A proper analysis would recognize that while income is declining, there is an excess demand for money, corresponding to the excess supply of commodities on which the description explicitly focuses. The decline in income will be halted when the excess demand for money and the excess supply of commodities simultaneously reach zero. Keynes' obscure discussion is to blame for the spread of the notion, implicitly accepted in analyses of the type just paraphrased, that the rate of interest will decline if and only if there has emerged an excess supply of money. In fact, shifts in saving and investment will either have a *direct* impact on securities markets and the rate of

---

it in the following way: "The above is closely analogous with the proposition which harmonizes the liberty, which every individual possesses, to change, whenever he chooses, the amount of money he holds, with the necessity for the total amount of money, which individual balances add up to, to be exactly equal to the amount of cash which the banking system has created. . . . This, indeed, is the fundamental proposition of monetary theory." Cf. *General Theory,* pp. 84–85.

interest, or the rate of interest will not be affected at all in the case considered, since the process does not generate an excess supply of money. Instances of this type of analysis, most often characterized by a mechanical manipulation of the IS-LM diagram or the corresponding simultaneous equation system, are extremely common in the income-expenditure literature.[27]

The Keynesian Revolution   Keynes envisaged a grand synthesis of the theory of value and the theory of money, as we have seen. The actual consequences of the *General Theory*, however, were to establish "Keynesianism" as a third body of analysis antithetical to traditional monetary approaches and unrelated to value theory.

It is all a very strange story. It is a story which can hardly be understood except by reference to the intellectual climate in which the *General Theory* made its appearance. For most economists, the experience of the thirties had been traumatic. The profession had been unable to come to a consensus on an action program squarely based on accepted economic analysis. In this atmosphere the *General Theory* was received as a liberating revelation and it was perhaps inevitable that the acceptance of the "New Faith" should be combined with a purge of the old doctrines, associated as they were with feelings of guilt and impotence.

This brings us back once more to the "legend" which still obstructs a clear perspective on Keynes' aims and accomplishments. In the revolutionary spirit of early Keynesianism, he was painted as the Redeemer untainted by earlier dogmas that had failed to provide salvation from the unparalleled catastrophe of the Great

---

27. This is amply demonstrated by Horwich's scholarly and thorough review of this literature. Cf. *op. cit.*, esp. Chapter X and its appendix ("A Reformulation of the Hicks IS-LM Diagram") and also the same author's earlier "Money, Prices, and the Theory of Interest Determination," *Economic Journal*, Dec. 1957.

Part of the problem above is, of course, that comparative static experiments with the standard simultaneous equation model cannot yield any statements relating to the process connecting the initial and terminal "equilibria." The seeming precision of the algebraic manipulations disguises the fact that "equation-skipping" sketches of intervening events are altogether impressionistic and—if careful attention is not paid to the implied distribution of excess demands over the markets of the system—will make sense only by pure chance.

Depression. Rather than having provided a new "monetary" explanation of unemployment linked to "our fundamental theory of value," Keynes—in this view—successfully demonstrated not only that the theory of value was not fundamental, but that it was *useless* in the analysis of macroeconomic problems. In addition, he was credited with having eliminated "monetary theories" of business fluctuations from serious consideration. From the standpoint of the development of economic analysis, the view was harmful—it contributed to the fragmentation of the body of general economic theory. The best that can be said for it is that it did not underestimate Keynes' capabilities as a professional economist. If anything, it offered instead a wildly exaggerated image of his intellectual capability.

In the course of the Neoclassical re-examination of Keynes' contribution, the estimate of his analytical capabilities and achievement veered towards the other extreme: from the standpoint of pure theory, Keynes' contributions were now considered trivial and not even original. To a considerable extent, Keynes was once again to blame. His propagandistic style and the polemics in which he engaged were most certainly conducive to this kind of appraisal. It was inevitable that the "Keynes and the Classics" debate would come to focus attention on the analytical "strawmen" Keynes had erected in considerable numbers as convenient targets for his polemics. Were it not for these "red herrings," one would expect the Neoclassical re-examination to have led to a re-evaluation of the role of money and relative prices in Keynes' thought. But the nature of his polemics stood in the way of such a reappraisal and seemed instead to point to another inference, namely that Keynes was simply not very familiar with received theory and had not mastered the tools of traditional economic analysis.

It is this inference which lies at the bottom of the patronizing attitude towards Keynes *qua* academic economist. Macroeconomic (monetary) problems, national and international, engaged Keynes' professional attention throughout his life, and microeconomics *per se* held little interest for him. But it is a far cry from this observation to the contention that he had little understanding of microeconomic tools. It should be remembered that he made contributions in various areas, for example, to the theory of index numbers and to the theory of forward markets. Undeniably, however, his writings on such problems leave one with the impression that he was interested in them only as building blocks for his macroeconomic structure. His work was almost never carried beyond the point absolutely necessary for the system-building effort.[28] Whenever the existing building blocks seem to fit his purpose, he was, as Mrs. Robinson notes, "content to leave orthodoxy alone"—a comment which would seem to suggest that the value-theoretical content of Keynes' thought was not insignificant, were it not that Mrs. Robinson in the same breath also perpetuates an old canard:

Gerald Shove used to say that Maynard had never spent the twenty minutes necessary to understand the theory of value.[29]

The assumption that Keynes lacked an adequate working knowledge of value theory grants the interpreter of the *General Theory* license to read into it practically whatever he wants. In matters of exegesis, such license should not be practiced too freely.

Keynes' knowledge of economic literature has also been questioned. As with the foregoing question, this is a matter of the standards of reference. On both counts he inevitably falls short if we measure him against his great contemporaries—Knight, Pigou, and Viner. With regard to the contemporary contributions, it should be recalled that Keynes was the long-time editor of the *Economic Journal* and did much to add stature to that publication. As for the "Classics," his education in the history of

---

28. In fact, Keynes did not always take it that far. His sketchy treatment of the determination of the flow-rate of investment is the most familiar example. Keynes' use of the Marginal Efficiency of Capital concept leaves the stock-flow dimensional problems unresolved. The subsequent work by Lerner, Haavelmo, Witte, and others demonstrates quite clearly the magnitude of the problems that Keynes skipped over in order to "get on with" the *General Theory*. There are many other instances where Keynes leaves only a brief sketch of his ideas without pursuing their ramifications. This is particularly true of the problems that will occupy us in Chapter IV.

29. J. Robinson, *Economic Philosophy, op. cit.*, p. 79.

doctrines was a great deal more thorough than is common today.

The lack of scholarly scruple evident in the polemical passages of the *General Theory* should be weighed against the well-balanced, beautifully written, and often moving tributes of his *Essays in Biography*, where Keynes certainly does not show a supercilious attitude towards his great predecessors. The doctrines the *General Theory* attacked as "Classical" were not representative of the best exponents of pre-Keynesian analysis. Nor was this really Keynes' target. His "assault" was directed towards "habitual modes of thought," towards the unimaginative and sterile discussion where, in a situation of dire emergency, lack of initiative was repeatedly defended by invoking "Classical Economics"—not the best thought that Classical economics could offer, but a stereotyped, cliché-ridden version of received doctrine.

Any author who attempts to express what he "feels" or "senses" is wrong with the way other people think, particularly if he employs the kind of drastic tactics used by Keynes, will expose himself to the counter-charge that through ignorance or lack of understanding he has misrepresented the best thinking on the subject. Of this risk, the present author has reason to be aware: in *some* respects, the discussion has dealt, and will deal, not with the best in Keynesian exegesis, but with what the author "feels" to be a widespread, stereotyped interpretation of Keynes and an interpretation that misses some of the most significant aspects of Keynes' contribution.

Thirty years after the start of the Keynesian Revolution we are farther away from, not closer to, achieving a theoretical synthesis than at the time Keynes was writing. Instead of the two-way split between the theories of value and of money that he deplored, we have to live with the three-way split [30] that the Revolution wrought. For some time now, contentment with this state

---

30. I.e., Income-expenditure theory, general equilibrium theory, and the New Quantity theory. The situation is hardly the more comfortable since it is the latter two that have been the source of the exciting new ideas in monetary theory over the last decade or so while the "majority school" seems to have run dry.

of the arts has rested on the motto: "The Theoretically Trivial is the Practically Important and the Practically Important is the Theoretically Trivial." It is a disturbing formula which can hardly be a permanent basis for the further development of the field.

Summary As a theorist and writer, Keynes had several characteristic flaws. At the same time, his *General Theory* caused an intellectual revolution in Economics. In analyzing the book, and in attempting to gain a critical perspective on the Keynesian Revolution, one should not overlook the flaws of the work or of the economist, but one must not exaggerate to the point where the interpretation is given unlimited "degrees of freedom." Otherwise the process whereby economic science progresses—if progress it is—will very likely be made incomprehensible. In particular, one must not approach a work with preconceptions about what the author "should have" said. Yet this has proved particularly tempting in the present case. Too frequently, the standard income-expenditure model has been *imposed* as the model which it is agreed the *General Theory* "should" contain. It has, in effect, become the Procrustean bed on which Keynes is put. If Keynes does not fit, so much the worse for him—the model represents what Keynes actually meant or really intended and, consequently, what he should have said. And when he says something plainly different? To the interpreter using this peculiar approach the answer is clear: "Again [sic!], as in the *Treatise,* Keynes *did not really understand what he had written.* . . ."[31] The impression of Keynes that one gains from such comments is that of a Delphic oracle, half hidden in billowing fumes, mouthing earth-shattering profundities whilst in a senseless trance—an oracle revered for his powers, to be sure, but not worthy of the same respect as that accorded the High Priests whose function it is to interpret the revelations.

If this be how Economics develops—where will it all end?

---

31. L. R. Klein, *op. cit.,* p. 83 (italics added).

I:3 Preview of Following Chapters

Chapter II considers an old issue, namely whether the *General Theory* is "static" or "dynamic." The issue is regarded here as one of form vs. substance. Keynes' formal method of analysis was in many respects "static" and retained a good deal of the corresponding traditional terminology. The theoretical problems with which he was concerned were problems of the "short run," i.e., of disequilibrium. His model was static, but his theory was dynamic. The income-expenditure theory has perpetuated the form but lost much of the substance.

The method is that of analyzing a dynamic adjustment process by breaking it down into "market day," "short run," and "long run" comparative static "equilibria." This method of period-analysis has a long history and was a favorite tool of Keynes' great teacher, Marshall. It has both advantages and disadvantages. Sequential period-analysis is simpler in that it substitutes step-functions for more complicated time-paths of the variables —a decisive advantage if the analysis relies on verbal argument to a substantial extent. But the simplicity can by the same token be misleading—one characteristic danger, for example, is that propositions referring to the average rate of change of a variable over the unit period tend to become indistinguishable from propositions relating to its average value or level.[1] The tools of equilibrium-analysis must be handled with much circumspection when what is being analyzed is not an equilibrium state but an equilibrating process, i.e., a succession of disequilibrium states. If the result is not to be ambiguous, great care must be taken in specifying—and justifying—the lag-structure assumed. This becomes especially difficult when the analysis involves *several* interrelated markets, a difficulty amply illustrated by the Liquidity Preference versus Loanable Funds Controversy.

Keynes, apparently, had little feel for the limitations of this method. One of his faults, when bent on economic-political "per-

---

1. Specifically, the proposition of *imperfect* wage-flexibility is easily confounded with that of wage-*rigidity*.

suasion," was impatience with technical detail. It is known for a fact that he had no patience at all with the technicalities of period-analysis.[2] In assuming that this was an area in which shortcuts could safely be taken, Keynes was certainly mistaken. The mistake has caused his ideas on the Theory of Markets to be misunderstood or overlooked.

Keynes inverted the ranking of price- and quantity-adjustment velocities characteristic of Marshall's period-analysis. The initial response to a decline in demand is a quantity adjustment. Clower has shown that the Keynesian income-constrained, or "multiplier," process can be explained in terms of a general equilibrium system of this dynamic specification. The standard "Keynes and the Classics" analysis places great stress on the restrictive nature of the "wage-rigidity" assumption. But this strong assumption is not necessary in order to explain system behavior of the Keynesian kind.[3] It is sufficient just to give up the equally strong assumption of instantaneous price adjustments.

The Keynesians have, in fact, reverted to explaining unemployment in a manner Keynes was quite critical of, namely by "blaming" depressions on monopolies, labor unions, minimum-wage laws, and the like. Reliance on such institutional constraints on the utility-maximizing behavior of individual transactors carries with it the suggestion that, if "competition" could only be restored, "automatic forces" would take care of the employment problem. Thus the modern appraisal that "Keynesianism" in effect involves the tacit acceptance of the traditional Theory of Markets with the proviso that today's economy corresponds to a "special case" of that theory, namely the case that assumes rigid wages. Keynes, in sharp contrast, sought to attack the foundations of that theory.

Chapter II goes on to examine the presumption that competitive markets would exhibit instantaneous price adjustment. Such

---

2. Schumpeter, *op. cit.*, p. 1184, quotes his advice to a student: "Forget all about periods."

3. I.e., use of Keynes' short-run model need not be predicated on the belief that wages in the real world are "rigid," any more than, say, use of Marshall's market-day construction requires the belief that flow rates of supply are "fixed."

pure price-adjustment behavior in the short run is implied only by models which postulate some version of the "recontract" mechanism. If this very restrictive assumption is relinquished, the generation of the *information* needed to coordinate economic activities in large systems where decision-making is decentralized is seen to take time and to involve economic costs. Alchian has shown that the emergence of unemployed resources is a predictable consequence of a decline in demand when traders do not have perfect information on what the new market-clearing price would be. No other assumption, we argue, need be relinquished in order to get from the Classical to Keynes' Theory of Markets.

The chapter's last section points out that the usual monopoly model implies only that a monopoly will charge a *higher* price than a competitive industry. In its most common version at least, it does not imply that profit-maximizing monopolies generally will respond more *slowly* in adjusting their prices to changes in demand than would competitive industries. This aspect of the income-expenditure model, therefore, would seem to require further analytical attention.

Chapter III also concerns the gulf between macrotheory and value theory. Where the discussion of Chapter II leads to a comparison of what may for the sake of brevity be called the "dynamic structure" of macrotheories, this chapter compares the "aggregative structures" of alternative macromodels. While both chapters focus on the differences between the income-expenditure model and Keynes' theory, the methods used should be equally applicable to the systematic comparison of other types of theories.

Chapter III begins with some simple illustrations of the principles of aggregation theory. The purpose is to emphasize that a major part of the value-theoretical content of a macromodel will often be hidden in the aggregates from which the explicit analysis starts. Controversies over the derived implications of alternative theories most often have their roots in the assumptions underlying competing models. But it sometimes proves difficult to trace such theoretical conflicts to assumptions which have been explicitly stated. This is partly because we habitually concentrate on making those assumptions explicit which specify the relationships between the variables actually appearing in the model. The immediately antecedent stage in model-construction, i.e., the selection of aggregates, is often the stage where implicit theorizing enters in.[4]

The behavioral assumptions underlying a particular mode of aggregation are, however, just as important as the behavioral relationships assumed to hold between the variables defined. The first type of assumption is often left implicit and particular aggregative structures are thus left to develop into undisputed conventions while at the same time controversies rage over the second type of assumption. The reason is, perhaps, that the first type is regarded as dealing merely with the problem of ruling out the "unimportant," whereas the second deals with the task of specifying the nature of the "important" economic relationships. We may refer again to Schumpeter's discussion of the "Vision" which the theorist seeks to embody in a model. In terms of this vision of how the world works, certain classes of events are regarded as of little or no significance in the over-all picture. An example of such a class of events may be changes in the relative prices of a given group of goods. If changes in these relative prices are regarded as having no significant consequences, or no significant *predictable* consequences, e.g., for aggregate employment, there is no reason for them to clutter up a model whose principal purpose is to provide an explanation of the forces determining employment. The "unimportant" price variables can then be removed by aggregating the corresponding group of goods.

An investigation of the aggregative structure of a macromodel will thus give us insight into what its author regards as unimpor-

---

4. The aggregation problem was one aspect of model-construction, at least, where one can hardly fault Keynes for being impatient with technicalities. His discussion of these problems is instead quite thorough and one can therefore rely directly on textual evidence in reconstructing his model and in comparing its aggregative structure with that of the income-expenditure model. Systematic attention to matters of aggregation has been one of the recognized virtues of the *Treatise*. Cf. A. G. Hart, "An Examination of Mr. Keynes's Price-Level Concepts," *Journal of Political Economy*, Oct. 1933.

tant. Such an investigation may not appear to be a very gainful type of employment. It becomes interesting, however, when we begin to compare models of different aggregative structure. Differences in aggregative structure mean that one author has left in relationships which another has removed by aggregation and *vice versa*. This, in turn, implies some disagreement on what classes of events play the most significant role in determining the values of the variables in which the macrotheorist or the policy-maker is ultimately concerned. Through this approach it will sometimes be possible to come to the root of macroeconomic controversies or, as in the present case of "Keynes and the Keynesians," to bring to the surface a conflict which has long remained dormant.

The major points that emerge from the comparison undertaken in the chapter's second section are the following. The aggregate production function makes the standard income-expenditure model a "one-commodity model." The price of capital goods in terms of consumer goods is fixed. The money wage is "rigid," and the current value of physical assets is tied down within the presumably narrow range of short-run fluctuations in the "real" wage rate. Relative values are, indeed, allowed little play in this construction. At the same time, however, this type of model allows us to define so-called "real" values for all nominal variables—a major convenience in dealing with many problems and one which Keynes' theory does not permit. In the standard model, "money" includes only means of payment, while all claims to cash come under the heading of "bonds."

The aggregative structure of the *General Theory* is a condensed version of the model of the *Treatise,* with its richer menu of short-term assets. As emphasized in the preceding section, the distinction between "capital goods" and "consumer goods" is essential—Keynes' initial decision to leave the fold of the Quantity Theory tradition was based principally on the importance he assigned to variations in the relative price of these two aggregates. Thus Keynes has a "two-commodity model." Keeping the level of aggregation the same (i.e., at four goods) for purposes of comparison, we must then find a corresponding difference in the treatment of non-produced goods between the two theories. The income-expenditure theory's distinction between physical and financial non-money assets must, we argue, be dropped in considering Keynes' model. In the latter, all titles to prospective income-streams are lumped together in what is here called "non-money assets." Bond-streams and equity-streams are treated as perfect substitutes, a simplification which Keynes achieved through some quite mechanical manipulations of risk and liquidity premia.

The fundamental property which distinguishes non-money assets, on the one hand from consumables, and on the other from "money," is that the former are "long" while the latter two are "short"—attributes which, in Keynes' usage, were consistently equated with "Fixed" (or "illiquid") and "Liquid" respectively. Basically, Keynes' method of aggregation differentiates between goods with a relatively high and a relatively low interest-elasticity of present value. Thus the two distinctions are not hard and fast but questions of degree. As a matter of course, the definition of "money" includes all types of deposits, since their interest-elasticity of present value is zero, but the term can be extended to cover also other types of short-term assets when convenient. The typical non-money assets are bonds with a long term to maturity and titles to physical assets with a very long "duration of use or consumption." Correspondingly, "the" interest rate in Keynes' works is always the long-term rate of interest.

The most straightforward application of these findings is to the question of the interest-elasticity of investment, an issue which has been central to the debates over the "effectiveness" of monetary policy ever since the Oxford Surveys of the late thirties. In the last section of Chapter III, we obtain the first piece of the puzzle of how Keynes, in contrast to the Keynesians, could regard low interest rates, in Harrod's words, as a matter "of the greatest significance of all."

The determination of the demand price of the representative "Fixed Capital" asset Keynes handled as an ordinary present value problem. On the one side, the price depends upon entrepreneurial expectations of the earnings stream in prospect. These expectations were discussed in terms of certainty-equivalents. On the other side, since such certainty-equivalent streams are regarded as perfect substitutes for bond-streams of comparable time-profile, the rate of interest for the appropriate maturity class of bonds is the discount rate by which the present value of prospective earnings is to be evaluated. In Keynes' analysis of the short run, the State of Expectation (*alias* the Marginal Efficiency of Capital) is assumed to be given, so that the price of assets varies simply (inversely) with "the" interest rate.

In Keynes' language, "a decline in the interest rate" *means* "a rise in the market prices of capital goods, equities, and bonds." Since the representative non-money asset is very long-lived, its interest-elasticity of present value is quite high. The price-elasticity of the output of augmentable income sources is very high. The interest-elasticity of investment is therefore necessarily significant, as a purely logical matter,[5] in terms of Keynes' model. There is no question here but that control over the long rate by the Central Bank would mean control over the rate of investment and, thereby, money income and employment. To Keynes, the problem with monetary policy lies not in the interest-inelasticity of investment but in the inflexibility of the long-term rate of interest.

Chapter IV. In Chapter II we analyzed Keynes' short-run contraction process in terms of a system which resembled the usual atemporal, general equilibrium model with which it was compared in that to all appearances it "had no future"—intertemporal decisions and prices, and the stock-flow relationships between current expenditures and net worth or real balances, etc., were ignored. Although this served to put the "multiplier" into price-theoretical perspective, the analysis thus shared the major weaknesses of the cruder versions of the income-expenditure model. This simplistic approach seems adequate to the analysis of the system's reaction-path once a disequilibrium has emerged.

Keynes' conception of the nature of the disequilibrium that forces contraction upon the economy is the very core of his theory. Without a firm grasp of this, it is almost impossible to see

---

5. Although the assumptions which make it so remain hidden in the aggregative structure that Keynes postulated.

any coherence or continuity in his expressed views on theoretical and empirical issues or questions of economic policy. His diagnosis of the malady, of which unemployment and other social ills are but the symptoms, will be the main concern of Chapter V. Keynes' diagnosis is an ambitious topic, however, for it deals with *intertemporal disequilibrium* and thus combines the difficulties of capital theory and of disequilibrium-analysis.

Before we try to discuss "what goes wrong" in Keynes' system, we must have a clear idea of how that system is supposed to work, i.e., of the mechanisms which are assumed to link income account to capital account variables. This is the subject of Chapter IV. This chapter will be a lengthy affair, partly because of the intrinsic difficulty of capital theory, partly because Keynes did not work out his ideas on the subject in much detail so that we are left with only what amounts to an unfinished sketch. The value-theoretical foundation of the relationships that he explicitly postulated is in some cases not at all clear and the interpretation essayed in this chapter will consequently be more speculative than in the rest of our study. The attempt must nonetheless be made, even though we have no illusions of having provided the last word on the issues involved.

The first order of business must be to establish that Keynes did pay some attention to the subject, for it is a widely held belief that the main analytical weaknesses of the Keynesian tradition are to be traced back to Keynes' own neglect of the influence of capital and "real" asset values on behavior.[6] The major impetus to this familiar criticism of early Keynesian economics derives from the modern theories of the consumption function, which have drastically modified the old consumption-income relation by their emphasis on variously formulated wealth-saving relationships. The criticisms of Keynes' alleged neglect of wealth as a variable influencing spending have similarly been directed specifically against the *ad hoc* "psychological law" on which he based his consumption-income relation. The first section of Chapter IV points out that this ignores Keynes' "windfall effect"

---

6. Cf., e.g., H. G. Johnson, "The *General Theory* After Twenty-Five Years," *American Economic Review*, May 1961, pp. 9, 11, 17; D. Patinkin, *Money, Interest, and Prices*, 2nd edn., New York, 1965, p. 636.

—a Second Psychological Law of Consumption which states simply that the propensity to consume out of current income will be higher the higher the value of household net worth in terms of consumer goods. A rise in the propensity to consume may therefore be caused either by an increase in the marginal efficiency of capital or by a decline in the long rate of interest. Since in the short run the marginal efficiency is taken as given, it is the latter relationship that concerns us: current saving does depend upon the interest rate.

The standard interpretation of Keynes focuses on the passages in which he argues that "changes in the rate of time-discount" will *not* significantly influence saving. On the present interpretation, these well-known passages express the assumption that household preferences exhibit a high degree of intertemporal complementarity, so that the intertemporal substitution effects of interest movements may be ignored. This is a negative conclusion at best, but it indicates that the windfall effect must be interpreted as a wealth effect.

The trouble is that it is far from obvious that there should be such a wealth effect. Keynes gave no clear account of the microtheoretical foundation of the effect—he just indicated his firm confidence in it as another "psychological law." Here the sketchiness of his capital theory becomes a bother. There is not much more than a number of scattered *obiter dicta* to work with. Up to this point, one has little difficulty in giving a price-theoretical interpretation to such pronouncements of Keynes, for it can be safely assumed that they refer to the generally accepted body of atemporal value theory produced by the Marginalist Revolution of Menger, Walras, and Marshall. But, in capital theory, there was no such generally accepted body of doctrine in Keynes' time. Instead, several furious controversies raged simultaneously in the thirties, concerning the very foundation of the subject, i.e., the "proper" choice of basic postulates that an acceptable theory of capital and interest "should" include. In the *General Theory,* one finds a mix of seemingly discordant echoes from Cassel, Fisher, Knight, Wicksell, and others. In the second section of Chapter IV we seek to provide some background to

Keynes' sketch by relating it to these other competing capital theories.[7]

Next, we take up Hicks' analysis of the wealth effect of interest rate movements. The wealth effect of a decline in interest will be positive, Hicks shows, if the average period of the anticipated income stream exceeds the average period of the transactor's planned consumption stream. Households that anticipate the receipt of streams which are, roughly speaking, "longer" than their planned consumption streams, are made wealthier by a decline in the interest rate. The present value of net worth increases in greater proportion than the present cost of the old consumption plan, and the consumption plan can thus be raised throughout.

There are a number of statements in Keynes' works which indicate his "Vision" of a world in which currently active households must, directly or indirectly, hold their net worth in the form of titles to streams that run beyond their consumption horizon. The duration of the relevant consumption plan is limited by the sad fact that "in the Long Run, we are all dead." But the great bulk of the "Fixed Capital of the modern world" is very long-term in nature and is thus destined to survive the generation which now owns it. This is the basis for the wealth effect of changes in asset values.

The interesting point about this interpretation of the wealth effect is that it also provides a price-theoretical basis for Keynes' Liquidity Preference theory. The last section of Chapter IV discusses the term structure of interest hypothesis, which is an integral part of that theory. In recent years, Keynes' (as well as Hicks') statement of this hypothesis has been repeatedly criticized for not providing any rationale for the presumption that the system *as a whole* wants to shed "capital uncertainty" rather than "income uncertainty." But Keynes' mortal consumers cannot hold land, buildings, corporate equities, British consols, or other

---

7. Many readers may want to skip this section entirely. After some vacillation I have included it in the text, rather than as a separate appendix, but it can be treated as an appendix with little loss to the continuity of the discussion of Keynes.

permanent income sources "to maturity." When the representative, risk-averting transactor is nonetheless induced by the
productivity of roundabout processes to invest his savings in
such income sources, he must be resigned to suffer capital uncertainty. Forward markets will therefore generally show what
Hicks called a "constitutional weakness" on the demand side.

Chapter V reaps the results of the long labors of Chapters III
and IV. It contains our reckoning with the "Neoclassical Synthesis." The synthesis has grown out of the debate over the Pigou-
effect. Keynes discussed the Pigou-effect in some detail. He concluded that it was of a secondary order of magnitude at best and
that, therefore, the only hope from deflation lies in the prospect
that it will lower the rate of interest and thereby raise aggregate
demand. This position of Keynes' has been regarded as entirely
unsatisfactory by the Neoclassicists, who have on the one hand
discounted the last-mentioned possibility (Keynes' "only hope")
and, on the other, strongly insisted that Keynes did not concede
nearly enough to the Pigou-effect.

This appraisal stems from a misconception about the aim and
content of Keynes' argument. Patinkin and Kuenne, for example,
take for granted that Keynes sought to oust all of received price
theory from macrotheory, that he was out to deny the position
basic to Classical theory, namely that there should be some
appropriate change in relative values possible so that full employment could prevail.

The second section explains Keynes' diagnosis of the problem:
the "trouble" arises from inappropriately low prices of augmentable non-money assets relative to both wages and consumer
goods prices. *Relative values are wrong.* Consequently, balanced
deflation (as implied by the Pigou argument) will not correct
the situation. This requires instead that asset demand prices fall
less than wages do, i.e., that asset prices are raised relative to
wages. If the deflation does not raise the marginal efficiency of
capital, this indeed requires—as Keynes insisted—that the long
rate of interest be brought down through "the effect of the
abundance of money in terms of the wage-unit."

This once more highlights the role of the rate of interest in

Keynes' theory and especially the role of the speculative activity which stabilizes yields and prevents the interest rate from adjusting in a "Classical" manner. The last section, therefore, considers those criticisms of Keynes' Speculative Demand for Money that have led modern monetary theorists to take an increasingly dim view of this idea and to rely on the inventory theory of the demand for money as the foundation for the interest-elasticity of the function. The criticism of Keynes focuses on his assumption of inelastic expectations on the part of bond-holders, an assumption, it is argued, for which there is no clear rationale and which therefore must be regarded as a "special case." We point out that the explanation of the emergence of unemployed resources in atomistic markets also relies on inelastic expectations and the consequent "speculative" reservation demand of suppliers. The assumption of inelastic expectations, we argue, is a natural one when dealing with a model that takes a realistic view of the market information on which transactors have to base their decisions. The assumption only looks contrived when the problem is formulated in terms of a Walrasian perfect information model.

Keynes had a very broad conception of "Liquidity Preference," but in the Keynesian literature the term has acquired the narrow meaning of "demand for money," and this demand is usually discussed in terms of the choice between means of payment and one of the close substitutes which Keynes included in his own definition of "money." In part, this is the result of the fact that the *General Theory* only distinguished two classes of assets— "money" and others. The *Treatise* is less aggregative and one has to go back to this work to get a detailed picture of how bear speculation prevents Keynes' system from adjusting to a decline in the marginal efficiency of capital without falling into contraction. Keynes' discussion of this topic affords some interesting parallels to more recent analyses, by Gurley and Shaw and others, on the role of financial intermediaries in income determination.

Chapter VI sums up the main line of our argument: Keynes, in the interpretation offered here, departed from the postulates of Classical doctrine on only one point. Furthermore, the postulate which he relinquished should have been recognized as objection-able in the first place. His model is characterized by the absence of a "Walrasian auctioneer" assumed to furnish, without charge and without delay, all the information needed to obtain the perfect coordination of the activities (both spot and future) of all traders. That his theory does without the contrived assump-tion of "recontracting" means that his claim to having attempted a more "general theory" is justified.

The first section ends with the suggestion that the "post-Keynesian" development of cybernetics as an interdisciplinary field studying communication and control in complex dynamic systems may provide valuable suggestions for economists inter-ested in exploring the "revolutionary" approach to monetary theory towards which Keynes was groping.

This study deals with what Keynes called his "Pure Theory." In the course of the discussion, however, we will repeatedly comment on various aspects of his "Applied Theory." The second section of Chapter VI attempts to pull these scattered comments together in order to elucidate Keynes' views on fiscal versus monetary policy, and on the type of situations in which primary reliance on one or the other set of policies is indicated. Keynes' Applied Theory, it is pointed out, does not deserve the accolade of "general"—not only are some of the empirical hypotheses invoked subject to dispute, but his arguments in favor of various policies are also based on a number of value judgments which are quite subjective in nature.

II · UNEMPLOYMENT DISEQUILIBRIUM: DYNAMIC PROCESSES AND THE COMPARATIVE STATIC METHOD

II:1 Price-Level and Income Adjustments

The phenomenal success of early Keynesianism, particularly in the United States, has often been attributed to the historical context in which the *General Theory* made its appearance. This is undoubtedly correct. Yet, it is also puzzling in at least two respects. Is it not rather strange, after all, that a model with wage-rigidity acknowledged to be its main distinguishing feature should become widely accepted as crystallizing the experience of the unprecedented wage-deflation of the Great Depression? And is the early Keynesian view that "money is unimportant" the natural conclusion to draw from the worst banking debacle in U.S. history?

This chapter deals with the first of these two puzzles. The second has to await a detailed discussion of Keynes' treatment of capital, wealth, and liquidity. Keynes' explanation of how "changing views about the future are capable of influencing the quantity of employment," [1] we have broken down into two stages: (1) the stock-flow analysis of the causes of changes in the rate of money expenditures, and (2) the analysis of the effects of changes in the rate of money expenditures on prices, output, and employment. The latter is the subject here; the analysis of this stage focuses almost exclusively on flow relationships.

The reaction of real output and employment to fluctuations in the money rate of aggregate demand is a problem in short-run dynamics on which an extensive literature exists. It is common in that literature to start from a hypothetical full employment equilibrium and to consider the adjustment process following a disequilibrating disturbance. We shall follow this convention and in addition specify that throughout, the disturbance considered is deflationary. Full adjustment to the disturbance entails restoration of full employment equilibrium. Our interest is in the nature of the disequilibrium situation at some point within the time-interval before the economy settles on a new equilibrium time-path.

"Pseudo-dynamics": Keynes versus Marshall Keynes dealt with dynamic processes by means of a "comparative statics" period-analysis. His employment of a static apparatus has frequently been criticized, but the critique has often suffered from a confusion of the method and substance of the *General Theory:* the subject of his work is not "unemployment equilibrium" but the nature of the macroeconomic process of *adjustment* to a disequilibrating disturbance. The method attempts to analyze this continuous process with the tools of static equilibrium theory. The device which makes such a method possible involves the conceptual partitioning of the continuous adjustment process into discrete stages or "periods." This device was not Keynes' invention. Marshall had made much use of it, and in this aspect of his method, as in many others, Keynes was very Marshallian.[2]

---

1. *General Theory*, p. vii.

2. Cf. H. G. Johnson, "The *General Theory* after Twenty-Five Years," *American Economic Review*, May 1961, p. 3, and J. Robinson, *loc. cit.*

But Keynes differed substantively from Marshall as well as from other price theorists in the use he made of this device.

In general equilibrium flow models, *prices* are the only endogenous variables which enter as arguments into the demand and supply functions of individual households. Tastes and initial resource endowments are parametric. In "Keynesian" flow models the corresponding arguments are *real income* and the interest rate. Of these, real income is a measure of *quantity*, not of price.[3] On a highly abstract level, the fundamental distinction between general equilibrium and Keynesian models lies in the appearance of this quantity variable in the excess demand relations of the latter.[4] The difference is due to the assumptions made about the adjustment behavior of the two systems. In the short run, the "Classical" system adjusts to changes in money expenditures by means of price-level movements; the Keynesian adjusts primarily by way of real income movements.

An analogy between price-level and real income movements in a macrosystem, and price and quantity adjustments in a single market will be helpful in illustrating the issues. Consider the Marshallian analysis of the adjustment process in a single market (for a perishable good) following a rightward shift of the demand schedule: (1) in the *market period*, the amount supplied is treated as given, and price moves to the corresponding point on the demand schedule; (2) in the *short run*, quantity supplied increases until supply and demand price are equal; (3) in the *long run*, capital stock grows, lowering unit cost and raising the rate of sales, until "normal" rates of profit are restored.

The partitioning of the adjustment process into periods is an ingenious and, in many applications, intuitively appealing device. But it is important to see what is going on. The common-sense observation that price can be altered more easily than the

---

3. In the usual income-expenditure model there is no problem in defining "real income." Within the framework of Keynes' theory, however, it is *impossible* to define a satisfactory quantity index for total output. This is a major point in our argument for rejecting the standard income-expenditure interpretation of the *General Theory*. This contrast between the two types of theories is not very significant in the context of this chapter and the issue will therefore be put aside until Chapter III.

4. Cf. R. W. Clower, "The Keynesian Counterrevolution . . . ," *op. cit.*

rate of output, which in turn can be altered faster than the size of plant, has been purified into the abstract assumptions that price reacts *infinitely* fast relative to output, and output relative to capital stock. Two steps are really involved here; the first is the assumption that prices do, in fact, adjust much more rapidly than output in response to any given disturbance; the second is the judgment that the essential elements of the process can be adequately analyzed by the comparative static period method.

In the Marshallian period-analysis of a single market, the reaction velocities of price, output rate, and capital stock are made subject to a qualitative ranking.[5] In the Marshallian short run, for example, the speed of price adjustment is regarded as infinite, that of capital stock as zero. ("Capital is a parameter in the short run.") The temporal length of the short run is regarded as determined in a rough way by the time it takes for quantity supplied to come into adjustment with demand at the short-run equilibrium price.

In an explicitly dynamic treatment of the adjustment process, the adjustment velocity of a variable is regarded as a dependent variable. The time dimension can be introduced into the optimizing problem, e.g., by making costs dependent not only upon the rate of output but also on its speed of change. *In dynamic models, the choice of speeds of adjustment of the decision variables enter into the optimizing problem of transactors on a par with the choice of their levels on which the conventional static theory focuses.* One must always keep in mind that period-analysis, far from being a way of attacking these dynamic problems, is an attempt to avoid them altogether.

In the Keynesian macrosystem the Marshallian ranking of price- and quantity-adjustment speeds is reversed: In the shortest period flow quantities are freely variable, but one or more prices are given, and the admissible range of variation for the rest of the prices is thereby limited.

The "revolutionary" element in the *General Theory* can perhaps not be stated in simpler terms. That the alternative dynamics which Keynes thus proposed would lead to a theoretical

---

5. Compare P. A. Samuelson, *Foundations of Economic Analysis,* Cambridge, Mass., 1947, esp. pp. 329 ff.

revolution in economic theory may on this basis seem paradoxical. It becomes understandable only when one realizes the full extent to which the Marshallian dynamics was entrenched in the thinking of Keynes' contemporaries. Fresh ideas are ever more powerful when simple.

The market period solution state for Marshall's isolated market implies an ongoing tendency for the rate of supply to change. Similarly, the unemployment solution state of the Keynesian short-run system implies in general an ongoing tendency for prices to fall in the non-clearing markets. Quite apart from the net accumulation of capital (positive or negative) which is taking place, the solution state is therefore not a full equilibrium state in the proper sense. It seems entirely beside the point, however, to criticize the theory on the grounds that "Keynes was unable . . . to solve the riddle of how to reconcile competition and unemployment . . . ," [6] or to argue that the *General Theory* contributed nothing new, since the possibility of unemployment in a system of rigid prices and wages had long been recognized. Keynes' predecessors had not attempted a comparably ambitious systematic investigation of the dynamic behavior of an interdependent macrosystem characterized by relatively inflexible prices and, consequently, by quantity (income) adjustments.

From this perspective, Keynes' "long struggle to escape" seems primarily to have been a struggle with the dynamics of the Marshallian period-analysis. Many critics as well as sympathetic interpreters of Keynes have had similar difficulties in freeing themselves from the intuitive plausibility of Marshall's ranking. A typical reaction to the quantity-adjustment type of theory has been that the implied short-run price-inflexibilities must be due to elements of "monopolistic restraints." [7] Such reaction would

---

6. G. Haberler in S. E. Harris, ed., *The New Economics,* New York, 1950, p. 176. The implied connotation that "competition" bears here—as well as in other similar appraisals—is that of "infinite price-flexibility." Since there is every reason to doubt that Keynes ever set out on the quixotic quest of reconciling perfect price-flexibility with unemployment of resources, this seems an inappropriate frame of reference for the evaluation of his contribution.

7. Haberler, *op. cit.,* is an example of a fairly moderate reaction along these lines. Emphasis on "monopolistic elements" puts the analytical diagnosis of depressions back to its pre-Keynesian stage. Cf. esp. L. Robbins, *The Great Depression,*

seem to reveal an "a prioristic" conviction that to rank quantity velocities higher than price velocities in the short-run analysis of markets with numerous transactors is to upset the "natural order of things." Despite the Keynesian Revolution, this is still an entrenched view and, therefore, one worth examining. This is done in section 3 of this chapter.

False trading   If prices are not "perfectly flexible"—that is, if they do not adjust instantly and fully "before any trade takes place"—transactions will be concluded at disequilibrium prices. This is Hicks' "false trading." Hicks notes that false trading creates analytically troublesome income effects: ". . . if there is a change in price in the midst of trading, the situation appears to elude the ordinary apparatus of demand-and-supply analysis." [8] The price at which trading starts on any particular "day" following a disturbance cannot be assumed to be the equilibrium price, it "can only be a guess." Some "false trading" will therefore take place, imparting "a certain degree of indeterminateness" to the ordinary analysis. Hicks argued, however, that such false transactions would be "limited in volume" [9] and these income effects could therefore be ignored as of secondary magnitude only. The

London, 1934—an account of the Depression in which history and economic analysis are skillfully interwoven, but the emphasis is wholly on the causal role of such obstacles to the automatic recuperative powers of an unhampered, competitive economic system. Cf. the reference to Professor Robbins, *General Theory*, p. 20.

The presumption underlying this kind of analysis—that, if monopolistic restraints can be removed, the system can be left alone by the policy-maker and no substantial quantity adjustments will be necessary—was undoubtedly the chief target of Keynes' often intemperate attacks on existing theory in the 1930's. Cf., e.g., *General Theory*, p. 276, and the last section of this chapter.

8. J. R. Hicks, *Value and Capital*, Oxford, 1939, p. 128.

9. *Op. cit.*, p. 129: "If any intelligence is shown in price-fixing, they will be." The whole of Chapter IX is of interest here, esp. pp. 119–22 and 127–29.

The dynamics of Part III of *Value and Capital* is characteristically built on a modified form of the Marshallian period-analysis.

In connection with Section II:2, below, it should be noted that Hicks developed his discussion of the formation of prices in the context of a model in which transactors have *single-valued* expectations about the future prices they will face. Implicit is the assumption that they expect to be able to sell or buy whatever quantities they desire at these anticipated prices. Hicks has provided a lucid

price vector established on "Monday"—to rule unchanged through the rest of the Hicksian week—could therefore be assumed to approximate closely the solution vector of a Walrasian system of offer and demand curves.

Since Hicks treats the supplies available on his market day as fixed stocks, in traditional fashion, the equilibrium price vector is assumed to be established before any changes in resource utilization take place. Thus, Hicks is concerned with *redistributive* income effects in his discussion of "false trading": buyers who make purchases at above equilibrium prices suffer a loss of real income; the corresponding sellers gain, etc. This explains his lack of concern with the false trading problem. With market-day resource utilization predetermined (and with the certainty-equivalent treatment of price expectations), there is no presumption that these distribution effects will affect real aggregate demand—and thereby real aggregate output during the rest of the "week"—in any particular direction.

The income-constrained process   Clower's contribution forces a drastic revision of this view of false trading. Here the attention is focused not on the distribution effects caused by transactions that *do* in fact take place at false prices, but on the aggregative income effects caused by the transactions which do *not* take place *because* of the false prices. Clower considers the specific instance of a disequilibrium price pertaining in the market for factor services supplied by households, thus staying close to the theoretical structure of the *General Theory*. ("Wages are rigid.") Current household receipts ("income") are determined not by the quantity of services a household would *want to* supply at the price at which such services are currently bought,[10] but by how

---

discussion of the strengths and weaknesses of the dynamic method of *Value and Capital* (and of the major alternatives). Cf. his "Methods of Dynamic Analysis," in *25 Economic Essays in Honour of Erik Lindahl*, Stockholm, 1956 (esp. pp. 143–45). The most comprehensive statement of Hicks' views is found in his *Capital and Growth*, New York, 1965, Part I.

10. In exchange equilibrium, a single price will equate supply and demand in the market for a homogenous good. When the market does not clear, there is no reason why all the transactions that do take place should do so at the same price. This problem, as well as the explanation of why a market-clearing price fails to emerge in the first place, is taken up in Section II:3.

much it will actually succeed in selling. Its *effective demand* in other markets will be *constrained* by the *income* actually achieved. This is the crucial point. *Realized transaction quantities* enter as arguments of the excess demand functions in addition to prices.[11]

The Keynesian consumption function embodies this dependence of aggregate demand on realized household income. The aggregate consumption function is often said to be the distinguishing feature of Keynesian Economics. Keynes himself insisted that the consumption function embodied the chief innovation of the *General Theory*. While more familiar, this contention is not at all inconsistent with the one made above, namely that the reversal of the Marshallian ranking of adjustment velocities is the revolutionary element of the *General Theory*. Emphasis on the underlying dynamic nature of Keynes' theoretical innovation is helpful in one respect at least. From this perspective the simple relation between consumption expenditures and measured income is viewed as a short-run, dynamic "reaction function." Since receipts from currently realized sales of household services do not in themselves constitute the budget-constraint on current household purchases, there is no presumption that this simple relation should be stable in the long run. Shifts in the simple consumption-income relation, or so-called "ratchet effects," are in fact to be expected.[12]

The constraint on household income, emerging through the inability of traders to sell all they want at "the" prevailing market price, leads to a reduction in effective demand in product markets *with further* ("multiplier") *repercussions on aggregate income*. This deviation-amplifying feedback-loop is characteristic of Keynesian quantity-adjustment models. The decline in income tends to proceed below the level to which it was brought by the initial shock. In the more common terminology (which is, however, sometimes misleading), the contraction is "cumulative." A "Classical" general equilibrium model, in contrast, presents the

---

11. Clower, *op. cit.*

12. For a further discussion of the operative budget-constraint on current purchases, cf. Chapter IV.

reassuring picture of an economic system equipped exclusively with deviation-counteracting feedback mechanisms.[13]

Implicit in this "multiplier" process is a short-run reaction function of producers—the "aggregate supply function," until recent years slighted in much of the income-expenditure literature.[14] The fall in effective demand for current output leads producers further to curtail their demand for labor, etc. Producer spending on current factor services is thus a function of current receipts from sales. This simple relation cannot be presumed to be stable in the long run either. In Keynesian disequilibrium, firms, like households, are to some extent constrained by their inability to sell what they want at the prices of the moment. Firms, like households also, are not dependent solely on current revenues to finance current purchases. A firm's willingness and ability to utilize other sources of funds at a particular time will depend on both the longer-run outlook and its financial position.[15] Since these are variable, the short-run reaction function of producers will usually shift over time.

The short-run solution state of the Keynesian model will find prices and wages falling. But they must now fall *below* the levels that, in the first period, would have brought clearance of all markets had prices been "perfectly flexible" to begin with. Once the deviation-amplifying feedbacks characteristic of this system have taken hold, the deviation-counteracting price adjustments become less effective. As an illustration suppose that, following the initial reduction in aggregate demand, an instantaneous across-the-board wage cut of X/unit time would have been sufficient to induce employers to maintain full employment through period 1. This did not happen; instead, some workers

---

13. This statement neglects the possibility of unstable market-clearing states. Throughout this study we will compare Keynes' theory only with "well-behaved" Classical systems.

14. Cf. A. L. Marty, "A Geometrical Exposition of the Keynesian Supply Function," *Economic Journal*, Sept. 1961.

15. It would be incongruous, of course, to combine the "imperfect" markets for current output and factor services with so-called "perfect capital markets" in the same model. "Perfect capital markets" presumes generally shared, certainty-equivalent expectations, and would naturally all but obviate the current income-constraints here under discussion.

lost their jobs and the income-constrained process came into operation, producing, in Schumpeter's term, a "secondary" decline in demand. With the demand conditions that employers thus perceive themselves as facing at the beginning of period 2, a wage reduction of X dollars would no longer be sufficient to induce them to reabsorb all the unemployed labor right away.[16] In the early stages of contraction, prices may then fail to keep pace with the fall in hypothetical market-clearing prices, with the gap between the actual and the short-run full employment price level widening instead of narrowing, even though the ongoing reduction be drastic to anyone but an observer obsessed with continuous full resource utilization as the Natural Order of the competitive system. In this phase, the contraction of real income would continue.

The alternatives Macroeconomic adjustment processes involving both price and income effects simultaneously in all markets are extremely complicated. To handle them empirically would require information of a kind and quality which, even today, seems beyond achievement. In constructing short-run macromodels, the economist therefore has to choose. At one extreme of a spectrum of possibilities are the traditional full employment models where the whole brunt of adjustments is borne by prices; at the other extreme are the "pure Keynesian"

---

16. Other possibilities might also have been adduced, e.g., the end of period 1 might find producers burdened with excess inventories and the system on the verge of the contraction phase of a Metzlerian inventory cycle, etc.

Implicitly the illustration used in the text assumes that a *balanced deflation of* appropriate magnitude would simultaneously erase the excess demand for money and corresponding excess supply of commodities (that constitute the "deflationary shock") *if* only this general price-level adjustment took place instantaneously. The reader should be warned, however, that *this would not do the trick* if the disequilibrium were of the type that Keynes postulated. The reasons for this have already been sketched in the outline of Chapter V above (Chapter I:3), but a full statement of the problem must await our discussion of Keynes' appraisal of the Pigou-effect in Chapter V.

Keynes' own best analysis of a disequilibrium situation which requires that a market price (the rate of interest) be forced *below* the level corresponding to its value in a hypothetical equilibrium price vector in order to jolt the system back towards full employment is found in his discussion of the "monetary policy à outrance" in the *Treatise*. Cf. Chapters I:2, V:2, and VI:2.

models where prices are essentially given and income moves. In between lie the complications of the real world which as yet have to be handled with one or the other type of model, modified by reliance on intuition and informed judgment. The choice is no doubt mainly a question of the "Long View and the Short." [17] The use of Keynesian models is in a sense predicated upon the judgment that the short run of pre-Keynesian theory is not so short after all—the ever-present endogenous, automatic forces that tend to bring the economy back to full employment are weak and sluggish when income and price effects interact in this manner. The social costs of passive government policies must be borne over relatively long periods even if no further disturbances occur. From the economist's viewpoint, Keynes' historical importance seems to lie in imposing his view that the "real world" lies closer to the income-model end of the spectrum. The "pure" income-adjustment model is the strategic simplification to make in the analysis of policy problems relating to full resource utilization on an aggregate level. Here the proof of the pudding has been in the eating. Although in the comparative statics of the New Economics the income-constrained process survives only in the form of the multiplier, that "inexhaustibly versatile mechanical toy" [18] is surely a major factor in the continued influence of this otherwise emasculated version of Keynes' theory.

---

17. As Professor Viner has repeatedly emphasized, Classical pre-Walrasian and pre-Marshallian price theory dealt with *long-run* problems. As an unequalled authority on this body of doctrine, Viner was far less disconcerted than many other contemporaries at Keynes' way of upsetting the widely accepted Marshallian ranking of adjustment speeds. In his remarkably incisive review of the *General Theory*, Viner took strong exception mostly to some of Keynes' sweeping long-run generalizations, e.g.: " . . . I would contend that over long periods, given a flexible price system, the propensity to consume will affect the rate of capital accumulation rather than the volume of employment . . . " (Cf. J. Viner, "Mr. Keynes on the Causes of Unemployment," *Quarterly Journal of Economics*, Nov. 1936, p. 164.)

18. H. G. Johnson, *op. cit.*, p. 11. But the amount of attention still accorded the multiplier in the literature dealing with the "Keynesian" simultaneous equation systems is, as Professor Johnson points out (p. 12), rather curious: " . . . the multiplier is a tiresome way of comparing general equilibrium positions."

Appendix: Problems of Period-Analysis

In Keynesian theory the traditional ranking of relative adjustment velocities is altered. This change in the dynamic structure of the basic model used for the analysis of short-run macroproblems has far-reaching implications. The long and involved debate over the relation between Keynesian and "Classical" theory, which followed the appearance of the *General Theory,* was to a great extent concerned with clarifying these implications. Not all of the issues raised in the course of this debate grew out of Keynes' use of a period model dynamically different from the traditional one; some of them involved difficulties generally inherent in the "period model" approach to the analysis of dynamic processes.[1]

The prime difficulty with period models is that actual reaction velocities need not be of a qualitatively different order of magnitude. This is true, for example, of price and output velocities in the case of a single market. Depending upon their relative magnitude, and the position of the initial disequilibrium point in relation to the equilibrium point, the actual adjustment process may involve oscillations (a) in price but not in output—the Marshallian case; (b) in output but not in price—a "micro-Keynesian" case; (c) in neither—i.e., both variables move directly to the equilibrium point; or (d) in both.[2]

The complexity of continuous adjustment models is a great incentive to adopting a discrete treatment of time. This necessitates a qualitative ranking of the reaction velocities in the system. If an unambiguous ranking can be obtained, a further "strategic" decision remains, namely to decide upon the variable whose adjustment speed will determine the period on which the model will focus. All other variables are then either "impounded in the *ceteris paribus*" or considered perfectly variable.

For a single market, alternative dynamic paths can be approximated by period models employing different lag structures. In macromodels with several distinct, composite markets, a strong ordering of all the adjustment speeds for all the markets may be nearly impossible. Cer-

---

1. For example, the controversy over Stock versus Flow Analysis which was part of the Liquidity Preference-Loanable Funds debate.

2. The last case has often been handled with period models with discrete behavioral lags—"cobweb" models.

For a continuous time treatment of the above cases, cf., e.g., D. W. Bushaw and R. W. Clower, *Introduction to Mathematical Economics,* Homewood, Ill., 1957, Chs. III and IV. There is a great increase in the complexity of the models in the latter chapter, where the authors deal with a system of *two* interrelated markets.

tainly no such ordering would command general assent [3] to the extent that the ordering of the Marshallian partial equilibrium model has done. It may be argued that a complete ranking is not necessary; all that is needed is that there be at least one period length which permits the economist to group the variables in two sets—those that are to be considered constant, and those to be considered perfectly variable.[4] Relative adjustment speeds within each of these sets could then be ignored.

The ranking of all the reaction velocities of an entire macrosystem must still generally be made on the basis only of incomplete evidence. But judgments differ among authors, and so do the dynamic structures of their models. A coherent theoretical discussion of short-run problems requires consensus on this ranking—a consensus which has not always been established. If there is *at least one* partitioning of the entire set of variables into "parameters" and "endogenous variables" on which agreement can be reached, then a common brand of short-run theory is also possible. If there is *only one* such partitioning, however, it will not be possible to handle problems of a relatively more "short-run" or "long-run" character.

The equilibrium condition defining the Keynesian short run is the equality of desired savings and investment rates. The actual calendar time counterpart of this short run would be "the time it takes for the multiplier to work itself out."[5] In relation to this period, Keynes assumed money wages, the capital stock, productive technology, and population constant. Consumption (saving), investment, and employment were considered freely variable. In the Keynesian tradition, the money price level and interest rates are usually considered variable, subject to the constraints due to the "fixed" money wage rate; in the *General Theory* itself the permissible short-run movements of the interest rate are restricted by the postulate of inelastic long-term expectations.[6]

---

3. Agreement on assumptions is not a proper *test* of a model. But much of the literature with which we are concerned deals with dynamic problems within a framework of period-analysis models, while at the same time devoting little attention to making these assumptions explicit. The lack of a generally agreed upon ranking has in several instances been an important obstacle to the resolution of past controversies.

4. Since the latter are assumed to adjust fully "within the unit period" of the model, it is clear that the application of this method presumes that the relevant short-run processes are always convergent.

5. Or, rather, for the income-expenditure-income repercussions to die down to a second-order magnitude—another matter on which judgments may differ. Cf. R. M. Goodwin, "The Multiplier," in S. E. Harris, ed., *The New Economics,* New York, 1950.

6. Cf. Chapters III:3 and V.

Consensus on the ranking of adjustment speeds is then one prerequisite for the construction of a generally acceptable short-run macro-model which can be discussed in a logically consistent fashion. Logical consistency of the basic model is not, however, the only requirement of an economic theory. Empirical relevance is another. For short-run "period" models this raises a problem closely related to that of ranking, namely what approximate calendar time interval the model's short run corresponds to. Some conception of the time interval implied by such a model is required for the purposes of testing it, since the data that the economist has to work with are recorded at discrete, and for some variables, rather long, intervals.

Keynesian models have been applied to both yearly and quarterly data, for example. Using quarterly data on an income-expenditure model usually means that it is assumed that desired saving and investment rates are brought into equality by endogenous forces within the quarterly time-span. At times Keynes referred to the multiplier as "instantaneous"—a usage to which many contemporaries reacted unfavorably, since it seemed to imply that *desired* saving and investment were always equal at each and every point in calendar time. On this interpretation the theory would assert that observed rates of income are always to be interpreted as short-run equilibrium rates. This would raise problems with respect to the explanation of movements in income, since such movements must be conceived of as essentially continuous and as adjustments in response to disequilibrium forces, saving and investment being the income-determining factors. Thus D. H. Robertson, for example, deplored Keynes' relinquishing of the *Treatise* approach, according to which the difference between saving and investment at a point in time determined the direction and speed of the change in income.[7]

The time-dimension problem became obscurely interwoven with that of causality in the voluminous "Savings equal Investment" debate. On this issue a broad consensus among "Keynesian" followers gradually emerged—based on the contention that Keynes was confused about the concepts of *"ex ante"* and *"ex post."*[8] But Keynes'

---

7. D. H. Robertson, *Essays in Monetary Theory*, London, 1940, I:1 and IX.

8. There is no doubt whatsoever that Keynes misunderstood completely the Swedish *"ex ante–ex post"* terminology. The semantic misunderstanding made him introduce some overly ingenious complications in an already confused debate. Thus, in his 1937 *Economic Journal* debate with Bertil Ohlin, he assumed *"ex ante"* to have a purely temporal connotation, i.e., meaning "in advance of," or "in anticipation of." He was much intrigued by what he took to be Ohlin's idea of how *"ex ante"* investment could influence *current* income. His two articles on the subject elaborate the notion that investment may influence income before it is actually carried out because entrepreneurs may decide to secure the needed

insistence on the continuous equality of actual savings and investment does serve a useful purpose in the analysis of the behavior of the system when out of short period "equilibrium." The purpose is simple— namely that of providing a check that descriptions of the disequilibrium process do not violate "Say's Principle." The "necessary saving-investment equality" is, as has so often been pointed out, a "tautology without causal significance." But such tautologies, expressing conditions which must be fulfilled, are not to be scorned. The principle has in fact frequently been violated in the income-expenditure literature, particularly in connection with some of the standard comparative statics exercises performed with the help of the well-known "IS-LM" diagram.[9]

The application of the tools of comparative statics to the construction of a model of a dynamic process leaves a result somewhat analogous to a movie cartoon—a series of "dated" snapshots of a process conceived to be continuous.[10] A comparison of two consecutive frames reveals the accumulated result of the processes taking place over a given interval of time, but the cartoon does not give information about the exact state of the portrayed system for any point in time within that interval. In the single market case referred to above, for example, linear interpolation between initial and terminal price-quantity values will only by accident yield the "half-time" situation—depending upon the unknown relative adjustment speed of the endogenous variables, the adjustment might, for instance, involve converging oscillations in both price and quantity traded.

Given the Keynesian model's partitioning of the variables into

---

"investment finance" *in advance* of actual expenditures, thereby raising the demand for money, etc. These ideas, being completely at cross-purposes with Ohlin's discussion, do give a surrealistic flavor to certain passages. Keynes' revealing statement that: "As for the concept of *'ex ante'* saving, I can attach no sound sense to it," is certainly understandable, since he interpreted the term to refer to current income withheld from consumption *in anticipation* of a future increase in income.

Keynes' manifest misunderstanding of this terminology does not prove that he was incapable of distinguishing between "desired" and "actual" magnitudes.

9. Compare Ch. I:2 above and the references to Horwich's work given in that context.

10. A cartoon rather than a film since the model does not record, but simulates the actual process. To spin out the imperfect analogy—the functions determining the values of the endogenous, "perfectly adjusting" variables could be regarded as a complete set of instructions to the draftsman for the drawing of any dated frame for which he is provided with the "parameter" values. A recursive model would give him a self-contained "plot"—the parameters themselves change value over time according to given rules, etc.

"short-run parameters" and "endogenous variables" (with no ordering of adjustment speeds postulated for the latter), the system will show equality of desired saving and investment for all points in time for which the given information permits a solution to be determined. A more detailed account of the dynamic process, which Robertson pleaded for, requires more detailed information on the dynamic structure of the system. If the endogenous variables of Keynes' model could be partitioned into "constants" and "perfectly adjusting variables," an ultrarapid version of the process could be drawn with a greater number of frames per unit calendar time. Robertson's suggestion was that consumption expenditures be regarded as the "slowest" adjusting of the endogenous variables in the Keynesian model. He therefore advocated treating consumption as a "short-run parameter," the value of which would at any point in time be historically determined by the level of income of the preceding period. This particular ordering of the adjustment speeds never did command the general agreement which was finally reached on the Keynesian model and, as a result, interest in "Robertsonian dynamics" waned.

The same type of problem can be equally bothersome when it is desired to extend the study from a given "short run" to some "longer run"—still falling short of the full equilibrium of the stationary state. Thus, if one started from a Robertsonian model there would be a number of possibilities. It might be assumed, for example, that income adjusted "infinitely fast relative to the capital stock," so that in the "longer run" savings and investment became equal "before" investment led to any addition to current capacity. This longer run would then correspond to the Keynesian model. If these two adjustment speeds were ranked in the reverse order, such a recursive Robertsonian model would contain no "frames" identical with a recursive Keynesian model. Starting from the Keynesian "short-run" model, the Harrod-Domar type of growth model presents a difference-equation system which assumes that capital stock "adjusts infinitely faster than the money wage rate," a ranking which for some reason has seldom been seriously questioned. Granted that the money wage is inflexible in the short run, it must still be remembered that "many short periods doth one long run make." Except for his "Notes on the Trade Cycle," Keynes hardly ventured beyond the presentation of the short-run solution of his system in any systematic way. The difference-equation approach to cyclical processes was developed by later Keynesians.

"Savings equal Investment" was hotly debated for a few years. But on the dynamic issues specific to the Keynesian choice of "period," a professional consensus was reached rather quickly. A similar widespread agreement was also reached on the "Keynesian" growth and business cycle models advanced by Harrod, Domar, Hicks and others.[11] In some other areas, the difficulties inherent in the application of comparative statics to essentially dynamic problems were not resolved—the "awkward complications hidden in plain view"[12] remained (and still remain) awkward. These problems have, in particular, haunted[13] the interminable Liquidity Preference versus Loanable Funds debate in which many of the issues still remain in dispute— primarily because of the time-dimension problem. A reading of Professor Johnson's well-known survey article[14] makes it clear how intimately the differences in implications of the many alternative models proposed in the course of the postwar discussion have been related to the choice of periods and the specification of lags.

The "Savings equal Investment" and "Loanable Funds versus Liquidity Preference" controversies, while important to the understanding of the development of the Keynesian tradition, do not excite much interest today. The problems of period-analysis are still with us in the literature on stock-flow analysis. The increasing emphasis on the use of capital concepts in modern theories of income determination makes stock-flow analysis more than ever an important tool.

---

11. Cf., however, A. F. Burns, *The Frontiers of Economic Knowledge*, Princeton, 1954, e.g., pp. 3–25, 207–67. Burns rather vehemently spurned the dynamic structure assumed in these models which he considered to be based on uneducated guesswork.

12. H. G. Johnson, *op. cit.*, p. 2.

13. In 1939 Robertson was already speaking of "the ghost of an old argument dating from the days of the *Treatise on Money*" which kept, as it were, upsetting the table (cf. *op. cit.*, p. 29). According to this argument, an increased rate of savings by consumers will not lower the rate of interest in the "short run"—the short run being defined as the length of lag before producers or distributors adjust their cash outflow to the new situation. Before this adjustment takes place, the producers will have to finance their unplanned increments in inventory by issuing securities so as to offset the excess flow demand for bonds at the old rate.

The postwar debate has been no less spirited. The argument reappears in somewhat different incarnations, for example, in J. Robinson, "The Rate of Interest," *Econometrica*, April 1951, and in H. Rose, "Liquidity Preference and Loanable Funds," *Review of Economic Studies*, Feb. 1957. Professor Johnson bemoans the willingness of British Keynesians to lend themselves as media to the old ghost: " . . . evident most notably in the prolonged defense . . . of the proposition that an increase in the propensity to save lowers the interest rate only by reducing the level of income, . . . a credit to their ingenuity rather than their scientific spirit." (*Op. cit.*, p. 7. Cf. also M. Burstein, *Money*, Cambridge, Mass., 1963, pp. 393, 604–6.)

14. H. G. Johnson, "Monetary Theory and Policy," *American Economic Review*, June 1962, pp. 359–65. Note, in particular, the comments on the models proposed by Hahn, Patinkin, Robinson, Rose, and Tsiang.

Many stock-flow models start from the explicit premise that "in the short run" the net rate of new output of a stock-flow commodity is "insignificant" in relation to the size of the existing stock and go on to postulate that this flow rate therefore can be ignored in the short-run analysis of price determination. One recognizes this as a period approach to price determination—the rate of change of existing stock is assumed to be a negligible variable in the short run. In general, the argument that the rates of output, "consumption," and net investment can be ignored in the short-run analysis of price determination in markets for stock-flow goods, stocks of which show a low average rate of turnover, is erroneous. The larger the stock quantity existing at any time, the lower—*ceteris paribus*—the price paid per unit of the services it yields; consequently, the faster a stock grows, the lower the returns that units of existing stock will earn over their remaining economic lives and the lower, therefore, *should* be their present market value. Even in the absence of future markets for the services of the stock, it can hardly be true *in general* that investors are unaware of this obvious relationship and the corresponding fact that the rate of growth of the stock will itself depend upon the level of present market values. Only if expectations of future earnings were completely unrelated to the present growth rate of the stock could present market values be unaffected, e.g., by a cost-reducing innovation shifting the flow-supply curve of the asset downward.

In models where future returns to assets and therefore their present market values are regarded by transactors as related to the level of net investment and where the rate of investment depends directly upon the market price, it is not safe simply to "rank" the capital stock as a constant in the short run. In general, the rate at which it grows will also have feedback effects on current prices. The main problem in keeping the system on an equilibrium path is that these feedbacks are apt to be distorted since they are filtered through expectations which are not based on "perfect foresight." [15]

---

15. This type of problem, however, will generally be less important in models of the income-expenditure type than in models of the *General Theory* type. Keynes did not deal with it very successfully in that work—his marginal efficiency of capital apparatus did not serve to clarify its stock-flow dimensional aspects. His "The Theory of the Rate of Interest," in *The Lessons of Monetary Experience; Essays in Honor of Irving Fisher*, 1937 (reprinted in Fellner and Haley, eds., *Readings in the Theory of Income Distribution*, Philadelphia, 1951), is a good deal more successful in this respect. Cf. section III:3, below.

II:2   Price Adjustments in Atomistic Markets

The revolutionary impact of Keynesian Economics on contemporary thought stemmed in the main, we have argued, from Keynes' reversal of the conventional ranking of price and quantity velocities. In the Keynesian models price velocities are not infinite; it is sometimes said that the implications of the model result from the assumption that money wages are "rigid." This usage can be misleading. Income-constrained processes result not only when price-level velocity is zero, *but whenever it is short of infinite.* Only if price flexibilities were almost "perfect"—i.e., if prices adjusted with a minimum of false trading—would income-constrained processes be of little interest to us. "Rigid" may carry the unfortunate connotation that the opposite extreme, "perfect flexibility," is the norm or the natural order in a freely competitive system and that, consequently, a theory incorporating the assumptions of such price-rigidity cannot claim to be "general." This is the presumption we must now examine.

Identifying imperfect flexibility of prices with the existence of "monopolistic practices" of one sort or another implies that, could such practices be suppressed, an otherwise active government policy would not be needed. Keynes would certainly have disagreed with this proposition. Nonetheless, it has become standard practice in the income-expenditure tradition to take the easy way out on this issue: the factual existence of minimum-wage laws, monopolistic unions, and administered pricing policies must be taken for granted in any discussion of aggregative policy issues. Since these institutional or structural facts would account for "rigidities" there is no need to look further; the "special assumption" underlying the Keynesian model is adequately motivated.

This kind of attitude does not give adequate recognition to the relevance of Keynesian, income-constrained models. Clower argues, for example, that Keynes' introductory attacks in the *General Theory* on "Say's Law" should be taken at face value, however obscure some of the supporting arguments advanced may be. The later distinction between "Say's Law" and "Walras' Law," made by Lange,[1] is not consonant with Keynes' intentions. Many of Keynes' *obiter dicta* become fully understandable only when interpreted as part of a critique of the short-run empirical relevance of the "Classical" equilibrium model of a freely competitive, *money-using* system.[2]

Problems of information and the "perfect competition" model
The intuitive plausibility of Marshall's period-dynamics seems to be due to the powerful sway which the static model of perfect competition holds over our thinking. This model is closely associated with many of the most powerful theorems in the field of economics. Whereas other theoretical tools of less general applicability are subject to steady scrutiny, it is perhaps natural that economists should be less self-conscious about the limitations of a tool which accounts for some of their greatest accomplishments. It is generally granted that the model applies only to markets with a particular structure. One specification of what is to constitute a "perfectly competitive market" is that the number of independent transactors be so large as to preclude the emergence of formal or informal collusive practices. To emphasize our contention that even with this structure markets would not generally show the infinite price velocity which is commonly assumed in the case of "perfect competition," we will refer to "atomistic" instead of "competitive" markets.

Actually nothing at all can be deduced about the rate of change of prices from the usual competitive model—unless it has

---

1. O. Lange, "Say's Law: A Restatement and Criticism," in Lange, McIntyre, and Yntema, eds., *Studies in Mathematical Economics and Econometrics*, Chicago, 1942. In Lange's well-known formulation Walras' Law states that all the market excess demands of the system sum to zero, Say's Law that the excess demands for all the *n—1* non-means-of-payment goods sum to zero. Say's "Law" therefore would not hold except in the special case where the excess demand for means of payment happens to be zero.

The distinction is new with Lange; it was not part of Keynes' analytical equipment. While there is ample evidence that Keynes was preoccupied with the inadequate treatment of money in much of received theory, Clower argues strongly that his attacks on Say's Law must be interpreted as attacks on Walras' Law in the sense of Lange. Cf. II:3 below.

2. Clower, *op. cit.*, Sections 1 and 2.

already been put in *ad hoc,* e.g., by assuming that the solution state for such a model holds true however short the unit period (in which case infinite price velocity is implied). The static model is completely inapplicable to the analysis of disequilibrium states, since—in addition to atomistic structure—a second condition of "perfect competition" is also specified, namely that all transactors always face infinitely elastic supply and demand curves at a given price. This condition that prices be parametric —that all transactors be "price-takers"—rules out the possibility of a state in which markets do not clear at the actual price of the moment. To make analysis of adjustment processes in an atomistic market possible, this condition must be relinquished.[3]

Perfect knowledge and absence of any costs connected with the act of changing price (or rate of output) would enable the traders in an atomistic market to detect and to move instantaneously to the new price equilibrium following a disturbance. In the absence of perfect knowledge on the part of transacting units or of any mechanism *unrelated to the trading process itself* that would supply the needed information *costlessly,* the presumption of infinite price velocity disappears.

This brings us to the crux of the matter. For simplicity, assume that transactors know their own preference maps and have perfect information on physical transformation possibilities. This is not enough to enable the individual transactor to make the right decisions—his actions have to be coordinated with those of others: "no one can decide upon his optimal activity without knowledge of what others (who are in the same difficulty) will do."[4] We focus on the information relevant to

---

3. For a further development of this line of criticism, see K. J. Arrow, "Towards a Theory of Price Adjustment," in M. Abramowitz *et al., The Allocation of Economic Resources,* Stanford, 1959; R. W. Clower, *op. cit.;* A. A. Alchian and W. R. Allen, *University Economics,* Belmont, Calif., 1964, Chapter 31; and D. C. Cogerty and G. C. Winston, "Patinkin, Perfect Competition and Unemployment Disequilibria," *Review of Economic Studies,* April 1964. Clower's essay is the one most relevant for our purposes since it develops the macroeconomic implications of the argument.

The opportunity to read an unpublished paper by Professor Alchian, "Unemployment and the Cost of Information," is gratefully acknowledged.

4. G. B. Richardson, "Equilibrium, Expectations and Information," *Economic Journal,* June 1959, p. 232.

exchange transformation possibilities (information which is, of course, needed also for production decisions).[5] The very core of the Theory of Resource Allocation is the demonstration of how prices may convey the necessary information:

> We must look at the price system as such *a mechanism for communicating information if we want to understand its real function.* . . . The most significant fact about this system is the economy of knowledge with which it operates, or how little the individual participants need to know in order to be able to take the right action. . . . only the most essential information is passed on, and passed on only to those concerned.[6]

What the individual transactor needs to know, however, are the *equilibrium prices.*[7] The "pure," atemporal theory of the competitive market usually concentrates on the description of an equilibrium state and its properties, i.e., that particular *state* in which the actual prices embody precisely the information that the transactors separately need to know. When one tries to interpret the classroom competitive model as one of an actual, continuous *process,* two interesting features emerge: (a) the information required by individual transactors is "produced" apart from the actual process of exchange (and production), and (b) it is "distributed" at no cost to transactors. In their attempts to abstract the essentials of the competitive model, both Walras and Edgeworth came to realize the necessity of providing assumptions yielding the first of these two features. Hence, the hypothetical "auction process" of Walras and "recontract process" of Edgeworth.[8]

---

5. The distinction made here corresponds to that between "primary" and "secondary" information made by Richardson, *op. cit.* We thus assume "perfect primary information" and concentrate on the problem of how the necessary secondary information would be generated and distributed.

6. Cf. F. A. Hayek's classic "The Use of Knowledge in Society," *American Economic Review,* Sept. 1945, pp. 526–27, italics added.

7. Even so, as Richardson rightly emphasizes, it is not clear that the individual entrepreneur would be able to decide either on which particular activity to engage in or (if his opportunity set is not strictly convex) exactly what quantity to produce.

8. Cf. L. Walras, *Elements of Pure Economics,* translated by W. Jaffé, Homewood, Ill., 1954, and F. Y. Edgeworth, *Mathematical Psychics,* London, 1881. The

Walras' general equilibrium in exchange and production The Walrasian *tâtonnement* is the more familiar idea. Professor Jaffé's recent demonstration of how differently Walras handled the problem, first, in his Pure Theory of Exchange and, later, in developing the Theory of General Equilibrium in Exchange *and* Production is very instructive for our present purposes.[9] Literally, *tâtonnement* means "groping"—the groping of the market for a point on the contract locus. In his theory of exchange, Walras retains the ambition of describing an auction process that is a realistic simulation of an actual market process. This process must be one of groping, of "blindly feeling its way, *since no one in the actual world is presumed to know in advance the parameters or the solution of the equations.*"[10] The actual trading process is described as an iterative search for the solution to the equation system. Walras' main concern here was simply whether the system will end up at the very point on the contract locus which represents the solution to the initially defined, static offer and demand curves. He realized that, for this to happen, the value of individual commodity holdings must not change as transactions are *successively* concluded. His "theorem of equivalent redistributions" demonstrates his awareness of the indeterminacy generated by the redistributive income effects mentioned in our discussion of Hicks' analysis. It might perhaps be argued that this constitutes implicit recognition on Walras' part of the "false trading" problem, but the problem was in fact

---

hypothetical sequence of events leading to the establishment of a market-clearing price, which the two authors outlined, were by no means identical. Walras appears to have been primarily interested in achieving a simplification which would enable him to proceed with the analysis of the entire general equilibrium system; Edgeworth's interest went deeper and concerned the process itself and its implications for different market structures. In recent years, the work of Shubik, Scarf, Debreu *et al.* has brought renewed attention to Edgeworth's efforts in this area. Cf. J. S. Chipman, "The Nature and Meaning of Equilibrium in Economic Theory," in D. Martingale, ed., *Functionalism in the Social Sciences*, Philadelphia, 1965, pp. 53–59.

9. W. Jaffé, "Walras' Theory of *Tâtonnement:* A Critique of Recent Interpretations," *Journal of Political Economy*, Feb. 1967.

10. This is Jaffé's apt characterization of the problem. Cf. *op. cit.*, p. 2, italics added.

never brought to the surface of his discussion and played no part in his analysis of *tâtonnement* in exchange.[11]

When expanding his model to include the current production of goods and services, however, Walras was forced to face up to the information problem. The "theorem of equivalent redistributions" obviously does not cope with the implications of having production commitments made on the basis of disequilibrium prices. The theory of exchange and the theory of production could not be fused in the way intended, if the connecting link— the holdings of produced commodities with which transactors enter the exchange process—were allowed to dissolve by permitting production to ensue in the creation of an essentially arbitrary set of *"false quantities."* [12] At this point, therefore, Walras found it necessary to resort to the device of *tâtonnement* by means of "fictive tickets." The description of this iterative, trial-and-error process makes no pretense of simulating the "groping" of real markets—the "tickets" are assumed to become valid contracts only when the equilibrium price vector has been found.[13] Thus the process involves "recontracting." But it is different from Edgeworth's recontract process.[14] Walrasian transactors do not bargain (as Edgeworth's do) but are described as acting throughout purely as "price-takers."

Walras' main concern was with the theory of value and resource allocation. In order to proceed with his demonstration of how economic activities can be smoothly coordinated in a system

---

11. Cf. Jaffé, *loc. cit.* As indicated in our discussion of Hicks' contribution, these redistributive income effects are of little relevance to theories of aggregate income and employment. In the usual, highly aggregative, macromodels the issue is entirely submerged, particularly when (as is often the case) total output is implicitly taken to be a measure of social income or "welfare"—an identification that most often involves the notion of some "representative transactor" and therefore, cannot be simultaneously entertained with the idea that redistribution effects are analytically significant. Cf. Chapter III:1.

12. This useful counterpart to the term "false prices" is suggested by Jaffé, *op. cit.*

13. Walras, *op. cit.*, p. 242.

14. With apologies to Professor Jaffé (who would reserve the term for the type of realistic use that Walras made of it in his theory of exchange) we will, therefore, continue to use the term *"tâtonnement"* with reference to fictitious recontracting processes in systems composed of price-takers.

where decision-making is utterly decentralized, he ignored information problems. "The famous *tâtonnements* are," as Solow has said, "a swindle, rigorously speaking. . . . But Walras' failure on this point was itself creditable." [15] Keynes' main objective, on the other hand, was to show how this coordination of individual activities could break down. These are two entirely different outlooks and they dictate different approaches. The following is a pertinent illustration:

The "fictive tickets" device ensures that Walras' system is suitably equipped with negative feedback mechanisms (i.e., the *tâtonnement* process will eliminate excess demand "errors" if the usual stability conditions are fulfilled). Having introduced this device, Walras senses that:

There is still another complication. . . . Production . . . requires a certain lapse of time. We shall resolve the second difficulty *purely and simply by ignoring the time element at this point.*[16]

The entire Chapter 5 of the *General Theory* is devoted to one simple point—that current production cannot be guided by what amounts to perfect foreknowledge, but must be based on expectations:

The *actually realised* results of the production and sale of output will only be relevant to employment in so far as they cause a modification of subsequent expectations. . . . Meanwhile the entrepreneur . . . has to form the best expectations he can . . . ; *he has no choice but to be guided by these expectations, if he is to produce at all by processes which occupy time.*[17]

The main point of this, however, was simply to deny producers the benefit of perfect information. The strongly stated *general* distinction between expected and realized results, Keynes proceeded to fudge:

---

15. Quoted by Jaffé, *op. cit.,* p. 5.

16. Walras, *op. cit.,* p. 242, italics added. Note that in the absence of backward-bending supply curves, etc., these assumptions ensure that *nothing can go wrong with the system*—all the feedback mechanisms of the system work to reduce "errors," none to amplify them, and there are *no lags.*

17. *General Theory,* pp. 47, 46, italics added.

Express reference to current long-term expectations can seldom be avoided. But it will often be safe to omit express reference to *short-term* expectation, in view of the fact that in practice the process of revision of short-term expectation is a gradual and continuous one, *carried on largely in the light of realised results;* so that expected and realised results run into and overlap one another in their influence.[18]

Later the distinction becomes virtually erased—for Keynes proceeded for the most part to treat consumption spending as a function of realized income, and production and employment as a function of realized expenditures. In this way he came to refer to the "multiplier" as though it were instantaneous—language to which D. H. Robertson and others took strong exception. Although it would have been cumbersome and tiresome to carry the distinction between expected and realized magnitudes through every passage of the book, it might still have been worthwhile to do so; many subsequent conundrums could have been avoided if Keynes had laid greater emphasis on process-analysis and less on the nature of the unemployment "equilibrium" state.

It is instructive to note that the assumption that expected and realized results completely "overlap" also implies a special information process, which, while far from leading to Pareto-optimal allocation, still is similar to the *tâtonnement* process in one respect. Thus, Clower's explanation of the income-constraint bases the financing of purchases on currently realized sales of labor services rather than on expected sales. In effect, therefore, households are assumed to be informed about the *quantities* they will be allowed to sell *before* making their decisions on purchases. This "dual decision hypothesis" Clower links to Keynes' "dichotomized account of spending and saving decisions."[19] This implies an information process which, like the Walrasian *tâtonnement*, functions apart from the trading process itself, but relates to quantities, not to prices. Households are informed of their real income "before any trade takes place." There are no

18. *General Theory*, p. 50, italics added. Also, p. 51: " . . . in practice there is a large overlap between the effects on employment of the realised sale-proceeds of recent output and those of the sale-proceeds expected from current input . . . " etc.

19. Clower, *op. cit.*, p. 117.

"false purchases" of consumption goods. If generalized to all markets, this would imply an instantaneous multiplier.

The two "pure" models differ in terms of the kind of information which they assume will be available to transactors in the short run when a previous equilibrium has been disturbed. Both types of models confine attention to information that is available at zero cost—if we adopt the convention of regarding as "costless" information that consists simply in registering events happening to the transactor, and for which he does not need to search or pay.

The costs to individual transactors of acquiring information should be explicitly considered in order to get a more realistic appreciation of the degree of price-flexibility that can be expected in a system of atomistic markets. We will deal first with individual behavior in a single market and later with the defects of the "communications network" of a multi-market system in which money is "the only good traded in all markets."

Information costs: individual behavior in a single market
The standard illustration of the hypothetical Walrasian auction process presents an appropriate point of departure: A price is "*crié au hazard*" and an auctioneer registers the buy and sell offers. If he finds that, in the aggregate, there is excess demand at the called price, a higher price is called out; if excess supply is registered, a lower price is tried. The process is repeated until a market-clearing price is found. *Only then are actual exchanges allowed to be carried out.*[20] Thus, in a market operating on such rules, no "false trading" is ever carried out. Such markets always clear; if we were to regard actual exchange as taking place continuously in calendar time, we would have to conceive of the *tâtonnement* as consuming *no* time, or as taking place "between innings" of a period model.

Two things are to be noted about this type of process:

(1) no transactor would ever face any constraint on the quan-

---

20. Compare Walras, *op. cit.*, pp. 84–86, where Walras considers the example of an auction market for government bonds. On p. 85 Walras twice posits instances of non-zero excess demand, commenting, "Theoretically, trading should come to a halt" and "Trading stops."

tities he can buy or sell at the market price at which trading actually takes place.

(2) no transactor is ever required to find terms for himself; traders make decisions only on the quantities they would want to buy or sell at the different prices tried out by the auctioneer.

But there is no auctioneer. The emperor, of course, *is* naked. Not all transactors can be completely passive in the way just described or the system could not adjust when markets fail to clear. If all traders are price-takers, Arrow points out, there is "no one left over whose job it is to make a decision on price." [21] Arrow proceeds to consider the problem facing price-setting sellers in an atomistic market in disequilibrium, noting that each such seller would regard himself as facing a downward-sloping demand curve, whose exact slope and position he would not be certain of. The traders who have the option of making price offers become, in effect, transitorily "monopolists" or "monopsonists" when the atomistic market does not clear.[22]

The analysis of the behavior of the individual trader in a disequilibrium situation can be advanced by bringing in *information costs* explicitly. This is what Alchian has done in the contributions cited. Alchian deals with a number of cases in which, for the sake of the economic argument, no non-economic constraints are assumed to be operative—there is always a price at which an economic good can be sold. The individual transactor does not know, however, what the best obtainable price is or from whom it can be obtained. This information is not available instantaneously nor at zero cost. The seller will normally be willing to hold his resources off the market while he investigates

21. Arrow, *op. cit.,* p. 43.

22. Cogerty and Winston have elaborated on Arrow's analysis in their critique of Patinkin. The terminology of monopolistic competition, whereby sellers are said to be transitorily monopolists, etc., does not appear very helpful in clearing matters up. Cogerty and Winston use it heavily. Admittedly, terminology is mostly a matter of taste, but it would seem less confusing if each particular market were allowed to fall in the same classificatory "box," whether in equilibrium or not.

To stay clear of this matter, we have used the term "atomistic market" for markets in which, when all traders have full information, no one has it in his power to improve his over-all gains from trade by restricting the quantity he supplies.

the environment, rather than sell at a price acceptable to whatever potential buyer or buyers he happens to be in contact with at the moment—e.g., the employer who has just laid him off. While sellers engage in such search behavior, unemployed resources would thus be observed.

Consider, for example, a seller of labor services who finds his old employment terminated, or a firm which finds its rate of sales falling off at the going price. How rapidly, and by how much, will these sellers cut their asking prices? The seller will not change his reservation price instantly but will first attempt to ascertain that the decline in sales was not simply a random event. The laid-off worker will spend *some* time in deciding that the rate of sales will not shortly pick up again by itself. Neither will the price cut be infinitesimal, when it once occurs, since an arbitrarily small price reduction will have little short-run effect in a market where buyers, too, lack full information. Since there is uncertainty on *both* sides of the market, an arbitrarily small price cut will not instantly re-establish "perfectly elastic" demand conditions for the individual sellers.

Descriptively the situation differs somewhat depending on the type of market in which sellers are engaged. In markets for most mass-manufactured products, for example, sellers quote prices, while buyers search for the best price, rather than bargaining with individual sellers. To these sellers, price is then the controlled variable and the rate of sales the dependent variable. In deciding when and by how much to cut his price, such a seller has to consider a whole complex of factors. A price cut will lead to a gradually rising rate of sales, as information about the new price spreads among buyers—as long as competitors do not cut their price and aggregate demand in this market is not further reduced. These *ceteris paribus* conditions are not realistic, however. With time his competitors will cut prices, which will tend to reduce his sales—by an amount which depends upon the speed with which buyers acquire information, etc. The individual seller is therefore interested also in the prices charged by other sellers. Thus, atomistic markets in disequilibrium present individual transactors with conjectural problems of immense complexity. Even if he could somehow process such information costlessly, a single seller would need a fantastic amount of information in order to arrive directly at an optimal pricing policy.

The seller in the labor market finds himself in a slightly different situation. Ordinarily, he will not regard his problem as one of choosing a price to quote, but as one of searching out the employer who will offer the best wage for a given rate of labor services.

In one case, the seller quotes a price, and buyers decide how much, if anything, to buy at this price. In the second case, buyers quote prices and it is up to the seller to decide whether or not to accept any of the prices known to him at the moment. Arrow notes that "the immediate location of price decisions is usually vested in the more concentrated side of the market, in sellers in the case of most commodities, in buyers in the case of unorganized labor.[23] Nonetheless, the two sellers face much the same problem: to decide on their *reservation price* while gathering more information.

Normally, a seller has no incentive to reduce the price he will accept to a level which would *immediately* raise his sales to some given level. The expectations which underlie his reservation price will be revised as he acquires more information on the market situation. Thus, the unemployed worker, for example, may start with a reservation price close or equal to his old wage, turning down employment opportunities which promise lower wage rates. As his search progresses, his sample of employment offers gets larger and the maximum wage offered increases.[24] The improvement achieved in the best offer known to the seller will decline with the extent of his search and with the cost devoted to information-gathering. The increased sample of current market opportunities will enable the seller to form a progressively better estimate of the best price potentially available to him. His reservation price will be adjusted in accordance with this estimate. Search—acquisition of information—is costly, both in direct expense and in foregone earnings. At some point, therefore, employment at the best wage then known will be accepted,

---

23. Arrow, *op. cit.*, p. 47.
24. Here the analysis paraphrases the paper by Alchian quoted above.

despite less-than-full information, in preference to continued expenditure of resources on information-gathering.

The price actually achieved thus depends upon the amount of information "purchased." The variable which the seller will attempt to maximize is the present value of achieved sales revenues *net* of search costs. Alchian points out the close connection between this idea and one aspect of the "liquidity" concept. If we assume that information is acquired at a constant rate, the maximum price known is, *ceteris paribus*, a function of time. "Liquidity" is often conceived as a relation between the proportion of the highest obtainable cash value which can be realized on an asset and the time spent in marketing the asset. An asset whose "full" market value can be instantly realized at zero transaction cost is said to be perfectly liquid.[25] Cash is *the* perfectly liquid asset. This suggests the "essential and peculiar" role that money plays in the Keynesian scheme.

Much of modern monetary theory deals with money as just one of the n goods in a general equilibrium model. It is now clear that *in general competitive equilibrium all goods are perfectly liquid.* All transactors face perfectly elastic demand functions; the full value of any good can be instantly realized. Money has no special status, and in a model which deals only with situations characterized by exchange equilibrium, money is (at most) "just another good." [26] In the present work, we deal with

---

25. We may again refer to the contributions of Arrow, and Cogerty and Winston: in the price-theoretical literature, the "monopolistic competitor" is usually regarded as having an advantage over firms selling in "competitive" markets. He is willing to devote part of his resources to preserving this advantage by advertising, etc. A competitive firm finding itself in a market thrown into excess supply disequilibrium is not "better off" than before surely. To avoid semantic snarls, problems of "illiquidity" and "imperfect information" in atomistic markets should be analyzed apart from the static problems of monopolistic competition.

26. Though general equilibrium models deal with the economy "as if" it were always in exchange equilibrium, the inclusion of "money" in such models—i.e., the explanation of why money is demanded at all—must be predicated on the illiquidity of earning assets, which is to say on the general prevalence of imperfect information and "uncertainty." Cf., e.g., Hicks, *op. cit.*, Chapter XIII, and Samuelson, *op. cit.*, pp. 122–24.

The current status of "pure" monetary theory is a curious one: The preferred analytical tool of many of its most distinguished practitioners is the general equi-

short-run disequilibrium processes. In the analysis of such processes, money—and "liquidity" generally—is of particular interest. (The Keynesian problem, after all, is to show how it can be that *all* the "false quantities" produced are too small.) Hence our emphasis on aggregate demand *in money terms*. Most Keynesians prefer to deal with the income-expenditure model in real terms, i.e., with nominal magnitudes entirely absent from the so-called "real sector" and, correspondingly, with the excess demand for money stated in terms of real balances. This procedure of dividing through "on both sides" with the GNP-deflator [27] is usually regarded as purely a matter of convenience, to be justified simply by reference to accepted postulates of "rational behavior," i.e., "absence of money illusion." When communication is far from perfect, however, it is not at all clear that *individual* "rationality" implies the kind of invariance propositions for the *system* as a whole that these models imply. "Absence of money illusion" has become one of the great fudge-phrases of economic theory—a "real veil," in effect, behind which some of the most basic and subtle issues of monetary theory lie concealed.

In a money exchange system, the means of payment is "a good traded in all markets." Herein, it is different from all other goods. The aesthetic attractions of modern general equilibrium models should not make us forget this fact. The first requirement of a relevant theory of a monetary economy should be that it reflects this singular property of money.[28] In order to come to grips with this problem, however, we must relinquish the present single-market framework and deal with a system of several interrelated markets.

---

librium model. But money cannot be "important" in theories which devote attention only to equilibrium situations. To a large extent, one finds this literature to be preoccupied with highly abstract and aesthetically satisfying but arid "invariance theorems." The predominance of this approach has been forcefully criticized, e.g., in an unpublished paper by M. L. Burstein, "Some Theory of Bank Rate" (1965).

27. What this amounts to, we will argue, is rather "dividing through" (cancelling) the means of payment function of money. Cf. R. W. Clower, "A Reconsideration of the Microfoundations of Monetary Theory," *Western Economic Journal*, Dec. 1967.

28. Clower, *op. cit.*

This is necessary also for another reason. Alchian's analysis of individual behavior in a single market demonstrates that when costs of information are taken into account, a disturbance of equilibrium will cause transitory unemployment of resources also in atomistic markets. Qualitatively, the analysis is as applicable to a hypothetical *barter* system as it is to a money economy. It makes clear that either system would exhibit a steady-state revolving pool of people "between jobs." This kind of "frictional" unemployment, however, Keynes explicitly excluded from his definition of "involuntary" unemployment and it was with the latter that his theory was concerned. Alchian's analysis remains perfectly applicable to the explanation of individual behavior in a state of "involuntary" unemployment, and the initial "inflexibility" of reservation prices that his analysis implies is, indeed, a necessary condition for the emergence of such a state. But it is not sufficient. Keynes' involuntary unemployment is fundamentally a product of the cumulative process which he assumed the initial increase in unemployment would trigger. The assumed deviation-amplifying feedbacks involved in this process cannot be explained in terms of an isolated labor-market model—the entire *money-using* system must be considered.

II:3   The Theory of "Involuntary" Unemployment

Notional versus Effective excess demands; the validity of Say's Principle and the irrelevance of Walras' Law   This brings us back to Clower's contribution. The excess demand relations of the conventional general equilibrium model, Clower emphasizes, are based on the assumption that all traders can buy and sell whatever quantities they desire at the market prices at which trading actually takes place. In a *tâtonnement* exchange model with multiple markets, the individual trader considers only the vector of "announced" prices in drawing up his budget plan. His demand curve for one of n commodities may be derived by holding $n - 2$ relative prices constant and varying the numeraire price of the commodity in question, registering the desired purchases of this commodity for each alternative numeraire price. Aggregation of such individual schedules (uncompensated for real income changes) gives the conventional market excess demand function. As Clower points out,[1] however, this procedure presupposes that the $n - 2$ other markets will "clear." In considering his purchases or sales of a particular good for any announced vector of prices, the trader is supposed to face infinitely elastic supply and demand functions in all markets. His trading plans are drawn up so that the total value of his purchases will be *financed* by the total value of his sales *and* on the presumption that he will be able to *realize* any sales he desires at the announced price vector. *Excess demand schedules derived in this manner Clower terms "notional" excess demand functions.*

The notional market excess demand functions thus represent the outcomes of a particular type of thought experiment, i.e., answers by individual transactors to hypothetical questionnaires which begin: "Suppose that you will encounter no problems in buying or selling whatever quantities you wish at the following list of prices . . ." etc.—answers which are then collated for each market. But *all* the notional transactions planned in this way can be carried out *only if* all markets clear at the price vector actually prevailing during trading. If actual demand falls short of notional supply in some markets, some suppliers in these markets find that they cannot finance their notional demands in other markets in the way originally planned.[2] They must therefore curtail their demand in the latter markets. Thus:

---

1. Clower, "The Keynesian Counterrevolution . . . ," esp. pp. 116-17, and "Keynes and the Classics: A Dynamical Perspective," *Quarterly Journal of Economics*, May 1960.

2. Cf. Clower, "The Keynesian Counterrevolution . . . ," p. 117: " . . . not every household can buy and sell just what it pleases if supply exceeds demand somewhere in the economy. *Do we nevertheless suppose that the facts of life never intrude upon the thought experiments of households?*" (italics added)

It is obvious from the previous discussion that, in addition to the observation of "idle" resources (which is the one we have stressed), market disequilibrium will also be observed in the occurrence of simultaneous exchanges at different prices for the same good. The uniqueness of price is a postulate belonging to equilibrium analysis. Jevons' Law of Indifference, on which it is based, rests on the assumption of perfect information on the part of all market participants. This assumption, in turn, precludes analysis of disequilibria of the type considered here.

Properly, therefore, we should not refer to the "prevailing market price" in the

. . . if realized current receipts are considered to impose any kind of constraint on current consumption plans, planned consumption as expressed in effective market offers to buy will necessarily be less than desired consumption as given by the demand functions of orthodox analysis.[3]

Market excess demand functions which take into account constraints on the transactions quantities that people expect to be able to realize, we term *"effective" excess demand functions.*

Effective excess demands coincide with notional excess demands only when both are zero in all markets, i.e., only in full exchange equilibrium. Recontract models postulate continuous exchange equilibrium. Individual traders in such models need never consider action on any other set of prices than that which will clear all markets. Actual prices are always market-clearing prices. Such constructions posit *pure price adjustment*—real income is always at a full employment level.[4]

Clower goes on to argue that "Walras' Law, although valid as usual with reference to *notional* market excess demands, *is in general irrelevant to any but full employment situations.*" [5] This, of course, is a most controversial assertion, mostly because no firmly established professional convention exists on a couple of relevant, terminological points. The lack of such conventions in itself reflects the fact that the substantive point made by Clower has not been recognized—and it is a point of great significance to the understanding of the economics of Keynes. Clower relies on a distinction between "Say's Principle" and "Walras' Law":

---

kind of deterministic terms used above. But since we will make no further use of the probabilistic nature of market prices, repetitive and cumbersome reminders to that effect may as well be avoided. Thus, we will follow the practice of referring to "price" *as if* it were a single-valued variable.

3. Clower, *op. cit.*, p. 118.

4. As Lindahl, Myrdal, Hayek, and others have amply shown, however, this does not mean that they necessarily behave "nicely" : the assumptions discussed at this point in the text only ensure the absence of income-constraints; the "daily" or "weekly" (as the case may be) *tâtonnement* clears the markets but not necessarily at the prices expected yesterday (or last week).

5. *Op. cit.*, p. 122, italics added. One should add that it is in the same sense irrelevant to inflationary (over-)full employment situations.

The familiar household budget constraint . . . asserts . . . that no transactor consciously *plans* to purchase units of any commodity without at the same time *planning* to finance the purchase either from profit receipts or from the sale of units of some other commodity.[6]

Consequently, the individual budget has the property that the values of net demands and net supplies will sum to zero (as usual). This is *Say's Principle*. Since it is assumed to hold for each and every transactor, it holds for the system as a whole.

The budget of a "pure" Walrasian price-taker is a *special case* of all budgets obeying Say's Principle. The quantities entering into this budget are "planned" by an individual who has not considered the possibility that, at the "given" prices, he may not succeed in selling all he wants to (in a deflationary disequilibrium) or in buying all he wants to (in an inflationary disequilibrium). The values of these "notional" net demands and supplies sum to zero. If everybody is like that, we get *Walras' Law* (in the sense of Clower) for the system as a whole—a usage to which Walras could hardly have objected.

Suppose the "facts of life" *do* intrude on the Walrasian price-taker—he fails to realize some of his notional sales. *Who is ever going to know what his notional demand quantities were?*

Assume that no one knows, so that notional demands do *not* "provide the relevant market signals." [7] The information which traders acquire is based primarily on the actually realized exchanges. The forces tending to make an initial contraction "cumulative" [8]—i.e., the income-constrained process—can now be sketched. Transactors with unemployed resources (current revenues curtailed by the initial "shock") will generally reduce their expenditures in other markets. *Effective demands* are thus reduced also in markets on which the initial disturbance may have had no impact. Unemployed resources emerge in these markets also and *the search instituted by unemployed workers*

---

6. Clower, *op. cit.*, p. 116.

7. *Op. cit., passim.*

8. This familiar term is not used to suggest that the system will "implode," only that the initial deviation of aggregate money demand will be amplified through endogenous mechanisms.

*and producers with excess capacity will yield information on
"effective" demands, not on "notional" demands.* The "multiplier"
repercussions thus set in motion make the information acquired
"dated" even while it is being gathered.

Consider a multi-market system initially at equilibrium with
an output vector, q, and a money price vector, p. Let there be a
change in some parameter—e.g., investors' expectations—such
that a new exchange-*cum*-production equilibrium can be defined
by the vectors, q' and p', the latter being associated with lower
aggregate demand in money terms. If information was perfect,
traders would act, individually, so as to establish the new equilibrium instantly. The first reaction, however, will be characterized by some inflexibility of reservation prices and corresponding
resource "unemployment" and inventory accumulation. If realized current receipts "impose any kind of constraint" on current
expenditure plans, this will entail more than merely a "frictional"
slowing down of the system's motion towards the new equilibrium. The new information generated by the income-constrained
process will not induce such a slow but direct movement towards
the new position. Instead, the "current income effects" operate to
compound the confusion: Not only are transactors misled about
potential aggregate money demand, but the contraction will
ordinarily enhance the general uncertainty by generating
changes in relative demands which are essentially unrelated to
the required movement from (p, q) to (p', q'). The elasticity of
demand with regard to current income will be of widely varying
magnitude in different markets. The "true" situation will be
further obscured if price velocities for given excess supplies are
highly unequal in different markets.[9] There is no *deus ex machina*
to straighten things out, no Walrasian auctioneer to ensure that
prices tell the truth (and nothing but the truth) about how
resources can and ought to be allocated. The cushion must be
sought in a fixed "outside" money stock or in a mixed inside-
outside money supply held steady by the monetary authorities. A

---

9. A depression may thus become more severe because of such induced "distortions." Cf., e.g., the excellent discussion of the "unbalanced deflation" in the U.S.
following the 1929 crash in Viner's pamphlet, "Balanced Deflation, Inflation, or
More Depression?" University of Minnesota, 1933.

purely inside money system might "implode" if the initial shock is heavy enough to set off a chain of defaults.[10]

To illustrate, consider the standard aggregative model, and the typical process which brings that system into a Keynesian unemployment "equilibrium." The money supply is assumed to be an exogenously determined constant in the usual manner:

Effective Excess Demand Table

	LABOR SERVICES	COMMODITIES	SECURITIES	MONEY	SUM
Initial equilibrium state	0	0	0	0	0
Stage 1	0	ES	ED	0	0
Stage 2	0	ES	0	ED	0
New income "equilibrium"	ES	0	0	0	<0

The initial state is one of full exchange-*cum*-production equilibrium. This is disturbed by an adverse shift in entrepreneurial expectations (a downward shift of the marginal efficiency of capital schedule). Entrepreneurs decide to order less investment goods and, correspondingly, to issue less securities. As yet, household income is unimpaired and their saving plans (demand for securities) unchanged. At Stage 1, therefore, we have effective excess supply of commodities coupled with an equal excess demand for securities. Next, the interest rate falls, the securities market being "ranked" as the fastest-adjusting in the system. Instead of having a constant-velocity money-demand function, however, we have Keynes' interest-elastic liquidity preference schedule. The funds channeled into security purchases by house-

---

10. Cf. I. Fisher, "The Debt-deflation Theory of Great Depressions," *Econometrica*, Oct. 1933, and *Booms and Depressions*, London, 1933. One of the most disturbing features of the consolidated balance-sheet models, which dominate contemporary monetary theory, is that they are incapable of generating the debt-deflation process sketched by Fisher. The term "credit-implosion" I have borrowed from David Meiselman.

holds are diverted into the hoards of bear speculators. At Stage 2, we consequently have excess supply of commodities—since the decline of market rate has stopped short of the new level of natural rate—and a corresponding effective excess demand for money. Inflexible reservation prices prevent the disequilibrium from being snuffed out simply by an appropriate change in the relative value of cash balances and commodities-labor services. The excess supply of commodities is removed instead by a contraction of output, which is amplified by the "multiplier" repercussions previously described, and halted finally when the excess supply of commodities and excess demand for money simultaneously reach zero. At the money income level where effective attempts to hoard cease, however, we are left with excess supply of labor—the unemployed looking for jobs.

The usual ambiguity surrounds the use of the term "unemployment equilibrium" with reference to the situation represented by the last line of the table. There are two ways in which the system may get out of this situation on its own: (a) The excess supply of labor implies some downward pressure on the wage rate. If wages were quite "rigid," nothing would happen. When they are not, the question arises whether wage deflation will lead only to a *pari passu* decline of aggregate demand in money terms or whether the Pigou-effect or some other mechanism will come into operation to propel the system back towards full employment. This question we must postpone, as Keynes did, until a later chapter. (b) Even with "rigid" money wages and no Central Bank or government action, an excess supply of money (spilling over ultimately into demand for commodities) should gradually develop in Keynes' case. Successive periods of persistently low short rates should cause the Keynesian bear speculators to revise their initial views of the future course of long rates. Such learning behavior would be reflected in a downward shift of the liquidity preference schedule and a corresponding decline of the (long-term) market rate. This, however, is a long-run phenomenon and we will be concerned here with the short-run situation.

The last line of the table is written the way Clower would have it: ". . . the *constrained demand* functions . . . and the *notional supply* functions . . . are the relevant providers of market signals." [11] And:

. . . in a state of involuntary unemployment, Walras' Law must be replaced by the more general condition . . . [that] *the sum of all* [effective] *market excess demands, valued at prevailing market prices, is at most equal to zero.*[12]

But the last line of our table, it must be noted, contradicts the usual [13] interpretation of the Keynesian unemployment "equilibrium" as one in which the excess supply of labor has a counterpart in an excess demand for money of equal value. This is again a matter of terminology, namely whether the money that the unemployed are seeking to obtain in exchange for their services should be represented as an "effective" excess demand for money. If we do so, obviously, we will be comforted to find that the last line "sums to zero" as we are used to having it, thus enabling us to shrug off Clower's contention:

Contrary to the findings of traditional theory, excess demand may fail to appear anywhere in the economy under conditions of less than full employment.[14]

From the standpoint of the information transmitted through the system, the unemployed indubitably do communicate to prospective employers the fact that they wish to earn some money. Yet I find the representation chosen in the table the more suitable because I prefer to associate the statement "there is an excess demand for money," with a situation in which there is an ongoing tendency either for velocity to fall, or for the interest rate to rise or, more generally, both. None of this is true about

---

11. Clower, *op. cit.*, p. 119. (Italics added).

12. *Op. cit.*, p. 122.

13. Cf., e.g., R. H. Kuenne, *The Theory of General Economic Equilibrium*, Princeton, 1963, pp. 354–61.

14. *Op. cit.*, p. 122. In contrast, Walras' Law asserts that (p. 121): " . . . in any disequilibrium situation there is always an element of excess demand *working directly on the price system* to offset prevailing elements of excess supply." (Italics added)

Keynes' short-period unemployment "equilibrium." So I choose to describe this as a situation in which the *effective* excess demand for money is zero.

Whatever one's preference with regard to terminology, however, Clower's substantive point remains. It concerns the dynamic forces determining the disequilibrium motion of a money-using system and brings out the rationale for the strictures against the neglect of the means of payment function of money presented above.

Suppose we make a "Walrasian questionnaire" investigation of the notional budgets (at the prices prevailing in Keynes' unemployment situation) of the unemployed. For simplicity (*only*), let us assume that the unemployed do *not* plan on building up their money balances (again) if they succeed in finding jobs. They plan just to restore their consumption and saving—in the form of accumulation of "securities"—to accustomed levels. Checking the results of this experiment, therefore, we would find the *notional excess demand distribution:*

	LABOR SERVICES	COMMODITIES	SECURITIES	MONEY	SUM
Keynesian unemployment "equilibrium"	ES	ED	ED	0	0

The experiment reveals, in Clower's words, that *"the other side of involuntary unemployment* [is] *involuntary under-consumption."* But Walras' Law is "obeyed": the excess supply of labor is equal in value to the sum of the unemployed workers' notional demand for consumption goods and for (indirect claims on) new investment goods. Assuming (with Keynes) that producers are always willing to pay labor its marginal product, that labor will accept jobs at a real wage equal to its marginal product, and that there are no unions or minimum-wage laws, etc., capable of preventing them from doing so, a "Classical" economist would now conclude that the situation can and will be remedied by an adjustment of the real wage rate that will simultaneously wipe out these excess supply and demand magnitudes.

Why, then, is this Walrasian portrayal of the situation irrelevant to the movement of the Keynesian system? Clearly, because in that system *all exchanges involve money on one side of the transaction.*[15] The workers looking for jobs ask for *money,* not for commodities. Their notional demand for commodities is *not communicated* to producers; not being able to perceive this potential demand for their products, producers will not be willing to absorb the excess supply of labor at a wage corresponding to the real wage that would "solve" the Walrasian problem above. The fact that there exists a potential barter bargain of goods for labor services that would be mutually agreeable to producers *as a group* and labor *as a group* is irrelevant to the motion of the system. The individual steel-producer cannot pay a newly hired worker by handing over to him his physical product (nor will the worker try to feed his family on a ton-and-a-half of cold-rolled sheet a week). The lack of any "mutual coincidence of wants" between pairs of individual employers and employees is what dictates the use of a means of payment in the first place.

Thus, *the dynamic properties of an economic system depend upon* what I will call *its "transaction structure."* That labor services are sold for money and that households obtain their consumption goods in exchange for money is one aspect of the transaction structure of Keynes' system. Another, equally important, lies in the postulate that savers and investors are "not the same persons"—but we will come to that in later chapters.[16]

In an economy of self-employed artisans our problem simply

---

15. Cf. Clower, "A Reconsideration of the Microfoundations of Monetary Theory," *Western Economic Journal,* Dec. 1967, which expands upon this aspect of the argument advanced in his "The Keynesian Counterrevolution . . . ."

16. This type of terminology, I know, may be becoming irritating. But it *is* necessary to specify one's "dynamic structure," "aggregative structure," and "transaction structure," in dealing with (at least short-run) macrotheory or the confusion will be endless. Considerable space is given in this study to discussing dynamic structure in terms of the ranking of adjustment speeds and aggregative structure in terms of index number theory. The transaction structure is no less important, but I am not clear on how it can be handled with economy and accuracy so that the implications stand out clearly. For a preliminary attack on this problem, cf. Clower, "A Reconsideration. . . ."

Apart from this paper, I am not acquainted with any recent work focusing upon this problem—with the single and most significant exception of Mrs. Robinson's *Essays in the Theory of Economic Growth,* esp. Chapter I and the Appendix to Chapter II. Cf. also A. H. Hansen, *A Guide to Keynes,* Chapter 1, esp. pp. 13–19.

cannot appear. If it does appear in a posited system, say, of big farmers "higgling and haggling" with prospective farm-hands over the room and board and other direct material benefits that are to constitute the real wage, it will be most smoothly solved in a thoroughly Walrasian manner.

The terminological thicket is a bother. Consider: *In the sense of Lange,* Walras' Law is the relation relevant to a money economy, whereas Say's Law applies only to barter systems and gives rise to "false dichotomies" and like troubles if misapplied to a money-using system. *In the sense of Clower,* Walras' Law is irrelevant to the stability properties of a money economy, whereas Say's Principle expresses the transactor budget-constraints not just in a barter system, but in a money system as well.[17]

All of this, it may be said, is fairly "modern" stuff, still not digested and absorbed into the contemporary teaching of macro-economics. It may help to make sense of Keynesian economics, but does it bear any relation to the 1936 efforts of that notoriously incompetent price theorist, John Maynard Keynes? This, obviously, must be our next question. In considering it, however, we must be realistic—we cannot expect or require the same analytical precision of Keynes that we find in the present-day discussion.[18]

Keynes on the second Classical postulate and Say's Law; his concept of "involuntary unemployment" The *General Theory* opens with Keynes' critique of "The Postulates of the Classical Economics." Initially, his attack focused on the second postulate of the Classical theory of employment, but by the end of Chap-

---

17. Cf., however, the reformulation of the traditional budget-constraint suggested in his "A Reconsideration . . . "

18. Cf. Clower, "The Keynesian Counterrevolution . . . ," (p. 104): "Unlike Keynes, who had to deal with doctrines of which no authoritative account had ever been given, we now have an extremely clear idea of the orthodox content of contemporary theory. We thus have a distinct advantage over Keynes in describing what has been said." Keynes did rely to a great extent on the most authoritative account in existence at the time—Pigou's *Theory of Unemployment*—and he has often been criticized for doing so. Cf., e.g., the introductory paragraphs of Hicks' "Mr. Keynes and the 'Classics.' "

ter 2 this attack is seen to have been but the preliminary opening of the breach through which an all-out assault on Say's Law is launched. The second Classical postulate Keynes put as follows:

The utility of the wage when a given volume of labour is employed is equal to the marginal disutility of that amount of employment.[19]

The principal links in Keynes' argument are the following: (1) The Classical theory recognizes only "voluntary" unemployment. It is extremely important to be clear on three things: (a) how very widely Keynes defined "voluntary" unemployment; (b) that his own concern was entirely with the residual category of "involuntary" unemployment and that it is with this unemployment that his theory of employment deals; (c) that his policy recommendations and remarks on the relative efficacy of fiscal and monetary policy measures refer specifically to the task of relieving "involuntary" unemployment, so that his judgments on the usefulness of monetary policy, for example, apply to such situations and not in general.

With regard to (a), Keynes followed up his definition of the second postulate by noting that

Disutility must here be understood to cover *every kind of reason* which might lead a man, *or a body of men,* to withhold their labour rather than accept a wage which had to them a utility below a certain minimum. (italics added)

The list of "every kind of reason" supplied by Keynes is very long. But it embraces "frictional" unemployment and seasonal unemployment in the broadest sense ("due to intermittent demand").[20] Most importantly here, the second postulate:

---

19. *General Theory,* p. 5. Page references to the passages from the *General Theory* quoted below will only be given when the quotes have not been taken from the relatively brief Chapter 2.

20. These two categories were designed to exclude Pigovian unemployment from the further discussion. Pigou's position was that: " . . . such unemployment as exists at any time is due wholly to the fact that changes in demand are continually taking place and that frictional resistances prevent the appropriate wage adjustments from being made instantaneously." *Theory of Unemployment,* p. 252. Cf. *General Theory,* p. 278, and Hansen, *A Guide to Keynes,* pp. 18–19: "Pigou

. . . is also compatible with "voluntary" unemployment due to the refusal *or inability* of a unit of labour, *as a result of legislation or social practices or of combination for collective bargaining* or of slow response to change or of mere human obstinacy, to accept a reward corresponding to the value of the product attributable to its marginal productivity. (italics added)

This third category, we may designate as "income-expenditure" unemployment. It is not, I think, unfair to do so—Keynes' followers have had persistent difficulties in assigning a clear meaning to his definition of "involuntary" unemployment. In today's textbooks "involuntary" generally means simply that the *individual* worker has no choice because unions or minimum-wage laws stand in his way. This to Keynes was an utterly "Classical" idea:

Thus writers in the classical tradition . . . have been driven inevitably to the conclusion . . . that apparent unemployment . . . must be due at bottom to a refusal by the unemployed factors to accept a reward which corresponds to their marginal productivity. A classical economist may sympathise with labour in refusing to accept a cut in its money-wage . . . ; but scientific integrity forces him to declare that this refusal is, nevertheless, at the bottom of the trouble.

The imperatives of scientific integrity are still with us. Modern Keynesians tend to save the notion of "involuntariness" by transferring the *blame* of the "refusal to accept a reward corresponding to the marginal product" from the individual to unions, monopolies, or governments.

Keynes lumped all the above three categories of unemployment into "voluntary" unemployment and paid no further attention to them *or to their causes*. The significance of his discussion of involuntary unemployment will be entirely missed unless one sees quite clearly that Keynes did not seek to assign "blame" to anyone or *any group*. Neither individually nor collectively do the transactors of the system that he dealt with "refuse to cooperate" in the way that a Classical economist would find "proper."

. . . distinguished between the *state* of Demand and *changes* in Demand . . . [and] believed that the state of Demand as such does not matter, as far as employment is concerned."

(2) This is the main import of his definition:

Men are involuntarily unemployed if, in the event of a small rise in the price of wage-goods relatively to the money-wage, both the aggregate supply of labour willing to work for the current money-wage and the aggregate demand for it at that wage would be greater than the existing volume of employment.

This definition has been regarded as most tortuously contrived by most later interpreters. Two points should be made about it:

(a) It proposes a thought-experiment to *test* for the presence of involuntary unemployment. Note that *both* labor *and* producers are "tested" for their willingness to cooperate in the way that the Classical theory of competitive markets would have them do. Producers are being tested for their willingness to employ labor up to the point where the product of the "last" worker hired is no higher than his real wage—the first Classical postulate, which Keynes insisted on keeping—and, consequently, on their willingness to hire more workers if the real wage were to decline. The relevance of this, I take it, is that *were producers to act otherwise, their "volition" would be to blame,* in which case employment would *not* be "involuntary" in Keynes' sense. And workers, of course, are being tested for their willingness to take a real wage cut in order to become re-employed.

(b) The test involves a cut in real wages, but Keynes *insists* on one of the two possible versions, namely that of a rise in the price of wage goods (money wages constant) rather than that of a decline in money wages (price of wage goods constant). Yet, *from a partial equilibrium standpoint,* either labor-market experiment ought to work as well. But Keynes reiterates again and again that the test of the "involuntary" nature of unemployment is that those unemployed "though willing to work at the current wage" would *not* "withdraw the offer of their labour in the event of even a small rise in the cost of living." [21]

On the other hand, he argued that there will be "some resistance to a cut in money-wages, however small." The juxtaposition of these two arguments seems to lead to the unavoidable

---

21. Chapter 2, and Appendix, Chapter 19, *passim.*

conclusion that Keynes' theory was based on the assumption of "money illusion" on the part of workers. Such an interpretation views his statements as referring to individual behavior in a single market. The appropriate perspective is that of the equilibrating tendencies of the entire system of interrelated markets. In disequilibrium, the system is "confused" and transactors act on the basis of faulty information. In a sense, then, though hardly a useful sense, they may be said to act under an "illusion" of one sort or another. But Keynes had no patience with this semantic point:

It is sometimes said that it would be illogical for labour to resist a reduction of money-wages but not to resist a reduction of real wages. For reasons given below, this might not be so illogical as it appears at first; and, as we shall see later, fortunately so. But, whether logical or illogical, experience shows that this is how labour in fact behaves.[22]

(3) Keynes had two separate objections to the second Classical postulate and the denial of the possibility of "involuntary" unemployment that it implied. The first of these "relates to the actual behaviour of labour" and "is not theoretically fundamental." [23] It concerns the resistance to money wage cuts. Consider the kind of individual adjustment problem discussed in the previous section. The immediate reservation price of a worker will be set on the basis of his expectations of obtainable prices. What information relevant to these expectations will be most cheaply available to him? Two sets of data appear relevant: (a) *past (money) prices received* for the same services, and (b) *prices currently obtained by successful sellers* of such services.

All that Keynes needed to assert is that the worker who is threatened with a lay-off will not offer to take *any* cut necessary

---

22 One should remember that Keynes insisted (*General Theory*, pp. 91–92) that "Consumption is obviously much more a function of (in some sense) *real* income than of money-income . . . " etc. Is it really plausible to interpret him as attributing at the same time "money illusion" to workers in planning to sell their services and sober "realism" in planning to spend the proceeds?

23. Actually, while it is not "fundamental" to Keynes' explanation of why a situation of involuntary unemployment is not quickly remedied by automatic forces, it *is* fundamental to the explanation of how the situation can develop that some lag in price adjustments is present. Cf. II:1 and II:2 above.

to retain his job. Nor, having been laid off, will he immediately resign himself to shining shoes or selling apples. One reason, of course, is that his views of what his services should be worth unavoidably are related to what he was paid only yesterday. His expectations are *"inelastic"* in the Hicksian sense and his decision to withhold his services from the market may therefore be described as *speculation* on the future course of (obtainable) wages. This is the way Keynes described the behavior of producers.[24] The further analogy with the important role that speculation based on inelastic expectations (of the future course of long rates) plays in his analysis of securities markets lends a pleasing unity of conception to a theory which stresses this reason for "some resistance" to money wage cuts. But, in dealing with the labor market (and labor services are, of course, "perishable"), Keynes chose to emphasize the second set of data.

The second reason why the unemployed worker will not accept an arbitrarily large wage cut in order to regain employment immediately is that he sees many of his former mates still at their jobs at much the same money wage as before:

Since there is imperfect mobility of labour . . . any individual or group of individuals, who consent to a reduction of money-wages relatively to others, will suffer a *relative* reduction in real wages, which is a sufficient justification for them to resist it.

This and other similar statements fail to make clear which of the following two hypotheses Keynes would stress: (a) the worker takes the wages of others purely as a piece of information on the remuneration that it is possible to obtain, or (b) his self-respect is involved—he simply will not accept that he suddenly is "worth" less than those with whom he worked so recently. Here, however, a third interpretation, for which Keynes' text hardly gives much evidence, has gained some currency, namely that he meant to invoke a "relative income hypothesis." This is a static version of (b) above—current usage bases the "relative income

---

24. "For although output and employment are determined by producer's short-term expectations and not by past results, *the most recent results* usually play a predominant part in determining what these expectations are . . . "etc. *General Theory*, pp. 50–51, italics added.

hypothesis" on the assumption that other people's earnings enter into the steady-state utility function of individuals. This interpretation seems implausible in view of the fact that Keynes' two chapters on the consumption function show no trace of such a "keep up with the Joneses" hypothesis.

In any case, the fact that workers watch each others' wages imparts sluggishness to the behavior of the general money wage level *despite* the assumed readiness of labor collectively to accept a required general wage cut. It is *because:*

> . . . there is, as a rule, no means of securing a simultaneous and equal reduction of money-wages in all industries [that] it is in the interest of all workers to resist a reduction in their own particular case.[25]

(4) Keynes' "theoretically fundamental" objection to the Classical theory of the labor market is that it *misrepresents the nature of the wage bargain* in presuming that it does not matter whether the analysis of the determination of wages is conducted in "real" or money terms (and in opting for the former as more convenient). That Keynes regarded this point as pivotal in his attack on Classical economics is unmistakable, for he hammers away at it again and again, using the same language:

> But there is a more fundamental objection. The second postulate flows from the idea that the real wages of labour depend on the wage bargains which labour makes with the entrepreneurs. It is admitted, of course, that the bargains are actually made in terms of money. . . . Nevertheless it is the money-wage thus arrived at which is held to determine the real wage. Thus the classical theory assumes that it is always open to labour to reduce its real wage by accepting a reduction in its money-wage.

> The traditional theory maintains, in short, *that the wage bargains between the entrepreneurs and the workers determine the real wage;* so that, assuming free competition amongst employers and no restrictive combination amongst workers, the latter can, if they wish, bring their real wages into conformity with the marginal disutility of the amount of employment offered . . .

---

25. *General Theory*, p. 264. Note: Whereas, on the other hand, each worker knows that all are equally affected by a rise in the price of wage goods.

But the . . . more fundamental objection . . . flows from our disputing the assumption that the general level of real wages is directly determined by the character of the wage bargain . . . [This is] an illicit assumption. For there may be *no* method available to labour as a whole. . . . There may exist no expedient by which labour as a whole can reduce its *real* wage to a given figure by making revised *money* bargains with the entrepreneurs.[26]

Thus, to repeat, the fact that there exists a potential barter bargain of goods for labor services that would be mutually agreeable to producers as a group and labor as a group is irrelevant to the motion of the system. In economies relying on a means of payment, the excess demand for wage goods corresponding to an excess supply of labor is but "notional"—it is not communicated to employers as effective demand for output. The resulting miseries are "involuntary" all around.

This, to my mind, is the only possible construction of Keynes' meaning. And it is, of course, recognized in the standard Keynesian argument that money wage cuts will, as Keynes had it, lead merely to a *pari passu* fall of aggregate demand in money terms as long as there do not emerge "indirect effects due to a lower wages-bill in terms of money having certain reactions on the banking system and the state of credit." [27] That Keynes' position has *not* been fully assimilated, however, is most clearly demonstrated by the superficial, and at the same time quite contrived, interpretation of his assault on Say's Law that has become commonly accepted.

(5) The attack on Say's Law follows directly upon the definition of involuntary unemployment. There are two prongs to the attack. Both arguments dispute the same "Classical" notion: that

---

26. Cf. also the Appendix to Chapter 19, pp. 272–79: *Eight* entire pages lambasting Professor Pigou with interminable variations on a single theme: Professor Pigou *knows* " . . . that workpeople in fact stipulate, not for a real rate of wages, but for a money-rate" ; yet, "in effect [he assumes] that the actual money-rate of wages divided by the price of wage-goods can be taken to measure the real rate demanded."

27. *General Theory*, p. 11. Cf. also p. 278 n., where the attack on Pigou's presumption that real wages can be adjusted directly by money wage adjustments is followed up: "There is no hint or suggestion [in Professor Pigou's argument] that this comes about through reactions on the rate of interest." Cf. Chapter V:1 and V:2, below.

excess supplies must have their counterpart somewhere (if only in the future) in *effective* excess demands of the same total value.

(a) The first argument again concerns the nature of the wage bargain. Keynes singled out a passage from J. S. Mill, the wording of which seems most flagrantly to assert that the offer of labor services constitutes effective demand for commodities:

What *constitutes the means of payment* for commodities is simply commodities. . . . Could we suddenly double the productive powers of the country. . . . Everybody would *bring* a double demand as well as supply; everybody *would be able to buy* twice as much, because everyone would have twice as much to offer in exchange. (italics added)

(b) The second argument became an almost incessant theme of later chapters:

As a corollary of the same doctrine, it has been supposed that any individual act of abstaining from consumption necessarily leads to, and amounts to the same thing as, causing the labour and commodities thus released from supplying consumption to be invested in the production of capital wealth.[28]

The "same doctrine" is of course Say's Law, applied in the latter case to an intertemporal general equilibrium construction.

Say's Law is irrelevant to a money economy:

The conviction, which runs, for example, through almost all Professor Pigou's work, *that money makes no real difference except frictionally,* and that the theory of production and employment can be worked out (like Mill's) *as being based on "real" exchanges* with money intro-

---

28. Compare, *General Theory,* e.g., pp. 104–5, where Keynes explicitly notes that "present provision for future consumption" will be a source of aggregate demand, except "in so far as our social and business organization separates financial provision for the future from physical provision for the future so that efforts to secure the former do not necessarily carry the latter with them . . . " etc. The problem is explicitly regarded as one of the effective transmittal of the relevant information (p. 210): "If saving consisted not merely in abstaining from present consumption but in placing simultaneously a specific order for future consumption, the effect might indeed be different." To these intertemporal problems we return in Chapters IV and V.

duced perfunctorily in a later chapter, is the modern version of the classical tradition. (italics added)

And the relevance of the prevailing transaction structure is taken note of:

> . . . these [Classical] conclusions may have been applied to the kind of economy in which we actually live by false analogy from some kind of non-exchange Robinson Crusoe economy, in which the income which individuals consume or retain as a result of their productive activity is, actually and exclusively, the output *in specie* of that activity.

According to the standard interpretation of these passages, Keynes accused the Classical economists of being addicted to Say's Law in the sense of Lange. It is assumed, in other words, that he sought to reaffirm Walras' Law, not to attack it. Say's Law in Lange's sense asserts that the sum of the values of the $n - 1$ notional excess demands for the system's non-money goods is identically equal to zero, whereas Walras' Law is the same proposition applied to all n goods. Now, as previously pointed out, traditional general equilibrium models do not accord "money" a special status—it is just one of n equally "liquid" goods. The point of the distinction between the two "Laws" has nothing specifically to do with the means of payment function of money. Walras' Law is logically correct simply because it reckons with all n goods. To assert that the sum of $n - 1$ excess demands is identically zero violates the principles of the theory of exchange for a barter system, just as it does for a money-using system. Say's Law is just as invalid if some non-money good is excluded from the summation—it is false, for example, if we fail to reckon with Lerner's fabled peanuts. The standard interpretation, consequently, fails to explain why Keynes should insist that the crucial error of the Classical economists lay in their misrepresentation of the nature of the wage bargain and in their conviction "that the theory of production and employment can be worked out as being based on 'real' [i.e., barter] exchanges." If there is money in the system, Say's Law is just as invalid, whether wage bargains are settled "*in specie*" or not.

From the perspective of the standard interpretation, moreover,

Keynes' statement that, "Nevertheless, [Say's Law] underlies the whole classical theory, which would collapse without it," is simply incomprehensible.[29] However many statements suggestive of the "invalid dichotomy," etc., may be found in pre-Keynesian writings, it is absurd to suggest that summing over $n - 1$ excess demands was an accepted convention "underlying the whole classical theory." And, even had this been true, of course, the discoverer of such a monumental blunder could never have argued that the theory "would collapse without it." Obviously, elimination of the error could only have strengthened received doctrine.

Keynes' charges against Classical theory were directed at three assumptions:

(1) that the real wage is equal to the marginal disutility of the existing employment;
(2) that there is no such thing as involuntary unemployment in the strict sense;
(3) that supply creates its own demand. . . .

One may, if one so wishes, piece together an interpretation of the *General Theory*'s second chapter by assuming that he invoked against Classical theory (a) the charge that Classical economists individually and generally were addicted to Say's Law in the sense of Lange, (b) the empirical hypothesis that workers seek to "keep up with the Joneses," and (c) the empirical hypothesis that they also suffer from "money illusion" (in the straightforward sense of being fooled by proportional changes in accounting prices). But one will then also have to assume that Keynes, basing his own position on this motley assortment of outlandish propositions, was brazen enough to argue that "These

---

29. By implication this interpretation also asserts that, having selected his quote from J. S. Mill's *Principles*, Keynes did not bother to finish reading the paragraph: "Besides, money is a commodity . . . "—much less the rest of that very brief chapter: "At such times there is really an excess of all commodities above the money demand: in other words, there is an under-supply of money. . . . so that there may really be . . . an extreme depression of general prices, from what may be indiscriminately called a glut of commodities or a dearth of money." For, surely, had he seen these statements, Keynes could not have attributed Say's Law in the sense of Lange to Mill.

three assumptions . . . all amount to the same thing in the sense that *they all stand and fall together,* any one of them logically involving the other two." [30]

One must conclude, I believe, that Keynes' theory, although obscurely expressed and doubtlessly not all that clear even in his own mind, was still in substance that to which Clower has recently given a precise statement.

Summary   We have attempted to show that *"reconciling competition with unemployment" appears as a "riddle" only when "competition" is implicitly equated with "perfect information."* When a more realistic view is taken of the information problem which traders face, the emergence of unemployed resources is a predictable consequence of changes in demand. This unemployment further constrains effective demand: a "cumulative" Keynesian process may be set in motion. Though the initial disturbance may have implied little change in the real wealth of the community had full employment equilibrium been continuously maintained, the "illiquidity" of real resources in a situation of market disequilibria induces a contraction of money and real rates of aggregate expenditures. This contraction constitutes a new set of "information inputs" causing adjustments by transactors which lead the system further away from equilibrium. This cybernetic chain of information feedbacks is the very essence of the income-constrained process.

II:4   Additional Notes on Price-Level Flexibility

We have seen that, once an effort is made to free the analysis of a static mode of thinking, there is no presumption that a system of atomistic markets will exhibit pure price-level adjustment behavior without painful, and costly, movements in real output and income. In the same way, it is far from evident that markets which are *not* atomistic will exhibit less short-run price flexibility than atomistic markets, under otherwise similar production and

---

30. *General Theory*, p. 22, italics added.

inventory cost conditions. The proposition that the optimizing monopolist will utilize his market power to charge a price above marginal cost—and therefore a price higher than would rule if the market were competitive—does not translate into the proposition that the same monopolist will find it to his advantage to keep his price "fixed" in the face of fluctuations in demand. Optimal price-setting policies over time depend upon a number of factors which would take us too far afield to pursue here. If, however, we assume the monopolist to market a highly perishable product—the assumption which underlies the application of the static, perfect competition model to short-run problems—then such a monopolist should normally respond to a decline in sales by quickly reducing price. With a very perishable product (near-prohibitive storage cost), wealth-maximizing implies continuous maximization of the flow-rate of net revenue.

There are all sorts of possible exceptions to this. Geometrically, it is quite easy to construct cases where a downward shift of a monopolist's demand curve results in a *higher* price becoming the short-run profit-maximizing one. Nor are such possibilities entirely academic. In 1933, Viner had to note that

Railroad freight rates have not only not decreased in the face of a fifty per cent decline in wholesale prices, but unbelievable though it should be, they have actually been permitted to rise since the beginning of the depression, and are pressing down as a crushing weight on all industries requiring long-distance hauling of bulky commodities.[1]

The price-theoretical questions are several: Under what conditions would a profit-maximizing monopoly respond to a decline in demand by lowering its price? By raising it? By maintaining it constant? How do we predict the speed of price adjustments? We cannot pursue all these questions here. The point is simply that if unemployment is to be blamed on the existence of monopolies, these points should be cleared up. One of the issues, however, is of particular relevance to the analysis of the previous section.

---

1. Viner, *op. cit.*, p. 8. Since the railroad industry was regulated, the freight-rate data do not reflect the unconstrained profit-maximizing solutions "before and after." But this hardly "explains away" the fact that rates *did* rise.

It is sometimes maintained that the competitive firm's information problem is simpler than that of the monopolist. The competitive seller needs to know only his cost function and "the" market price of his product in order to maximize profits. The monopolist, it is argued, needs information on his entire demand function. This argument can be examined from either of two standpoints: the information needs of the two types of sellers (1) in equilibrium or (2) in disequilibrium.

In equilibrium, the information problem is trivial. Least-cost functions being known with certainty (by assumption), once the sellers are in equilibrium—and the entire system must then be in general exchange equilibrium—neither the competitive, nor the monopolist firm need spend any resources on active search for information. The only information needed—confirmation of the fact that the rate of output is the "correct" one (equal to the rate of sales)—is automatically available through the outcome of current trading. As long as the rate of sales holds steady at the given price, no price and output adjustments are called for.[2]

In disequilibrium, it is hard to see how it can be argued that sellers in atomistic markets have simpler information problems than the monopolist. Since the monopolist makes the market, the actual outcomes of all trading constitute information automatically available to him. He does not need to find out what a multitude of other sellers are doing; if there are multiple prices in the market at any time, it is because he, the monopolist, is discriminating; he does not have to devote resources to finding out where and by whom what price is paid. When the atomistic market is in disequilibrium, the individual seller can no longer regard price as "parametric"—he must attempt to form an estimate of how *industry demand* is developing in order to formu-

---

2. The one possible exception—a rotation of the monopolist's demand curve around the present trading point (which would make his current price-output policy inoptimal)—is hardly worth detailed consideration. Only if this change in demand conditions in the monopolized market did *not* lead to changes in actual trading outcomes *anywhere* in the whole system, would the monopolist continue to be unaware of the need for adjustment. If the amount traded at the given prices changes somewhere in the system, the information needs of both types of sellers increase.

late a rational pricing policy. Changes in his own rate of sales give the atomistic seller less accurate indications of the relevant demand changes than in the monopolist's case, since multiple prices will be charged in the market at any one time. The information which he would need for an optimal pricing policy includes a lot of data, freely available to the monopolist, but which he can only acquire at formidable cost.[3]

Atomistic markets functioning through organized exchanges constitute exceptions to the above argument. For our purposes it is sufficient to note that the existence of such institutions is in itself evidence of the high cost of information in unorganized, atomistic markets.[4]

Nonetheless, price may be more volatile in atomistic markets than in highly concentrated markets. If so, the reason is not that sellers in such markets have better information or need less information, but that their information costs are very high. In the previous section we argued that the seller will continue his search as long as the costs of further information gathering do not outweigh prospective gains in sales revenues. Thus, if information costs are very high, the atomistic seller may reduce his quoted (reservation) price sooner. But since the new reservation price is set on the basis of highly imperfect information, such price volatility is not necessarily to be preferred from a welfare point of view to the price policies pursued by sellers in concentrated markets on the basis of more adequate knowledge. Drastic transitory price falls may create exaggerated, adverse expectations harmful in the short run to employment in such industries. Static welfare theory tells us that monopolistic price-setting is Pareto-inefficient in the stationary state. Welfare theorists have devoted less energy to the problem of the efficiency of the adjustment processes characterizing alternative market struc-

---

3. In the disequilibrium case, the assumption that sellers know their cost functions with certainty, which we have used in order to deal only with output markets, cannot be maintained. As buyers of factor services, however, the two types of sellers face similar information problems.

4. Cf., e.g., H. S. Houthakker, "The Scope and Limits of Futures Trading," in Abramowitz et al., The Allocation of Economic Resources, op. cit.

tures. In a rapidly changing world, these problems seem to merit serious attention.[5]

It is possible that highly concentrated industries are also industries where optimal pricing policies over time dictate a combination of infrequent price changes and short-run adjustments by way of changes in order backlogs, inventories and—conceivably—output rates. Concentration and perishability of product may be inversely correlated, for example. If concentration and inflexibility of prices are found to be correlated, however, we would expect the same underlying factors to account for both these industry characteristics, rather than the market structure to explain the degree of price-flexibility.

The above argument can be extended from monopoly to industries characterized by price-leadership or by "monopolistic competition." An oligopolistic industry without a recognized price-leader may be so perilously perched at a particular time that the individual firms might temporarily abstain from any act of changing price for fear of destroying the industry's "egg-on-end" equilibrium. In our aggregative context this case is of little interest.

An argument may even be made for expecting increased price competition in times of depression in "monopolistically competitive" industries which exhibit mainly non-price competition in more normal times. For example, income-elasticity of demand may be much higher for bucket seats, car radios, and other "extras" than for "transportation pure and simple." [6] Low levels of income would then leave little scope for this type of product differentiation, and other similar methods of non-price competition. Ordinary price competition might therefore be intensified.

The power of labor unions vis-à-vis both workers and employers may be similarly eroded at low levels of real income and in periods of widespread unemployment. The prospective costs and benefits which both workers and employers have to consider

---

5. Cf. D. McCord Wright, "Some Notes on Ideal Output," *Quarterly Journal of Economics*, May 1962, esp. section V.

6. Compare J. R. Hicks, *A Revision of Demand Theory*, Oxford, 1956, pp. 166–68. Though the argument does not bring in income-elasticities it is similar in conception to the one used here—and it is stated more fully.

in dealing with unions—or in refusing to deal with unions—change to the disadvantage of the union leadership. But the facts on this matter, as well as the hypotheses usually adduced to account for the facts, are well known and we need not dwell on the point.

In this chapter, we have argued that Keynes' theory constitutes an attack on, not an elaboration of, those explanations of depressions which stress monopolistic restraints on the movements of prices. A system of atomistic markets will not always work "perfectly." To completely insure against movements of real income and output that may be self-amplifying (or "cumulative"), prices would have to move *instantaneously* in response to a deflationary disturbance so that no "false trading" occurs. Transactors have to watch the actual outcomes of trading for their most important information; real world markets, however, yield information on effective excess demands—there are no actual mechanisms, like the Walrasian *tâtonnement*, that permit notional excess demands to be registered for transactors to act upon. If buoyant medium-term and long-term expectations do not prevent it, "false trading" will therefore lead into an income-constrained process.

The "Economics of Keynes," as we have interpreted it, has not permeated "Keynesian Economics" on the issues discussed in this chapter. One frequently finds statements to the effect that Keynesian theory is worthwhile because downward price "rigidities" are with us whether we like it or not. Many "Keynesians" appear to agree that Keynesian Economics would not be very relevant to a truly competitive economy. But the short-run behavior of a system of atomistic markets, however competitive, may be better explained by a model closer to the pure income adjustment than to the pure price-level adjustment end of the spectrum.

The considerations on which we judge the relative merits of alternative market structures in static welfare theory are not directly relevant to the social evaluation of their adjustment behavior when the system is out of equilibrium. From conventional welfare theory we know that rigidities of the *relative* prices of factors and commodities are undesirable from the standpoint of resource allocation. If the wealth distribution which the automatic working of the system brings about is accepted, behavior that interferes with the adjustment of relative prices is dysfunctional to the system and can be condemned on ethical grounds. Academic economists have been the high priests of this ethic. This kind of value judgment has sometimes been extended from the static problems of optimal resource *allocation* to the problem of aggregate resource *utilization* over time. It may seem natural to assume that if we cannot have the best of all worlds—i.e., the kind of instant price-level flexibility which would keep the economy from ever entering upon an income-constrained process—the desirable objective is still the highest possible degree of such flexibility.

It is well known that Keynes was adamant in attacking such a conclusion.[7] There were, characteristically, two prongs to his attack. The first was the argument, phrased in exceedingly polemical language, that a *pari passu* fall of money wages and money prices would not get us anywhere. An immense amount of ammunition has been fired at this argument, particularly in the course of the debate over the Pigou-effect.[8] The second was the argument, subsequently elaborated by Lerner,[9] that too high a

---

7. One must guard against the (unfounded) impression that, in so doing, Keynes was also attacking a predominant view among economists and policy-makers in the thirties. Opposition to a policy of drastic, *general* wage cuts, was, in fact, quite widespread. Cf., e.g., J. R. Schlesinger, "After Twenty Years: The *General Theory*," *Quarterly Journal of Economics*, Nov. 1956, pp. 599–601.

8. For a recent, critical appraisal of this literature, essentially on its own terms, cf. J. H. Power, "Price Expectations, Money Illusion, and the Real Balance Effect," *Journal of Political Economy*, April 1959.

9. Cf. *General Theory*, Chapter 17. It must be noted that many eminent economists have taken a dim view of this part of the *General Theory*. Johnson, *op. cit.*, dismisses it as "pretentious philosophizing"; A. H. Hansen in his *A Guide to Keynes*, New York, 1953, pp. 155 and 159, expresses much the same sentiment. A less tortuous statement of Keynes' views can be found in his "Social Consequences of Changes in the Value of Money," in *Essays in Persuasion* (Norton edn.), New York, 1963.

Cf. A. P. Lerner, "The Essential Properties of Interest and Money," *Quarterly Journal of Economics*, May 1952. In "Comment" (on H. G. Johnson, *op. cit.*), *American Economic Review*, May 1961, Lerner distinguishes four orders of price-flexibility. (Lerner, however, appears to subscribe to the monopoly explanation of price-rigidities.) Also, M. L. Burstein, *Money*, Cambridge, Mass., 1963, pp. 504 ff.

degree of price-level flexibility is incompatible with the maintenance of a money exchange system.

The crux of Keynes' position is simply that *balanced* deflation will not do if relative values are wrong to begin with. But this flat statement anticipates the argument to be developed in the next two chapters. The Pigou-effect and associated issues will be taken up in Chapter V.

III·THE AGGREGATIVE STRUCTURE OF ALTERNATIVE MODELS

III:1 Aggregation and the Construction of Macromodels

Aggregation implies abstraction—certain particularistic features of the elements of the aggregate are suppressed, while "representative" characteristics assume exclusive significance. The aggregation procedure is, therefore, as important in determining the properties of an economic model as are the assumptions made about the relationships between the aggregates. Yet, economists habitually pay far more attention to specifying and defending the qualitative relationships among the aggregates of their models than to giving their reasons for the particular choice of aggregates. The aggregates used tend to become professional conventions which are seldom examined.

The standard income-expenditure model embodies many such long-established conventions. Its aggregative structure is different from that of Keynes' model. In the chapters to follow, we will find repeatedly that important substantive differences between the two types of model derive from the different aggregation procedures employed. Income-expenditure doctrine conflicts with Keynes' theory on numerous points. The concept of "aggregative structure" will prove helpful in distinguishing the systematic pattern that these later "Keynesian" departures from Keynes' theory have followed. But ultimately we are interested not so much in this pattern *per se* as in the differences in basic assumptions that account for it.

Since these assumptions have seldom been systematically spelled out, we begin by discussing and illustrating some of the basic principles involved in aggregation. There exists an extensive, technical literature on this subject.[1] The following notes are designed simply to show how this literature can be helpful to the non-specialist economist in investigating the reasons underlying the conflicts among alternative models—a perspective that but seldom comes to the fore in the technical literature, e.g., on the construction of index numbers.

Aggregation is based on judgments about what is of primary and what of secondary importance—about what to include and what to leave out. It poses statistical decision problems that should, in principle, be settled by empirical test.[2] Analytically, the benefits lie in the simplifications of model structure which make it easier to understand and manipulate; the costs lie in the potentially significant causal relationships which vanish from sight. Empirically, the benefits lie in the reduced data and computation requirements, the costs in lessened predictive power.[3]

The choice of a specific aggregation will depend on the objectives of inquiry and on the limits of tolerable approximation that this context imposes. The justification, stated or implied, for a given mode of aggregation may be more or less sweeping and it is frequently important to distinguish the two levels on which it

---

1. H. A. J. Green, *Aggregation in Economic Analysis*, Princeton, 1964, is an excellent survey of the field.

2. One virtue of Green, *op. cit.*, is the steady emphasis on this point.

3. This is the perspective of the "pure" theory of aggregation, from which "throwing away" any set of potentially relevant data always means throwing away the ambition of explaining 100 percent of the variance of the variable to be explained. But, in practice, results may be *improved* if this ambition is given up—it is better to be "roughly right than exactly wrong." Cf., e.g., Y. Grunfeld and Z. Griliches, "Is Aggregation Necessarily Bad?" *Review of Economics and Statistics*, Feb. 1960.

may be advanced: (1) the relationships suppressed and, correspondingly the information that is thrown away (or not gathered) may be *irrelevant in any event*. The mean or total may be the only "number" that counts, whereas other characteristics of the population of basic observations do not. The characteristics that are asserted not to count may include, for example, the variance around the mean and other, higher moments of the distribution. (2) The information neglected may be *relevant in principle* but unnecessary in the context of a particular application. It may be recognized, for example, that the dependent variable of the theory does depend on the distribution around the mean of a certain independent variable, but it is either known or assumed that this distribution does not change in the particular system and during the particular time-period under study.

In one case, the value of the dependent variable is assumed to be invariant to a certain class of events. In the other, certain events that would be relevant to the outcome are assumed not to happen. This latter type of assumption we will meet in several different disguises. On either level, it is rarely the case that the assumption is strictly justified—tacitly or explicitly, a standard of tolerable approximation is generally invoked.

This, however, is by no means the only twofold division of the subject that is relevant. The following list will indicate how extensive the subject of aggregation is:

1) aggregation
   (a) "over transactors," i.e., aggregation of individual demand or supply functions, or
   (b) "over goods," i.e., aggregation reducing the number of market demand and supply functions;
2) the conditions imposed may apply to
   (a) consumer goods, or
   (b) assets;
3) they may impose restrictions on the form of
   (a) production functions (supply side), or
   (b) utility functions (demand side);
4) the conditions may be of either
   (a) strict complementarity, or

(b) perfect substitutability;
5) a given aggregation procedure
   (a) may be valid only if certain equilibrium conditions are fulfilled, or
   (b) may be equally applicable to situations of disequilibrium.

Clearly, we cannot possibly survey the whole problem-complex. The following illustrations are the ones deemed most relevant to the issues dividing Keynes from the "Keynesians."

Aggregation over transactors   The offer curves of an individual trader are functions of his tastes, of his resource endowment, and of market prices. The typical problem is whether market excess demand functions can be written as dependent upon prices and the *sum* of endowments. The vital assumption that has to be made is that of "no distribution effects," i.e., that aggregate demand depends upon the sum of resources, not on their distribution among transactors. With reference to the simple consumption-income relation of early Keynesian models, for example, the question is whether aggregate consumption depends only on total current income or also on the distribution of this total income among consumers.

The assumption of no distribution effects may be justified on either of the two levels mentioned above. (1) Changes in distribution are irrelevant if utility functions fulfill certain restrictive assumptions. For simple aggregate demand functions, the necessary assumption generally is that all transactors have utility functions of the same form and that these functions be homogeneous [4] with respect to the endowment variable. If, for example,

---

4. That is, homogeneous of some degree: it is not necessary that the utility functions be linear homogeneous. Linear homogeneity is otherwise the condition most frequently encountered. It is generally necessary, for example, in the case of aggregation of firms' supply functions. In this case the dependent variable (supply) itself enters directly into the determination of the model's equilibrium solution. Fortunately, we do not require of our models that they give a solution for "total utility."

Most often, then, linearity conditions have to be imposed. It should be noted that there exists a special class of aggregation theorems which deals, not with linearity in the variables, but with linearity in the logarithms of the variables. Cf.,

for any given price vector, the Engel-curves of all traders are straight lines through the origin with the same slope, a redistribution of resources from A to B will induce B to expand his demand for all goods in exactly the same amounts as A contracts his. Hence market excess demands—and the equilibrium solution for the system—will be unaffected. These conditions imposed on "tastes" permit total demand to be written as a function of total "income," regardless of the distribution of that income among households.

(2) Alternatively, less stringent conditions on "tastes" will suffice if it may be assumed that the distribution of income will remain constant. It may be recognized, for example, that *per capita* consumption depends not only on *mean* income but in principle also on the second and, perhaps, higher moments of the distribution. Aggregate consumption can then still be written simply as a function of total income, if it can be assumed (a) that, except for the mean, the parameters of the distribution are fixed, and (b) that all Engel-curves are linear. In this instance it is not necessary to require that the Engel-curves also have the same slope.

The consumption function literature illustrates how the amount of professional attention paid to a particular aggregation problem varies with time and circumstances.

In the early income-expenditure literature, the "propensity to save" was regarded as markedly higher in high income groups than in low ones. The so-called "Keynesian stagnationists" were interested in the possibility of raising the aggregate propensity to consume—and thereby escape the posited fate of "mature economies"—by fiscal redistribution of income from rich to poor. As the "Bogey of Economic Maturity" has waned and been replaced by concern with the problem of inflation, interest in this issue among American "Keynesians" [5] has declined drastically.

---

e.g., the work by Klein, May, *et al.* on Divisia indices and Cobb-Douglas functions, cited by Green, *op. cit.*, Chapter 5. The discussion in the text is less than general since we confine ourselves to a subclass of aggregation problems, i.e., those dealing with the straightforward summation of variables.

5. In Britain, the situation is different. There, the theoretical work on growth and cycles associated particularly with the names of Robinson and Kaldor assigns a

(It has not been proposed to deal with inflation by redistribution from poor to rich.) This reflects advances in both empirical knowledge and theoretical sophistication: Kuznets' finding of an approximately constant long-run saving-income ratio and the development of the "modern" approaches to the consumption function with their new implications for the interpretation of cross-section consumption data. The new theories relate cross-sectional differences in savings ratios to underlying determinants that are less volatile than current income, particularly factors involving different dimensions of demographic structure. Since the change in demographic variables is relatively slow, the consumption function can, for many purposes, be developed in terms of simple aggregates of expenditures, income, net worth, etc.

One of the most important issues of modern monetary theory revolves around the "aggregation over transactors" problem. A seldom examined, though highly questionable, convention of contemporary monetary theory is the assumption that "real" aggregate demand is independent of the "real" value of intra-private-sector financial contracts. Redistribution of real net worth between creditors and debtors, due to price-level movements, is assumed to have no qualitatively predictable effects on aggregate demand, output, and employment. These variables are assumed to depend, apart from current income, only on the variables contained in the private sector's *consolidated* balance sheet. The "interior" of the "matrix of claims" is ignored.[6] This convention occupies a central place in modern monetary theory. When the assumption of "no distribution effects" is mentioned without further explanation in contemporary literature, it usually

---

crucially important role to the distribution of current and anticipated income among capitalists and wage-earners. American interest in this school of thought has been light. The neglect of it in this work reflects, not a judgment of its relevance or importance, but a consciously parochial concern with the development of the American "Keynesian tradition"—though this tradition is certainly not to be considered "purer" than the British.

6. The method of describing the financial structure of the economy as a matrix of claims and liabilities appears to be due to A. G. Hart. Cf. his "Uses of National Wealth Estimates and the Structure of Claims," National Bureau of Economic Research (NBER), *Studies in Income and Wealth*, Vol. XIV, New York, 1950.

refers to the consolidation of the private sector's balance sheet. The writers who systematically rely on it have given no account of the subsidiary, restrictive, behavioral assumptions on which it is founded. It is at least questionable whether it has a legitimate place outside the long-run context of the comparative static analysis of full stock-flow equilibria or short-run "perfect information" models.[7] But it is a standard feature of income-expenditure models, and was only occasionally relaxed (in a most *ad hoc* manner) in the *General Theory*. Hence, it will be employed consistently throughout the following chapters.

Aggregation over goods   Aggregation over a particular group of goods replaces the distinct quantities of the separate goods with a quantity-index. The corresponding relative prices disappear from the model and are replaced with a price-index for the composite bundle.

On what grounds can the exclusion of certain relative prices be justified? As usual, there are two ways out: *either* changes in relative prices are assumed to have no (predictable) consequences relevant to the analysis, *or* such changes are assumed not to occur. Although we deal explicitly only with the "pure"

---

7. In the previous chapter, we commented on some of the disturbing features of the modern general equilibrium approach to "pure" monetary theory, particularly the preoccupation shown in this literature with the formal conditions for the static "neutrality of money." The analysis of these comparative statics conditions has been universally based on the assumption of "no distribution effects." It is important for monetary theorists to be clear on those conceivable circumstances under which the quantity of money and other nominal variables are of no significance to the determination of the system's "real" equilibrium. But these problems must by now be regarded as settled—yet there have been few if any signs of the adherents of this approach being willing to turn to problems of greater relevance to the functioning of actually existing systems.

One way to break out of the present arid framework would be to examine the value-theoretical foundations of the "no distribution effects" assumption in order eventually to proceed with the *dynamic* analysis of systems in which the conditions implicit in this assumption do not hold. This may be the most important task in this field. A persuasive case can be made that a theory incorporating this assumption—and based ultimately upon the type of "perfect information" postulates criticized in Chapter II—is inherently incapable of dealing with the majority of problems that have traditionally been the preserve of monetary theorists. But a more detailed development of this case must be left for another occasion.

cases, some standard of satisfactory approximation is always involved in practice—i.e., the effects of a change in certain relative prices are so minor that they can be ignored, or the price changes are themselves so minor that their effects can be ignored.

The first case, in its pure form, involves strictly complementary goods. When two or more goods are consumed in fixed proportions, produced as joint outputs, or used in fixed proportions as inputs, their relative prices do not matter—only the total price of the fixed bundle is relevant to the various decisions involved. Whereas this class of aggregation conditions is important—for example, in input-output models—and looms large in the literature on the theory of index numbers, conditions of this type are not very relevant to the issues considered in this chapter.

We will be concerned instead with the conditions underlying Hicks' theorem. Hicks' theorem states that the separate quantities of a group of goods, the prices of which always vary in proportion, can be aggregated without loss of information or introduction of predictive error. Aggregate quantity can then be measured as a weighted sum of the separate quantities of component goods.[8] This type of aggregation thus presupposes the constancy of the relative prices of the goods involved. These relative prices then "disappear" as endogenous variables of the model, though they remain implicit in the measurement of the aggregated quantities.

As before, we must look beyond the assumption of constant relative prices to the deeper assumptions about the system's behavior which would imply this constancy. The potential conditions that would establish constancy of relative prices for a given group of goods may be classified according to whether they impose restrictions on (a) *production functions,* or on (b) *preferences.*

(a) The relative price of two goods x and y, will be constant if the cost of production of x always stands in a given proportion, k, to the production cost of y. For this condition to hold, irre-

---

8. J. R. Hicks, *Value and Capital,* Mathematical Appendix, ¶10, pp. 312–13.

spective of relative factor prices, restrictions on the two production functions are implied. Again, conditions of linear homogeneity are encountered. Clearly, x must require k times the factor inputs required for the production of one unit of y. This must hold irrespective of the scale of output in the two industries. Hence, the two production functions must be linear homogeneous and identical except for the factor of proportionality, k.[9]

For any two goods satisfying these conditions, the production possibilities corresponding to any given vector of inputs can be portrayed as a straight line transformation curve. Opportunity costs are constant. The slope of the transformation line is given by the constant k and reflects only the conventional units of measurement for the two commodities. Market prices must, in equilibrium, conform to the slope of this transformation line.

In our context, it is of special interest that these conditions are generally implied whenever an aggregate production function is postulated. Such functions have aggregate output as a function of a number of total input quantities. The proportionality factors, corresponding to k above, are all submerged in the index adopted for the measurement of aggregate output. Identification of this measure of output with "real income" presumes that the system is in "equilibrium." The index of aggregate output measures merely the distance of the transformation plane from the origin along some straight line ray. "Real income" is a monotonic function of this measure only if it can be assumed that the optimal consumption point on any given transformation plane always obtains.[10] If at any time this is not true, rates of exchange would diverge from rates of transformation in production, and the Hicksian theorem cannot be applied.[11] Thus, although it is convenient to discuss the problem from the two

---

9. Here the simplest case would involve fixed coefficient production functions requiring the same ratios of inputs.

10. We may be permitted, here, to dodge the problems of "community indifference maps," etc. In the Crusoe case it is clear that many "disequilibrium" points on a higher transformation plane are inferior to the best point on a lower plane.

11. The possibility should perhaps be pointed out that the system could be in an equilibrium with a corner solution so that one of the goods is not produced at all. Special cases of this sort will, however, be ignored in the following discussion.

separate standpoints of production and preferences, no "clean" dividing line can be drawn between the two.[12]

(b) Constancy of relative prices can also be deduced if certain restrictions are imposed on the utility functions of transactors. The condition, in the simplest, two-goods case, is that the two goods be perfect substitutes in consumption at some given rate of substitution which is independent of the quantities consumed of all other goods. Here it is the indifference curves, rather than the physical transformation curve, which show up as straight lines if a cross-section of the map is taken in the plane of the two goods involved. If all traders' utility functions are identical in this respect, demand can be non-zero for both the goods only if the market price equals the given rate of substitution. If the goods cannot be produced at costs standing in this relation, one of them would not be produced in equilibrium. In recent years general equilibrium theorists have become more ambitious in requiring that their models explain also what goods will appear in the equilibrium output vector; hence, one reason for the growth of interest in linear programming analysis of general equilibrium problems.

The condition of perfect substitutability is a stringent one, and it may be questioned whether the proper definition of "a good" does not preclude its strict application between goods.[13] The

---

12. This conclusion is familiar from some of the perennial issues of capital theory—it unavoidably crops up in discussions on the measurement of capital, or "average roundaboutness," on the technical superiority of present goods, and on the possibility of a pure productivity theory of capital . . . *et hoc genus omne.* A simple Wicksellian case of maturing timber, for example, may seem to involve only productivity considerations. If the illustrative example is changed to aging cheese or wine, however, rates of substitution in consumption between wines of different ages must be brought in, since it is "intuitively obvious" that these represent "different goods." It is then realized that the timber case involves a hidden postulate involving "tastes," namely that one cu. ft. of timber is a perfect substitute for any other cu. ft. of timber in final use, etc.

All aggregation theorems use postulates about preferences, and aggregation theorems dealing with production functions are not an independent class of such propositions.

13. Conversely one may compare the point made by H. G. Johnson and recently quoted by K. J. Lancaster: ". . . Johnson [has] suggested, somewhat tongue-in-cheek, that the determinateness of the sign of the substitution effect (the only substantive result of the theory of consumer behavior) could be derived from the proposition that goods are goods." Cf. Lancaster, "A New Approach to Consumer

proper definition of a good involves basically the definition of a unit of quantity measurement. Ponder the case of eggs, for example. If, for every household, one pound of eggs is a perfect substitute for any other pound, egg quantities should be measured in number of pounds. If, for some reason, however, they were actually measured in dozens, cartons of a dozen eggs would be found to trade at different prices depending upon weight. A moderately clever economist would then find scope for the application of Hicks' theorem. All he need do is to discard the prevailing convention of measurement and redefine it in terms of weight to get a unit for which there would be only one egg price (in equilibrium). If, on the other hand, households regarded any dozen eggs as a perfect substitute for any other and weight as irrelevant, while for some reason the conventional unit of measurement was stated in terms of weight, the same reasoning applies *mutatis mutandis*. Finally, if households have preferences both about weight and numbers, there is nothing for the economist to do but to look the index number problem "firmly in the face and pass on." [14]

Of greater practical interest is the case where *some*, but not

---

Theory," *Journal of Political Economy*, April 1966, p. 132. Lancaster's promising effort to reconstruct the theory of demand is based on a redefinition of the basic objects of choice and utilizes the methods of activity analysis. A unit of a good is treated as a fixed coefficient "bundle of *properties*" and the utility function is defined in terms of these underlying properties rather than directly in terms of quantities of "goods."

The simple illustrations which follow in the text consider questions of the following type: Are two objects (or collections of objects) good enough substitutes to allow aggregation? ("Good enough" should be understood as referring to standards of approximation imposed by the ultimate purpose for which a model is constructed.) Note that the discussion of this sort of question runs in terms of those "properties" which the objects do *not* have in common. The concrete question becomes whether these distinguishing characteristics are of "much" significance in terms of the utility functions of traders. ("Criterion function" is perhaps a more helpful term than "utility function" here—two objects are perfect substitutes if the individual does not perceive any *subjectively meaningful criteria* on which to make a choice between the two.)

14. As Green notes, insistence on complete rigor in these matters leads to a particularly unfruitful nihilism: "it is possible to argue that no two commodity units can be alike in all respects . . . ," etc. (p. 9.) To search for aggregates which do not sacrifice *any* potentially relevant information is simply a quixotic quest. Cf. *op. cit.*, Ch. 1, and P. A. Samuelson, *Foundations of Economic Analysis*, *op. cit.*, pp. 144–45.

all, traders regard the two goods as perfect substitutes at some given price ratio. To continue with the egg market(s): one group of households may prefer pounds of eggs with as many (small) eggs as possible, another with few eggs as large as possible, and a third group—the omelet consumers—may be completely indifferent about the number of eggs in a pound. The third group would then always buy at the cheapest price per pound and if this group exercises a large enough part of the total market demand it would arbitrage any per pound price differentials that might otherwise develop.[15] In a case of this sort, the problem for the model-builder is to form a judgment about what kind of structural (or distributional) changes are likely to be relevant, considering the "reference coordinates" in time, space, and so forth for which his model is designed to yield predictions. As long as the third group is large enough relative to the total market, for example, supply and demand quantities can be measured simply in terms of weight and there will be a single exchange-equilibrium price in the market. This aggregation might break down, however, if the income of omelet consumers were to decline drastically relative to the income of the other groups. If, on the production side the number of eggs per pound were a purely random variable, the initial market would become fragmented as the first two groups bid up the prices of both very small and very large eggs.

Aggregation over assets   So far we have dealt with the aggregation of goods destined for direct consumption, paying particular attention to the aggregation of close ("approximately perfect") substitutes. In dealing with the aggregation of assets, the only conditions we need consider are those of substitutability. The considerations relevant to the aggregation of assets are, however, somewhat different from those applying to consumption goods.

---

15. Here again, it is not enough to look at only one side of the market. If production is monopolized, for example, there may be an opportunity for discriminatory pricing. Even with competition on the supply side, the different groups have to pay different prices if there exist separate production and cost functions for the "different goods" which they demand.

In the case of consumption goods, the focus is on those concrete, inherent properties which make goods distinguishable and the question is whether these differentiating characteristics are of much significance to the "representative consumer's" choice between two goods. While people may attach a "prestige value" to some assets which other types of assets are not accorded, such Veblenesque issues will be ignored here—as they generally are. As a general rule, the choice *between* assets (and, therefore, the determination of *relative* asset prices) is assumed to be independent of the concrete characteristics of the assets as objects in themselves.[16] The utility-relevant characteristics of different asset classes pertain instead to the consumption "outcomes" *in the future* which current ownership of alternative portfolios is perceived to entail.

In considering the aggregation of assets, one must therefore distinguish the various *prospective return streams* from the *sources* of these streams. While observable market prices pertain to the sources, it is the substitutability-relationships between return streams with which we must be concerned. This distinction between the source itself and the stream "attached" to the source is of little or no significance as long as transactor expectations about returns to various assets are taken as "given" for the immediate purposes of the analysis. Under this condition, the change in the price of a source means a corresponding change in the price of a given return stream. When expectations about the earnings to be derived from a given source change, this simple correspondence does not hold. The two extreme cases illustrate the range of possibilities: the price of a specified future stream of prospective receipts may not change while the price per unit of the sources from which streams of this nature can be derived does change; or the price of sources does not change while the present value of a given future return stream does. In discussing the determination of short-run income equilibrium, Keynes pre-

---

16. In dealing with the choice between consumption in general and accumulation of assets in general, there is a real issue of whether it should be assumed that traders are concerned wholely with future consumption or whether they also "just like to be wealthy." This issue will be considered in Chapter IV.

ferred to work with the simple case holding "the State of Long-Term Expectations" constant.

In dealing with assets, therefore, one is concerned with the aggregation of future prospects rather than of currently existing sources. For present purposes, it is convenient to assume that we need to deal with only one future date. The population of assets from which a portfolio is to be chosen consists entirely of assets which mature at this future date. An aggregation problem arises only if these prospects are "risky." If the future were foreseen with certainty, the present price of a given amount of consumer goods for delivery on a specified future date would be the same, no matter what concrete form current investment would take. The various types of assets—which provide the current owner with command over future consumption goods—would all trade at prices proportional to their net return per unit. At these relative prices all assets would be regarded as perfect substitutes. Under the assumption of "no uncertainty," one would have to regard the composition of individual portfolios as indeterminate and would thus deal with a model with but a single asset aggregate. The "aggregation problem" evidently hinges upon differences in "risk" among assets—or, better, among return streams. At this point, it is useful to distinguish between *"degrees of risk"* and *"types of risk."*

The utility-relevant outcome, which we may refer to as the "payoff," is contingent upon the state of the world that will obtain at the future date. Risk means that it is uncertain which state of the world will, in fact, obtain. Most modern approaches to the problem of decision-making under uncertainty start from the assumption that the decision-maker assigns probabilities to the various possible states of the world.[17] With the payoffs to

---

17. Keynes' treatment of the uncertainty problem is entirely unencumbered by the technical apparatus which modern theorists have erected on the basis of this assumption. Modern readers have often found his analysis "crude" in its use of certainty-equivalents, etc. It should be remembered that he explicitly rejected the "actuarial calculus" as a permissible basis for an attack on the problem. Cf., e.g., his "The General Theory of Employment," *Quarterly Journal of Economics*, Feb. 1937, reprinted in S. E. Harris, *The New Economics*, New York, 1952. His analytical method in later years reflects the position developed in his *Treatise on Probability*, London, 1921.

presently held assets dependent upon the future state of the world, one can derive probability distributions of payoffs for different asset classes. The degree of risk of an asset, or its "riskiness" in the abstract, may then be associated with some measure of the statistical dispersion of the perceived probability distribution of payoffs, e.g., its standard deviation.

In the approach which has been the most common one in recent years, the criterion function underlying the choice between risky prospects is formulated in terms of the mean and standard deviation of such a probability distribution. The basic objects of choice are entire portfolios rather than individual assets. This Mean-Variability approach has recently been so predominant that it is known as "the portfolio approach." [18] The approach provides an explanation for the observed diversification of portfolios. Efficient portfolios are those which, for any over-all expected mean rate of return, minimize the standard deviation, or, conversely, maximize the expected rate of return for any given value of the standard deviation. It can then be shown that one-asset portfolios are, as a rule, not efficient portfolios. In our context, two implications should be stressed. If we take the coefficient of variation as the measure of the "degree of risk" of an asset, it can be shown that (a) any two assets which differ in their respective degrees of risk will, for all practical purposes, never be regarded as perfect substitutes, and (b) as a consequence, relative asset prices will generally be dependent on relative asset supplies.

It might appear that the simplest way of forming aggregates would involve lumping together assets with "approximately the same degree of risk" on the presumption that these are "good," though not perfect, substitutes. But this is, of course, misleading. Two assets with the same coefficients of variation would be perfect substitutes at prices proportional to the mean values of the respective prospects only if the risks were perfectly (and posi-

---

18. The Mean-Variability approach is the label used by J. Hirshleifer, "Investment Decision Under Uncertainty—Choice-Theoretic Approaches," *Quarterly Journal of Economics*, Nov. 1965. Since alternative approaches to the problem of portfolio composition do exist, this label seems to be preferable. For a critical scrutiny of the Mean-Variability approach, cf. esp. pp. 517–23 of the article.

tively) correlated. If the risks were to be inversely correlated—so that one asset promises low payoffs for states of the world for which the other asset promises high payoffs, and *vice versa*—the standard deviation of the whole portfolio will depend upon the mix of the two assets included, although the mean payoff does not. Differences purely in degree of risk among assets are therefore of little significance to the aggregation problem. In the construction of macromodels it is instead the extent to which risks are correlated which turns out to be important. This means that the classification of asset aggregates will be based on "types of risk."

The type of risk we identify with the type of event that has the greatest influence on the utility-relevant payoff of a given asset. To take the illustrations relevant to the following sections, one would draw a line, for example, between physical and financial assets, because a decline in the money prices of commodities will raise the "real" value of financial assets relative to that of physical assets. Similarly, one would distinguish between short-term and long-term assets, because changes in "the" rate of interest affect the value of the former much less than that of the latter. Assets which are affected in the same way by one set of events and are insensitive to other events would be lumped together in one aggregate.

Different prospects can be aggregated if their relative prices can be assumed to remain constant. This is, again, the Hicksian condition. In the case of consumables, it was found sufficient to postulate that the goods involved were "close" substitutes to a well-financed subset of transactors. These transactors would then be induced to switch their purchases from one component of the aggregate to the other by changes in the price ratio of only "secondary magnitude." In the case of assets, the corresponding function is fulfilled by transactors willing to vary the size of their "positions" in certain types of risky prospects in response to minor changes in prospective yields. Financial institutions willing to provide the services of intermediaries at near-zero or approximately constant cost play the role of the "omelet consumers" of our previous illustration—the recipe for the omelet in this case being based on the pooling of risks.

Aggregation procedures of this sort are found, for example, in models which ignore the differential between the lending and borrowing rates and also the total assets and total liabilities of banks and/or intermediaries. The most far-reaching application of this procedure—models involving the consolidation of the entire financial structure—has already been mentioned.

Sweeping aggregation procedures of this kind tend to develop into conventions. These conventions often remain unquestioned simply because the theoretical conditions which would justify their use have not been investigated. It is worth noting the reception accorded two recent, important contributions to the theory of finance. Both propose hypotheses that would justify aggregation procedures in general use among macroeconomists, but both have stimulated considerable controversy. When made explicit, the assumptions needed to justify the respective aggregation procedures have been found quite stringent. The two contributions in question are the work of Modigliani and Miller [19] on the cost of capital to the firm and Meiselman's investigation of the expectations hypothesis of the term structure of interest.[20] The Modigliani-Miller hypothesis asserts that the cost of capital to a firm, while dependent upon the "risk class" to which the firm belongs, does not depend upon its debt-equity, or leverage, ratio. The hypothesis rests on an arbitrage possibility: investors have the option of substituting unlevered stock bought on margin for levered stock in their portfolios,[21] Modigliani and Miller assume that there will be enough investors in the market

---

19. F. Modigliani and M. H. Miller, "The Cost of Capital, Corporation Finance, and the Theory of Investment," *American Economic Review*, June 1958.

20. D. Meiselman, *The Term Structure of Interest Rates*, Englewood Cliffs, N. J., 1962.

21. The two alternatives are not equivalent in all respects; e.g., holding stock in a company with a debt-equity ratio of 20 percent or "taking a position" in an unlevered company's stock using 20 percent borrowed money are not "by definition" perfectly substitutable alternatives, since the personal debt in the latter case is not subject to limited liability. The Modigliani-Miller hypothesis must therefore be understood to assert that these alternatives are regarded as "very good substitutes" by some investors and that these investors are sufficiently important in the market for the hypothesis to be valid. Cf. the discussion in A. Barges, *The Effect of Capital Structure on the Cost of Capital*, Englewood Cliffs, N. J., 1963, Ch. 6. Also R. L. Slighton's review of Barges, *American Economic Review*, June 1964.

willing to increase the leverage of their personal portfolios to prevent the market value of unlevered firms from ever differing substantially from the value of otherwise identical, levered firms. Thus, the implication is that the market would put the same value on a given constellation of productive assets, constituting a firm, regardless of how this aspect of the firm's financing is handled. The hypothesis assumes that the financial markets be "perfect" in the sense of treating identical combinations of productive capital as "perfect substitutes."

Meiselman's work concerns another aspect of the economy's balance-sheet structure: the distribution of available assets according to term to maturity. Bonds of different term to maturity —or capital goods of different durability—cannot by definition be considered different quantities of the "same good." Meiselman's hypothesis asserts, however, that the market does, in fact, treat them as the same good: for any group of assets which do not differ in any other respect (such as default risk) than by terms to maturity, the market will establish a set of current prices proportional to expected one-period holding yields. Again an arbitrage mechanism is postulated which implies this behavior in the market. It is *not* assumed that bonds with equal expected holding yields are perfect substitutes to every transactor in the market, but it is assumed that transactors with such tastes "bulk sufficiently large" in the market to eliminate differentials in expected holding yields.[22]

It is of particular interest to note that Meiselman's theory gives meaning to that familiar construct of macromodels, namely "the" interest rate, for the class of bonds devoid of default risk. The expected holding yield—which is the same variable usually termed "the" interest rate in static models—is here

---

22. Meiselman, *op. cit.*, p. 10. The most important contribution of this work, one which does not directly concern us here, lies in Meiselman's effort to give operational content to "expected yields" by an ingenious adaptation of the error-learning mechanism developed by Cagan *et al.* It is this part of the book which explains the great amount of further work which Meiselman's contribution has stimulated. Cf. esp. J. H. Wood, "Expectations, Errors, and the Term Structure of Interest Rates," *Journal of Political Economy*, April 1963; and R. A. Kessel, *The Cyclical Behavior of the Term Structure of Interest Rates* (NBER, Occasional Paper 91), New York, 1965.

an (inverse) *index* of the level of bond prices in the sense that the price of default-risk-free bonds, of whatever maturity, can be inferred once this "index" is known. Note, also, that were the holding yields of risky assets to be assumed to stand in a similarly rigid relation to the yields of assets free from default risk, "the" interest rate would be an index of the *"general level of asset prices."* [23] One more piece of information would be needed in that connection, namely information on the term to maturity of the "representative asset." The change in the market value of short assets is small compared with that of long assets when "the" interest rate changes. If the "representative asset" is long, therefore, the "real value" of the economy's net worth rises substantially with a one-point decline in the interest rate; if it is short, the corresponding change in real net worth will be relatively insignificant. [24] In order to properly assess a macromodel, it is important to have a general idea of whether its existing assets are assumed to be on the average very long or very short. [25]

The contributions of both Modigliani and Miller and Meiselman have stimulated critical attention and further empirical investigations. The hypotheses have encountered opposition particularly from specialists in finance, and the controversies which they have engendered in this field are not yet settled. Our perspective is different: where the Business Finance specialist is going to reject the Modigliani-Miller theory if he can devise a test discriminating enough to unambiguously reject the null-hypothesis that leverage has no effect *at all* on the firm's cost of capital, the macroeconomist (conscious of the quality of the other aggregates which enter his model) will use the theory to simplify the capital accounts of his model if he is satisfied that it

---

23. Cf. the discussion of the aggregates used by Keynes in the *General Theory* in the following section.

24. "Real net worth" of a transactor will be defined in this work as the money value of his net worth divided by the money price level of consumer goods. Cf. Chapter IV for a discussion of the concept.

25. It is well known that concepts such as "the average term to maturity," "the average duration of a loan," or "average roundaboutness" in themselves pose index-number problems which are not always capable of a tidy solution. At present, the discussion does not yet require a precise measurement. This type of index problem will be discussed in the following chapter.

represents a "reasonable approximation," e.g., for the period of U.S. history in which he is primarily interested. The statistical decision problem is quite different for the macrotheorist and for the researcher specializing in the market in question.

III:2 Aggregation and the Interpretation of Macromodels: The "General Theory" and the Income-Expenditure Theory

The simple principles of aggregation may now be applied to an examination of "Keynesian" macromodels. Verbal expositions of the standard, closed-economy model generally refer to five aggregates:

> consumer goods;
> capital goods;
> labor services;
> money;
> government debt ("bonds").

We are here associating the various functions of the standard simultaneous equation model with the demand (or excess demand) for different goods aggregates. In much of the older income-expenditure literature this is not done, at least not in a clear and consistent fashion.[1] It is primarily due to Patinkin, and through the extensive debate stimulated by his contributions, that the Keynesian model has come to be generally treated as a

---

1. Compare, e.g., Samuelson's 1947 comment, in his discussion of index numbers, on the "various simplified versions of the Keynesian system" as being "of no interest in this connection *since we cannot pair a set of 'price' variables as 'conjugate' variables to 'quantities.'*" *Foundations of Economic Analysis*, pp. 138–39 (italics added). Here Keynesian theory is regarded as *sui generis*—as a brand of theory which we cannot relate to the general theory of value. "There is no way to get there from here."

In this section we take the other tack and attempt to undertake this "pairing" of prices and quantities for various Keynesian models. Thus, we do not regard value theory as entirely "foreign" to such models but regard them, rather, as leaving an important part of their value-theoretical content implicit in the aggregates adopted. By examining the mode of aggregation, we try to bring the implied value-theoretical propositions out in the open in order to examine the relationship of these models to pre-Keynesian or Neoclassical ideas.

simplified, highly aggregative general equilibrium system characterized by certain postulated "imperfections."

But the standard simultaneous equation model cannot without further ado be taken as an aggregative version of a general equilibrium model. The reason is clear: above we identified *five* aggregates with which "Keynesian" theory conventionally deals; a general equilibrium model with five goods should have *four* relative values. The standard income-expenditure model, however, contains only *three* variables which can be interpreted as price relations, i.e., the money price level, the money wage rate, and the interest rate.[2]

With only three prices, we cannot very well construct a model with more than four goods which is also consistent with value theory. We will therefore presume that, in cases where only three prices are explicitly mentioned, the basic model contains but four goods, and that when one or more additional good(s) is brought into the verbal discussion of a model, this only represents an *ad hoc* effort at putting a modest amount of realistic flesh on an otherwise bare mathematical skeleton.[3] Of the five goods on our list, therefore, one should be found on inspection to be assimilated into one of the others. We then come to a rather interesting question: In the three-price models belonging to the "Keynesian tradition," is the fifth good always eliminated, by aggregation, in the same way? This, as we shall see, is where Keynes and the Keynesians part company.

---

2. Some terminological matters: (a) All values are relative. We have no particular occasion to use the term "absolute prices" and it will be convenient to refer to the value of a good in terms of money simply as another "relative price." (b) The text deals at this point with present goods only and consequently counts relative *spot* prices. (c) Following Keynes' usage, "the interest rate" refers to the spot price of titles to given income-streams, e.g., the price of bonds.

3. Cf. Samuelson's comment, *op. cit.*, p. 144: "Any economic system when viewed carefully will be found to consist of an almost uncountably large number of variables. It is almost a necessity . . . to simplify matters artificially. . . . Some authors retreat to a one or two commodity world [one might add here: and a Robinson Crusoe world] in order to derive more precise results; the penalty for this lies in the difficulty in establishing the relation between the simplified construct and complex reality. This, however, is at least an honest procedure. Other writers wish to have their cake and eat it too: to work with only a few variables and at the same time retain an air of realism and versimilitude."

Two aggregative structures   One good has to go. The question is where. First, we may note one place where we need not look: labor services are treated in the same way in Keynes' model and in the income-expenditure model. The supply curve for labor is given and demand is derived simply from aggregate expenditures on current output. In neither model do households consume any labor services directly. This good can therefore be ignored in the following discussion.[4] We have to identify the three aggregates formed from the four: consumer goods, capital goods, bonds, and money.

There is no "mystery of a missing price" in the standard income-expenditure model. The most common formulation incorporates an *aggregate production function* that is lacking in the *General Theory* and, indeed, conspicuous by its absence.[5] Thus, our two first aggregates, "consumer goods" and "capital goods" are lumped together under the homogeneous label of "output." Some of the best statements we have of this model take care to follow Samuelson's "honest procedure": it is explicitly assumed that only one commodity—the "shmoo"—is produced in the

---

4. We can dismiss labor services thus summarily only while staying strictly within the confines of Keynes' short-run model and while dealing only with those disturbances that he postulated. The discussion of Chapter II must be kept in mind: The "short-run equilibrium state" emerging in the unit period is not determined *ab ovo* (as in a simultaneous equation model which makes no reference to past states of the system). Keynes' short-run equilibrium is to be understood as the terminal state of an adjustment process which starts from a historically given state. The analysis focuses upon the *changes* in the price and quantity vectors defining system states with particular interest traditionally attaching to changes in employment. In ignoring the labor market both here and in the following chapters, we proceed on the assumption that changes in employment will occur only if there is a change in the rate of money expenditures on currently produced commodities. Note that this implies, *inter alia,* that labor-saving innovations and "exogenous" wage-push disturbances, as well as current wage-rate adjustments due to an inherited labor market disequilibrium are ignored. The only disturbances which would lead away from the (closed) system's initial state that the analysis will accommodate are (1) changes in entrepreneurial expectations (in the "Marginal Efficiency of Capital"), (2) changes in the supply of outside money, and (3) changes in household saving behavior.

5. For Keynes' refusal to use the "vague concept of the general price-level" and to treat "incommensurable collections of miscellaneous objects" as a single "numerical quantity," cf. *General Theory,* Chapter 4, *passim.*

system.[6] For brevity, we label this kind of model a "*one-commodity model.*"

The use of an aggregate production function implies a straight-line transformation curve between "capital goods" and "consumer goods," there being one such locus for each level of employment. Hicks' theorem applies—the two goods must trade at money prices that stand in fixed proportion to each other. "The price level" is hence a perfectly unambiguous concept. The composition of output [7] into capital goods and consumer goods must therefore be determined by factors other than relative prices. Relative values are allowed little play in this type of model. Since the price of capital goods in terms of consumer goods is constant, and the money wage is assumed to be "rigid," the present money value of capital goods is tied down within the range of short-run fluctuations in the "real" wage rate. The model still uses two functions to determine demand for the one-commodity aggregate: what distinguishes the investment function from the consumption function is, however, the "autonomous" character of the former compared with the "induced" character of the latter within the short-run period. The distinction is not between the types of goods demanded; the investment function, for example, includes expenditures for the accumulation of stocks of consumables.

In attempting general statements about the *General Theory*, it has become customary to insert the modest caveat that such generalizations fail to do justice to the "richness" of the work. Evasive as such caveats may appear, they are unavoidable. The *General Theory* is not just a lengthy statement of one tidy model; indeed, Keynes goes out of his way to express a skeptical attitude towards mathematical model-building as an approach to macroeconomics. Whatever the justification for this attitude, it is

---

6. Notably, F. Modigliani, "The Monetary Mechanism and Its Interaction with Real Phenomena," *Review of Economics and Statistics*, Feb. 1963.

7. Patently an absurd phrase with respect to "shmoo models"—where we have to talk about the uses of the output instead—but sensible in cases where the two goods are assumed to be distinguishable and the slope of the transformation line, while constant, differs from (minus) unity.

relevant to an understanding of his work. The standard commentaries on the *General Theory* also distinguish at least two models in the book: the simple flow model in the introductory chapters—i.e., basically the analysis of the income-constrained, or multiplier, process—and the full-scale theory of the latter parts of the book. But of far more importance than this distinction is the great discrepancy between Keynes' approaches to "pure" problems and to policy problems. In the realm of pure theory, he takes great pains to explain the nature of contraction processes and depressed states in a closed system in which the government does not play an active role. For this purpose he develops a simple, highly aggregative model of the private sector. Some of the most significant of these aggregations, as we shall see, are based on all-encompassing assumptions about the "perfect substitutability" e.g., of all non-money assets. But when he discusses policy measures he seldom sticks to this simple model. The book is fairly sprinkled with passages dealing with policy questions in which all the simplifying assumptions about the substitutability of assets, etc., are relinquished—often without warning to the reader. In arriving at a diagnosis of the economy's ills, Keynes is willing to rely on a very simplified theory; but when it comes to devising cures for the patient, the experienced general practitioner conscious of his responsibility shuns the generalizations of the textbook.[8]

While thus recognizing that to force the *General Theory* into the mold of a four-good model may be to do considerable violence to the "richness" of the work, it is still possible to discern the aggregative structure of the "basic model" of the *General*

---

8. In addition, one must always keep in mind that the *General Theory* is full of analytical shortcuts by-passing problems dealt with at length in the *Treatise on Money*. Keynes insisted that the *General Theory* should be read as a further development of the ideas advanced in his earlier works. One cannot, therefore, presume that the many problems adequately dealt with in the *Treatise,* but excluded from the *General Theory*, are excluded because Keynes had changed his mind on their relevance to problems of income-determination.

Unfortunately, his insistence on the close links between the two works has hardly been taken seriously by most American "Keynesians." With the latter, the "revolutionary" character of the *General Theory* has been an article of faith—the book is regarded as a "clean break," not only with the "Classics," but also with Keynes' own earlier work.

Theory. We will focus entirely upon the "diagnostic" model. Only in a few passages will we consider the realistic modifications of the basic model which Keynes regarded as necessary for "prescriptive" purposes.

Keynes' discussion in the *General Theory* also names five "goods," yet it too deals with but three relative values. The same question may again be raised: In what manner is the fifth good eliminated?

Three features of Keynes' aggregation scheme are essential:

(1) *The model of the "General Theory" is a "two-commodity model."* Consumer goods (or wage goods) and capital goods are distinct. The productive transformation curve must be conceived as being concave to the origin. The relative price of consumer goods and capital goods is, as will become apparent, a most significant variable, also in the short run.

(2) *Keynes' basic model treats capital goods and "bonds" as one aggregate.* Apart from money, the model has only this one asset aggregate. We will therefore refer to it as "non-money assets" henceforth. Bonds and capital goods are titles to prospective income-streams. The same interest rate is applied to calculating the present market value of both bond-streams and equity-streams. "The" interest rate is therefore an (inverse) index of the money price level of non-money assets.

(3) *Keynes' "representative" non-money asset is a long-term asset.* Thus the representative bond has a long term to maturity, the representative capital good is very durable. The long-term nature of non-money assets is the principal characteristic which distinguishes capital goods from consumer goods as well as non-money stores of value from "money."

We can now schematically indicate the aggregative structures of the two types of models by listing the aggregates with which the analysis in each case operates, as follows:

INCOME-EXPENDITURE MODEL	THE "GENERAL THEORY"
Commodities	Consumer goods
Labor services	Non-Money assets
Bonds	Labor services
Money	Money

Both have four goods and three prices.[9] Nonetheless, the differences are major. The respective "visions" which these two aggregative models reflect—or call forth—are surely quite different.

Keynes' aggregation procedure   The income-expenditure model is stripped down to four goods by lumping together consumer goods and capital goods. The relative price of the two disappears from the model. The procedure is characterized by the restrictive conditions imposed on the system's production functions.

Keynes gets down to four goods by lumping capital goods and bonds together. The relative value of bond-streams and equity-streams falls out of the model. Here we must look to preferences rather than production functions in order to find the assumptions underlying the particular aggregative structure used. The assumption is that bond-streams and equity-streams are (to a satisfactory approximation) perfect substitutes to wealth-owners. In the short run, the prices of bonds and capital goods should therefore fulfill the condition of Hicks' theorem— "if the prices of a group of goods change in the same proportion, that group of goods behaves just as if it were a single commodity." [10]

This is the crucial point. Keynes' aggregative structure is different also in other respects from that of the standard model, but the whole issue revolves around his treatment of non-money assets. This part of his procedure, therefore, requires further discussion. The definitions of "consumer goods" and "money" appropriate to his theory will fall into place without much fur-

---

9. It has already been indicated that Keynes, in many passages of the *General Theory,* discusses a larger "menu" of goods. Similarly, not all contributions to the income-expenditure literature confine the analysis to the four goods listed above. Yet, for a coherent comparative analysis it is necessary to keep the "level of aggregation" the same for the two brands of theory. Possibly, a case could be made for the five goods/four prices level of aggregation as being more appropriate for the comparison than the four goods/three prices level chosen here. The analytical distinctions to be drawn stand out in sharper relief when the present approach is taken. This is desirable *per se.* In my opinion, this does not involve us in significant distortions of the analytical content of the two types of theories nor in substantial exaggeration of the differences between them.

10. Hicks, *Value and Capital, op. cit.,* p. 313.

ther ado once the treatment of "non-money assets" is clear.

Keynes treated the determination of current asset prices as an ordinary present value problem. It is important to note that his analysis of the determination of short-run equilibrium always presumes a *given* "State of Long-Term Expectation." This assumption is vital to his aggregation procedure. Without it, his habit of using "the rate of interest" as a synonym for "the general level of asset prices" could not be defended. A simple illustration will clarify these points:

The present value of a T-year stream of a dollars per year depends upon (a) the percentage rate at which the stream is discounted, and (b) the size of the prospective "annuity," a. The State of Long-Term Expectation (*alias* the Marginal Efficiency of Capital) gives the value of a in the current period. The value of a is different for different classes of assets. Since, for each asset class, the number of dollars per year that is expected to accrue to the owner of such an asset is a constant, their prices will vary in the short run only (inversely) with changes in "the" interest rate, i.e., with the price *per dollar of T*-year streams.

Consequently, Keynes used "the" interest rate as an index of the general level of asset prices in the short run. Much confusion would have been avoided if he had, at least occasionally, used the latter term instead. This had indeed been his usage in the *Treatise*. His reason for the change was that the *Treatise*'s terminology was misleading in the analysis of liquidity preference:

For "bearishness" is there defined as the functional relationship, not between the rate of interest (or price of debts) and the quantity of money, but between the price of assets and debts, taken together, and the quantity of money. This treatment, however, involved a confusion between results due to a change in the rate of interest and those due to a change in the schedule of the marginal efficiency of capital, which I hope I have here avoided.[11]

He did indeed avoid giving the impression that the demand for money depended upon the price of assets rather than on the price per dollar of returns to non-money assets, but only at the

---

11. *General Theory*, pp. 173–74.

expense of obscuring the aggregation procedure utilized in both his major works.

Keynes calculated the present value or demand price for a capital good by discounting the good's prospective return stream net of user cost by (unity plus) "the" bond rate. Hence, the yields from bonds and capital goods are the same, and the current price of bond-streams and capital-streams with the same time-profiles are equal. Any discrepancy will be eliminated by arbitrage.

In the first part of Chapter 11, where the topic is first introduced, Keynes stays close to the traditional view of investment in a competitive market under certainty. In the latter type of static model, it is also assumed that the yield on capital goods will not diverge from the yield on bonds. In this traditional model the rather superfluous distinction between households doing the saving, and supplying loanable funds, and entrepreneurs investing and demanding loanable funds was usually made. Entrepreneurs were assumed to stand ready to take an "infinite position" in capital goods—i.e., to undertake unlimited leverage—if they were to be faced with a rate of interest below the marginal efficiency of investment.[12] Hence, the behavior of profit-maximizing competitive entrepreneurs would always eliminate any yield-differentials.

Evidently, this cannot be all there is to it. There are a number of difficulties with Keynes' procedure:

(1) The assumption of a given State of Expectation is supposed to define the return streams expected to accrue to different classes of assets. The concept is not without its problems. In other contexts, Keynes stressed the differences in opinion among investors. The determination of asset prices he nonetheless treated much as if there existed an observable "market view" of return streams which is at the same time unanimous and uncertain.

---

12. Lerner has done much to clarify Keynes' discussion of the determination of investment, and Lerner's terminology is today the accepted one. Cf. A. P. Lerner, "On the Marginal Product of Capital and the Marginal Efficiency of Investment," *Journal of Political Economy*, Feb. 1953. Lerner would probably be the foremost authority to refer to in defense of the present interpretation of the *General Theory*'s treatment of consumer goods and capital goods as distinct commodities.

(2) The same assumption also tends to obscure a stock-flow dimensional problem. The income per unit of a given type of capital goods at a given time will depend on the aggregate stock of such goods in existence at that time. The quantity that will exist in the future depends on the current rate of net investment which, in turn, depends on the current market price of such goods. That the state of long-term expectations is "given" cannot, therefore, be interpreted to mean simply that the time-profiles of returns for various asset classes may be treated as constant for the purposes of short-run analysis. In the *General Theory* this point is taken care of by the downward slope of the marginal efficiency of capital schedule, but for the rest, Keynes' MEC-apparatus was designed to avoid, rather than to elucidate, the stock-flow aspects of the investment problem.

(3) The time-profiles of return streams differ in a number of ways. Generally, we have to deal with bonds of a range of different maturities and capital goods of different durability. Also, the expected returns net of operating costs to a capital good usually tail off over its lifetime, whereas a bond that is not a perpetuity has the repayment of principal as the last and largest item in the time pattern of returns. Keynes explicitly acknowledged that his statement "slurred" these points, but argued that "it is not difficult to restate the argument so as to cover this point." [13] The "slur" remained, however. In Chapter 17, where Keynes went through the motions of lumping all assets into the two aggregates, "money" and "non-money assets," he avoided the problem of the duration of streams by stating his aggregation conditions in terms of one-period holding yields. In the immediate context, this was sufficient. But, as a whole, his theory really requires that the whole range of different "maturities" be considered—as in the *Treatise*. To stick with the simplified two-asset structure of the *General Theory* model, one must provisionally assume that each of the two asset classes can be characterized by reference to a "representative" term to maturity.

(4) All this still neglects a number of differences between different types of non-money assets, in particular, the risks or uncertainties pertaining to the prospective streams and the short-

---

13. *General Theory,* p. 137 n.

run "liquidity" of the different assets in their respective markets. (Two assets with the same variance of return may "have different liquidity"—the market for one may be "thinner" than for the other.) Though the *General Theory* abounds with statements emphasizing the significance of the uncertainty of expectations, the actual treatment of this particular aspect of the uncertainty problem is cursory. Though Keynes recognizes that capital goods and government bonds differ in both marketability and variability of prospective returns, the heterogeneity of non-money assets plays no role in his discussion of the aggregative model. The marginal efficiency concept, as we have seen, is first developed using *single-valued expectations* of prospective returns without reference to uncertainty. When considerations of risk and uncertainty are brought in, Keynes sticks to single-valued expectations by resorting to the device of "certainty-equivalents." This device allows him to treat two assets with the *same certainty-equivalent streams as perfect substitutes*.[14] Thus, a bond and a capital good with the same mathematical expectation of returns will no longer trade at the same price, if the capital good is "riskier." But the aggregation rule is simply restated in terms of certainty-equivalent returns.

The discussion of liquidity in the *General Theory* is similarly sketchy. "Liquidity" is defined as the "potential convenience" which the "power of disposal over an asset during a period may offer." To enjoy this convenience, people are willing to bear an opportunity cost in terms of income which might have been earned on less liquid assets—or, alternatively expressed, to pay a "liquidity premium." The "total return" on an asset, measured "in terms of itself," is defined as equal to its (certainty-equivalent) yield minus its carrying cost plus its liquidity premium. To make these "total own-rates of return" commensurable in terms of money, they must be further adjusted for their "expected percentage appreciation" (or depreciation) in money value over the period. In the short run, the factors underlying the liquidity

---

14. Cf. A. G. Hart, "Keynes' Analysis of Expectations and Uncertainty," S. E. Harris, ed., *The New Economics*, particularly pp. 419–22, where Hart links Keynes' neglect of the heterogeneity of assets to his use of the certainty-equivalent representation of expectations.

premia can be assumed given—"changing from time to time
. . . depending upon social practices and institutions." [15] In
equilibrium the demand prices for different assets will be such
that their percentage rate of "total return" in terms of money will
be equal.

In this mechanical fashion, the expected value of returns on
different assets are "adjusted" for differences in the degree of risk
and liquidity to obtain (superficially) *homogeneous* "total returns." The homogeneity of returns means that assets would be
regarded as perfect substitutes at prices proportional to their
respective total returns. This relationship between asset prices
then becomes a condition of short-run equilibrium which must
hold, whatever the equilibrium value of the "pure" rate of interest. Given the State of Expectation, "the" rate of interest serves
as an index of the general level of (non-money) asset prices.

Thus, the *General Theory* model contains only two asset
aggregates: money and non-money assets. The income-expenditure model, in contrast, has three: stocks of the "shmoo" commodity, bonds, and money.

Keynes' model ignores the distinction between *physical* and
financial non-money assets. Neglect of a distinction of this sort
means that the behavioral implications of certain risks or contingencies, according to which the subaggregates are differentiated,
are ignored. The relevant risk in this case is that of changes in
the money prices of commodities which would change the relative "real" values of physical and financial assets. Keynes' use of
percentage appreciation coefficients is designed to "take care of"
this risk. This device is hardly satisfactory even within Keynes'
own framework. To treat these appreciation coefficients as constants independent of the current level of the interest rate implies unit-elastic price expectations. This fits ill with Keynes'
theory of Liquidity Preference which is based on the assumption
of inelastic expectations.

Another point is perhaps more important. In terms of the ranking of adjustment speeds characteristic of Keynes' theory, it is
appropriate to regard the relevance of the physical-financial dis-

---

15. *General Theory*, p. 240.

tinction as hinging entirely upon the risk of changes in the money prices of commodities *in future periods*. With the wage unit "rigid" within the current unit period, the real par-value of the given volume of outstanding bonds may be regarded as a constant to a satisfactory approximation. But in a different dynamic context, such as the Hicksian "week," the "real quantity" of financial assets is an endogenous variable. Keynes' habit of aggregating physical and financial assets is inappropriate in such a context and mars his discussion of the adjustment behavior of a "Classic" system with fully flexible money wages and prices.[16]

The evidence for the contention that Keynes worked with this physical-financial asset aggregate does not derive only from Chapter 17, although this chapter has been found useful as a basis for our discussion, or even from the *General Theory* alone. This analytical habit goes back, at least, to the *Treatise*. Whereas the *Treatise* deals with a capital accounts structure which is in many other respects richer than that of the *General Theory*, Keynes also in the former work lumped together "fixed capital" and long-term bonds. The terminology of the *Treatise* is particularly revealing in that Keynes chose to refer to the "existing stock of wealth" as the "volume of securities." [17]

Keynes and the Keynesians: contrasting visions of the economic system Providing the specific assumptions needed to justify a particular mode of aggregation is a rather mechanical task—merely a matter of stripping down the model to a manageable, simplified form. There is little reason to scrutinize Keynes' (or anybody else's) procedures in detail for their own sake or even to discuss at length how carefully the task is executed. A highly aggregative model is grossly oversimplified and there is always a range of important problems to the analysis of which it is not at all suited. This being the case, questions concerning

---

16. Cf. Chapter V:1, below.

17. Cf. *Treatise,* Vol. I, p. 248. One should note that the definition of this variable excludes "liquid claims on cash." It is significant that the richer menu of assets in the *Treatise,* compared with the *General Theory*'s two-asset system, is based entirely on a more detailed differentiation according to term to maturity or durability.

whether its originator "hedged" his simplifying assumptions with elaborate care or only very carelessly are of academic interest at most.

What interests us is, instead, the "vision" of economic processes that motivates the adoption of a particular set of—often blatantly "unrealistic"—simplifying assumptions, i.e., the broad theoretical considerations determining the aggregative structure of the model used.

The aggregative structure of Keynes' model has been discussed by Professor Tobin in a well-known paper.[18] This paper is of particular interest here since it also seeks to demonstrate how even apparently minor differences in the aggregative structure of alternative models may embody quite different "visions" of the way in which the economy works. Tobin poses the following question: consider three stores of value—money, bonds, and capital goods. Suppose it is desired to construct a macromodel with only two stores of value. This may be done by assimilating "bonds" either to physical capital or to money. The decision, Tobin notes, hinges upon the judgment of whether bonds are in fact closer substitutes for capital goods or for money, since the resulting model will, as an approximation, treat bonds as perfect substitutes for that store of value to which they are assimilated.

There are thus two options. Here, Tobin argues, Keynes—and after him the Keynesians—took a different approach from the older Cambridge monetary tradition as represented by Lavington and Pigou. In the older approach, bonds are lumped together with money and the problem of portfolio balance is posed as the choice, on the margin, between money and capital goods. In

---

18. J. Tobin, "Money, Capital, and Other Stores of Value," *American Economic Review*, May 1961. This paper is concerned with the aggregation of the capital accounts. In order to see the implications of Tobin's discussion for the income account variables, one has to relate it to his earlier contributions, in particular "A Dynamic Aggregative Model," *Journal of Political Economy*, April 1955, to which the 1961 paper also makes frequent references.

To my knowledge, Professor Tobin is just about alone among modern monetary theorists in his explicit attention to the aspect of model-construction that is the subject of this chapter. That I disagree with him on the doctrine-historical matter of how the aggregative structure of Keynes' theory is to be interpreted should (hopefully) not obscure the extent of my intellectual indebtedness.

both types of models there are but two yields to consider: The uniform yield on all non-money assets and the imputed liquidity yield on money in the Keynesian model; the uniform yield on money (imputed) *cum* bonds and the yield on capital goods in Tobin's pre-Keynesian model. But for the purposes of analyzing monetary policy measures, the two models are, as Tobin shows, in important respects quite different.[19]

In comparing the aggregative structure of these models, Tobin thus draws a line between Keynes and the "Keynesians" on the one hand and certain "pre-Keynesians" on the other. The validity of this distinction is not to be disputed, but if a single such distinction is to be drawn, the major difference would seem to lie between Keynes and the "Keynesians." The aggregative structure of the standard income-expenditure model, we maintain, is more "foreign" to the *General Theory* than are older "Classical" models.

How can this proposition be supported? First, we should recall our previous argument that, in employing the aggregate production function and thus using a scalar measure of output, the income-expenditure model treats capital goods and consumer goods as one aggregate. There is only one (stock-flow) commodity. According to Tobin, the income-expenditure model also treats bonds as perfect substitutes for the stocks of this commodity. The result would be a three-good model, the two market prices being the money price level and the money wage rate. Such a model does give a solution value to the yield on non-money assets, but "the" interest rate is not properly to be regarded as a market price.[20] Tobin's own 1955 model is a three-

---

19. Tobin, "Money, Capital, . . . ," *op. cit.*, pp. 30–34.

20. For the interest rate to be a "price" in this sense, a fourth market would have to be explicitly included, such as a forward market—e.g., in consumer goods—or a private-sector loanable funds market. Intra-private-sector debts and claims are eliminated from these models by the ubiquitous assumption of "no distribution effect." We may note that this assumption Keynes himself made in the *Treatise* (cf. Vol. I, p. 129): "When we are dealing with a closed system as a whole, [claims on money and the corresponding debts or obligations] can be neglected, since they cancel out." In the *General Theory*, in my opinion, the same assumption is implicit in the "basic model"; yet, the experiences of the early thirties have left their trace—scattered through the text one finds numerous comments on

good model, albeit of a Lavington-Pigou variety, the aggregates being labor, the stock-flow commodity, and financial stores of value. We will argue that the standard income-expenditure model is more appropriately regarded as a four-good model and will stick to discussing this class, avoiding both "smaller" and "larger" models.

We have talked rather blandly about "aggregates" or "goods" so far, and have discussed how the four aggregates (disregarding labor services) money, consumer goods, capital goods, and bonds can be reduced to three by making specific assumptions about substitutability (in consumption or among outputs). In judging whether to believe that a is a better substitute for b than for c, or vice versa, we must relate these concepts of labeled aggregates to the bewildering variety of goods in a real economic system. What do the labels mean? Implicitly we have some rules of identification at the back of our minds whereby the goods of the real world can be sorted in a rough way into the labeled boxes of our abstract categories. We arrive at these rules of identification or aggregation criteria in a most *ad hoc* manner—by, as Tobin says, "reflection on the characteristic properties" of the various goods. What, then, is meant by a "characteristic property"? It is a property which makes people discriminate *in their behavior* between the good and other goods—i.e., something which makes people *not* treat "other" goods as perfect substitutes. If the output of *a priori* model-building of this traditional brand is a "guide to instinct," one must be ever conscious that the inputs consist not only of first-year calculus but also of "casual empiricism," the coefficients being fairly fixed—a 50–50 mix after the manner of the classic recipe for pigeon pie: one pigeon to one horse. A plump, young pigeon, one might add, will still make rather awful pie if the horse is rotten.

A population of economic goods may be conceived of as distributed in a space of many dimensions where, along each axis, some aspect of structure or characteristic property, potentially relevant to economic behavior, is measured. A "good" is defined

---

"lenders' confidence," the asymmetry of "moral risk," "the excessive burden of many types of debt," etc. Cf. e.g., pp. 144–45, 157–58, 208, 264, 268.

by a unique set of "coordinates" in this space. The problem of aggregation is to reduce the number of dimensions of the space to a manageable number by suppressing those aspects of the population's structure deemed least significant to economic behavior.

Now, consider the task of reducing the population of all possible stores of value to two "representative" assets. Observe first that this does not necessarily demand that we retain only one dimension: some variables may "bear an invariant, 'perfectly joint' relationship to each other." [21] To take the illustration of most direct relevance: suppose that people discriminate both between "short" and "long" assets and between "physical" and "financial" assets, but that at the same time *all* physical capital is extremely durable while *all* "bonds" are very short-term bills. In such a case, it would be unnecessary for the model-builder (restricted to using only two stores of value) to decide whether the "most important" aspect of asset structure involves the distinction between longs and shorts or between physical and financial. Whatever factors within the model affect the excess demand for "long assets" will also *a fortiori* affect the excess demand for physical assets, etc.

This is the easy way out. In practice, however, some decision would have to be made. Consider the following "empty boxes":

	PHYSICAL ASSETS	FINANCIAL ASSETS
"SHORTS"		
"LONGS"		

If all the various stores of value in the economy were to be sorted into these boxes, hardly anyone would argue *a priori* that one or more of them would remain empty. (A "perfectly joint relationship" would leave the two on one of the diagonals empty.)

---

21. Samuelson, *op. cit.*, p. 145. The class of aggregation propositions based on perfect complementarity in consumption or on fixed coefficients in production we generally ignored in the previous section as of little immediate interest. References may be made to Samuelson, *loc. cit.*, and Green, *op. cit.*, esp. Chapter 9.

We may then fill in the boxes from top/left to bottom/right as follows: (1) consumer goods, (2) money, (3) capital goods, and (4) bonds. Note that the rules of identification remain to be spelled out: Should shares in limited liability companies be considered as similar to private ownership of physical capital or as easily marketable paper? Should consumer durables be classified as "short" or "long" commodities? [22] Are time-deposits part of the money supply? These, and many other questions of the sort, are left open for the moment.

First suppose that for some reason it is desired to make do without at least one of these boxes. What should be done? Tobin, as we have seen, chose in this situation to "collapse" the short-long dimension of the structure, and to deal explicitly just with a stock-flow commodity and "money." [23] The judgment here is that, in terms of actual behavior, the distinction between physical and financial assets is the most significant one to make. Keynes and the Keynesians do away with just one of the boxes, thus:

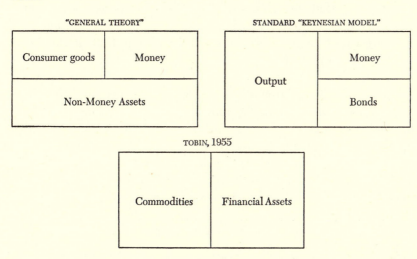

22. Econometricians have much to contemplate. The Department of Commerce series on Personal Consumption Expenditures includes, for example, rental value of housing on the one hand but purchases of new cars and expenditures on private research and education on the other. The item "religious and other welfare activities," one suspects, is treated with discretion, whatever the decision.

23. One could collapse the structure also the other way, while still retaining money in the model after a fashion i.e., by treating money as "complementary" to

In contemplating the aggregation of capital account variables, the judgment to be made hinges upon *what kind of "events,"* determining the potential advantages and disadvantages of holding different types of assets, are likely to be the most important within the context of a given model. Thus, Tobin stresses the distinction between claims with a par-value fixed in nominal terms and commodities *because* the "risks of price level changes" are the most significant in the context of his work. The underlying empirical judgment is made quite explicit in his comparison of "Keynesian" models and models of the Lavington-Pigou variety:

Granted that both models are over-simplified, which is the better guide to instinct? . . . . Reflection on the characteristic properties of these assets—in particular how they stand vis-à-vis *risks of price level changes*—surely suggests that if government securities must be assimilated to capital or money, one or the other, the better bet is money.[24]

In contrast, when Keynes in the *General Theory* turns to the discussion of the capital accounts he has already settled on the assumption that the short-run flexibility of money wages and prices is very limited, and when later he turns back to wage and price flexibility issues he is concerned to argue that, if this flexibility were in fact great, a policy to reduce that flexibility would be desirable. In his context, therefore, the distinction between physical and financial assets is of less significance, and the characteristic event which does loom large in his thinking about the capital accounts is a *change in "the" rate of interest*. Tobin's quoted statement may be paraphrased to reflect, instead, Keynes' vision of the economic system: "reflection on the characteristic properties of these assets—in particular how they stand vis-à-vis *risks of interest rate changes*—surely suggests that long-term

---

output as it is, in a sense, in constant-velocity models. The model would emphasize the dichotomy between "sources" and "services"—or perhaps Kaldor's *"Gebrauchsgüter"* vs. *"Verbrauchsgüter"* comes closer to the desired distinction—it would stress the importance of the interest rate as a market price and would employ a constant-velocity money-demand function. Among major authors (who are still widely read), Irving Fisher would seem to conform most closely to a schema of this sort. But it is, of course, at best a very rough characterization of his work.

24. Tobin, *op. cit.*, p. 34, italics added.

bonds be assimilated to capital." A movement of "the" rate of interest implies large changes in the current market value of "long" assets, but only insignificant changes in the value of "short" assets.

Which of these models is to be preferred obviously depends upon the problem at hand. The complaint has often been made, for example, that Keynes' depression theory is ill-suited to the analysis of the primary problem of the postwar period—inflation. Although we have here advanced an interpretation of Keynes' model which differs from the standard one, this judgment still holds. Clearly, models emphasizing, as Tobin's does, the distinction between physical and financial assets are needed to deal with these problems. But the alternatives are, of course, not mutually exclusive. Because the distinction between "shorts" and "longs" to which Keynes attached almost exclusive significance has been largely neglected in the subsequent Keynesian literature, it is with this that we will be concerned in what follows. But the following argument is only designed to urge that his distinction be given due consideration, not that it replace the other one. We can have both.

"Liquid" and "Illiquid" goods   In Keynes' thinking, the dichotomy of "short" vs. "long" overrode in importance all other distinctions between properties of stores of value. Large and important sections of the *General Theory* can hardly be properly appreciated if the significance of this aspect of his approach is not realized. Nor will his dependence on earlier writings be seen in proper perspective, for it is in this respect, above all, that the *General Theory* does *not* make a clean break with the past but where, instead, links go back to the *Treatise,* to D. H. Robertson, Wicksell, and other "pre-Keynesian" authors. Keynes' emphasis on the long-short differentiation is most readily discernible in the *Treatise* where a number of distinct assets are differentiated along the maturity continuum: On the financial side, "means of payment," "business and saving deposits," and "bonds"; on the physical asset side, "liquid capital," "working capital," and "fixed capital"—all distinctions that are not just mere realistic orna-

ments, but are integrated into the analysis of money income determination in the book.[25]

Though these detailed distinctions are dispensed with in the *General Theory*, the distinction between "long" and "short" assets is still vital. Yield-differentials based on any other characteristic asset properties Keynes habitually treated as constants and not as truly endogenous variables. Apart from *ad hoc* observations of a less than systematic nature, his theory of relative asset prices was basically a theory of the term structure of interest rates. In the *Treatise* this is obvious enough, but the simplified two-asset structure of the *General Theory* tends to obscure it. With only "money" representing the short end of the maturity continuum, and "non-money assets" representing the long end, the term structure of rates becomes indistinguishable from "the" level of the money rate of interest. Keynes' conception

---

25. The aggregative structure of Keynes' model, we argued above, has less in common with the income-expenditure model than with some of the influential pre-Keynesian business cycle theories. With respect to the Cambridge School, he should be linked with D. H. Robertson, rather than with Lavington and Pigou. The asset collection of the *Treatise* is borrowed from the former's *Banking Policy and the Price Level*, London, 1926, though Keynes took pains to disentangle his aggregates from the veritable Wonderland terminology of Robertson's book.

In *Banking Policy and the Price Level*, Robertson found the old-fashioned variables of Saving, Investment, and Hoarding too confining. "Lacking" and "Stinting" were added, and of these he distinguished not only "long" and "short" —i.e., a distinction between the *kinds of assets* supplied or demanded—but between "Automatic," "Imposed," and "Induced," etc.—all distinctions having to do with the *type of act or circumstances surrounding an act* of demanding or supplying an asset. This work is a virtuoso performance on that peculiar Cantabrigian instrument, the "period model" of dynamic processes, but it is played *allegro furioso*. The cumbersome terminology is adopted "in the interests of desperate abbreviation"; once installed it permits the author to lead his readers at a most merry pace through any number of short-run variations on the theme of monetary disequilibrium. The discussion plunges heedlessly from one analytical possibility to the next, while the assumptions ruling the applicable leads and lags of the model are continuously being altered—but the author goes on serene in the knowledge that these are all built into the terminology in any case. Few readers then or now have shared Robertson's initial joy at the many complicated patterns a shake or two of his kaleidoscope could bring—a sobering reception, no doubt, and Robertson was ever afterwards to be famous for having the reader's entertainment at heart.

of Liquidity Preference encompasses at the same time the explanation of both the term structure and the "general level" of rates.

In the *Treatise*, other dimensions of the structure of goods are suppressed. The *General Theory* simplifies things further by substituting the *dichotomy* of short versus long, or "liquid" versus "fixed," for the maturity continuum of the *Treatise:*

> There is, of course, no sharp line of division between fixed and liquid goods; we have a continuous series, each member of which has more duration of use or consumption than its predecessor—services, food, clothing, ships, furniture, houses, and so on. But the broad distinction is clear enough.[26]

The *General Theory* had little, if anything, to add to the *Treatise's* treatment of money and banking issues. As previously noted, the novelty of the *General Theory* lay in the analysis of quantity-adjustment dynamics and the income-constrained process. It was by simplifying the aggregative structure, in the manner just described, that Keynes in the later work so drastically condensed "the technical monetary detail" of the *Treatise*.

The long-short dichotomy provides the qualitative criterion for distinguishing both consumer goods and money from non-money assets. The distinguishing characteristic of consumption goods in the *Treatise* was that they were "liquid." There was, as noted by Hart, "some ambiguity as to the disposition of durable consumers' goods."[27] The same ambiguity remains in the *General Theory*. As a general rule, the consumption aggregate is treated simply as a pure *Verbrauchsgut*. The stock-flow analysis of the markets for "liquid goods" of the *Treatise* is missing in the *Gen-*

---

26. *Treatise*, Vol. I, pp. 128–29. Note that the term "liquid" is applied equally to physical goods and financial claims. Compare the usage, e.g., *General Theory*, p. 240: ". . . capital equipments will differ from one another . . . in the rapidity with which the wealth embodied in them can become liquid, in the sense of producing output, the proceeds of which can be re-embodied if desired in quite a different form."

27. A. G. Hart, "An Examination of Mr. Keynes's Price-Level Concepts," *Journal of Political Economy*, Oct. 1933, p. 625.

eral Theory—the consumption aggregate is treated also as a pure flow-good.[28] The preceding discussion of the asset structure of Keynes' model has, therefore, not taken the existence of liquid capital into account. In considering the basic model of the *General Theory* this seems permissible, and we shall continue to regard money and long-term non-money assets as the only two assets of the model.

Where on the maturity continuum is the line between "shorts" and "longs" drawn in Keynes' model? What is to be regarded as the "representative short asset," what as the "representative long asset"? It is all very well to label these two "money" and "non-money assets" respectively, but is the representative non-money asset a ninety-day bill, a five-year bond, or a perpetuity, an inventory of consumer goods, a machine, a building, or the "eternal soil"? To give the labels meaning, we must have some rules of identification to allow us to sort the real world's bewildering variety of assets into the two conceptual boxes of "money" and "non-money assets." In addition, we need to have an idea of where on the continuum the two maturities considered as "representative" of the two aggregates are assumed to be located and how far apart these two points are.

In some passages of the *General Theory,* these questions are, in Keynes' own words, "slurred over." But they are important questions, since we are vitally interested in the relative price at which the two representative assets will exchange currently in the market. The short-long dimension of asset structure is significant in Keynes' model because, with the State of Long-Term Expectation given, the interest rate plays the role of an index of

---

28. Keynes' Chapter 22, "Notes on the Trade Cycle," does, however, make reference to the *Treatise*'s analysis of "Liquid Capital" (p. 318). Cf. also pp. 331–32: "Recent American experience has also afforded good examples of the part played by fluctuations in the stocks of finished and unfinished goods—'inventories' as it is becoming usual to call them—in causing the minor oscillations within the main movement of the Trade Cycle." Keynes, however, was much less interested in these "minor oscillations" than in finding a way to avoid major catastrophes.

The distinction made in the text may be unfamiliar to some: A *Verbrauchsgut* is a good which is "used up when it is used"—rates of production and consumption are measured in the same units as the existing stock. Milk is an example. A pure flow-good is a non-storable service—no stock exists. A pure *Gebrauchsgut* is characterized by zero use-depreciation.

the value of non-money assets in terms of money or in terms of wage units. This is what makes the question about the approximate term to maturity of the "representative" non-money asset assumed by Keynes so important to the proper understanding of his theory.[29] The interest-elasticity of the present value of a perpetual income-stream is unity; the same elasticity for money and all kinds of deposits is zero; the interest-elasticity of the present value of a short-lived capital instrument or short-term credit instrument is very low.[30] Deposits and short assets provide certainty of real capital value—*given the price level;* long assets offer income-certainty and this is true also of extremely durable capital goods—given the State of Long-Term Expectation.[31]

Consider the following two alternatives of representing the maturity continuum by two assets: (1) a means of payment and a title to a permanent income-stream, and (2) a means of payment and a title to a one-year stream. These are somewhat extreme alternatives. They represent strongly contrasting visions of the structure of the actual economic system. Our contention here is that the model of the *General Theory* comes close to the first alternative, while the standard income-expenditure model comes closer to the second alternative. The representative physical asset envisioned in income-expenditure models may, perhaps, be a machine lasting five years or so. Reading the income-expenditure literature chronologically gives one an impression of a gradual "unfunding" of the representative financial asset over time, ending in the "bills only" models of recent and current money-demand theory.

There is hardly any difficulty in documenting the long-term nature of Keynes' representative non-money asset. That Keynes

---

29. Since interest rates must enter into the weighting in the computation of any average term to maturity of a group of assets, the "representative" asset's term to maturity must vary with changes in "the" rate of interest. This point will be considered in some detail in Chapter IV. At present, it is sufficient to put the question in the broadly qualitative manner of the text.

30. Cf., e.g., G. L. S. Shackle, "Interest Rates and the Pace of Investment," *Economic Journal*, March 1946.

31. This, as always, means the state of *certainty-equivalent* long-term expectations, *nota bene.*

chooses a consol as his example in discussing the determination of "the" interest rate inevitably comes first to mind. But evidence for the assertion made is abundant throughout the book. For example:

It is by reason of the existence of *durable equipment* that the economic future is linked to the present.

. . . open-market operations [in] very short-dated securities [may] have but little reaction on the much more important long-term rates of interest.

Perhaps the most revealing statement of all occurs when Keynes explicitly reminds himself:

. . . that capital-assets are of various ages, wear out with time and are *not all* [sic!] *very long-lived*.[32]

The following discussion will provide more abundant and, *in toto*, more conclusive textual evidence. At this point, we may just infer that, while the representative non-money asset is not a perpetuity or a title to an "infinitely durable," rent-earning natural resource of the more or less non-augmentable kind, it is evidently a quite long-lived asset with an interest-elasticity of present value quite significantly different from zero.

This difference between the two theories in the term to maturity of non-money assets assumed is quite significant. That they differ also in the treatment of "money" is, in comparison, less important. It is well known that in the *Treatise* "money" was defined to include not only means of payment, i.e., currency and checking deposits, but also all other kinds of deposits, i.e., Keynes' business and saving deposits. It has frequently been forgotten that this is the case also in the *General Theory*. The definition there is, if anything, even more inclusive:

. . . we can draw the line between "money" and "debts" at whatever point is most convenient for handling a particular problem. For example, we can treat as *money* any command over general purchasing power which the owner has not parted with for a period in excess of three months, and as *debt* what cannot be recovered for a longer

---

32. Quotations from the *General Theory*, pp. 146, 197, and 253 respectively. Italics in each case added.

period than this; or we can substitute for "three months" one month or three days or three hours or any other period; or we can exclude from *money* whatever is not legal tender on the spot. It is often convenient in practice to include in *money* the time-deposits with banks and, occasionally, even such instruments as e.g., treasury bills. As a rule, I shall, as in my *Treatise on Money* assume that money is co-extensive with bank deposits.[33]

The reason for this lack of insistence on a single, specific definition is clear. Keynes' two-asset model simply divides the population of all assets into two classes—"money": assets with a low interest-elasticity of present value; and "non-money assets" : those with a high interest-elasticity of present value. "Low" versus "high" is unavoidably a matter of degree. The "liquidity" of Keynes' Liquidity Preference theory is a matter of degree as well. There is nothing in his analysis which dictates that the line between "money" and "non-money assets" must be drawn at, say, a zero value for the interest-elasticity of the former asset class.

The last quotation provides another illustration of the thesis which has been stressed from the beginning of this chapter, namely that many of the important implications of a model will follow simply from the assumptions built into its aggregative structure. Thus, if in a model of the *General Theory* type, "money" is defined to include treasury bills, it follows as a matter of course that open market operations in such bills will have no effect whatsoever on the all-important long-term rate of interest. Keynes' repeated urgings, both in the *Treatise* and in the *General Theory*, that the Central Bank should conduct its contra-cyclical operations in the long end of the market should be recalled in this context.

It is worth noting, finally, how conscientiously Keynes refrained from defining "output" as a single-valued "real" variable and, correspondingly, from employing the notion of "the" price level. He did not find it easy to abstain from this convenience:

The three perplexities which most impeded my progress in writing this book, . . . are: firstly, *the choice of the units of quantity* appro-

---

33. *General Theory*, p. 167 n. Cf. also pp. 194–95.

priate to the problems of the economic system as a whole; secondly, the part played by expectation in economic analysis; and, thirdly, *the definition of income.*[34]

Few income-expenditure theorists have been noticeably "perplexed" by these difficulties. Some readers may doubt—as the author has reason to know—that Keynes bothered enough about aggregation problems to justify comparing the aggregative structures of his model and the income-expenditure model in such detail as we have done in this chapter. That he allowed his progress with the *General Theory* to be "most impeded" by the three issues listed should be enough to indicate that he took great pains with them, and we will refrain from quoting the many other passages which could be adduced in support of the present interpretation. One might add, however, that Keynes' reasons for allowing these problems to perplex him can be inferred with some degree of psychological plausibility: in the *Treatise,* as in the *General Theory,* the relative price of "Liquid" and "Fixed" goods was a function of the interest rate and thus a variable in the short run. In setting up his "Fundamental Equations," Keynes did not let this deter him from defining the "quantity of output" as a single-valued variable. Hayek's withering criticism of this procedure[35] left the theory of the *Treatise* in tatters, in the opinion of a very influential segment of the profession. Keynes was not about to commit the same mistake twice!

That the "solution" which Keynes adopted—namely that of falling back on an old habit of his and measuring "real quantities" in terms of labor—is not wholly satisfactory is another matter. In terms of his model, it is quite reasonable to postulate that employment is some monotonic function of aggregate money expenditures in the short run (when the MEC-schedule is regarded as given). But in general, the amount of employment associated with a given rate of money expenditures will depend not only on the real wage rate but also on the division of that expenditure on the production of consumer goods and of capital goods. Keynes devoted the better part of Chapter 20 to a discus-

---

34. *General Theory,* p. 37, italics added.
35. Cf. the references given in Chapter I:2.

sion of these points. To correctly appreciate the care with which Keynes handled problems of measurement, one must recall that the *General Theory* antedated all the work on index numbers by Hicks, Samuelson, *et al.* Between the Wars this field was still full of mysteries.[36] That Keynes himself was a distinguished contributor to its development furnishes further proof of the importance he assigned to meaningful aggregation in the construction of macromodels.[37]

III:3   Investment and The Rate of Interest

In the preceding section we contrasted the aggregative structures of the standard income-expenditure model and Keynes' "basic" model. The analysis of macroeconomic processes may be carried out in terms of either type of model. What difference does it make?

This is the main question. The most obvious application of the findings of the last section concerns the analysis of the determination of current investment expenditures and, in particular, the question of the magnitude of the interest-elasticity of investment. This is the subject of the present section. On the basis of the preceding discussion, the development of this issue will be quite straightforward. Other issues on which the two approaches differ are considerably more complicated. This is particularly true of Keynes' so-called "windfall effect" and its relationship to his theory of Liquidity Preference, which become the topic of the next chapter.

Background   There is another question of subsidiary interest: How did the "Keynesian tradition" develop from the model of

---

36. Professor Frisch's famous article on the subject appeared the very same year as the *General Theory*. Cf. R. Frisch, "Annual Survey of General Economic Theory: The Problem of Index Numbers," *Econometrica*, Jan. 1936.

37. The entire Book II of the *Treatise*, Vol. I, is devoted to the subject. In critique of Edgeworth and others, it lays great stress on the concept of an index number as the price of a "composite commodity." For a contemporary appraisal of this effort, cf. Hart, *op. cit.*

the *General Theory* to the standard income-expenditure model? It would take us altogether too far afield to try to pursue this doctrine-historical question in adequate detail. With respect to the present topic, however, the story is well known. The discussion of the interest-elasticity of investment has proceeded within the debate over the efficacy of monetary policies in combating business fluctuations. Keynes' pessimism on the latter issue and his propaganda for various fiscal policies were two of the most prominent features of the *General Theory*. In the hands of many early "Keynesians," these elements of his thought hardened into simplified dogmas—monetary policy came to be regarded as completely ineffective in recession while fiscal policies were propounded as the universal and only cure for macroeconomic problems. In the course of this evolution, there was an important change of emphasis in the explanation offered for the presumed inefficacy of monetary measures. It is this shift of emphasis which concerns us here.

Keynes' explanation ran altogether in terms of his Theory of Liquidity Preference and was a rationalization of his fears that conventional monetary policies would not suffice to bring about a large enough and rapid enough change in the long rate of interest.[1] The Liquidity Trap notion—explicitly repudiated by Keynes—was admittedly part of early income-expenditure doctrine. But it would explain the uselessness of monetary policy only in the so-called "Keynesian special case." In the income-expenditure literature, therefore, the general case against reliance on monetary policy was based on the postulate of a very low interest-elasticity of investment. The decisive impetus to this latter thesis came from the famous Oxford Surveys which seemed to indicate that variations in borrowing costs had very

---

1. A complete statement of his views, we have argued, would include his premises with regard to the behavior of central bankers. It would stress their unwillingness both to undertake operations of sufficient magnitude to deal with the situation of the thirties and to operate in "unconventional" segments of the maturity continuum. As a corollary to the unwillingness of the Central Bank to operate in the long end, his explanation would lay great stress on the length of the lag before changes in short rates had an appreciable effect on long rates. Cf. Chapter I:2 above, and Chapter VI:2.

little influence on the investment plans of businessmen.[2] During the forties, the "Stagnationist school" was quite influential. That secular stagnation could not be relieved simply by monetary injection was naturally an integral part of this doctrine. Within this school, the assumption of low interest-elasticity of investment was sharpened into the thesis of the "lack of investment opportunities," or "lack of outlets for saving," presumed to be characteristic of "mature economies." In its more simplistic formulations, this thesis makes no reference at all to the level of interest rates.[3] In the conventional type of comparative statics exercises with the standard income-expenditure model, the only apparent role for the "monetary" subset of equations is to obtain the value of the interest rate. This, in turn, is only of interest insofar as the interest rate has an effect on investment which is of more than a "secondary magnitude." It is consequently in works that lay great stress on the interest-inelasticity of investment that we find the so-called "vulgar Keynesian" short-run models consisting of "autonomous" private-sector investment, the multiplier, and, apart from fiscal policy variables, nothing else.

The 1940's represented the low ebb of "Keynesian" interest in monetary theory and policy. This interest as well as the belief in money's importance has since undergone a remarkable revival— remarkable not least in that it has not been accompanied by an

---

2. Cf. J. E. Meade and P. W. S. Andrews, "Summary of Replies to Questions on Effects of Interest Rates," *Oxford Economic Papers*, Oct. 1938; Andrews, "A Further Inquiry into the Effects of Rates of Interest," *ibid.*, Feb. 1940; also the American study by J. F. Ebersole, "The Influence of Interest Rates upon Entrepreneurial Decisions in Business—A Case Study," *Harvard Business Review*, No. 1, 1938. The results and implications of the Oxford studies were discussed by H. D. Henderson, "The Significance of the Rate of Interest," *Oxford Economic Papers*, Oct. 1938, and R. S. Sayers, "Business Men and the Terms of Borrowing," *ibid.*, Feb. 1940.

3. Keynes' judgment on a forerunner of the "Keynesian Stagnationists" is of interest here. Referring to N. Johannsen, *A Neglected Point in Connection with Crises*, 1908, and other pamphlets by the same author, as espousing a doctrine which "seems to me to come very near the truth," Keynes commented: "But Mr. Johannsen regarded the failure of current savings to be embodied in capital expenditure as a more or less permanent condition in the modern world . . . and overlooks the fact that a fall in the rate of interest would be the cure for the malady if it were what he diagnoses it to be." Cf. *Treatise*, Vol. II, p. 100n.

equally dramatic groundswell of optimism with regard to the magnitude of the interest-elasticity of investment.

While the interest-elasticity of investment is most often discussed in relation to the issue of the "effectiveness" of monetary policy, for our purposes the main relevance of the topic lies in the realm of "pure" rather than "applied" theory and concerns the appraisal of the relationship between Keynes and the Classics. The main theme of Classical economic theory, from Adam Smith onwards, has been the demonstration of how innumerable production and consumption decisions, made by transactors who have full discretion in making the choices they want, can be efficiently coordinated through the movement of prices in a system of free markets. Keynes' objective was to show how such a system could malfunction in a way consistent with those observations of an economy in depression, to which he assigned the most significance.

The Classical theory of how individual activities are *controlled* so as to make coordination feasible is constructed on two broad assumptions:

(1) price-incentives are effective—transactors do respond to movements of prices by changing the quantities produced and consumed in a qualitatively predictable manner;

(2) prices tend to move, and are "free" to do so, in response to excess demands or supplies in such a manner as to induce transactors to alter their behavior in the directions required for all activities to "mesh."

Whether the actual economic system of a given time and place is such as to conform to these broad Classical specifications is an empirical issue of great and obvious significance. But, from a purely theoretical standpoint, it is a most trivial exercise to construct a model that incorporates a number of assumptions directly contrary to the Classical specifications and which, consequently, will not at all be as "nicely behaved" as the Classical system. The standard interpretation of Keynes concedes him practical significance but consigns his pure theory to the category of such trivial exercises. According to this interpretation, Keynes simply took a sledge-hammer to the delicate Classical mechanism wrecking it at several crucial points:

(1) by postulating that intertemporal price incentives were almost completely ineffective—neither savers nor investors respond to changes in interest rates; [4]

(2) by postulating wage-rigidity and the Liquidity Trap.

In Chapter II, we have already disputed that Keynes invoked institutional obstacles to the adjustment of money wages. We have also mentioned that he specifically rejected the idea of an unyielding floor under the long rate having been a strategic factor in the great depressions up to that time. So, his attack on Classical theory was *not* based on the assumption that prices, in fact, are rigid. When the economic system fails to behave in the manner of the Classical model, it is *not* due simply to the absence of the feedback mechanisms assumed by the Classics.

The notion that Keynes assumed saving and investment to be interest-inelastic is also unfounded.[5] Price incentives are effective. When coordination of activities breaks down, it is *not* simply because the feedback of "errors" fails to trigger the responses assumed by the Classics.

In Keynes' theory, then, the homeostatic mechanisms postulated by the Classics are neither "out of order" nor just missing. This means that *a purely static interpretation of his "unemployment equilibrium" is impossible*. His theory *must* be interpreted as dynamic in nature and, on today's usage, as dealing with unemployment *dis*equilibrium.[6]

---

4. While the present study deals only with the closed system, Professor Machlup's apt term "elasticity pressimism" fits very well in this context, although coined in connection with Machlup's critique of income-expenditure models of balance of payment adjustments. It is worth recalling the frequently made observation that in the great Keynes-Ohlin debate it was Ohlin who was the "Keynesian" while Keynes emerged the Classicist.

5. Cf., e.g., *General Theory*, p. 64: "It might be, of course, that individuals were so *tête montée* in their decisions as to how much they themselves would save and invest respectively, that there would be no point of price equilibrium at which transactions could take place. In this case our terms would cease to be applicable . . . prices would find no resting-place between zero and infinity. *Experience shows, however, that this, in fact, is not so* . . ." (italics added).

6. This is not a novel point, of course. It has been consistently emphasized by Patinkin, for example, beginning with his 1948 "Price Flexibility and Full Employment." Cf. his *Money, Interest, and Prices*, 2nd edn., pp. 337–43. The above states the imperative for a dynamic interpretation in stronger and more general

The slope of the marginal efficiency of capital schedule   In a way, Keynes' MEC-construction is to be admired for the compactness with which the determinants of investment are summarized in a simple schedule, and for the ruthlessness with which a shortcut is taken through all the complexities of stock-flow analysis. But the very economy of means makes it that much harder to "decompose" the analysis so that the separate assumptions relevant to the interest-elasticity of the function can be examined. Keynes did not provide a systematic discussion of these assumptions. But then he could not have anticipated much disagreement with his confident enunciation of conventional wisdom: " . . . we are . . . entitled [to regard the rate of interest] as exercising, . . . a great, though not decisive, influence on the rate of investment." [7]

Keynes has given us several accounts of his theory of the determination of investment and the role of the rate of interest in this connection. [8] His most comprehensive effort reveals more of his method of reasoning than the *General Theory's* exposition and is worth quoting *in extenso:*

The owner of wealth, who has been induced not to hold his wealth in the shape of hoarded money, still has two alternatives between which to choose. He can lend his money at the current rate of money-interest or he can purchase some kind of capital-asset. Clearly in equilibrium these two alternatives must offer equal advantage to the marginal investor in each of them. This is brought about by shifts in the money-price of capital assets relative to the prices of money-loans.

---

terms, however. Note that Patinkin's discussion lays great weight on the interest-inelasticity of investment (e.g., p. 338) as a characteristic and strategic property of "the" Keynesian system.

7. *General Theory*, p. 164. While "great," the influence is not "decisive" since shifts of the MEC-schedule will generally be of a magnitude that is not offset by movements along the schedule, taking into account the *"practicable* changes in the rate of interest." Compare also *op. cit.,* p. 316, and *Treatise,* e.g., Vol. II, pp. 346 and 364.

8. The passages of the *Treatise* which are directly relevant here concern investment in "Fixed Capital"—cf. esp. Vol. I, pp. 255–57. In the *General Theory* the main part of the argument is contained in Chapter 11. The analysis quoted in the text appears in his "The General Theory of Employment," *Quarterly Journal of Economics,* Feb. 1937; page references here pertain to the reprint in S. E. Harris, ed., *The New Economics, op. cit.*

. . . This, then, is the first repercussion of the rate of interest, . . . namely, on the prices of capital-assets. This does not mean, of course, that the rate of interest is the only fluctuating influence on these prices. Opinions as to their prospective yield are themselves subject to sharp fluctuations. . . . It is these opinions taken in conjunction with the rate of interest which fix their price. . . . Now for [the next] stage. Capital-assets are capable, in general, of being newly produced. The scale on which they are produced depends, of course, on the relation between their costs of production and the prices which they are expected to realize in the market. Thus if the level of the rate of interest taken in conjunction with opinions about their prospective yield raise the prices of capital-assets, the volume of current investment . . . will be increased; while if, on the other hand, these influences reduce the prices of capital-assets, the volume of current investment will be diminished.[9]

The marginal efficiency of capital is defined as "equal to that rate of discount which would make the present value of the series of annuities expected from the capital-asset during its life just equal to its supply price." [10] If by "the" interest rate we mean the observed rate on government bonds, the slope of the marginal efficiency of capital schedule depends on the magnitude of the following four elasticities:

(1) the elasticity of the demand price for capital goods, for some given rate of discount, with respect to the rate of growth of the capital stock;

(2) the interest-elasticity of the discount rate applied to the evaluation of income-streams accruing to physical capital; [11]

(3) the discount rate elasticity of the present value of a given anticipated "capital stream" or "investment prospect";

(4) the price-elasticity of the rate of supply of new capital goods.

Consider diagrams A and B. A demand-price schedule is drawn for a given capital stock in existence, a given State of Expectation, and a given rate of interest. It shows the present value assigned to successive prospective additions to the capital stock, acquired in

---

9. *Op. cit.*, p. 188.

10. *General Theory*, p. 135.

11. The latter rate is the "socially required rate of return to capital" of Ando and Modigliani or the "supply price of capital" of Friedman and Tobin.

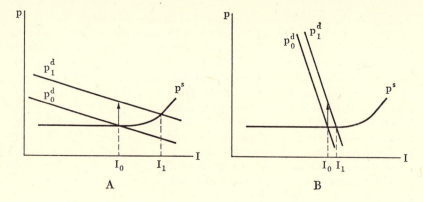

A

B

the present period, under these conditions. Everything else equal, a decline in the applicable rate of discount will shift the demand-price schedule upward. The extent of the shift—made equal in diagrams *A* and *B*—will depend upon elasticities (2) and (3). The rate of investment is determined by the condition that the demand price will be driven to the point of equality with the supply price. For a given upward shift in the demand-price schedule, the change in the rate of investment will depend upon elasticities (1) and (4) as illustrated in the figures.

We have to consider the assumptions, stated or implied, made by Keynes with regard to these four elasticities and then to compare them with the assumptions more typical of the "Keynesian" literature.

Elasticity (1) would be zero (the curve a horizontal line), if entrepreneurs expected each successive increment to their capital stock to yield the same stream of revenues over its life as that expected on the average from already existing units of capital. The more rapidly the expected marginal amounts of future revenues fall off, as further increments to the capital stock are contemplated, the steeper the curve. Thus, the nature of sales expectations is crucial. If the investment under consideration is in equipment of a type for which there is already excess capacity and that excess capacity is not expected to be absorbed for the better part of the short life of the assets, the prospective addition to future revenues net of operating costs will be almost nil. This is the kind of situation envisaged in much of the income-expenditure literature. But, although this sales-constraint is an idea quite consonant with the Keynesian quantity-constraint analysis considered in Chapter II, Keynes' conception of investment in "Fixed Capital" is quite different:

> Willingness to invest more or less in manufacturing plant is not likely to be very sensitive to small changes in bond-rate. *But the quantity of new fixed capital required by industry is relatively trifling even at the best times, and is not a big factor in the situation.* Almost the whole of the fixed capital of the world is represented by buildings, transport and public utilities; and the sensitiveness of these activities even to small changes in the long-term rate of interest, though with an appreciable time-lag, is surely considerable.[12]

We have further evidence on Keynes' assumptions with regard to elasticity (1) from his comparison of the slopes of the demand-price and supply-price schedules. The marginal efficiency of a given type of capital will decrease as investment is increased partly:

> . . . because the prospective yield will fall as the supply of that capital is increased, and partly because . . . its supply price [will] increase; *the second of these factors being usually the more important in producing equilibrium in the short run. . . .*[13]

Most of the time, in fact, Keynes ignored any downward slope of the demand-price schedule and treated it as horizontal. As a general rule, his discussion will simply equate the current market valuation of existing units of capital with the demand price for new units facing the capital goods producing sector.[14]

---

12. *Treatise,* Vol. II, p. 364, italics added. Compare *General Theory,* p. 163, where the classes of "very long-term investments" discussed are, again, buildings, public utilities, and investments of public authorities: "In the case of . . . public utilities, a substantial proportion of the prospective yield is practically guaranteed by monopoly privileges coupled with the right to charge such rates as will provide a certain stipulated margin"—a point directly relevant to the elasticity of the demand-price schedule.

13. *General Theory,* p. 136, italics added.

14. For example, in "The General Theory of Employment," *op. cit.,* p. 183: "The mischief is done when the rate of interest . . . leads to a market-capitalization of [an] asset which is less than its cost of production." Statements which, like this one,

When the demand price is treated as independent of the con-current rate of investment, the interest-elasticity of investment becomes a matter simply of the product of the remaining three elasticities. The assumptions of Keynes and of the Keynesians can be contrasted with score-sheet brevity:

	(2)	(3)	(4)	PRODUCT
General Theory:	High	High	High	High
Standard Model:	Low	Low	High	Low

The value of (2) is unity when the elasticity of substitution of bond-streams for capital-streams is infinite. This is characteristic of the *General Theory*—on the proviso that the expected return streams to capital goods are "adjusted for risk," etc., in the manner discussed in the previous section.[15] The standard income-expenditure model, in contrast, treats bonds and capital goods as imperfect substitutes.

In the *General Theory*, elasticity (3)—that of capital goods values with respect to the required rate of return—is quite significantly different from zero by virtue of the assumption that the representative capital good is long-lived. Thus, a decline in the interest rate, in Keynes' model, does imply a very considerable increase in the demand price for capital goods, given the expected returns to such goods and the "confidence" with which these expectations are held. The representative capital good of the standard model, on the other hand, is short-lived. Consequently, the interest-elasticity of capital goods values is insignificant, quite apart from the assumption made in regard to the

---

make no reference to the rate of investment (where this would be absolutely necessary if the demand price were assumed to depend on it), appear very frequently in Keynes' writings.

15. The assumption of perfect elasticity of substitution between bond-streams and certainty-equivalent capital-streams, in conjunction with the assumption that the market value of existing assets is also the demand price for newly produced assets, is quite relevant to the fiscal vs. monetary policy issue: An open market purchase of *long* bonds will be just as stimulating to aggregate demand as a direct purchase of capital goods by the government financed by "new" money. It will naturally be *more* effective than the same government investment financed by borrowed money, and still more effective than when financed by new taxes.

elasticity of substitution between bond-streams and capital-streams.[16]

On the price-elasticity of the flow-supply of new capital goods, finally, the two theories do not seem to differ—elasticity (4) is high within either framework. Keynes comments on this elasticity only to note that its value should be less than infinite even in a situation of unemployment. It is a condition of the stability of the system, he noted, that "a moderate change in the prospective yield of capital-assets or in the rate of interest [should] not involve an indefinitely great change in the rate of investment." The capital goods industry operates under conditions of increasing costs (wage costs plus "User Cost"). But if the volume of unemployment is substantial, "there may be considerable instability within a certain range." [17] That Keynes saw a need to argue that the interest-elasticity of investment *will not be infinite* shows more clearly than anything else how very different his conception of this issue was from that of his followers.

The price relation to which elasticity (4) refers is the money price of Fixed Capital in terms of the (constant) money wage unit. In order to obtain the effects of the change in the interest rate on aggregate income and employment in the context of the *General Theory* model, one cannot simply apply the "multiplier" to the change in the *quantity* of capital goods produced. The change in the rate of output of capital goods has first to be translated into a change in the *value* of that output either in terms of money or in terms of wage units. The consumer goods/capital goods transformation curve is concave to the origin; a change in

---

16. When Keynes' device of representing uncertain expectations about return streams to capital goods by certainty-equivalents is not adopted, it is difficult to draw a clear distinction between elasticities (2) and (3). The device is not a very satisfactory one and most income-expenditure authors have not been willing to go along with it. But the position of most "Keynesians" on the *product* of (2) and (3) seems clear in any case: the interest-elasticity of the present value of the representative capital good is assumed to be relatively insignificant.

17. *General Theory*, p. 252. This, of course, is relevant to the earlier discussion of the slope of the demand price schedule. The above concedes that in a situation of unemployment, the capital goods producing sector may find itself operating in a range of approximately constant costs. Nonetheless, Keynes argued that the supply schedule was "usually the more important in producing equilibrium in the short run."

the rate of interest is a change in the relative price of Liquid and Fixed commodities; these are consequently not commensurable in terms of physical quantities. No over-all GNP-deflator can be defined for this two-commodity model. In this respect, the income-expenditure model is much simpler. Elasticity (3) is simply the money price level elasticity of the aggregate supply function.

The differences between Keynes and the Keynesians on this issue can now be illustrated geometrically by reference to diagrams A and B above. The supply schedule we would draw the same in either case. It should show a substantial range of very high elasticity (near-constant cost). Keynes' demand-price schedule should be horizontal or nearly so, while the "Keynesian" one slopes steeply downward to the right. For a given change in the rate of interest, Keynes' demand-price schedule should show a vertical displacement substantially greater than that of the corresponding income-expenditure function. "The" interest rate is thus seen to be far more important as a determinant of the current rate of investment in Keynes' framework than in the income-expenditure model.

The elasticity of substitution of bond-streams for capital-streams   One's intuitive judgment about the "plausibility" of a relatively high interest-elasticity of investment is easily colored by the way in which the economic behavior relevant to the issue is described. Semantics is never more important than when "introspection" is admitted as empirical evidence. The issue of the substitutability of bonds for capital goods is a case in point. Consider an initial equilibrium in which the non-banking sector's State of Expectation is given and the "total rates of return" on bonds and capital goods are equal. This situation is disturbed by a rise in the banking system's demand for bonds which increases bond prices and lowers the rate of return on bonds.[18] Three

---

18. In the context of Keynes' theory, where bonds and capital goods are treated as perfect substitutes, the only reason for recognizing the distinction between the two lies in the assumption that the banking system is constrained from holding capital goods and demands only bonds, and that consequently the effects of "monetary" disturbances have a recognizable time-sequence leading first to

aspects of the description of the system's adjustment to this event should be considered.

(a) The disturbance will induce two types of adjustment responses by the non-banking sector. On the one hand, some transactors who initially hold claims on others will be induced to sell these in order to reinvest in capital goods (or equities) which now promise a higher rate of return. This is the type of adjustment discussed by Keynes in the quoted passages. On the other hand, some transactors will be induced to issue claims on themselves in order to increase their holdings of capital goods. This latter "borrowing cost" version is the one most often stressed in textbook discussions of the issue. Exclusive emphasis on this possibility may bias one's judgment on the magnitude of the interest-elasticity—the knowledge that transactors are not indifferent to their debt-equity ratios implicitly creeps into one's consideration of the issue. The businessmen responding to questionnaires, framed on the basis of the "borrowing cost" version, must almost certainly have had considerations of this sort in mind. Actually, both types of adjustment will be involved. It is worth pointing out, then, that the first type of adjustment implies that the supply of equity capital will also be increased and its cost to the firm lowered.[19]

(b) The adjustment according to either one of the two above versions may be discussed either in terms of a change in the relative rates of yield on bonds and capital goods or in terms of a change in the relative prices of bond-streams and capital-streams. In the former case, the discussion concerns the value of the elasticity under (2), in the latter the value of the elasticity of substitution between bonds and capital goods. From a theo-

changes in bond prices and later, through adjustments of the non-banking sector, to changes in capital goods prices. Cf. Chapter V:1, below.

19. To elicit answers appropriate to the theoretical issue, the question put to businessmen would therefore have to be formulated somewhat as follows: "Suppose that (a) the required rate of return on equity capital fell, (b) the prices at which new bonds with given coupons and of any desired term to maturity could be issued by your company rose, (c) the cost of borrowing at banks and financial intermediaries fell, and (d) the market prices of securities currently held by your company rose—would you then undertake any investment projects that are not now being considered?"

retical standpoint, the two formulations are equivalent. Taking
the expected return stream as given, the two remaining variables
—the present value and the rate of discount are uniquely related.[20] For various reasons, however, most economists have
found it convenient to discuss problems of this sort in terms of
variations in discount rates rather than in terms of changes in the
present prices of streams. From a heuristic standpoint, however, it is not completely a matter of indifference what tack is
taken. Few people find the proposition strange that an investor
"wavering," as Keynes put it, between two alternative portfolios
will be influenced in his decision by a change in the cost of one
relative to the other. The traditional analysis of the investment
decision, in which the demand prices are arrived at by discounting single-valued expectations of future return streams, etc., is on
the other hand regarded by most people as involving an "unrealistic description" of the mental processes and administrative procedures by which investment decisions are actually reached.
From this judgment it is (apparently) a short step to the view
that changes in the theorist's discount rate are "unlikely" to influence investment decisions and, from there, to the position that
the interest-elasticity of investment is, most likely, insignificant.

The "descriptive realism" of the model should naturally have
nothing to do with the issue. To the economist the transactor en-
tities of the model are simply "Black Boxes." The task is to construct a model which enables one to predict the response or "output" of the Box to specific events or "inputs." The qualitative
predictions can frequently be arrived at by several more or less
distinct chains of reasoning. When two such chains of reasoning
are "formally equivalent," in the sense that it can be demonstrated that they will always lead to the same predictions, the
theorist is likely to make a habit of the alternative which he finds
most convenient. The most convenient chain of reasoning is not
necessarily the one which most closely resembles peoples' intuitive ideas of "what goes on inside the Box." Properly, this should

---

20. This statement, of course, rests on the assumption which is conventional in
this context, namely that the same discount rate is to be applied to all elements of
the return stream, independent of their distance in time from the present.

have no bearing on an issue such as the present one. But it may not be too fanciful to suggest that it sometimes does, i.e., that the economist's description of the way in which he arrives at a *qualitative* prediction of the response to a certain event sometimes influences our judgment about the likely *quantitative* significance of the response.[21]

(c) The alternatives of choice relevant to the evaluation of Keynes' assumption of a high elasticity of substitution between bonds and capital goods must consist of streams of approximately the same duration.[22] In the Liquidity Preference theory, physical stores of value with a low rate of turnover are not good substitutes for those with a high rate of turnover, nor are long bonds good substitutes for short bonds. Obviously, then, short bonds cannot be close substitutes for long-lived capital goods. A transactor who borrows short to invest in durable capital goods runs the risk of having to refinance at higher rates later. The existence of this risk, according to the Liquidity Preference theory, definitely implies that the elasticity of investment in durable capital with respect to short rates of interest will be modest. Consequently, this risk is very relevant to the issue of the counter-cyclical efficacy of a "bills only" monetary policy. It is a pivotal point in Keynes' pessimistic appraisal of traditional monetary policy measures. But it would be to confound the issues to treat the "efficacy of monetary policy" and "the interest elasticity of investment" as synonymous (and then "explain" the former by reference to the latter). The substitutability between

---

21. One should note also that the habit of dealing with asset choice and investment decision in terms of asset yields instead of asset prices is inconvenient and even inappropriate in some contexts. This is particularly the case with regard to the problem of the formulation of optimal investment criteria. Keynes' suggested rule of equating the marginal efficiency of capital with the interest rate, for example, produces some conundrums in cases of investment prospects for which the marginal efficiency rate is not single-valued. More importantly, it can be shown that whenever the maximization of present value rule leads to results different from the maximization of the internal rate of return rule, the former is (as always) correct and the latter wrong. Cf. J. Hirschleifer, "On the Theory of Optimal Investment Decision," *Journal of Political Economy*, Aug. 1958.

22. This is put very loosely. The comparison of the "duration" or "average period" of two streams involves an index number problem which will be postponed to the next chapter.

assets of different maturities should be distinguished from the substitutability between physical and financial assets.

Liquidity Preference and the demand price for capital goods
Keynes' made a very sharp distinction between the two sets of factors determining the demand price for capital goods, i.e., the State of Liquidity Preference and the marginal efficiency of capital:

I would . . . ask the reader to note at once that neither the knowledge of an asset's prospective yield nor the knowledge of the marginal efficiency of the asset enables us to deduce either the rate of interest or the present value of the asset. We must ascertain the rate of interest from some other source, and only then can we value the asset by "capitalising" its prospective yield.[23]

The independent "source" from which the interest rate is ascertained is Keynes' Theory of Liquidity Preference. "The" interest rate of the *General Theory*'s two-asset model is then the rate corresponding to the term to maturity of the "representative" non-money asset. Keynes' analytical procedure may be schematically illustrated in the following way. For our immediate purposes, we may think of the representative income-stream simply as a constant stream of one "certainty-equivalent" dollar per year running for T years. This "standard stream" [24] thus defines the unit quantity needed for the supply and demand analysis of asset prices. Knowledge of the value of "the" interest rate is tantamount to knowing the market price of this "unit stream." The second factor, Keynes' marginal efficiency of capital, then serves

23. *General Theory*, p. 137. Cf. also his "The General Theory . . . ," *op. cit.*, p. 188. For a contrasting approach, consider, e.g., Tobin's 1955 "Aggregative Model" in which the marginal productivity of capital in the current period, derived from the aggregate production function, determines the real rate of interest and the opportunity cost of holding cash balances. Note also that models with this feature are a major target of Keynes' criticism in his chapter on the marginal efficiency of capital. Cf. *General Theory*, pp. 138 ff.

24. If T is less than infinite, it obviously cannot possibly be the case that all existing assets have T years of yield left. This and related problems we postpone to Chapter IV in which the "standard stream" concept is discussed in more detail.

to define the number of such unit streams that entrepreneurs expect from reproducible physical sources. The number of unit streams per capital good and the value which society puts on a unit stream together determine the demand price of capital goods.

In Keynes' short period, the marginal efficiency schedule is given, and movements in the demand price of capital goods are then due entirely to changes in the interest rate. The *General Theory's* analysis of the comparative statics of investment determination is less general and less clear than it might have been principally because of Keynes' preoccupation with a particular dynamic issue, namely whether or not the rate of interest would "equate Saving and Investment." Keynes' regarded it as a "Classical" thesis that it would. His own explanation of how an unemployment state comes to emerge required that it would not. Without this denial of the supposed Classical proposition, he would have no theory of fluctuations in employment. His whole discussion of the two sets of factors which determine the demand price for capital goods has this "Classical proposition" as its target. To Keynes the invalidity of this proposition was by no means a foregone conclusion—it posed an issue requiring serious analytical attention. This is in marked contrast to how the matter appears from the standpoint of the income-expenditure model. With the latter model's postulate of the interest-elasticity of investment (and of saving), the possibility that despite inflexible money wages, interest rate adjustments might keep the economy at full employment in the face of a decline in the marginal efficiency of capital, can be dismissed almost out of hand.[25]

The dynamic setting of Keynes' analysis of the emergence of unemployment may be described in the following manner. It is presumed that the marginal efficiency of capital in the current short period is lower than in the preceding period. For employ-

---

25. Compare, e.g., the unique, "knife-edge," growth-path of the Harrod-Domar models. The structure of the *General Theory* model allows the possibility of the system's responding to fluctuations in the marginal efficiency of capital by changes in the composition of output and, thus, in the rate of growth—induced by interest rate adjustments—rather than by changes in employment. Keynes had to go to great lengths to show why this possibility will not be a probability.

ment to remain at the previous period's level, current investment must be approximately the same as in the previous period. The rate of investment will be the same only if the money demand price for capital goods remains the same. The decline in the marginal efficiency of capital means that the number of prospective unit streams per unit capital has declined. For the demand price for capital goods to remain the same, therefore, the demand price per unit stream must be correspondingly increased, i.e., the interest rate must fall. The interest rate, however, will not fall without creating an excess demand for money—thus liquidity preference will prevent it from falling enough.

As seen above, we can replace Keynes' "interest rate" with the price of a suitably standardized income-stream. In many passages of the *General Theory*, it appears that this price is determined solely by the State of Liquidity Preference and the supply of "money." This notion is naturally a bit disturbing. Surely, factors other than the demand and supply of money must enter into the determination of the value (in terms of current consumer goods or in terms of wage units) which society puts on its resources. Even admitting that "Liquidity" plays a role in the short run, the Classical factors of "Productivity" and "Thrift" must still be considered.

On "Productivity," one must first recall Keynes' critique of models which equate the rate of interest with the marginal productivity of capital.[26] What counts are the "opinions about prospective yield," and productivity is relevant only as it affects these opinions. Keynes' position here is eminently reasonable. On the other hand, these opinions must clearly affect the demand side of the loanable funds market, and in this way, enter into the determination of the interest rate. The short-run assumption of given opinions about prospective yields—a given MEC-schedule —we may translate somewhat schematically into the postulate of a given stock supply of standard income-streams. The habit of working out the short-run analysis on the basis of the assumption that this important stock variable was *constant*, occasionally misled Keynes into statements which to all appearances imply that

---

26. *General Theory, loc. cit.*

the interest rate would be *independent* of the perceived stock of income-streams—e.g., that it would be determined "from some other source." A decline in the MEC-schedule means, in effect, that the perceived stock supply of streams is reduced. There is no reason why the demand for such streams should fall exactly to the same extent so as to keep the price per unit stream ("the" interest rate) unaffected. The simplified two-asset structure of the *General Theory* model tends to be misleading here. With only "money" and "non-money assets" and with the supply (in the relevant sense of "unit streams") of the latter fixed, the Liquidity Preference theory *degenerates* into the theory that the interest rate is determined by the demand and supply of money. "The" interest rate is here the difference in the rate of yield on long assets over "money"; with this framework, as previously remarked, there is nothing to distinguish the two concepts of the level and the term structure of interest rates. With a richer menu of assets—differentiated, as always, by term to maturity—the point becomes all but self-evident. The shape of the yield curve, in the Keynes-Hicks theory, depends apart from the State of Liquidity Preference on *relative* asset supplies. The supply of money and short streams relative to the supply of long streams can be altered just as well by a change in the supply of the latter as in the supply of money.

In the above discussion, the "Productivity" of the Classical theory is identified with the supply of the various stores of value that wealth-owners demand. The *General Theory*'s treatment of this supply side of the problem is, then, far from fully satisfactory, the objection being with the almost exclusive emphasis on the supply of "money" to the neglect of the supply of non-money assets.

We should turn then to the demand side—to the Classical "Thrift." It might be thought that much the same objection applies here, i.e., that Keynes focuses too exclusively on the demand for money. But this would be wide of the mark. In income-expenditure usage "Liquidity Preference" and "money demand" have come to be virtually synonymous terms. Keynes' Liquidity Preference, however, is not just a fanciful or flamboyant term for the demand for money. The later usage reflects a very narrow interpretation of his Theory of Liquidity Preference. The General Theory of Liquidity Preference does *not* ignore "Thrift," i.e., the preference patterns underlying the choice between current consumption and the accumulation of wealth. But the connections between Keynes' theory of saving (and consumption) and his Theory of Liquidity Preference is a complicated affair which will be the subject of the next chapter.

Investment in long-lived capital assets   An argument repeatedly advanced in the income-expenditure literature asserts that, once unemployment has arisen, the interest rate would have to be negative to again equate saving and investment at a full employment rate of output.[27] If, in order to discuss this issue, we assume that the elasticity of substitution between bonds and capital goods is perfect, the argument implies that the relevant class of capital goods is short-lived; consequently, the interest-elasticity of present value is slight, and demand price will be completely dominated by expectations about returns in the near future.

It is quite true that if full employment were to be maintained without a reduction in money wages, through the maintenance of a certain rate of investment specifically in inventories and short-lived capital equipment, then a negative interest rate would, on occasion, be necessary to provide the requisite "subsidy" to continuing investment of this sort. As a general proposition applying to all "maturity classes" of investment, however, the negative rate case is basically the same as the Stagnationist notion of "lack of investment opportunities."

The Stagnationist position has been examined by Bailey, whose analysis of the "outlets for saving" which would open up at very low positive rates of interest conclusively shows that a sufficient fall in the level of long rates would stave off unemployment indefinitely.[28] In evaluating the results of questionnaire

---

27. Cf., e.g., D. Patinkin, "Price Flexibility and Full Employment," *American Economic Review*, Sept. 1948, reprinted in *Readings in Monetary Theory*.

28. M. J. Bailey, *National Income and the Price Level*, New York, 1962, pp. 107–14 and 123–30. One would be tempted to call Bailey's discussion of the topic "definitive" were it not that the argument had previously been stated just as

studies on this problem, the differences in the technical type of the investments which would be optimal at normal and very low rates respectively are worth noting. Bailey's illustrations of low interest rate investment opportunities are to the point: use of stainless steel and other costly, durable alloys in many uses where these are uneconomical at normal rates, or coastline fill-ins—i.e., production of "land," the factor of production traditionally used both as an example of a resource in perfectly inelastic supply and as an illustration of a pure *Gebrauchsgut*. These possibilities are obviously relevant to any evaluation of the "Specter of Secular Stagnation." Yet, one must ask: Do businessmen, who in their responses to questionnaires deny that movements of interest rates are significant in their investment planning, base their answers on the premises relevant to the economist interested in secular stagnation, namely (a) that the individual firm can float large issues of perpetuities, (b) that the interest rate on these perpetuities is a mere fraction of the borrowing rates historically experienced on very long private-sector issues, and (c) that the marginal efficiency of projects utilizing a technology so radically different from the one prevailing should be contemplated? These are the questions that should be asked (if need be)—"*secular* stagnation" certainly would provide time for the relevant learning process. Yet one suspects that the answers garnered in these efforts merely echo what the economist knew already, namely that the interest-elasticity for given anticipated *short* streams is very low.

Having "ruled out" the interest rate, and in addition having nailed down the relative price of consumer and capital goods as a constant, early income-expenditure theorists were left with an "autonomous" investment variable in the short run. The theory of prices in many "Keynesian" models of the forties was on the verge of extinction. But "autonomous" variables do not give much scope to the talents of those theoretically inclined, and this development did have a worthwhile by-product: the development of recursive business cycle models. Since nothing else influ-

---

forcefully and then been forgotten—cf. G. Cassel, *The Nature and Necessity of Interest*, London, 1903, esp. p. 109.

enced investment in this model, the early "Keynesian" writers *a fortiori* came to concentrate on the formation of expectations. The accelerator mechanism was near at hand, since the assumption of an approximate constancy of the desired capital-output ratio makes some sense in a model where the representative capital good is of only moderate durability. In the "short end" of the asset-spectrum, the accelerator is dominant and the interest rate marginal; in the "long end" these roles are reversed. From the present-day perspective, the significance of these models for the development of macrotheory has little to do with the soon emerging, very voluminous literature which debated the accelerator from the standpoint of the theory of production. Its importance lies in the fact that the problem of predicting revisions of expectations within the model was tackled—in a very simplistic fashion at first, as was natural, but it nevertheless was tackled.

Keynes' theory of expectations was sketchy at best [29] and this he was certainly aware of. He could therefore appreciate the work being done in the years following the *General Theory* on relating investment demand to income and changes in income. But he could *not* at all accept the proposition, which was often advanced almost as a corollary of the new approaches, that the interest-elasticity of investment was very low. His *theoretical* reasons for not accepting these propositions are, by now, quite clear. The early "Keynesians" would, however, have disputed the "empirical soundness" of his judgment on this point.

A priori reasoning and time-series evidence   It has become commonplace to maintain that the significance of the interest-elasticity of investment is an "empirical issue"—meaning that the burden of proof rests upon the theorist who assumes that the re-

---

29. He may not have regarded it as "inoperational" exactly. It is unlikely that he would have been content with a modern econometrician's confining definition of "operationality." Compare his attitude in "Professor Tinbergen's Method," *Economic Journal*, Sept. 1939 and "Comment," *ibid.*, March 1940. A fall in the marginal efficiency of capital a gentleman could observe at his Club, no doubt. But, while in many respects he was a "tone-and-feel of the City" man in these matters, the Bursar of King's was no fool in judging investment opportunities.

lationship is not to be ignored. The situation is a rather curious one. Any macromodel will contain a large number of partial relationships of this kind. Normally the decision to take any one of these into account is based simply on introspective evidence and casual empiricism—the usual raw materials of *a priori* theory construction—and is also accepted on such grounds. In the present case, *a priori* reasoning tells us that the elasticity of investment in short-lived capital with respect to the short rate will be slight, but that the long rate elasticity of investment in durable capital should be significant. In the "Keynesian" literature, the position that the interest-elasticity of investment is not small enough to be ignored has most often not been accorded the conventional measure of "suspension of disbelief," while in the same literature many other partial relationships are accepted on the basis of choice-theoretical reasoning.[30]

It is always possible to dispute the relevance of any price-theoretical proposition and to take the position that its quantitative significance must first be empirically established before it is incorporated in a macromodel. One would then start from the proposition that "the interest-elasticity of investment is slight" —in itself a straightforward proposition in static, partial equilibrium analysis. Others of its kind would be, e.g., "changes in the price of houses lead to changes in demand so slight that they can be ignored," or "gasoline is a Giffen-good." These we do not in fact pose as "empirical issues," since to do so would be to advertise a complete lack of faith in economic theory in general, whereas we do have reason to believe that price theory possesses considerable predictive power. If all propositions of price theory had to be independently "verified," economics would be turned into a purely lexicographic endeavor, i.e., a body of knowledge from which nothing can be inferred about facts or relationships which have not already been registered and classified.

A large number of econometric studies of the investment function have failed to find a significant partial relationship between

---

30. Notably, the proposition that the elasticity of demand for "transaction balances" with respect to the short rate is significant. Cf. the discussion in Chapter V:3 of the Baumol and Tobin rationalizations of this proposition.

aggregate investment and "the" interest rate. This is the major factor in the case made against Keynes' assumption. But one must realize how formidable the identification problems are which must be overcome in any attempt to obtain a reliable measurement of the interest-elasticity of investment from aggregative time-series data. The hypothesis which is characteristic of all "Keynesian" theories of economic fluctuations is that it is typically and primarily shifts in the marginal efficiency of capital schedule which account for short-run movements in investment, income, and the interest rate. In a typical Keynesian contraction, the observed values of these three endogenous variables will decline together as a consequence of an adverse shift in "opinions about prospective yields." In order to isolate the "deviation-dampening" effect on investment and income of the fall in the interest rate, a very exact and reliable method of estimating the movements of the investment schedule would be required. The best that can be done with this problem is usually to include a number of lagged income terms in the investment function. Since the same event accounts for the decline in all three variables, it is perhaps not surprising that findings relating to the partial relationship between investment and interest rate will be inconclusive once investment has been regressed on income.

We may note that the "Keynesians" have generally shown themselves as less impressed with similar evidence on the unimportance of interest in another area. Professor Friedman has reported that in his investigations of the "permanent income hypothesis" of the money-demand function, no significantly better fit is obtained by including the interest rate as an argument of the function, once the result of a regression based only on lagged income terms has been obtained.[31] All "Keynesian" models have

---

31. M. Friedman, "The Demand for Money: Some Theoretical and Empirical Results," *Journal of Political Economy*, Aug. 1959, reprinted in R. A. Gordon and L. R. Klein, eds., *Readings in Business Cycles*, Homewood, Ill., 1965; and M. Friedman and Anna J. Schwartz, "Money and Business Cycles," *Review of Economics and Statistics*, Feb. 1963.

Cf. A. M. Okun's "Comment," on the latter article, p. 75: "Nor can I accept the procedures in Friedman's quantitative work on the demand function for money. There, other variables get the first chance to explain demand while interest rates wait in line and are given only the opportunity to eat the leftovers, the residuals of the basic equations. . . ."

one requirement in common—that this interest-elasticity be significant. If it were not, the whole family of models would be irrelevant exercises. In this case, therefore, the inconclusive findings have not been generally accepted. There exist, of course, other econometric studies of the money-demand function which find the interest rate to be quite significant,[32] but the extent to which choice-theoretical reasoning and casual empiricism are injected into the discussion of the issue is notable in comparison with the way in which such considerations are often shoved aside in considering the interest-elasticity of investment.

When general considerations of this sort enter into the discussion of the latter topic, the tenor of the argument sometimes gives the impression that the *a priori* expectation is that empirical research would *not* show the interest-elasticity to be of significant magnitude, i.e., that the *a priori* expected result runs directly counter to the implication to be derived from price theory.[33] If this is the expectation, the inconclusive test results are likely to be accepted as proof of the interest-inelasticity of investment. It is hard to say exactly on what grounds such an expectation would be held. It does not seem unlikely that it may rest in part on judgments of how the system would behave if the interest-elasticity of investment were substantial, e.g., of the following kind: if the interest-elasticity were in fact significant, we would be living in a more nearly "Classical" world, in which (a) fluctuations in output and employment would have a smaller amplitude than we in fact observe, and (b) monetary policy would prove a more convenient and effective stabilization device than experience shows to be the case.

Not much is to be gained from trying to ascertain whether, or to what extent, such presumptions have played a part in the development of income-expenditure doctrine. But the thesis of the

---

32. H. A. Latané, "Cash Balances and the Interest Rate—A Pragmatic Approach," *Review of Economics and Statistics,* Nov. 1954, is probably the one most often cited as a counterweight to Friedman's findings. In work on the money-demand function, there does not exist the same compulsion to use lagged income terms as in work on the investment function. With the latter, it is necessary somehow to correct for shifts in the marginal efficiency of capital—there is hardly any choice but to have the interest rate "wait in line."

33. Again, it is only the long rate and durable capital that are relevant to the issue.

inefficacy of monetary policy in reversing a contraction has been historically antecedent to the thesis of the interest-inelasticity of investment in this development—the first thesis is found in Keynes, the other is not. Here we need only point out that the response of the system to a decline in the marginal efficiency of capital and to a monetary injection will in either case depend, in the first instance, on the interest-elasticity of the demand for money, not on that of investment. A dynamic question will also be involved, namely the strength of the feedback effect that a decline in income will have upon "opinions of prospective yields." Thus, casual observation of the *dynamic* behavior of the system as a *whole* cannot provide a basis for a judgment on the *static, partial* equilibrium problem in question.

The type of sequence-analysis of the contraction process which we have previously criticized as inconsistent with Say's Principle may lead to some misunderstanding here. The sequence of events according to this rationalization of the usual IS-LM exercise should be recalled: (1) the MEC declines, and investment is reduced, (2) income declines as the "multiplier" sets in, (3) the decline in income "frees" transaction balances, and (4) "in order to have these balances absorbed into speculative balances," the interest rate will fall. This is the excess supply of money explanation of endogenous reductions in the interest rate. It is false: a fall in income does not create an excess supply of money; it is due to an excess demand for money, and will go on only until the excess demand for money becomes zero. But if this sequence-analysis is accepted, it is natural to conclude that, once the initial decline in income has taken place, the "subsequent" reduction in the interest rate will stimulate investment and thus act in a "deviation-counteracting" manner. On this kind of analysis, it would then appear that a system with an interest-elasticity of investment of substantial magnitude would show little or no tendency to develop "cumulative" income-constrained processes. The "initial" decline of income will be regarded as triggering two immediate feedback responses—(a) the deviation-amplifying accelerator effect through the dependence of entrepreneurial expectations on the rate of change of income, and (b) the deviation-counteracting effect of the reduction in interest. If the second of these is strong, the over-all tendency for the system to propagate the initial deflationary impulse should be weak. Since the system actually seems to develop cumulative processes, one might then conclude that the interest-elasticity of investment "must" be slight.

A correct sequence-analysis would not include the second, counteracting feedback loop that this description of the process presumes. In the short run, therefore, there is nothing immediately to offset the amplifying effect of the accelerator mechanism and cut the cumulative process short. For reductions in the interest rate to contribute towards pushing the system back towards full employment, one must instead await the much slower process of a gradual revision of expectations about future long rates which will reduce the "speculative demand for money" and thus create an excess supply of money at the prevailing level of income. But, in the shorter run, no such deviation-counteracting effects can be expected, whatever the interest-elasticity of expenditures.

Keynes through income-expenditure glasses   To return to Keynes, then, the interest-elasticity of investment was assumed to be quantitatively highly significant in Keynes' model. A volume of investment inadequate to sustain full employment could not, within his system, be blamed on low interest-elasticity. Consequently, inadequate investment was to Keynes a *problem of interest rate inflexibility;* the problem was that the interest rate—the all-important *long* rate—did not adjust adequately on its own accord. This idea was central to his thinking over many years. He was always a "low interest rate man." Two things distinguish the *General Theory* from the *Treatise:* the analysis of the nature of income-constrained processes and resource unemployment, and the doubts, which the Great Depression had amplified in his mind, that *conventional* monetary operations could budge the long rate *rapidly* enough to avoid prolonged periods of unemployment. The "vision" of how the system works which we get from the *General Theory* is thus quite different from the one embodied in the income-expenditure model. In the latter theory, the problem is that variations in the interest rate "do not mean anything."

As is usual in "Keynesian" literature, one finds on this issue also an extraordinary conviction that the standard income-expenditure model is the "true" model of the *General Theory*. Against this standard, Keynes himself is measured and often found wanting. Frequently the inference is drawn that his theoretical thinking was internally inconsistent, at other times that, while it might be consistent at any one time, Keynes changed his mind back and forth on issues of major importance so that, over time, his recorded views show major discrepancies.

An illustration of the latter type of biographical interpretation and theoretical exegesis is found in Klein's discussion of Keynes' views on investment and interest. If the income-expenditure theory of the forties is taken to be the correct interpretation of what Keynes tried to say in the *General Theory*, then that work "should say" that monetary policy is ineffective because of the interest-inelasticity of the investment function. Klein notes Keynes' earlier views on the efficacy of low rates, then quotes from the *General Theory*:

For my own part, I am now somewhat sceptical of the success of a purely monetary policy directed towards influencing the rate of interest. . . . it seems likely that the fluctuations in the market estimation of the marginal efficiency of different types of capital . . . will be too great to be offset by any practicable changes in the rate of interest.[34]

Klein offers the following passage from a later letter by Keynes to Dr. Ezekiel as a *contrast*:

I am far from fully convinced by the recent thesis that interest rates play a small part in determining the volume of investment. It may be that other influences, such as an increase in demand, often dominate it in starting a movement. But I am quite unconvinced that low interest rates cannot play an enormous part in sustaining investment at a given figure, and when there is a movement from a higher to a lower rate in allowing a greater scale of investment to proceed over a very much longer period than would otherwise be possible.

On this basis, Klein argues that the views on interest and investment expressed in the *General Theory* were "evidently just a

---

34. *General Theory*, p. 164. Only part of the passage used by Klein is given here.

temporary lapse in his theoretical development, for a few years later *he changed his mind again* and returned to his former optimistic faiths."[35] The Procrustean Bed in operation! The quoted statements give no evidence of a "lapse" or "change of mind" since they deal with entirely different questions. The first is a statement of Keynes' fears that there may be insurmountable difficulties in the way of exerting a sufficiently flexible control of the long rate so as successfully to offset changes in the marginal efficiency of capital. The second statement simply asserts that, in his view, *if* the long rate *can* be made to change, the effect on investment would *ceteris paribus* be "enormous." One refers to shifts of the MEC-schedule, the other to its slope. The two are entirely consistent, and state Keynes' long-held views precisely and concisely.

---

35. L. R. Klein, *The Keynesian Revolution*, New York, 1960, pp. 66–67, italics added.

IV·THE GENERAL THEORY
OF LIQUIDITY PREFERENCE

IV:1   Keynes' "Windfall Effect"

In the *General Theory,* consumption is most frequently treated simply as a function of current income. In most contexts, this simplification is adequate for Keynes' immediate analytical purposes. Keynes referred to this consumption-income relation as based on a "psychological law," and made no attempt to deduce it from conventional choice-theoretical principles. This *ad hoc* procedure obscured the distinction between the short-run and the long-run consumption-income relation. Early contributors to "Keynesian" theory generally presumed the long-run stability of the short-run relation.

The postwar forecasting debacle forced a revision of these optimistic beliefs about the predictive accuracy of simplistic income-expenditure models which had been a natural part of the emotional climate of the Keynesian Revolution. At the same time, Kuznets' findings clearly demonstrated the necessity of distinguishing between the long-run consumption-income relation and the short-run reaction of consumption to cyclical changes in income. The reconciliations of the short-run and long-run evidence proposed by Duesenberry, Friedman, Modigliani, and others have a strong family resemblance in their emphasis on longer run income prospects, or the value of wealth, as the variables explaining the shifts over time of the short-run consumption-income relation. The forceful demonstration of the importance of wealth and capital variables provided by the new theories of the consumption function has done much to determine the direction taken by modern research in other areas, notably research on the money-demand function. This increasing reliance on capital theory is the most prominent and seems the most promising development in recent macroeconomic work.

From our present standpoint, therefore, the early "Keynesian" literature's preoccupation with flows appears as its major analytical weakness. The emphasis in the more recent exegetical criticism of Keynes' work has shifted correspondingly. Thus, Professor Johnson concludes his retrospective evaluation of the *General Theory* by stressing that ". . . the book was weak at a crucial point, in its neglect of the influence of capital on behavior." [1]

It is usually recognized that Keynes did provide for a wealth effect on consumption in the very long run. In Keynes' discussion of possible stationary states, the effect of the growth in the stock of capital was considered. Keynes concluded that, even with rigidity of money wages and the disappearance of "investment opportunities" yielding a positive return, stagnation with unemployment may be avoided if

. . . a situation in which a stock of capital sufficiently great to have a marginal efficiency of zero also represents an amount of wealth sufficiently great to satiate to the full the aggregate desire on the part of the public to make provision for the future.

A stationary state with zero marginal efficiency of capital would, however, be "an unlikely coincidence":

If . . . this more favourable possibility comes to the rescue, it will probably take effect, not just at the point where the rate of interest is

---

1. Johnson, "The General Theory . . . ," *op. cit.*, p. 11. Compare P. A. Samuelson, "A Brief Survey of Post-Keynesian Developments," J. E. Stiglitz, ed., *The Collected Scientific Papers of Paul A. Samuelson*, Cambridge, Mass., 1966, pp. 1537 ff.

vanishing, but at some previous point during the gradual decline of the rate of interest.[2]

The modern criticism of Keynes therefore attacks the *General Theory* from a slightly different angle. Johnson, for example, notes that the new theories of the consumption function have had to be

. . . concerned with the . . . shortcoming of the theory as Keynes presented it, the neglect of the influence of wealth on consumption, a *neglect inherent in Keynes's short-period approach* and concealed by his deduction of the shape of the propensity to consume from an unexplored "psychological law." [3]

The contentions underlying Johnson's criticism are still clearer when he considers Keynes' Liquidity Preference theory:

His concern with *the short run in which the stock of physical capital is given,* together with his assumption of a given wage level, enabled him . . . [to proceed] *without explicitly introducing the value of assets.* . . . [T]he significance of the oversight lies . . . in the neglect of the effects of the increase in real wealth on aggregate demand.[4]

Several distinct contentions are involved in this judgment. The first is that Keynes' preoccupation with short-run problems led him to develop certain analytical habits inappropriate to the analysis of long-run problems and that he was not sufficiently aware of their limitations. He therefore showed a tendency to generalize in a rather reckless fashion from the results of his short-run analysis to problems of the long run. With this conten-

---

2. *General Theory,* p. 218. With respect to Chapter III:3 above, it may be noted that Keynes' discussion of the possible disappearance of "investment opportunities" pays more attention than the "Keynesian Stagnationists" generally did to the possibility that the growth in wealth might make the continuing provision of new "outlets for saving" unnecessary. On the other hand, Keynes' position was quite distinct also from that of Cassel and Bailey in that he believed that one or two generations of capital accumulation uninterrupted by depressions would suffice to bring about virtual capital saturation—a possibility which, it may plainly be inferred, Bailey rejects and which Cassel went to great lengths to dispute.

3. Johnson, *op. cit.,* p. 11, italics added.

4. *Op. cit.,* p. 9, italics added.

tion one can hardly quarrel.[5] The second contention is that the dynamic structure of Keynes' short-run model predisposed him to overlook the consequences of changes in the real value of financial assets due to proportional variations in money prices. The validity of this point we have also acknowledged in discussing Keynes' neglect of the distinction between physical and financial non-money assets. The third contention is that Keynes neglected changes in the real value of asset holdings since the stock of physical capital is a constant in the short-run context with which he was habitually concerned.[6]

This last assertion is not warranted. The reason is clear. We already know that the "real value" of the existing stock of physical capital is not a constant in Keynes' model. The purpose of the present section is, first, to document the fact that Keynes recognized that this variable would affect current consumption and, second, to make a preliminary investigation of the nature of the wealth-saving relation which Keynes postulated.

A second psychological law of consumption Keynes' wealth-saving relation has been almost universally overlooked [7] simply because the *General Theory* has for a long time been read through the glasses of the income-expenditure model. In this one-commodity model, the value of the capital stock in terms of current commodities is not a variable in the short run. But this is the concept of "real wealth" to which both Johnson and Patinkin refer.[8]

---

5. Cf. also Viner's 1936 judgment quoted in Chapter II:1 above.

6. It should be noted that Patinkin's critique of Keynes' handling of the role of the capital accounts in income determination is based on exactly the same contentions as that of Johnson. Patinkin's argument is quoted below, Chapter V:1.

7. The signal exception is B. P. Pesek and T. R. Saving, *Money, Wealth, and Economic Theory*, New York, 1967. In revising the present study for publication, I have not been able to take sufficient account of this recent work.

8. There is no obvious justification for the presumption that this is an analytically satisfactory measure of "wealth" or "capital." Until recently, too little attention has been devoted to the question of whether the current commodity value of net worth is really the "wealth" variable theoretically appropriate to the formulation of the relevant behavior functions.

We will continue to follow conventional usage in referring to money values deflated by present period consumer goods prices as "real values." Such terms are

Clearly, the value of the capital stock in terms of present consumer goods is, in principle, a variable in Keynes' two-commodity model. A failure to take the "influence of capital on behavior" into account is consequently not a weakness *"inherent"* in Keynes' short-period approach. "Real net worth" will be constant in this type of model only if the short run is defined in such a way that *both* expected return streams *and* the interest rate are assumed not to change. The value of capital goods in terms of consumer goods is not a constant "by virtue" of the aggregates chosen. The contention that Keynes did not introduce this variable explicitly is also false, but the common misconception on this point is understandable in view of the fact that, once having assumed given "opinions about prospective yields," Keynes in most instances preferred to express his analysis in terms of changes in the rate of interest rather than in terms of changes in asset prices. Recognition of this price relation as a short-run variable, however, does not *per se* disprove "neglect" of its influence on aggregate demand. But Keynes is as explicit as can be desired on the point:

Windfall changes in capital-values . . . should be classified amongst *the major factors* capable of causing *short-period* changes in the propensity to consume.[9]

Capital values depend on two factors: "opinions about prospective yields" and "the" interest rate. The apparent reasons why the significance of Keynes' wealth-saving relation has not been recognized are worth noting. First, his short-run analysis treated the marginal efficiency schedule as given. Second, his discussion of the consumption function was immediately followed by his exposition of the truncated model, i.e., the simple autonomous investment *cum* multiplier model. To explain the simple case, Keynes had to anticipate the major conclusion of his discussion of the relation between the capital accounts and the income ac-

---

used only as convenient abbreviations, however, and the usage here does not presume that present "real net worth" is an analytically satisfactory measure of "wealth."

9. *General Theory*, pp. 92–93, italics added.

counts in the complete model, namely the inflexibility of long rates. Third, as we shall see, Keynes dismissed as of no significance changes in the rate of interest that do not work through changes in the "real value" of the existing capital stock—thus dismissing the intertemporal substitution effect usually emphasized by theorists confined to one-commodity models.

Keynes' "windfall effect" may be initiated either by a revision of "opinions"—i.e., a shift in the MEC-schedule—or by a change in the long rate. The first possibility falls outside the purview of the theory of income determination in the short period with which the great bulk of the *General Theory* is concerned. It finally makes its appearance in Keynes' chapter on the Trade Cycle:

> Unfortunately a serious fall in the marginal efficiency of capital also tends to affect adversely the propensity to consume. For it involves a severe decline in the market value of Stock Exchange Equities.

For present purposes it is important to note that Keynes' discussion does not indicate that he regarded the "real net worth" variable as only a minor refinement on the consumption-income relation. On the contrary:

> These people [who take an active interest in their stock exchange investments] are, perhaps, *even more influenced in their readiness to spend by rises and falls in the value of their investments than by the state of their income.*[10]

In the present study we are mainly interested in Keynes' short-period theory and, hence, in the second possibility—that of "given opinions" but changes in the rate at which perceived income prospects are discounted in the market. The last quotation given suggests a reference to the "Great Crash" of 1929. Actually, Keynes is thinking of the years following 1930 in which contracting and low incomes did account for a "serious fall in the marginal efficiency of capital." He blamed the onset of the Great Depression on a misguided monetary policy. The "punitive rate

---

10. *General Theory*, p. 319, italics added.

of interest" through which the Federal Reserve System sought to curb stock market speculation "could not be prevented from having its repercussion on the rate of new investment."[11] A high rate of interest will thus depress both the demand prices for capital goods and the market value of equities. In Keynes' view:

> The last point is important and . . . may suggest a generalisation of permanent value. A country is no richer when, for purposes of swopping titles to prospective gain between one of its citizens and another, people choose to value the prospects at twenty years' purchase, than when these are valued at ten years' purchase; but the citizens, beyond question, *feel* richer. Who can doubt that a man is more likely to buy a new motor-car if his investments have doubled in money-value during the past year than if they have been halved? He feels far less necessity or obligation to save out of his normal income, and his whole standard of expenditures is raised.[12]

The general import of all this is quite clear. It is asserted that a rise in asset values due entirely to a fall in interest rates—the "country is no richer"—will raise the propensity to consume out of current income. But the analytical foundations of the postulate are unclear. In establishing his consumption-income relation, Keynes was content to invoke an intuitively obvious "psychological law" and did not bother to provide a choice-theoretical derivation of the relationship. In the quoted passage he operates in the same manner: "Who can doubt that . . ." the propensity to consume out of current income depends upon the real value of assets? One might refer, then, to this wealth-saving relation as Keynes' Second Psychological Law of Consumption.

Preliminary discussion of the value-theoretical content of the Second Law   The Second Law is as ambiguous as the First. Keynes was satisfied to postulate it as a relation simply between consumption demand and the value of net worth (given the rate of money income). This *may* be all there is to it—Keynes' hypothesis may simply assert that consumption demand is uniquely

---

11. *Treatise*, Vol. II, p. 196.
12. *Op. cit.*, p. 197.

related to real net worth.[13] Criterion functions for households may be specified which would imply such behavior.[14]

The value of net worth may, as we have seen, change either as a consequence of changes in the marginal efficiency of capital or as a consequence of changes in the rate of interest (the demand price for unit streams). In the case of the types of utility functions specified by Chase and Thompson, it is not necessary to distinguish between these two possibilities. But otherwise it must be done. One possibility refers to the *supply* of future streams—an upward re-evaluation of the marginal efficiency of capital does "make the country richer," in Keynes' sense, at least if these more optimistic opinions are warranted. The other possibility refers to changes in the *demand* for income streams due, for example, to monetary expansion. In this instance, the productive transformation possibilities of the system are unchanged. In general there is then no presumption that, given current income, current consumption will respond in the same way to a given increase in the value of net worth due to an increase in anticipated future income-receipts as to an equivalent increase in net worth due to a reduction in interest, perceived future receipts constant. There is, in other words, no presumption that current consumption will be a single-valued function of current real net worth as Keynes' formulation of his Second Psychological Law would seem to suggest.

---

13. It is convenient here to follow S. B. Chase, Jr., *Asset Prices in Economic Analysis*, Berkeley, 1963, and use a Robertsonian lag in the consumption-income relation and thus to include last period's income in current net worth. The Robertsonian lag is for that matter very much in the right spirit: households have to obtain means of payment before they can exert *effective* demand for consumer goods (cf. Chapter II:2–3).

14. Two distinct possibilities have been developed. Cf. (a) Chase, *op. cit.*, and (b) E. A. Thompson, "Intertemporal Utility Functions and the Long Run Consumption Function," *Econometrica*, April 1967. The arguments of Chase's criterion function are current consumption and the current consumption value of net worth. Thompson's objects of choice, in accordance with more conventional analytic procedure, are consumption in the current and future periods, the criterion function having the property that, for any given current value of net worth, current consumption is completely inelastic while consumption in future periods is unit-elastic with respect to changes in intertemporal rates of transformation. I am indebted to Thompson for making me realize that this type of utility function is not such a "special" or "unrealistic" case as I was first inclined to regard it.

In the short period, with which Keynes was mainly concerned, the marginal efficiency of capital is taken as given and the "windfall effects" that may occur are due to movements of the long rate. The ambiguities of Keynes' discussion of this effect of interest rate changes are particularly unfortunate, since later "Keynesians" have been in all but unanimous agreement on the proposition that interest rates have only a negligible influence on consumption demand. The discussion in the *General Theory* improves upon the *Treatise* in some respects, although it still leaves important questions in need of clarification:

The influence of this factor [changes in the rate of time-discounting, i.e., the ratio of exchange between present and future goods] on the rate of spending out of a given income is open to a good deal of doubt. . . . There are not many people who will alter their way of living because the rate of interest has fallen from 5 to 4 per cent . . . . [But] if a man is enjoying a windfall increment in the value of his capital, it is natural that his motives towards current spending should be strengthened, *even though in terms of income his capital is worth no more than before;* . . . Apart from this, the main conclusion suggested by experience is, I think, that the short-period influence of the rate of interest . . . is secondary and relatively unimportant, except, perhaps, where unusually large changes are in question.[15]

Again, one notices the recourse to the "intuitive plausibility" of the postulated relationship: "it is natural that" capital gains should induce increased consumption spending. But the cited passages do give us a few things to go on in the search for the value-theoretical premises of the consumption-interest relation. Thus we have to deal purely with a change in relative prices. The clause which has here been italicized unambiguously asserts

---

15. *General Theory*, pp. 93–94, italics added. For future reference, it may be noted that Keynes continues with an obvious paraphrase of Cassel: "When the rate of interest falls very low indeed, the increase in the ratio between an annuity purchasable for a given sum and the annual interest on that sum may, however, provide an important source of negative saving by encouraging the practice of providing for old age by the purchase of an annuity." For anyone not acquainted with Cassel's work, this is a rather cryptic summary of his famous argument for a lower limit to the movements of the long rate—i.e., "The Necessity of [positive] Interest." We will have occasion to return to this argument later in the chapter.

that the stock of receipt streams held by households is regarded as unchanging.

Since the appearance of Hicks' *Value and Capital*, it has been customary to decompose the total effect on trading plans of changes in relative prices into "substitution effects" and "income effects." Hicks' famous work post-dated the *General Theory* and his analytical apparatus was not available to Keynes. When judging Keynes' abilities as a price theorist, it is worth recalling that the type of ambiguity which we have lamented above is to be found almost everywhere in the theoretical literature in this and earlier periods.

The quoted argument will be interpreted here in the following way: Keynes regards the substitution effect of interest changes as "open to a good deal of doubt," as "secondary and relatively unimportant"—a phrase which in his works means, in effect, that the relation is ruled out of consideration.[16] The statement that people "will not alter their way of living" in response to changes in the price of future consumption goods in terms of present consumption goods is interpreted to mean that preference functions defined for alternative time-paths of consumption are assumed to exhibit a considerable degree of intertemporal complementarity.

The passage re-emphasizes the contention made in the *Treatise*, namely that interest rate changes exert their influence on saving through (and *only* through) "the appreciation or depreciation in the price of securities and other assets." [17] This implies, once more, that these securities and capital goods are of *long term*. If the representative non-money asset is not a title to a relatively long stream, the "windfall effect" of interest movements would surely have to be classified in the same category that Keynes, according to the present interpretation, placed the intertemporal substitution effect, i.e, as secondary and unimportant.

If, then, intertemporal substitution effects are to be ruled out, the windfall effect in question must be regarded purely as an income effect, or more appropriately a "wealth effect." Thus we

---

16. The repeated statements to this effect are, of course, the passages of Keynes' discussion of the relationship between saving and the interest rate which later Keynesians have fastened upon.

17. *General Theory, loc. cit.*

would regard the rise in current consumption, which Keynes postulates, as due not to a rearrangement of the preferred time-path through which a given amount of wealth (in some sense) is consumed, but to the assumed fact that the decline in the interest rate makes "the citizens feel richer," i.e., makes them wealthier. From here on we will refer to "wealth effects" rather than to "windfall effects." Throughout the remainder of this chapter, these wealth effects are to be understood as caused by interest rate movements. Changes in "opinions of prospective yields" will naturally also have wealth effects, but the following discussion assumes this State of Expectation to be given.

This alteration of Keynes' terminology is made in order to emphasize that we are proceeding on a particular interpretation of the value-theoretical underpinnings of Keynes' windfall effect. The salient characteristic of this interpretation is the neglect of the intertemporal substitution effect, i.e., the assumption of the intertemporal complementarity of preferences. Although the present author "feels" this interpretation to be the correct one, the quoted passages do not allow us to reject categorically the possibility that Keynes would have accepted the type of criterion function explored by Thompson as the appropriate formalization of his behavior hypothesis. On this alternative interpretation, the intertemporal substitution effect is not to be ignored. The characteristic feature of this type of model is that current consumption is uniquely related to the real value of current net worth so that, given the value of the latter variable, it is independent of the rate of intertemporal transformation. This means, therefore, that the substitution effects and wealth effects of changes in "the interest rate" must interact in such a manner as to leave the propensity to consume out of current net worth unchanged, while the entire effect of the change in the opportunity cost of current consumption in terms of future consumption falls on planned consumption in future periods.

The theory advanced by Chase has the important feature in common with Thompson's model that current consumption is simply a single-valued function of current net worth. Our interpretation, according to which Keynes chose to "assume away" the intertemporal substitution effect, is incompatible with an interpretation based on the Thompson model which requires the substitution effect to be significant. Our interpretation is not in the same way incompatible with Chase's theory. This is because Chase's treatment of the consumption-accumulation decision simply does not specify anything about intertemporal consumption opportunities and preferences. The decision problem is dealt with exclusively in terms of choices between currently attainable combinations of present period consumption and real net worth. Chase's model suppresses what Wicksell would call the "longitudinal" dimension of the time-commodity space; the characteristic feature of the model lies in the reduction of the problem to the immediate choice between consumption goods and assets in the current period "cross-section" of the time-commodity space. Thus, the questions about the degree of intertemporal complementarity of preferences that are at issue between the present interpretation of Keynes and the alternative interpretation based on the Thompson model, have little or no meaning within Chase's framework.

This is enough to indicate that the *General Theory* contains problems in the area traditionally labeled as "the" Theory of Capital and Interest which have been almost completely ignored by Keynesian interpreters. In view of the current emphasis on the use of capital concepts in all areas of macroeconomics, an exploration of Keynes' wealth-saving relation should be of considerable interest.

Interest rates and central banking   At this point, one of the main objectives of our comparative study of Keynesian Economics and the Economics of Keynes has been by and large achieved. In Chapter I, the drastic contrast between Keynes and the later Keynesians with regard to the significance of the interest rate was stressed as one of the major puzzles which must be confronted in trying to understand the development of the "Keynesian tradition." Keynes, in Harrod's words, held low interest rates to be a matter "of the greatest importance of all," a position which has not been characteristic of (at least American) Keynesianism. The present interpretation of Keynes' theory provides a rationalization of the efficacy of low rates. The basic income-expenditure model, in contrast, has in uncountable instances been the vehicle for arguing the general unimportance of the interest rate.

It is clear how the assumptions which on the present interpretation are fundamental to the model of the *General Theory* provide the theoretical underpinnings for Keynes' position on interest rates. Given the State of Long Term Expectations, low interest rates will stimulate both investment and consumption demand. If the long rate can be controlled, it should provide an effective regulator of aggregate demand. Thus, the present section's discussion of the relation between saving and the interest rate comes to much the same conclusion as the analysis of the interest-elasticity of investment in the previous chapter. Keynes' problem is not that interest rates do not significantly affect expenditures. It is that the level of long rates cannot, in the short run, be made to move with sufficient speed, at least not through use of the conventional instruments of Central Bank policy.

In considering the development of Keynes' views on monetary policy it is necessary to distinguish clearly between monetary policy in the short run and in the long run. Since Keynes always found the problems of the short run more theoretically fascinating, his pronouncements on the former issue are more prominent and have attracted the most attention. In the *Treatise,* his convictions of the potentially powerful effects of interest rate movements still dominate his search for better counter-cyclical policies. But already in this work, one can trace a growing realization that *the very factors which account for these powerful effects will also tend to make the level of long rate quite stable in the short run and, therefore, difficult to control.*[18] Investors are regarded as taking a considerable time-span of past experience into account in forming their views of what is currently a "safe"

---

18. Consider the simple analogy: If the price-elasticity of excess demand for a commodity is very great, this means—in the loose terminology of the text—that price changes have "powerful effects" on this market. It also means that if, e.g., some government agency wants to affect this price and has to do so by "open market" sales and purchases of the commodity, its transactions must be on a quite substantial scale to have a significant effect. Here, naturally, the Central Bank has an important advantage in that a fractional reserve banking system normally will act as a powerful amplifier of Central Bank action.

price for a unit standard stream, i.e., of the value of the "normal rate of interest." Differences of opinion exist—without them the Central Bank would have to dominate the market completely in order to have any influence at all over the long rate—but an attempt to shift the rate significantly in the short run will normally set in motion such a mass migration from the bull to the bear camp, or vice versa, that conventional methods will prove to be of little avail.

But if it can be done, it will work—in Keynes' theory—and the search for counter-cyclical policy instruments in the *Treatise* is still a search for ways to do it. The way out of a depression, consequently, is a monetary policy *à outrance*—open market purchases of long assets and of risky assets, and purchases to the "point of saturation." In the *General Theory*, Keynes' views on the short-run inflexibility of the long rate are a good deal firmer and more doctrinaire. The bull-bear argument of the *Treatise* is correspondingly simplified and sharpened into the later book's theory of the Speculative Demand for Money.[19] The attempt to devise effective short-run monetary policies is given up and, instead, Keynes preaches the case for various fiscal measures.

There is little to indicate that Keynes changed his mind about the importance of monetary policy in the longer run. The Central Bank's ability to control aggregate demand in the short run may be limited, but it still holds awesome powers for good or ill over the longer run. Although it may not be feasible to manipulate the long rate deftly enough in the short run, it is as important as ever that the Central Bank act vigorously so as to hold market rate in the near neighborhood of the average level of (an appropriately defined [20]) "natural rate." By maintaining an inappropriately high level of interest rates on the average over several cycles (e.g., for balance of payments reasons) the Bank would be responsible for a succession of deep recessions and weak or abortive booms as well as for a correspondingly low long-run growth rate. To Keynes, Britain's economic problems in the late twenties and early thirties were a story of "the obstinate

---

19. The subject of Chapter V:3, below.
20. On the appropriate definition, cf. V:2 and VI:2, below.

maintenance of misguided monetary policies" which had contributed to keeping "rates up for fifteen years to a level which would
have seemed a generation ago quite beyond reasonable probability." [21] If, instead, rates had been kept lower, the growth rate
would have been higher, booms would have reached full employment and recession would have been weak. Low rates are
"of the utmost importance."

This, again, is quite different from more recently influential
theories, whether these have a strongly "Keynesian" flavor or not.
The standard doctrine is here that the Bank has no control over
"real" market rates of interest over the longer run but that these
are determined entirely by "real" (as opposed to "monetary")
factors. [22] If the Bank tries to maintain some other level of rates
(on the average over the longer run), the effects of such a policy
will be reflected mainly in the rate of change of money prices,
whereas real income, employment, and real rates of growth will
not be significantly affected.

To a considerable extent, the difference between Keynes and
later Keynesians on this issue lies in the way in which the aggregate money-demand function is specified. The textbook Keynesian model assumes real money demand to be dependent upon
real income and the interest rate. This "liquidity preference
schedule" is assumed stable in the long run—the Bank has no
influence on its position. [23] The function specifies the conditions

---

21. *Treatise*, Vol. II, p. 384.

22. This is another issue, then, on which we may observe that Keynes attached
far more importance to "monetary phenomena" than his later followers. An explanation of his position on this matter is suggested in the text. That an explanation of sorts can be provided does not mean that Keynes' judgment on the relative
importance of "real" and "monetary factors" in the generation of fluctuations is
justified. Professor Hayek criticized Keynes on this important point in the early
thirties. Cf. F. A. Hayek, "Reflections on the Pure Theory of Money of Mr. J. M.
Keynes," Parts I and II, *Economica*, Aug. 1931 and Feb. 1932. The Austrian
perspective from which Hayek attacks the *Treatise* will appear "foreign" to later
Keynesians. Our previous discussion should make clear however that it is
appropriate—term to maturity or "roundaboutness" is the most important dimension of Keynes' theoretical structure just as in the writings of the Austrian
school.

23. A more adequate statement would *inter alia* take expected rates of change of
the price level into account. Cf., e.g., A. L. Marty's review of Gurley and Shaw,

under which the Bank may depress money rates of interest in the short run by monetary injection. In the "medium run," however, this will have the effect of raising the money price level, thereby reducing the real stock of money again and restoring the initial rate of interest. This is a short paraphrase of the most common formulation of the "neutrality of money" argument according to which money will not lastingly affect the "real" equilibrium values of the system's variables.[24] To maintain a lower money rate, the Bank must thus continue to generate inflation.

In Keynes' theory, on the other hand, the money-demand function depends not only upon income and the market rate of interest but also, and importantly, on a third variable, namely investor opinions with regard to the "normal rate":

. . . what matters is not the *absolute* level of r but the degree of its divergence from what is considered a fairly *safe* level of r . . . etc.[25]

In the long run of Keynes' model, consequently, the income-expenditure liquidity preference schedule will be found to *shift* as these investor opinions are revised over time.[26] The inclusion

---

Money in a Theory of Finance, in *Journal of Political Economy*, Feb. 1961. This is not the place to bring in such complications, however.

24. We will not here go into the controversial questions opened up by L. A. Metzler's famous, "Wealth, Saving, and the Rate of Interest," *Journal of Political Economy*, April 1951. To the extent that a Metzler-type wealth effect should be acknowledged, we may for present purposes assume that it is of "secondary magnitude" and that the neutrality of money is "approximate."

25. *General Theory*, p. 201. Note that, whereas in Wicksell the terms "natural rate" and "normal rate" are used interchangeably, the "normal rate" here denotes a concept quite distinct from the "natural rate" of the *Treatise*. The former indicates the security prices which investors at any time regard as "fairly safe" against capital losses; the latter indicates that hypothetical price for "unit streams" which, if it can be established at the moment when aggregate activity is about to decline, will mean the maintenance of aggregate demand in money terms. The problem for conventional counter-cyclical monetary policy arises in situations where these two rates are too far apart—i.e., when speculation based on the belief of a given long rate being "normal" prevents the market rate from being brought into line with the natural rate.

26. The "Liquidity Trap" notion is anti-Keynesian not only in that Keynes explicitly rejected the idea that the money-demand function would be perfectly interest-elastic within any range that we would possibly be interested in, but also in its

of the "normal rate" in Keynes' money-demand function is another element of his monetary theory that has been neglected by later Keynesians.

In the short period, the power of the Central Bank to affect the long rate is limited by the opinions about its "normal" level inherited from the past. This, then, limits its ability quickly to reverse, e.g., a cyclical contraction that is already under way. In the longer run, however, the monetary authority, in Keynes' opinion, has considerable influence over these opinions about normal rate and it has a most important responsibility in nudging the normal rate to a level consistent with the underlying, basic non-monetary interest determinants of Thrift and Productivity. For the automatic forces tending to bring this about are weak, and investors learn but slowly:

. . . the failure of employment to attain an optimum level being in no way associated, in the minds either of the public or of authority, with the prevalence of an inappropriate range of rates of interest.[27]

If the Bank consistently pursues this objective, it will also find that the recessions that it has to deal with in the short run are less severe. By the same token, however, it may, if it is not careful, act in such a way as to validate false opinions about the normal level of long rate and thereby postpone the required adjustment almost indefinitely: "[the rate of interest] may fluctuate *for decades* about a level which is chronically too high for full employment."[28] If the normal rate stays persistently above the natural rate, the consequences will be a steady deflationary pressure, weak booms, and deep recessions.[29]

---

neglect of the downward shift of the entire schedule that, in a continuing state of depression, "at long last . . . will doubtless come by itself." Cf. *Treatise, loc. cit.*

27. *General Theory*, p. 204.

28. *Loc. cit.*, italics added. Note the contrast: Over a time-span of *decades*, modern "neutrality" reasoning would surely lead one to expect only nominal and no "real" magnitudes to remain under Central Bank influence.

29. On these matters, Professor Sayers would appear to be almost alone among prominent monetary theorists since Keynes who can be regarded as "truly Keynesian." In this respect, Keynesianism has not been the mass movement that it is so often depicted as being. Since the late 1930's, Sayers has consistently argued that

Summary Keynes' saving function does depend upon interest rates. But the quantitative significance of the wealth effect—as long as moderate variations in the rate are considered—should not be exaggerated. Keynes' attitude can be seen in his discussion of the differences between himself and the "Classics" on the theory of interest:

> But they would, presumably, not wish to deny that the level of income also has an important influence on the amount saved; whilst I, for my part, would not deny that the rate of interest may perhaps have an influence (though perhaps not of the kind which they suppose) on the amount saved *out of a given income*.[30]

Thus, the quantitatively significant effect of interest rate movements is still the effect on investment.

Our theoretical interest in a functional relationship is not determined simply by its quantitative significance in this sense, particularly not if we find that the proviso of "within the normal range of variation" is involved, as it is here. Many influential theorists have, for instance, been preoccupied for more than two decades with the Pigou-effect, or real balance effect, a relationship that is commonly regarded as of very modest quantitative significance within a normal range of price-level variation. Theoretically, Keynes' wealth effect is at least as interesting as the real balance effect.

At this point, however, the basis for this wealth effect is still unclear. It poses a problem in the theory of value and capital

---

monetary policy measures are ineffective in the short run and that their use should be reserved for longer run objectives. The similarities go a good deal farther. Sayers is known as the major author of the famous Radcliffe Report. The report is quite Keynesian in its emphasis on analyzing the economic situation with which the monetary authority is at any time confronted in terms of a broader concept of private-sector "liquidity," instead of in terms of the demand and supply of cash only.

30. *General Theory*, p. 178. (On the present interpretation, the parenthetical statement refers to Keynes' denial of the significance of the intertemporal substitution effect.) But cf. also p. 377: "It may turn out that the propensity to consume will be so easily strengthened by the effects of a falling rate of interest, that full employment can be reached with a rate of accumulation little greater than at present."

which Keynes did not tackle explicitly and which later Keynesians have in the main ignored completely. As we will see, the issue provides an important "missing link" between general value theory and Keynesian macroeconomics. The rest of this chapter will be devoted to exploring this issue.

IV:2   The Wealth-Saving Relation and the Theory of Capital and Interest

In section III:2 we contrasted the aggregative structure of Keynes' model with that of the standard income-expenditure model. In order to emphasize the most salient distinction between the two, we labeled the former a "two-commodity model," the latter a "one-commodity model." Two-commodity models of the Keynesian type—i.e., models which distinguish between consumables and capital goods—pose a number of analytical problems that are unfamiliar from the standpoint of the conventional macromodel. On these issues, the *General Theory* has far more in common with such "pre-Keynesians" (and post-Wicksellians) as Lindahl, Myrdal, and Hayek—and the author of the *Treatise on Money*—than with the Keynesian tradition as it developed from the late thirties on.

In the income-expenditure model, the relative price of consumables and capital goods is a constant. The same price relation is a key variable in Keynes' analysis. Given the inflexible money wage rate and the capital stock inherited from the past, both the rate of investment and of consumption, and consequently income and employment, depend upon the demand price of sources established in the current period. The higher this price, the higher the rate of output of capital goods and, with Keynes' wealth-saving relation as set forth in the preceding section, the higher the demand for consumables. Hence, this price provides the key to the determination of income and employment in the short run. Keynes' discussion of the employment problem is organized accordingly.[1] It focuses upon the determination of a

---

1. This is obvious in the *Treatise,* where the whole discussion revolves around the relation between the Natural Rate and the Market Rate. In the *General Theory,*

price which the usual textbook "Keynesian" model treats as a constant.

When "opinions about prospective yields" are treated as given, the variable determining the present value of sources is the (long) rate of interest. Given the money wage rate and entrepreneurial expectations, there will be some positive long rate such that, if it could be established, aggregate money expenditures would be sufficient for full employment. A higher rate means unemployment and a low rate of growth. A lower rate means inflation. A sufficiently low rate is a matter of "the greatest importance of all."

Keynes' wealth-saving relation poses a problem which must be considered on two different levels. On the first level, the problem is that of providing a choice-theoretical explanation of the relationship between consumption and the interest rate which Keynes postulated. It is then posed as an individual decision problem for which the appropriate framework, in Patinkin's term, is that of an "individual experiment." The question is simply under what conditions a lowering of the rate of interest which an individual faces will have a positive wealth effect and a corresponding tendency to increase his current consumption. This will be the subject of our discussion in section IV:3. Next, Keynes postulated that this wealth-saving relation was relevant to the determination of *aggregate* consumption. On the second level, therefore, the question is whether the conditions implying an inverse relation between wealth and the interest rate in the individual case can be applicable to the "representative transactor," i.e., to the system as a whole. This has been disputed. In part this question must be considered in the context of a "market experiment." This we will do in section IV:4. On the individual experiment level, the interest rate (or, in Keynes' short run, "the general level of asset prices") is simply an independent variable. In considering the question whether a short-run wealth effect in

---

the emphasis on the main innovation of that work, namely the Multiplier, tends to obscure it, but it is still the case that the income-constrained process will not come into play unless (or until) the market (long) rate fails to reach the "natural" level at which *ex ante* aggregate money demand would be of the same magnitude as in the previous period. Cf. *General Theory*, pp. 242 ff.

the aggregate is a meaningful possibility, we unavoidably have to deal with questions that pertain to the determination of the interest rate itself. Consequently, it is necessary to enter the controversial area of "the" Theory of Capital and Interest.

Keynes, however, did not provide a clear statement of the microtheoretical foundations of his wealth-saving relation, and the sum total of his many scattered remarks on this and other related topics amounts only to a very loose sketch of his ideas on capital theory. As long as one deals only with the functioning of spot markets in the way of Chapter II above, it is a relatively easy task to provide a price-theoretical interpretation of Keynes' expressed views, for it can be presumed that his various *obiter dicta* were either based on, or directed against, the body of atemporal value theory commonly accepted at the time. There is no such presumption with regard to the appropriate frame of reference to guide one's interpretation of his capital theoretic ideas. No generally accepted theory of capital and interest existed in the thirties. One does not have to read far in Keynes' works, moreover, to find evidence of his eclectic attitude towards the conflicting theories in the field. The *General Theory* echoes propositions variously associated with Cassel, Fisher, Hayek, Knight, and Wicksell.

In the future sections of this chapter we will try to piece together a coherent interpretation of Keynes' views. The present section attempts to provide the needed background for this venture. Three areas of the literature will concern us: (a) the modern theories of the consumption function, (b) the capital theories current in Keynes' time, and (c) the modern so-called "metastatic" models, i.e., the generalizations of the atemporal general equilibrium model to deal with the problem of optimal intertemporal allocation.

The post-Keynesian theories of the consumption function
Keynes' "windfall effect" is our point of departure for the examination of his ideas on capital theory. In trying to interpret the microtheoretical foundation of this effect, the first impulse is naturally to turn to the modern theories of the consumption function, since what these theories all have in common is the en-

deavor to improve on the naive consumption-income relation by systematically taking "the influence of wealth on behavior" into account. But this literature proves to be of little help on either the individual or the market experiment level of the problem.

On the individual experiment level, the contributors to this literature all make use of the choice-theoretical paradigm to dissect the consumption-income relation and to arrive at a post-mortem diagnosis of its fatal weakness. These diagnoses differ in the emphasis put on the various aspects in which Keynes' First Psychological Law may be shown to be unsatisfactory from a choice-theoretical standpoint. The diagnosis will suggest the treatment, and these differences are reflected in the various improved hypotheses which this research has produced.

In developing hypotheses superior to the naive consumption-income relation, the various contributors have elaborated on the choice-theoretical foundations of the macrohypotheses in varying degree. Modigliani, Brumberg, and Ando, as well as Friedman, pay more attention to the price-theoretical underpinnings than does Spiro, for example.[2] Modigliani, Brumberg, and Ando are perhaps the most systematic in this regard. Their work contains the more thorough attempt to derive the aggregate consumption function, step by step, from the individual behavior assumptions characteristic of the "Life Cycle" hypothesis.[3] Modigliani *et al.* have concentrated on the implications of explicitly introducing an intertemporal *preference function* for households with specific qualitative properties, while Friedman has concentrated on the formulation of the relevant intertemporal *budget-constraint.* With respect to the choice-theoretical development of the empirical hypothesis, Spiro's work is the least ambitious of those mentioned. The *a priori* foundation on which he builds consists mainly in the application of the basic convention of stock-flow analysis: " . . . savings are the result of a discrepancy between

2. Cf. A. Ando and F. Modigliani, "The 'Life Cycle' Hypothesis of Saving," *American Economic Review,* March 1963. This article provides references to the earlier papers on the Life Cycle hypothesis. M. Friedman, *A Theory of the Consumption Function,* Princeton, 1957; A. Spiro, "Wealth and the Consumption Function," *Journal of Political Economy,* Aug. 1962.

3. With respect to the price-theoretical interpretation of Friedman's hypothesis, however, his *Price Theory,* Chicago, 1962, Chapter 13, is in many respects more helpful than his book on the consumption function.

the actual and the desired stock of wealth; when there is no discrepancy, savings equal zero."[4]

Despite the fact that the various hypotheses have been arrived at by quite different routes of *a priori* reasoning, it has proved very difficult to discriminate between them empirically. Consequently, the "right" theoretical interpretation of the body of econometric findings is left in doubt, except for the evidence presented by all investigators that the use of broader conceptions of "wealth" yield much better results in the prediction of consumption (or, for that matter, money demand) than the use of simply current income. The reason for these difficulties is that the development of the various approaches into hypotheses operational in terms of obtainable data, force the authors to use a number of simplifying assumptions, mathematical manipulations, and "proxy" variables, etc. The final product of this process is a regression equation stating current consumption as a function of a number of variables for which data (of varying quality) exist. The end results for different contributors will be difficult to judge between partly because the existing data dictate that unobservables are translated into pretty much the same observables, partly because the three crucial variables—income, wealth, and the interest rate—are interdependent.[5]

The upshot of all this is twofold. On the one hand, the transformations which must be undertaken in order to put a theoretical hypothesis into operational form are such that the relationship between the final empirical hypothesis and a "pure" choice-theoretical model, such as Fisher's, will be quite tenuous.[6] On

---

4. A. Spiro, *op. cit.*, p. 339. The application is also somewhat mechanical—the reader is apt to be puzzled by several formulations which seem to pose some strange "chicken-or-egg" problems. Cf., e.g., the conclusions: "The analysis of this paper has shown that both economic theory and the available evidence are consistent with a model in which (a) the desired wealth/consumption ratio has remained constant so that (b) *all savings has in fact arisen from an increase of income* that has raised the desired wealth yielding this ratio and hence (c) *if income should cease rising, saving would decline to zero.*" *Op. cit.*, p. 348, italics added.

5. Cf. H. G. Johnson, "Monetary Theory and Policy," *op. cit.*, pp. 349-51, 356.

6. Cf. I. Fisher, *The Theory of Interest*, New York, 1930. Though the approaches of Modigliani and Friedman soon diverge, both start out by juxtaposing the basic Fisher model of individual consumption planning against Keynes' First Psychological Law.

the other hand, the necessity of going through these transformations also tends to remove the incentive for elaborating on the pure theory. The objective of this research has been to improve on the predictive performance of the early formulations of the consumption function. Thus, Friedman appropriately insists that the "permanent income hypothesis" be judged solely on the predictive power of the regression equation that he arrives at and apart from the pure choice-theoretical arguments that initially suggested the approach.

One does not, therefore, find much discussion of the theoretical problems relevant to Keynes' wealth-saving relation in this literature. Relatively little attention is devoted to the interest rate in the consumption-function literature, perhaps because of a general conviction that it in any case plays a very subordinate role. The *ceteris paribus* conditions relevant to our problem—that endowed resources and perceived productive transformation possibilities be held "constant"—are seldom isolated and the substitution and wealth effects of interest rate movements are not disentangled.

On the "market experiment" level of our problem, the modern consumption-function literature is even less helpful. The objective is to predict aggregate consumption. Choice-theoretical reasoning is used (to a varying extent) to suggest the form of the consumption function for an individual household. At this stage of the argument, the interest rate is an independent variable. In this research, it is still treated as an independent variable when, through aggregation, etc., the regression equation is obtained. The identification problem involved has received little attention, and it is not clear what kind of relation between the interest rate and consumption the various hypotheses predict—whether the propensity to consume will be high when the interest rate is low (because of the interest-elasticity of individual consumption), or, whether the interest rate will be high when the propensity to consume is high (because, *ceteris paribus,* a reduction in the aggregate propensity to save will drive asset prices down).[7]

---

7. Disregard for this identification problem may, of course, be based on the presumption that the relationship between consumption and interest is so weak

There is in fact nowhere to go in the econometric macroliterature "to find out about" developments in interest theory. There has arisen a professional division of labor in this research which largely parallels the equation structure of the standard income-expenditure model: consumption function, investment function, money-demand function, and so on. The volume of empirical work on each of these has become so large that they have evolved into virtually distinct specialties, into distinct subfields of macroeconomics. In each of these areas, the trend in recent years has been towards the increasing use of capital-theoretic concepts in the construction of improved hypotheses and a corresponding tendency to try out various new stock variables as arguments in the equations designed to predict the core variables of the standard system. But, although in all of these fields economists have come increasingly to utilize "wealth," "permanent income," the value of net worth, and interest rates, the Theory of Capital and Interest in the traditional sense does not fall within the province of any of these specialties. Whether interest rates are introduced explicitly or remain implicit in asset price indices, they are almost always treated everywhere as independent and nowhere as dependent variables. The results of this body of research have demonstrated the importance of taking "the influence of capital on behavior" systematically into account. But it seems very doubtful that an integrated theory of the income and capital accounts can be achieved if work continues indefinitely in all these subareas separately and simultaneously on the notion that the interest rate and asset prices are determined "somewhere else in the system." From a value-theoretical standpoint, a fruitful development of "capital theory" independent of the theory of interest seems a contradiction in terms. This study seeks to absolve Keynes from a variety of sins for which he has been

---

that it hardly matters. But once the existence of the problem is recognized, one cannot turn around and use a low partial correlation coefficient to "prove" that the presumption is, indeed, warranted. Compare the discussion of the interest-elasticity of investment in III:3.

The time-series utilized often cover many decades over which a large number of government programs and policies affecting private "thrift attitudes" have been adopted.

blamed. But he does seem to have cast a lasting spell of confusion over the subject of interest theory.

Remarks on the state of capital theory in Keynes' time   The problems around which theoretical interest and debate revolved in the decades antecedent to the Keynesian Revolution fell into two areas—Capital and Interest, and Monetary Dynamics. This combination immediately evokes the name of Wicksell. Wicksell's life work proceeded from a diagnosis of the "state of economics" in his time, namely that these were two of the three major problems left in an unsatisfactory state by the great Neoclassical system-builders Walras, Menger, Jevons, and Marshall.[8] The theory of capital and interest was the subject of a great debate in the early thirties involving the most famous theorists of that time—Fisher, Hayek, Kaldor, and Knight, as well as several lesser names. The issues were not resolved. Keynes' *General Theory* had the effect of cutting the debate short. The capital-theoretic controversies were buried under the avalanche of pro-, anti-, and (soon enough) post-Keynesian writings, and the issues were to remain in abeyance for some twenty years. The explanation for this incubation of the problems of capital and interest cannot rest simply on the content of the *General Theory*. In retrospect, it appears that one must also adduce a state of widespread exasperation with a debate at the same time so technically difficult and so inconclusive as a major reason for the fact that Keynes' work was made the excuse for dismissing the problem.

Keynes subjected what he regarded as received doctrine to a vigorous attack. His main point was that "Classical" interest theory generally dealt with a barter system and ignored the store-of-value role of money. This point was generally accepted. At the same time, however, Keynes did not achieve a satisfactory statement of his own theory of interest that could be substituted for the doctrines he had sought to demolish. The critiques of Robertson, Somers, *et al.* soon made it clear that Keynes had over-

---

8. To Wicksell the third problem was "the population question," which will not concern us here.

stated the role of liquidity preference in interest determination. But this criticism did not put new life into the earlier debate on capital and interest. It failed to do so largely because the reformulation of the "Keynesian system" provided by Hansen and others was widely accepted as a successful "integration" of Keynesian and Classical interest theory.[9]

Keynes' Liquidity Preference conception, or some alternative version of the basic idea, is a necessary element of any macrodynamic theory which attributes the instability of income and employment primarily to shifts in entrepreneurial expectations with regard to the return to investment. It is therefore a very important contribution. But it must be understood that the Liquidity Preference theory is *not*, and cannot be, a complete theory of the determination of the level of interest rates. It deals merely with the determination of the *movement* of "the" interest rate from some historically given level which will occur when the system as a whole is exposed to some specified disturbance. It is a theory of the dynamics of interest movements—of short-run fluctuations in the rate. It does not explain the average level around which these short-run fluctuations take place. It would be a gross exaggeration to say that Keynes had no more of a theory of the rate of interest "in the longer run" than he had a theory of the level of money wage rates. Nonetheless, there is a modicum of truth in such an allegation: in Keynes' model we

---

9. Cf. Chapter I:2 above. The "IS-LM formulation" of the matter replaced the Classical economists' "Thrift" and "Productivity"—the exogenous data of the problem—with the endogenous flow rates of saving and investment, and made no reference to the stock concepts of "wealth" and "capital." In addition, saving and investment were regarded as affecting the interest rate only *indirectly*, through their influence on income and the demand for money. *Directly*, the interest rate was treated as determined by portfolio-*composition* preferences of ultimate wealthholders in conjunction with the stock supplies of "bonds" and money. In discussing the behavioral underpinnings of this theory, the income-expenditure theorists thus dealt with the choice of alternative ways of holding a "given" net worth. In the older theories of value, on the other hand, the discussion of the behavior of ultimate wealth-holders focused on the consumption-accumulation decision, on the choice between alternative consumption time-paths. (But many of the earlier capital theorists never arrived at discussing the consumption-accumulation decision—Wicksell being only the most prominent of the ones who got hung up on the productivity side of the problem.)

inherit some money wage level of which we know nothing except that, for certain given disturbances, it will "crumble" at some fairly slow rate. What the liquidity preference apparatus can tell us is also the *reaction* of the interest rate to a specified disturbance of the initial "short-run equilibrium."

It may seem curious that the income-expenditure theory has been able to go along for this extended period of time on such a sketchy and incomplete theory of interest. But for anyone committed to the one-commodity macroframework, the urge to venture into the murky muddles of the pre-Keynesian literature on capital and interest is not likely to be compelling.

To the pre-Keynesian guardians of the Neoclassical heritage, the situation looked quite different. Walras, Marshall, *et al.* had left a by-and-large satisfactory solution to the problem of the determination of prices for "final" outputs and factor services and of the allocation of resource flows under the (arbitrary) condition of "fixed" resource endowments. The achievement was incomplete in one obvious respect: the determination of the prices of the stocks of productive resources from which flow the factor services of the static general equilibrium model. This was *the* problem of capital and interest[10]—the major lacuna which must be filled before the capstone could be put on the grand structure of value theory on which all major theorists since Adam Smith had labored.

This problem simply does not arise in the one-commodity macromodels. Such models presume from the outset that consumer goods and capital goods (and, presumably, the services of capital goods) can be measured in the same units. This basic unit of quantity is at the same time the unit measure of "real value." Thus, where the older capital theorists perceived two difficult problems—that of defining the "quantity of capital" and that of devising a theory of the determination of the "value of capital"—the income-expenditure theorist sees no problem at all. The "real value" of physical wealth simply is what it is and there

---

10. The problem of determining the value of resource stocks also embraces the problems of optimal saving and accumulation of such stocks.

is no need to analyze it.[11] There remains a rate of interest in the model, but when it is not associated with the value of "capital," the theory of interest determination loses most of its intrinsic interest.

Up to this point, we have sided with the value theorists in bewailing the often-tenuous links between macroeconomics and general value theory based on the paradigm of choice theory. As Tobin puts it:

Twenty-five years after Hicks's eloquent call for a marginal revolution in monetary theory our students still detect that their mastery of the presumed fundamental, theoretical apparatus of economics is put to very little test in their studies of monetary economics and aggregative models. As Hicks complained, anything seems to go in a subject where propositions do not have to be grounded in someone's optimizing behavior . . .

But as long as we are juxtaposing value theory and macrotheory in this way, the shoe should also be put on the other foot:

From the other side of the chasm, the student of monetary phenomena can complain that pure economic theory has never delivered the tools to build a structure of Hicks's brilliant design.[12]

This point is even more applicable in our present context. The call for a marginal revolution in consumption-function theory is

---

11. Possibly, the tone of Mrs. Robinson's comment may be found deplorably lacking in "scientific detachment," but she has a point (*Economic Philosophy, op. cit.*, p. 68): "Just as the problem of giving operational meaning to *utility* used to be avoided by putting it into a diagram, so the problem of giving meaning to the quantity of 'capital' is evaded by putting it into algebra. K is capital, ΔK is investment. Then what is K? Why, capital of course. It must mean something, so let us go on with the analysis, and do not bother about these officious prigs who ask us to say what it means."

12. J. Tobin, "Money, Capital, and Other Stores of Value," *op. cit.*, p. 26. Tobin's further comments will be found pertinent to our discussion later on: "The utility maximizing individual and the profit maximizing firm know everything relevant about the present and future and about the consequences of their decisions. They buy and sell, borrow and lend, save and consume, work and play, live and let live, in a frictionless world; information, transactions, and decisions are costless."

anything but "A Suggestion for Simplifying the Theory of Saving."

The most immediate and, at the same time, most important reason for this disturbing state of affairs is quite forcefully brought home by Friedman. In explaining why he did not find it worthwhile to attempt to derive his operational hypothesis from the stated choice-theoretical considerations in a more "rigorous" manner, he notes that the paradigm of traditional choice theory loses a good deal of its power when the existence of uncertainty about the future is explicitly taken into account: "The sharp dichotomy between tastes and opportunities that is the central attraction of indifference analysis under certainty is shattered." [13] This is a most devastating point, which we will sidestep in the next section by simply not mentioning uncertainty, but which must be brought up again later.

But this is far from being the only reason why a synthesis of traditional value theory and modern macroeconomics cannot be promoted by hounding the empirically oriented macroeconomists with complaints concerning the use they make, or fail to make, of value theory. Even if the uncertainty problem could somehow be put aside, a macroeconomist concerned with the problems of capital and interest discussed above would not necessarily know where to turn. A number of difficult issues in "pure" capital theory remain to be settled. The debate on capital and interest in the early thirties may again be recalled. In this debate several partial models were espoused, each dealing with different aspects of "capital," each providing a distinct approach to the problem of interest determination.[14]

The most uncomfortable fact about this famous debate, as with the many others which preceded it, is that the hot controversies in which it abounded did not concern alternative solutions to defined problems. It is not only that the discussions failed to produce a generally accepted theory of capital and interest. They failed to produce a generally acceptable paradigm

---

13. *A Theory of the Consumption Function, op. cit.*, p. 15.
14. Cf., e.g., R. M. Solow, *Capital Theory and the Rate of Return*, Amsterdam, 1963, pp. 11–16, 25.

within which agreement on the definition of the unresolved issues could be reached. The choice of paradigm, in fact, was what the controversy was all about. The field of capital and interest was in what Professor Kuhn has termed the "pre-paradigm state"—a state from which it cannot be said to have fully emerged even in the sixties.[15]

The Marginalist Revolution in the latter part of the nineteenth century established a paradigm for the field of statics. The fields of capital and interest, however, remained on a more "primitive" level of discourse. The establishment of a generally accepted paradigm means, among other things, that the phenomena to be explained and, equally important, those phenomena which it is permissible to ignore, are specified. It also means that the general method—the conceptual apparatus—to be employed in seeking to explain these phenomena is agreed upon. In static (*timeless*) value theory, these conditions have existed since the so-called Marginalist Revolution.[16] There have existed a set of informal professional rules, which determine the tools routinely to be employed in attacking a specific price-theoretical problem. Similarly there are rules which determine what aspects of a social problem (and what phenomena) the member of the profession may without objection ignore and leave to political scien-

---

15. Kuhn's concept may be illustrated by quoting what he says about pre-Newtonian optics: "Being able to take no common body of belief for granted, each writer on physical optics felt forced to build his field anew from its foundations. In doing so, his choice of supporting observation and experiment was relatively free, for there was no standard set of methods or of phenomena that every optical writer felt forced to employ and explain. Under these circumstances, the dialogue of the resulting books was often directed as much to members of other schools as it was to nature. That pattern is not unfamiliar in a number of creative fields today, nor is it incompatible with significant discovery and invention." *Mutatis mutandis*, Kuhn's statement serves admirably as a description of the state of capital theory at least up until recent years. T. S. Kuhn, *The Structure of Scientific Revolutions*, Chicago, 1962, p. 13.

16. It should not be inferred, of course, that paradigms spring into being complete and "correct" in all particulars. What Kuhn calls "Normal Science" is a process (to be distinguished from "Scientific Revolutions") through which (a) the paradigm is employed in the solution of a range of specific problems, and (b) the paradigm is gradually modified and improved upon. The developments in Utility and Demand theory since the time of Walras, Marshall, *et al.* should be looked on as such modifications of the Neoclassical paradigm.

tists, sociologists, or social psychologists to handle. In contrast, the controversies which abound in the area of capital and interest concern, to a very great extent, such issues as the "basic" postulates which "ought to be" adopted as a part of the foundation of a general theory—a stage of development all but completely surmounted in static value theory. It is, moreover, symptomatic of the "pre-paradigm state" of the field that the discussants make battle at one and the same time on *empirical* judgments of "what the world is like" (and, therefore, what is to be explained) and on *methodological* judgments of "what economic theory should be all about"—and that it is almost impossible to separate the two sets of issues.

It is therefore not surprising (though it is significant) that these past controversies were at the same time so heated and so indecisive. Economists are used to sharp and acrimonious debate where the issues are of more or less immediate political concern. But such matters of policy can hardly be said to have been involved, for example, in Böhm-Bawerk's many wrangles—his attacks on practically all predecessors, his debates with J. B. Clark and Fisher, his controversy with Schumpeter,[17] etc. The same sharp tone recurs in Cassel's attacks on Böhm-Bawerk, in the usually considerate Wicksell's retaliatory critique of Cassel, and in the multilateral controversy between Knight, Hayek, Kaldor, and others.[18] In the absence of a paradigm by which differences

---

17. The last-mentioned debate is perhaps the least well known in the United States. (It took place in *Zeitschrift für Volkwirtschaft, Sozialpolitik, und Verwaltung*, 1913.) As these things go, however, it actually makes very entertaining reading, mainly because of the veiled ferociousness of the exchange between the exceedingly patronizing and senior Böhm-Bawerk and the correspondingly impatient Schumpeter—all carried out in accordance with the stately rules of overt conduct governing nineteenth-century academic jousts of this sort. The Imperial Austro-Hungarian flavor is heightened further by the subject of the controversy—would the rate of interest necessarily be zero in the "static state"? —and by the inability of the adversaries through three long Acts of the operetta to come to grips with the issues. (Neither was at all sure what should be meant by "static state.")

18. For references to the most important contributions to the early thirties debate, cf. N. Kaldor, "The Controversy on the Theory of Capital," reprinted with "A Rejoinder to Professor Knight," in his *Essays on Value and Distribution*, London, 1960, pp. 153–205. These papers originally appeared in *Econometrica* in July 1937 and April 1938 respectively.

can be adjudicated, controversies will be heated—by the nature
of his trade, the capital theorist has always had the argument *ad
hominem* at his elbow. By the same token, it is not surprising
that these controversies have shed so little light. The absence of a
shared framework means that the judgments underlying the di-
vergent approaches will be personal and subjective. In addition,
the very complexity of the (variously defined) subject area
means that these judgments will be almost impossible to communicate accurately. When they are nonetheless enunciated, with
more or less profundity, the ensuing debate more often than not
acquires an almost metaphysical character.

It would be a highly interesting task to attempt a census of all
the propositions—relating either to the phenomena which "the"
theory of capital and interest "must" explain or to the postulates
from which it "should" proceed—which have been advanced by
the authors in this field. It would also be a Herculean task (one
thinks, perhaps, primarily of the Augean stables). The following
paraphrases will serve as illustrations: (1) "The pure theory of
capital should assume that 'consumption is the ultimate objective
of all economic activity' and that 'assets are not valued for their
own sake' "; (2) "The theory of capital must make a clear distinction between sources and services, between capital goods and
consumables. A model which assumes the only distinction between instruments of production and consumption to be that of
stock-flow dimensionality has not tackled the 'central' problem";
(3) "The 'proper' definition of 'capital' is that of 'economic resources in general.' Consequently, the 'pure' theory of capital
should be based on the Law of Constant Returns"; (4) "The
greater 'productivity' of roundabout methods of production is the
'basic fact,' the implications of which it is the principal objective
of capital theory to investigate"; (5) "No 'meaningful' theory of
accumulation is possible without taking the distribution of income between social classes into account"; etc. The formulations
of such propositions vary, as does the extent to which a particular author labors to give them more exact meaning. But, underlying the various distinct approaches to capital theory, we do
find, explicitly or implicitly, each author's acceptance or rejection of a number of generalizations of this sweeping (and hard

to interpret) nature. Professor Knight, for example, is eloquent in his rejection of (1), ardent in his argumentation for (3), and scornful in his criticism of (4). The judgment paraphrased in (5) one associates today particularly with Mrs. Robinson and "the later" Kaldor. Similarly, (4) is the hallmark of the Austrian school. The distinction between "sources" and "services" is a basic ingredient in recent work by Friedman and by Lerner,[19] whereas this distinction is at the very most incidental in the modern "metastatic" models of intertemporal pricing and resource allocation. Fisher's basic two-period model takes a tack directly contrary to Knight's on both (1) and (3) . . . , and so on. Thus the elementary models on which, for example, Wicksell, Fisher, and Knight concentrated their capital-theoretic investigations differ profoundly and represent quite distinct approaches to the field—approaches which have in varying degrees been pursued by later contributors.

Knight's "Crusonia plant" model, for example, may be regarded as the prototype of von Neumann growth models—the characteristic feature in each case being that the real rate of interest is determined independently of preferences by the system's given maximum possible rate of expansion. The "Turnpike theorem" literature which has grown rapidly in recent years also belongs in this tradition.[20] Knight's—or von Neumann's—progeny is thus very impressive. Still, it would seem that that of Fisher—or of Ramsey[21]—has been even more numerous and

---

19. M. Friedman, *Price Theory*, Chapter 13; A. P. Lerner, "On Some Recent Developments in Capital Theory," *American Economic Review*, May 1965.

20. We have mentioned the reference to Fisher in Friedman's work on the consumption function. Friedman is principally a "Knightian," however—the "permanent income" wealth concept brings to mind Knight's permanent capital. Cf. also Friedman's insistence on the "inclusive capital" concept (i.e., inclusive of human capital), and the attention paid to the case of constant long-run returns to (inclusive) capital in his *Price Theory, loc. cit.*

21. The modern mathematical economists who have advanced the theory of capital along these two lines are wont to quote von Neumann and Ramsey, rather than Knight and Fisher. The two former were not only the first to give clear mathematical statements of the basic models, their contributions were also (subjectively) quite "original." Cf. F. P. Ramsey, "A Mathematical Theory of Saving," *Economic Journal*, Dec. 1928, and J. von Neumann, "A Model of General Economic Equilibrium," *Review of Economic Studies*, No. 1, 1945–46 (translation of a 1937 article in German.)

influential since the war. The Fisher-Ramsey brand of model has been the one to lend itself most readily to the generalization of the traditional analytical techniques of static general equilibrium theory—albeit in modern high-powered mathematical dress—to intertemporal allocation problems. Models of this type are often referred to as "metastatic." [22] Of all the "old" writers on capital theory, Wicksell may be the one who has most often received "honorable mention" from present-day capital theorists—perhaps because he was clear on the partial nature of his model [23] and made no extravagant claims for it. But the Austrian theory of which Wicksell was an exponent has received far less attention since the war than the approaches linked with Knight and Fisher. The time structure of capital, or turnover of the capital stock, with which the Austrians were so preoccupied, are concepts that have not figured prominently in the modern debate.

We have already discussed at some length the significance Keynes attached to time-to-maturity or durability as a dimension of structure according to which economic goods are differentiated. Since these concepts are similar, though not quite analogous, to the Austrian period of production, the decline of interest in this school of thought is worth commenting on. From the start the Austrian school got bogged down in problems of the measurement of capital, which other approaches to a large extent allow to be circumvented. At a time when index number theory was hardly even in its infancy, the idea may have seemed "natural" that an inquiry into capital theory should start with defining the *quantity* of capital before tackling the determinants of the *"price* of capital." Böhm-Bawerk's dubious doctrine of

---

22. If one reference is to be selected from this large literature, it should be E. Malinvaud, "Capital Accumulation and Efficient Allocation of Resources," *Econometrica*, April 1953. Cf. T. Koopmans, *Three Essays on the State of Economic Science*, New York, 1957, esp. pp. 105–26.

23. Cf., e.g., R. M. Solow, "Notes Toward a Wicksellian Model of Distributive Shares," in Lutz and Hague, eds., *The Theory of Capital*, London, 1961, esp. p. 249: "Wicksell's procedure amounts to taking (the value of the stock of capital in terms of 'commodities') as a parameter and observing how the whole system's equilibrium shifts as [this parameter] is varied." Thus the demand for "real net worth" is not dealt with by Wicksell and the model therefore does not determine the rate of interest. Cf. also J. Hirshleifer, "A Note on the Böhm-Wicksell Theory of Interest," *Review of Economic Studies*, April 1967.

"Original Factors" demanded, however, that the quantity of capital be measured in terms of either labor or wage units (consumption goods). But this concept of the quantity of capital cannot be measured either in terms of inputs or of outputs without bringing in the interest rate—i.e., the "price" the determination of which was to be the second step of Böhm-Bawerk's analysis. As the extent of the measurement difficulties gradually became clearer, the Austrians increasingly had to take resort to "special cases" where the index number problem caused only a minimum of embarrassment—notably the point-input point-output case, as in Wicksell's growing timber and aging wine illustrations.[24] But the result reached for the point-input point-output case, as Hicks points out, "does not generalize in the sort of way in which it might have been expected to generalize." [25] Böhm-Bawerk, who was far from fully realizing the difficulties, also attempted some analysis of the time preference or "abstinence" part of the general equilibrium problem, although he could not put the two together in a satisfactory form. Wicksell did not have the mentality that would allow him, once he had run into the snags of Böhm-Bawerk's period of production concept, blithely to skip them and go on to the next part of the problem, and had very little to say about the preference side.[26]

---

24. Similarly, they found it necessary to impose stationarity as a condition in order to extend the analysis beyond the microanalysis of the point-input point-output case. This convention proved somewhat unfortunate, since it made a convenient target for the argument of J. B. Clark, and later, Knight, according to which the synchronism of inputs and outputs in a stationary state made concepts like the period of production or "waiting" superfluous or even meaningless with reference to such a state. This attack can be countered, but only with reference to a model in which stationarity is determined as part of the over-all equilibrium solution, rather than used as an arbitrarily imposed condition. As pointed out by Solow in the passage quoted above, however, Wicksell's system was incomplete and Wicksell used stationarity as an auxiliary assumption to make it determinate. Consequently, the wrangle between Knight and the Austrians has proven an exasperating drawn-out affair.

25. J. R. Hicks, *Value and Capital*, op. cit., p. 222.

26. Cf. K. Wicksell, *Lectures on Political Economy*, English edn., London, 1934, Vol. I, pp. 207 ff. In my judgment—as the reader will in any case perceive below—Wicksell underestimated the significance of what Cassel had to contribute

It is interesting to note that, though these concepts do not play any important role in the capital-theoretical models which have received most attention in recent years, the conviction remains in many quarters that the characteristic Austrian *duration problems* must—somehow—be essential to the theory of capital and interest.[27] Again and again, however, the typical Austrian path has been retraced by later theorists only to wind up in the same *cul-de-sac*—thus belying, it seems, Wicksell's hunch that "as long as the *time-element* is given its appropriate place, the starting-point for the construction of a theory of interest can be chosen almost at random." [28]

Of the three approaches to capital theory mentioned above, the two that we have associated with the names of Knight and Wicksell deal principally with the production side of the problem. There is a difference, however, because while Knight's model does determine the rate of interest independently of preferences, Wicksell's theory, despite his preoccupation with the production possibilities aspects, cannot properly be labeled a

---

to the analysis of the preference side of the interest-determination problem. As pointed out by G. Arvidsson in his "On the Reasons for A Rate of Interest," *International Economic Papers*, No. 6, 1956 (originally in *Ekonomisk Tidskrift*, 1953), Wicksell was also too hasty in dismissing Böhm-Bawerk's "First Ground," a matter of some significance, since the second and third "Grounds" left him with only the postulates of myopia and the productivity of increased roundaboutness. Arvidsson's inference that Wicksell's error in this case resulted from his analytical habit of imposing (rather than determining) stationarity seems justified.

27. Cf., e.g., Kuenne, *op. cit.*, p. 287: "In spite of one's knowledge that the Austrian period of investment is nonoperational, it is difficult to escape the feeling that the 'vision' of economic process contained in the Austrians' productivity analysis comes closer to capturing the essence of capital than the analyses of the pure productivity school." Cf. Hicks, *op. cit.*, esp. pp. 192–93, 222–24. Also, E. Malinvaud, "Interest Rates in the Allocation of Resources," in F. H. Hahn and F. P. R. Brechling, eds., *The Theory of Interest Rates*, London, 1965, where Malinvaud points out that for many purposes of qualitative comparative static analysis, the scalar measure of the *total* capital stock, with which the Austrians struggled in vain, will not be needed: (p. 238) "It is not, as a general rule, possible to define the period of production in an unequivocal manner. . . . Nevertheless, it might still be possible to find a sensible criterion which would enable us to say whether, in passing from one [production] programme to another neighbouring programme, the productive process is extended or shortened."

28. *Op. cit.*, p. 236. This is Wicksell's review of Cassel's *Theory of Social Economy*, included as an appendix in the English edn. of the *Lectures*.

"productivity theory of interest." It is simply an incomplete theory of interest, an unfinished structure. Of the three, it is Fisher who alone achieved a complete model in which both the preference and the productivity part of the choice-theoretical paradigm were integrated. To the extent, therefore, that modern consumption-function theorists have drawn at all upon the older capital-theoretical literature, it is quite natural that they should turn to Fisher. The other two approaches have almost nothing to offer on the problem of the *rate* of saving. It should be emphasized also that the three approaches mentioned are not intended as a general classification of theories in this area—the works of Cassel and Chase, for examle, simply do not fit into any of the three.[29]

Metastatics   The modern "metastatic" models are a blend of Walras and Fisher. Walras' static *n*-good system is extended to cover the intertemporal transformation and substitution possibilities elaborated by Fisher. Quantities of physically identical commodities available at different dates are treated as distinct goods so that with T such dates considered we have an nT-dimensional system. Once formulated in this way the model is handled just as the standard general equilibrium system. In general, *certainty* is assumed. Given some initial resource-constraint, the physical transformation possibilities inherent in current and future (foreseen) technology, and some preference function(s),[30] an equilibrium solution is specified in the usual manner. The usual continuity and convexity properties of transformation and preference functions are assumed; imposition of the appropriate "tangency" (optimality) conditions on producers and consumers yield the needed supply and demand functions, and the condition that supply equal demand for all goods in all periods then determines the solution of the system. The solution

29. G. Cassel, *The Nature and Necessity of Interest*, New York, 1957 (originally published in 1903). S. B. Chase, Jr., *Asset Prices in Economic Analysis*, Berkeley, 1963.

30. The preference functions will be defined over an mT-dimensional commodity space ($m < n$), where m is the number of consumer goods, presumably including leisure.

defines the *efficient time-path*. The duality-property characteristic of optimum states of the static model is found here also—to
the optimal output and consumption vectors corresponds a given
price vector which, under the given assumptions of certainty,
etc., if once established, would induce the transactors in a system where production and consumption decisions are decentralized to reproduce the appropriate quantity vectors.

It is quite clear that these highly formalized models could
hardly be further removed from the problems with which "Keynesian" macroeconomics has to wrestle. The principal contributors can hardly be accused of having made claims for its usefulness in this area, however. Malinvaud's frank appraisal is, for
example, that: " . . . one cannot but be impressed by the inad-
equacy of these models as describing the actual working of our
economies." [31] The metastatic model is nonetheless a remarkable
achievement. It belongs, it is true, to Welfare Theory rather than
to "positive theory"—that is, this literature explores how the
intertemporal allocation problem would be solved efficiently under highly idealized conditions, not how it is actually handled.
This is no ground for complaints since it is the lack of such an
ideal solution as a point of reference that accounts for much of
the confusion in the early capital-theoretical debate. One thing
in particular has been demonstrated, namely that the shortcuts
to the problem typically attempted by earlier writers were, in
fact, detours. The early capital theorists also sought the solution
of an "idealized" case—assuming, e.g., perfect foresight—as a
first approximation. A problem with the innumerable margins of
choice, characteristic of the nT-dimensional metastatic model,
could not very well be tackled with the sort of numerical illustration to which Böhm-Bawerk, for example, was limited. Various "simplifications" were therefore sought from the start, involving attempts to define aggregates such as "capital," "income,"
and "saving," and correspondingly, an index for "the" interest
rate. To determine the solution of the system, some single "universal" equilibrium condition was envisaged such as making "the
marginal productivity of capital equal to the interest rate."

31. Malinvaud, *op. cit.*, p. 215.

These "simplifications," as we have seen in the Austrian case, led to nothing but trouble.

The modern mathematical economists who have worked on the metastatic model have, in contrast, solved the more "general" problem first, showing that this can be done if one does not get embroiled with aggregates of the kind indicated. The model, moreover, yields a price vector with a very large number of relative, intertemporal prices, none of which has any special claim to being identified as "the" interest rate. In general, no normalization will be possible which would yield a single real rate of interest relating any two periods. Similarly, the term structure of own rates for a single physical commodity may be quite irregular—the own-rate need not be smoothly increasing (or decreasing) as a function of the time-interval, nor in particular need it be a constant rate independent of this interval. Thus, the model does not depend upon the definition of aggregates and indices of this sort, but it does provide a framework within which it is possible, if desired, to consider in a systematic manner whether such indices can be defined in a precise and meaningful manner.

This type of model thus avoids the aggregation problems involved in such all-embracing stock concepts as "capital." It also avoids dealing explicitly with stock variables altogether. The alternatives of choice, from which "the system selects" in one fell swoop the optimal time-path, are formulated completely in terms of flow variables—time-profiles of input, output, and consumption streams. The chosen production programme does indeed imply the existence of stocks, technologically required for its execution. In principle, it should be possible to find out what the "structure of capital" will have to be at any date along the time-path. Similarly, one could in principle find out the value, in terms of some specified numeraire, of the stocks in existence at any such date. But the data thus obtained on stock quantities and asset values are a pure by-product of the model. The stock variables play no part in the analysis of behavior. As in Fisher's elemental two-period model, the quantities of capital goods are subsumed under the intertemporal productive transformation possibilities set which is defined in terms of "final goods." It is therefore difficult to say what lessons can be drawn from these models in trying to solve the problem that would seem to have priority in "Keynesian" macroeconomics today, namely the construction of an integrated stock-flow theory of the income and capital accounts.

Three postulates that are commonly, if not always, used in the construction of metastatic models will concern us: (a) the postulate, mentioned above, that *consumption is the ultimate purpose of economic activity,*" (b) the postulate that the relevant preference function is to be specified over consumption of all consumer goods at all dates up to an *infinitely distant horizon,* and (c) the *certainty* postulate.

(a) The postulate that consumption is the end-all of all economic activity is mentioned with surprising frequency in the recent capital-theoretic discussion as casually as if it were a self-evident proposition. Perhaps one can see this as a symptom of an accepted paradigm at last emerging in this field—of increasing professional consensus on what is "good" or "bad" economics in dealing with the problems of capital and interest. But it is not always clear what the postulate is supposed to mean; it can be interpreted as a simple tautology defining "consumption" as embracing everything that is asserted to affect "utility."

The postulate does become meaningful if interpreted as restrictive and, more specifically, (1) as asserting that there is a definite subset of goods and services such that only the members of this set have the property of "possessing utility" and (2) as denying the possibility that there are any significant services belonging to this set which can only be "enjoyed" through the actual possession of assets or through command over asset values and thus cannot be purchased or sold apart from their sources. If the postulate is interpreted in this way, its increasingly general acceptance means that a rich and diverse school of thought on the subject of saving is being read out of economics. We tend to forget how many great names in our field have maintained that the postulate must be denied, i.e., have argued that saving is *not* solely motivated by the desire to command "consumption goods" in the future.

Pareto, for example, viewed saving "as a product largely of instinctive or compulsive factors." [32] Veblen and Weber explained saving behavior largely in terms of social acculturation, Veblen stressing the prestige and power that goes with wealth in a capitalistic system, Weber the Protestant Ethic. Cassel put great weight on the Veblenian motives as well as the desire for future consumption. Knight stressed both "instinctive behavior" and social motives for saving. Pigou postulated that the possession of assets yielded "amenities" which could be enjoyed in no other way. Knight's colleague at Chicago, Professor Simons, held a position closely akin to Knight's:

Now the observable fact is that many people save instead of consuming, just as some smoke pipes instead of cigarettes; that it seems reasonable to hold that the choices are of the same order in the two cases. . . . There is raised here a most difficult problem of social psychology and culture history; and it hardly becomes the economist to make a pretense of competence by resort to verbal legerdemain. To assume that all economic behavior is motivated by desire for consumption goods, present and future, is to introduce a teleology which is both useless and false . . .[33]

Models of accumulation that would take motives such as these into account *in addition* to intertemporal consumption planning become very complicated and unwieldy. If it is recognized, for example, that command over physical resources gives the social "power" of ordering other people about and that this is an enjoyment for which certain individuals are willing to forsake consumption goods, then physical assets enter the utility function. This has the consequence of making the expression for the intertemporal budget-constraint quite complicated. If the "amenities" of being wealthy are related to the quantity of consumer goods which could potentially be commanded, relative prices will have to be introduced into the utility function and "the sharp distinction between tastes and opportunities that is the central attrac-

32. Cf. R. E. Kuenne, *The Theory of General Economic Equilibrium*, Princeton, 1963, p. 234.

33. Henry Simons, *Personal Income Taxation*, Chicago, 1938, pp. 94–99. Quoted from Chase, *op. cit.*, pp. 17–18.

tion" of the choice-theoretical paradigm is shattered even without bringing in uncertainty. If "prestige" depends not just on the individual's wealth, but on his wealth relative to that of others, the interdependence of saving decisions will greatly complicate the general equilibrium system . . . etc.

Since choice-theoretical saving models based on *both* "social" motives *and* intertemporal consumption preferences are so unmanageable, the "pure" intertemporal consumption choice approach is the one usually taken. Chase's work represents the other extreme: intertemporal consumption planning is ignored altogether—traders save because they "just like to be wealthy." This may be too extreme to be acceptable as "the" theory of saving and asset prices,[34] but in the absence of useful "compromise models" Chase's model (which appears to be the only one of this type to have been explicitly worked out) is worthwhile as an antidote to the dominant analytical approach.

(b) The "infinite horizon" postulate of the usual metastatic model is subsidiary to the postulate just discussed. The latter involves a means-ends distinction[35]; the rationale for holding stocks must then always lie in *future* "consumption." The "infinite horizon" postulate then becomes, more or less, a mathematical necessity (albeit a behavioral embarrassment). The equilibrium path of the system over a finite interval of time cannot be deduced if terminal stocks are not defined as one of the conditions of the optimization problem. But any specification of such terminal stocks that is not made with reference to anticipated consumption *beyond* the finite horizon must be quite "arbitrary"—an argument which holds for any finite horizon however distant. No cut-off point has anything to recommend it over all others. The way out of this formal dilemma is, then, to define preference functions "from Here to Eternity." The only determinate solution, which is not "arbitrary" in this sense, is that which settles the future of the system 'til Kingdom come. It is

---

34. For some disturbing implications of Chase's "Simple Taste Approach," cf. *op. cit.*, e.g., pp. 50 ff.

35. For a further discussion of the significance of this means-ends dichotomy, cf. the introductory pages to the following section.

this device which makes the stock variables disappear from view. Once we decide to tackle the problems of capital theory by seeking a generalization of Walrasian static general equilibrium analysis, this is where we must end up. The system must be solved for all the future for the same reason that the static Walrasian model must be solved simultaneously for all "markets."

(c) Correspondingly, the certainty assumption of the metastatic theory is the needed extension of the perfect market-information postulate of the static general equilibrium model, which we discussed in some detail in Chapter II. In the metastatic world, in fact, all transactions for all the future are settled on the Eighth Day of Genesis at the latest. What comes after involves nothing but the contracted delivery of goods. No dynamic decision-making is involved. The metastatic theory has, indeed, a disturbingly teleological flavor—as Simons hinted that a fully developed model based on these postulates would have. The term "metastatic" has also been chosen to denote that the system is not truly dynamic. The model represents a "clockwork mechanism"—the term used in cybernetics for "machines" that are not "dynamic systems."

Current research in the area seems in many cases to proceed on the assumption that the most promising route towards the development of a "useful" dynamic theory is to start by accepting the metastatic model as the basic "pure" case, and then to proceed by stages of successive modifications towards a more "realistic" theory. The stages would presumably involve first introducing Knightian risk—the actuarial calculus which Keynes spurned—and, subsequently, Knightian uncertainty. Capital theorists have, however, frequently been wrong in the past in their intuitions of the best research strategy. There is some danger that this may turn out to be the case here as well. A cybernetist would certainly maintain that almost *nothing* can be learned about dynamic systems from the study of "clockworks" and that research based on the presumption that dynamic systems are modified clockworks will have little prospect of success. In Chapter II, we saw that relinquishing the implicit Classical assumption of perfect information leads to systems with a qualitatively different—radically different—dynamic behavior, i.e., to "Keynesian" systems.

IV:3   The Wealth Effect of Interest Rate Movements

Section IV:1 raised the question of the value-theoretical basis of Keynes' wealth effect. This is a problem in the general area of capital and interest. The previous section shows, however, that there is no such thing as "the" theory of capital and interest. There exists, instead, a large, heterogeneous, and difficult literature filled with unresolved controversies pertaining to the central postulates which should be made the basis for "the" pure theory of capital. From this literature a set of postulates must be selected for the analysis of the wealth effect.

Means and ends   Our discussion of the wealth effects of interest rate changes will be based first on the assumption that "consumption is the ultimate purpose of all economic activity." The assumption is to be understood as restrictive, as ruling out certain possible types of behavior. Thus, sociological motives for saving of the kind discussed, for example, by Veblen and Weber are ruled out. The transactors of the system to be considered here do not save for the power, prestige, and influence which command over wealth "yields" in society. Nor do they accumulate wealth in the expectation of rewards in the hereafter (or in the case of Weberian Calvinists, at least to reduce post-mortem liabilities). Nor do they act on the similar motives considered by Knight, Pareto, Pigou, and Chase, i.e., because they "just like to be wealthy."

In the following argument, "consumption" is taken to *exclude* such things as "amenity yields" or "liquidity yields" enjoyed through the holding of assets. It refers to a definite subset of goods, "consumption goods" as distinct from "assets." Thus we deal with an exaggeratedly "Neoclassical" type of value theory, the structure of which is characterized by an hierarchical ordering of three mutually exclusive classes of goods: (1) consumption goods from which "utility" is derived and which are "valued for their own sake"; (2) the services of productive agents, the value of which must be "imputed" from their marginal contribution to the (efficient) production of the first class of goods; (3)

the productive agents themselves, whence the factor services flow, the value of which may also be imputed, once "the" interest rate is known, from the value of services which these stocks render over time.

In Böhm-Bawerk's formulation, the "pure" Theory of Capital and Interest reduces to an "imputation of value" problem set in a framework of this sort. Apart from Böhm-Bawerk and perhaps some of his followers, it is hard to find capital theorists who are unambiguously committed to the above view of "what the world is like." We must note, however, that it becomes difficult, if not impossible, to assign any definite meaning to the proposition that "assets are not wanted for their own sake" if some framework such as this is not presumed.[1] This conception of the capital-theoretic problem is particularly difficult to entertain when dealing with education and the accumulation of human capital. But we will deal with certain problems in the area of capital and interest as they used to be formulated before the recent and dramatic growth of theoretical and empirical interest in investment in human capital. Thus, human capital is treated as a God-given endowment, in which no investment is possible, but which is consumed in the course of the individual's life cycle. The consumption-accumulation decision in the following pages deals only with the accumulation of physical capital.

The ordering of the three classes of goods which characterizes the "imputation" approach to capital theory is based on the notion of a definite hierarchy of means and ends. The set of consumption goods comprises all "ends" of economic activity. All choices are made with these "ultimate ends" in view. Quantities of consumption goods obtained in the present and in future periods are the only arguments entering into utility functions. Assets are accumulated and held solely because they are the "means" through which individuals can command consumption goods in the future. For the closed system as a whole, consump-

---

1. Statements of this sort could, of course, be interpreted just as trite reminders not to get the stock-flow dimensions confused, i.e., that if stock variables are included among the arguments of the utility function they must be interpreted, for example, as proxies for unobservable flows. If this is all that is meant, such statements would appear to be mere mnemotechnic jingles.

tion goods cannot be commanded by direct disposal of assets, but only by the consumption of the factor services they "contain" through their use in the production of consumer goods. On this societal level, therefore, factor services are an "intermediate end" motivating the accumulation of capital. But the "ultimate end" always remains "consumption." Factor services cannot be "consumed" and do not yield "utility"; all services yielded by every type of asset are factor services.

To anyone with a secure, if unpremeditated, belief in this brand of capital theory, Keynes will appear at his eclectic worst in his discussion of the motives for saving. The *General Theory* recognizes *eight* such motives: "Precaution, Foresight, Calculation, Improvement, Independence, Enterprise, Pride, and Avarice" [2] and conveys the impression that, given the time to philosophize on the human condition, Keynes might well have added to the list. Some of these motives are included in recognition of the uncertainty of Man's affairs—a problem which we will ignore for the better part of this section—but it is by no means the case that by assuming perfect information we could reduce his list to the one item: provision for future consumption. Consequently, the following discussion of the wealth effect deals only with one element of Keynes' thought on accumulation and wealth-holding. Some will question whether it deals with the most important element. Mrs. Robinson and Kaldor, who have been the guardians of his less "purely economic" ideas on the subject, could make a persuasive case that it is not. This is an important caveat, but having made it, we proceed with the problem as defined.

The sharp means-ends distinction outlined above is one of the devices economists use in order to effect a clear separation of Economics from the other social science disciplines—and to put the problems of the latter in the *ceteris paribus* dustbin. This separation can be pernicious if its artificiality is not kept in mind.[3] It is, however, largely due to this drastic abstraction of

2. *General Theory*, p. 108.

3. Cf. F. H. Knight, *Risk, Uncertainty, and Profit*, London, 1933, "Preface to the Re-Issue," *passim*. For Knight's opinion on the conventional means-ends distinc-

the "purely economic" from the totality of social interactions that economists have been able to get so far ahead of the other social sciences in theory construction. The clear delineation of what is to be considered the realm of discourse provides the necessary foundation for the construction of a theoretical paradigm which can be shared by the persons active in a given scientific field. Such a shared paradigm is in turn necessary to prevent theoretical conflicts from simmering on interminably—it provides the "rules" according to which decisions can be made on what constitutes the "solution" to a problem.[4]

The paradigm we are concerned with here is that of the "general" theory of value, which has emerged historically on the basis of the twin distinctions between means and ends and between "economic" and "other" types of social interactions. *Ex post*, the second distinction no longer appears fundamental—the choice-theoretical toolbox proves to have its uses, not only in areas traditionally regarded as in the sphere of economics, but also in other areas where one is willing, at least provisionally, to make a reasonably clear distinction between means and ends.[5] In the traditionally economic sphere, the paradigm has proved very useful in dealing with a wide range of problems—a fact which provides an *ex post* justification for the underlying abstractions which *ex ante* could with reason be regarded with a good deal of

---

tion, cf., e.g., p. xiii: "The classical economists fell into two disastrous errors . . . connected with taking food and eating as the type of economic interest . . . " etc.

4. Cf. T. S. Kuhn, *op. cit.*, Chapters II–V.

5. The paradigm does not become completely useless if the hierarchy of means and ends (and, perhaps, intermediate ends which are the means to ultimate ends, etc.) is less than absolutely clear. But the "economy of thought" that its use affords rapidly diminishes as one allows means to be "to some extent ends in themselves." It becomes increasingly more difficult to derive the logical implications of the model and the results of correct deduction are more and more likely to be of the variety "the effects may go this way or that way depending upon circumstances"—where "circumstances" means a long list of "factors." The best illustration of this is exactly the issue in capital theory which bothers us here—intertemporal allocation models become extremely nasty to deal with when we allow saving and asset-holding to be motivated *both* by a desire to make provision for future consumption *and* by "enjoying" the command over assets for its own sake.

apprehension. When a paradigm has proven itself successful in one area, it is always tempting to expand the realm of discourse within which it is applied. One must be wary of yielding to this cosmological temptation. It is certainly not a foregone conclusion that such extensions of a theory will be worthwhile, and it must remain a serious question to what extent this traditional price-theoretical approach can contribute to our understanding of the central substantive problems in the areas of Growth and Development for example. This, then, is our second caveat and of more importance than the first since it pertains not only to the exegetical appropriateness of the following line of argument, but also to its substantive worth.

The question is, however, whether Keynes' wealth effect and his theory of Liquidity Preference has an interpretation consistent with "Classical" price theory. The value-theoretical paradigm will be used in an entirely traditional manner to investigate this question.

The wealth effect in the context of an individual experiment
The paradigm of the theory of individual choice consists of three elements: the criterion function, the initial endowment, and the given transformation possibilities—(a) in exchange, and (b) in production. The specification of all of these must include "future dated" values of price and/or quantity variables. All such expected magnitudes will be treated as single-valued. This certainty-equivalent treatment of expectations means that, for all practical purposes, the discussion of the individual experiment proceeds "as if" the individual trader had access to perfect information.

Four assumptions are pertinent to the individual criterion function: (1) the arguments of the function are the quantities consumed at different dates, "consumption" as of a given date being treated as one homogeneous good; (2) the function is homogeneous of some degree in these arguments, so that indifference surfaces may be represented as radial projections (from the origin) of each other; (3) the function is assumed to exhibit strict intertemporal complementarity, the planned consumption time-paths always showing the same ratio between quantities to be consumed in any two given periods; (4) the consumption plan has a finite horizon.[6]

The initial endowment consists of a stock of income-streams, specified as a given sequence of gross receipts. The total gross income-stream with which the individual is at any time endowed may be considered as a sequence of expected money values with each item deflated by the corresponding expected money price of the consumer goods aggregate. For the most part, we will consider these "earnings" as accruing simply in the form of consumer goods bundles.

With respect to the transformation possibilities the argument will proceed in two stages, dealing first with the case of exchange transformations only and thereafter introducing productive transformation opportunities.

The meaning of "wealth"   The analysis will utilize the tools developed by Hicks for the analysis of the effects of changes in the rate of interest, particularly the concepts of the Average Periods of receipt streams and preferred consumption streams which he has used to dissect the income effects of such events.[7] Keynes' wealth effect will be interpreted as a Hicksian income effect of this type. Thus, we define a "wealth effect" (e.g., on current consumption) as an adjustment of individual (consump-

---

6. Both (2) and (3) are assumed merely for analytical convenience and are not necessary for the argument to follow. The effects of relaxing (3) will be considered briefly. (3) is used here because Keynes assumed (we have argued) that the intertemporal substitution effects of changes in "the rate of time-discount" are negligible. (1) and (4) are quite central to the discussion.

With regard to (4) we may just as well go along with the simplifying assumption of "zero planned bequests" made by Modigliani and Brumberg. This sets an arbitrary terminal stock value to the individual household's temporal allocation plan, but this fact is really of little or no consequence to the argument. It also avoids the issue of defining the variable to represent "bequests" in the criterion function—i.e., the question of whether the "real bequest unit" should be a "unit of real net worth" (as defined previously) or a "unit permanent income-stream" or some intermediate alternative such as a "unit twenty-year annuity." There is, as we know, no *a priori* "rationality" postulate that will settle questions of this sort.

7. J. R. Hicks, *Value and Capital*, esp. Chapter XIV, Appendix B (where the tools are first developed), and Chapters XVII and XVIII.

tion) plans following from any event which makes the individuals involved "better off." The question is whether a reduction in the long rate of interest is such an event, as Keynes postulated.

Before proceeding to this question we must digress, however, for this definition of "wealth" is different from at least two other wealth concepts frequently encountered in the macroliterature. There is, in fact, no firmly established usage at present, despite the increasing emphasis in recent years on the influence of "wealth" on every conceivable type of economic behavior.

In the context of the standard one-commodity model, the term usually refers to the quantity of physical capital plus "real" financial claims held by an individual. Usually, only net outside claims are considered on the aggregate level, so that the first component is by far the predominant one. The quantity of physical capital is, of course, a short-run constant and "wealth," thus measured, does not vary with changes in intertemporal rates of transformation. This wealth concept is irrelevant to our discussion of Keynes' two-commodity model.

Alternatively, an individual's "wealth" is often defined as the *present value* of his income prospects. This variable is not just a constant in the short run. We will refer to it not as "wealth," but as "net worth." Keynes, of course, postulated that a rise in the value of net worth in terms of present consumer goods (a rise in "real net worth") would have a positive wealth effect on current consumption. The reason for nonetheless insisting upon this distinction is that it would be to prejudge the issue of this section to identify the present value of endowments with "wealth." *A priori*, an increase in this present value magnitude, which is due solely to a fall in the rate of interest, may have either a positive *or* a negative Hicksian "income effect."

The variable used to measure "wealth" should be some index of the individual's command over goods *over time*.[8] The general concept of "wealth" is measurable only as a vector—the preferred vector of "amounts consumed" of all those vectors that the intertemporal budget-constraint allows. In the present case, our

---

8. Here "consumption goods" only, given the means-ends distinction set forth above.

restrictive assumption of strict intertemporal complementarity allows us to substitute a simple scalar for this vector. But the present value measure of "wealth" would be uniquely related to this scalar variable only in special cases.

Generally speaking, the present value measure represents an index number with an extreme choice of weights—unity for potential consumption in the present period, zero for all others. The same objection applies to any other measure which indicates only the maximum potential consumption in some arbitrarily selected period. "Wealth" in such cases is measured by the intersection of the intertemporal budget-constraint with one particular axis of the relevant commodity space (and without regard to the "angle" of the intersection). The axes represent consumption in different periods and the present value definition measures "wealth" along the current consumption axis. If additional assumptions about the time-distribution of individual endowments and preferred consumption time-profiles are not introduced, there is no basis for presuming that the intersection of the budget-constraint with one such axis has any particular claim to our attention over that accorded any other such intersection. With this type of wealth definition, a fall in the "rate of time-discount," for example, will always raise the value of an endowment of prospective streams discounted into the present, but it will also lower its value capitalized into some period sufficiently far into the future.[9] Without additional assumptions, there is

---

9. In the present context, "Productivity and Thrift" are "impounded in the *ceteris paribus*." The desirability of distinguishing clearly between "net worth" and "wealth" is perhaps nonetheless best illustrated by considering changes in "productivity," particularly in the context of the Knight-von Neumann class of models. Knight's "Crusonia plant" is both the only good consumed and the only type of "capital" in his model. It is assumed to grow in volume at a fixed compound rate. The rate of interest must be equal to the maximum potential rate of growth—a pure productivity theory of interest. Consequently, the present value of an individual's resources is equal to the physical volume of Crusonia plants that he possesses. If, then, at some moment there occurred some instantaneous technological change which raised the exponential growth rate from, say, 3 to 5 percent, this would leave his "wealth" unchanged if measured in present value terms. Yet, as long as he had not planned to consume his entire endowment in the current instant (which one might perhaps argue to be impossible on dimensional grounds), he is definitely "better off" since his command over resources in general over time has increased.

nothing to tell us whether the wealth effect of the event is positive or negative.

Given the endowment of prospective receipt streams, a fall in the interest rate will raise the present value of net worth. The question is whether this would ordinarily make people in general better off or not. In both the *Treatise* and the *General Theory*, it is assumed that the representative transactor "feels richer" at higher capital values—i.e., that net worth changes, endowment constant, are typically associated with wealth effects of the same sign. The proposition that changes in the present value of an individual's endowment are associated with "wealth effects" which are typically—or for the *representative transactor*—of the same sign, is a statement pertaining to the system *as a whole*. Thus it implies some assumptions about the system which are stronger than the mere postulates of convexity of individual preferences, etc. Implicitly, a more specific view of "what the world is like" is asserted. It is the price-theoretical rationale for this aggregative wealth effect with which we must ultimately come to grips.

Keynes versus the Keynesians on the relationship between saving and the rate of interest   In Keynes' theory, the intertemporal substitution effect of interest rate movements is not entirely absent, but it is assumed to be very weak. But his wealth effect is assumed to affect current consumption *in the same direction* as the substitution effect. There remains, therefore, a significant inverse relationship between consumption and interest. This dependence of the propensity to save out of current income on (long) rates of interest was one analytical reason, albeit not the main one, for Keynes' life-long belief in the efficacy of low rates in stimulating economic activity. Hence, it is also one of the reasons why the *General Theory* devotes so much space to the exposition of the factors which in Keynes' view cause long rates to be inflexible in the short run and thus tend to "neutralize" the

---

Note also that this is the type of model in which the above two approaches to the measurement of "wealth"—the present physical stock of capital and the present real value of capital—would be interchangeable.

interest rate mechanism which would otherwise contribute to the stabilization of aggregate demand and employment.

There is hardly a sharper contrast to be found between Keynes and the income-expenditure theorists than that between the two positions on this matter. Keynes' belief in the *potentially* powerful effect of interest rate movements made him regard the question of why the rate of interest would not "equalize saving and investment" as one of the crucial questions of macrodynamic theory. He was preoccupied with providing as effective an answer as possible to it. The early "Keynesians," on the other hand, tended to regard the answer as completely self-evident, so self-evident that it destroyed the original question by depriving it of analytical meaning. But the answer which they presumed was quite different from that given by Keynes. In the early income-expenditure literature, the emphasis is not on the short-run inflexibility of the interest rate. Apart from the Liquidity Trap case, the interest rate may vary "all over" but, it was argued, interest effects on both saving and investment are at best of only secondary magnitude, at least "within the normal range of interest fluctuations." In this view, the problem was not that the interest rate does not move, it was that such movements have no appreciable effects on the system's "real" variables.[10]

---

10. The proposition that the interest-elasticities of both saving and investment are insignificant within the "normal range" of interest variations puts a heavy burden on the interest-elasticity of the liquidity preference function. It is far from obvious that the presumption of a relatively restricted range of variation is compatible with the assumption of highly interest-inelastic investment and saving functions. Why should there be such a narrow "normal range" for a price which hardly affects people's "real" behavior?

Note that, by and large, the burden falls on the "transactions demand" for money. The assumption of inelastic expectations underlying Keynes' speculative demand are hard to rationalize in the context of a system where interest does not affect savings and investment—people's "real behavior" as the income-expenditure literature would have it. From a purely algebraic standpoint, there is nothing to prevent us from incorporating both a "speculative demand" for money and interest-inelastic "real" demand functions, but on a "deeper" economic level the two elements of the model seem incompatible. Fortunately, the ill-understood process which generates economic doctrines, seems at least to have the reassuring property of ultimately bringing such "deeper incompatibilities" to the surface. In recent years this has also happened with this issue: Keynes' speculative demand has fallen into disfavor and the arguments advanced against it are, indeed, based

The interest effect on the saving-propensity was frequently dismissed in such an offhand, impressionistic manner by the early "Keynesians" that it is difficult to ascertain the underlying combination of assumptions with respect to wealth and substitution effects on which the postulate of interest-inelasticity rests. One particular argument appeared with such frequency, however, that it ought to be considered here. Professor Klein has recently sought to revive it:

We disposed of the interest effect on savings or consumption early in the Keynesian debate by means of a logical argument showing that the effect could go either way . . . depending upon the rational choice of savings plans by individuals.[11]

The logical argument to which Klein refers suggests that the wealth effects of reductions in long rate may be predominantly negative and that consequently wealth effects and substitution effects tend systematically to offset one another. This, then, runs directly counter to Keynes' belief that both effects would generally work in the same direction.

It had long been recognized that for *some* transactors the wealth effect of a reduction in interest will be negative, tending to reduce present consumption. Marshall's exposition of this possibility, for example, was often cited by the early Keynesians. Marshall's case assumed an individual who had set himself a fixed wealth-accumulation target defined in terms of an income-stream of a given sum per year *indefinitely*.[12] For the following discussion it is important to note that the standard illustration of a negative wealth effect from a lowering of the interest rate presumes that *saving constitutes a demand for "permanent" income-*

---

on the presumption that there are no strong underlying "real factors" to justify strong beliefs about some "normal" level of long rate. This criticism of Keynes will be discussed in Chapter V. At this point, we only note that it necessarily raises the question why past observed movements of long rate do, after all, seem to have been confined within a relatively narrow "normal range."

11. L. R. Klein, "Comment" (on H. G. Johnson, "The General Theory . . . ," *op. cit.*), *American Economic Review*, May 1961, p. 25.

12. Cf. A. Marshall, *Principles of Economics*, 8th (variorum) edn., London, 1961, p. 235.

streams. Implicitly, the individual's criterion function extends in time to infinity. As pointed out above, "wealth" will be positively, rather than inversely, related to the interest rate if the transactor is more interested in the command over consumption goods which his endowment makes possible at points in time which lie on the average far into the future, than he is in the "real value" of the endowment streams discounted into a period close to the present. This would be the case, for example, for households in the early part of their life cycle that have yet to transform their inevitably wasting human assets into non-human capital on which to live after retirement when the original endowment of human capital has been "run down." These people, then, will be made "poorer" by a lower interest rate—having planned to purchase (direct or indirect) claims on capital goods, they become worse off when the prices of sources of future income rise relative to current and near-future consumption.

Having taken note of this possibility, it was still Marshall's considered judgment that present consumption and the rate of interest were likely to be inversely related *in the aggregate,* although he deemed the relation to be rather weak. In the early Keynesian literature, the discussion seems seldom to have gone beyond mentioning the point that for some transactors the wealth effect will go in the direction opposite to the substitution effect. The position indicated by Klein appears not to have been uncommon, i.e., the theorist "ought to" dismiss the interest effect on aggregate saving on grounds of "equal ignorance": some transactors will curtail, others will increase their current consumption when faced with a decline in the rate of interest. This type of argument makes it difficult to infer what significance was attributed to the wealth effect on the individual experiment level. Usually, it was explicitly assumed that the intertemporal substitution effect was weak enough to be ignored—a position which we have argued was shared by Keynes. With the exception of Hicks, no one seems to have attempted a systematic appraisal of the wealth effects. In order to justify the postulate of a zero total interest effect, the assumption should be that individual wealth effects approximately cancel in the aggregate—with enough of a net wealth effect to offset also the weak substitution effect. Since the matter was seldom considered in any detail, however, this is only an *ex post* rationalization of the position. It does not allow us to infer whether individual wealth effects were regarded as potentially quite sizable, though offsetting, or as negligible and offsetting.

The Hicksian analysis Hicks is to be credited for providing the analytical tools necessary to give some precision to the notions of "nearer" versus "farther" future on which the wealth effect issue is now seen to hinge. His method of dealing with the "income effects" of interest changes starts from the problem of calculating income—"wealth" in our teminology—which "consists in finding some sort of *standard* stream of values whose present capitalized value equals the present value of the stream of receipts which is actually in prospect."[13] Events which make it possible for the transactor "to raise the standard stream, still keeping it to its old standard shape, but raising it throughout," have positive income effects. In the general case, the substitution effects of interest changes will mean that the "shape" of the standard stream varies with interest rates. In the special case of a "fixed coefficient" utility function, which we are assuming here, references to the "standard shape" of the planned consumption path are perfectly unambiguous. It permits us to choose a certain (arbitrary) amount of period 1 consumption as defining the "unit standard stream." The corresponding quantities of goods consumed in other periods are then also defined by the assumption of "fixed proportions." Any event, then, which permits command over a greater number of such unit streams is said to have a positive wealth effect, since this unit provides a scalar measure of which the individual's "utility" must be a monotonic function.

The question then is whether, with *given* prospective receipt streams, the representative transactor will be able to command a greater or smaller number of standard streams after a decline in the interest rate.

13. *Value and Capital*, p. 184. Quotations below for which no references are given are taken from pp. 184–88, comprising Appendix B of Hicks' Chapter XIV.

We deal first with the case in which the individual can only transform his endowed streams through exchange and has no productive transformation opportunities. He is considered to hold title to a number of specific capital goods which, together with his sales of labor services, are going to yield a given series of gross receipts. At some initial interest rate this stream has a certain capital value, x. If the rate of interest falls, the capital value of the *same* sequence of gross receipts increases to x'. The time-profile of receipts is assumed "frozen" in the sense that, once the new interest rate is established, it is not possible for the trader to rearrange the stream over time in such a manner that its present value would exceed x'.[14] He is, however, able to re-distribute receipts over time, e.g., by selling off capital goods or by reinvesting gross earnings at the going rate of interest, etc., in any of a large number of ways which preserve the capital value x'. The assumptions are contrived, but allow us the convenience of starting with the simple case in which the individual's original endowment can be represented as a single point in the commodity space. Changes in the rate of interest merely rotate the intertemporal budget-constraint around this fixed point.

Whether a reduction in interest has a positive, a negative, or a zero wealth effect now becomes, as Hicks has shown, a matter of the relation between the *Average Periods* of the receipt stream and the standard stream (consumption plan). A reduction in interest raises the present value of any receipt stream which includes some future receipt, but also raises the "present cost" of a given standard stream. The individual is better off only if he can purchase a greater number of unit standard streams than before at the new interest rate. Thus, if the cost of a unit standard stream increases by a smaller proportion than the capital value of receipts, the wealth effect is positive. The direction of the wealth effect consequently depends upon the relative interest- (or discount factor) elasticities of the two streams. The measure

---

14. I.e., while capital assets are durable, their services are regarded as "perishable." Use and age depreciation functions for both human and non-human assets are assumed to be such that opportunities for profitably "stretching out" the consumption of existing assets over a longer time-period are nonexistent.

of this discount factor elasticity has, as Hicks demonstrates, the dimension of time—its arithmetical value represents the "average period" of the stream.

In comparisons between streams which have constant flow rates over time ("rectangular time-profiles"), the longer stream will have the greater interest-elasticity of present value. Hicks' concept of the Average Period is the generalization of this well-known fact to streams with more complicated time-profiles. The streams considered here consist of time-sequences of money values with each item deflated by some anticipated money price of consumer goods corresponding to the date of each item. The Average Period is a weighted average of the temporal distances by which the various payments (or receipts) in a given stream are deferred from the present. The weight applicable, for example, to a payment due two years hence would be the present value of that single payment divided by the present value of the entire stream (or "the share of the two-year deferred payment in the total present value of the stream"). Thus, the Average Period is the "*average length of time for which the various payments are deferred from the present, when the times of deferment are weighted by the discounted values of the payments.*" The arithmetical expression for this index of the Average Period is identical with the expression for the discount factor elasticity of present value of the stream. It should be noted that the discount factors do not cancel out in the calculation of the index—the average period even of a "frozen" stream will vary (positively) with the discount factor (and thus inversely with the interest rate). This lesson was drummed in in the course of the debate over the Austrian theory of capital—"average roundaboutness" or the "average period of production" cannot be uniquely defined independently of the interest rate.

The Hicksian tools are most simply illustrated in the context of the Fisherian two-period case. In the figure, the initial budget-constraint is indicated by the line $x_1'-x_2'$; planned consumption is (c_1', c_2') at a utility level $U = U'$. The indifference curve reflects our assumption of perfect complementarity of period 1 and period 2 consumption. Two alternative "frozen" receipt

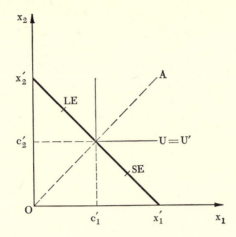

streams are indicated by LE and SE, the former having a longer, the latter a shorter average period than the standard stream. Individual "wealth," given the homogeneity of the utility function, is measured from the origin along O–A. With the present complementarity assumption, we have chosen to measure it, instead, in number of "unit standard streams"—O–c_1—along the x_1-axis.

A decline in the interest rate is represented by a counter-clockwise rotation of the budget line around the relevant endowment point. Hence, if LE represents the endowment stream, a reduction in interest will have a positive wealth effect. It enables the individual to move to a higher indifference level along O–A. If the budget-constraint were rotated around SE, however, it would intersect O–A nearer to the origin and the wealth effect would be negative. Note that if we have two individuals one of whom had the endowment LE and the other SE, and if both had the same homogeneous utility function (i.e., "in the absence of distribution effects"), wealth effects of changes in the interest rate would cancel—"aggregate" current consumption demand would be unaffected. The effects on aggregate demand will be exactly zero when the average period of the two endowments together equals that of the "representative" standard stream. In the system comprising just these two individuals, the interest rate would thus be in neutral equilibrium. This curious result is due simply to the fact that, in addition to assuming offsetting wealth effects, we have contrived to assume away intertemporal substitution effects *both* on the production plan *and* on the consumption plan.

Substitution effects on the production plan will enter in as soon as we consider "unfreezing" the endowment streams. If, then, individual Y is instead endowed with a production possibilities set smoothly concave to the origin, etc., and tangent to the initial budget-constraint at LE, the decline in the interest rate will induce him to choose a new production plan along this locus. The new production plan would yield a gross receipt stream with a longer average period than LE (whether the comparison is made at the old or at the new interest rate). Allowing a degree of intertemporal substitution in the production plan in this manner will, as a consequence, amplify the positive wealth effect experienced by this individual. If the other individual, Z, similarly has production possibilities tangent to the old budget line at SE, his adjustment of the production plan will moderate the negative wealth effect of the change in interest. In this case, therefore, the wealth effects would not cancel, although for the two traders together, the average period of the sum of their receipt streams was initially equal to that of their summed consumption plans. Even without allowing any substitution effects at all on consumption plans, the decline in the rate of interest will here cause a rise in the "aggregate demand" for current consumption.

The following points should be emphasized: The average period of a "frozen" stream is lengthened by a decline in the interest rate. This effect is purely arithmetic—it results from the changes in the weights used to compute the average period index. A decline in interest will also tend to lengthen the production plan and thus the average period of the proceeds of the plan, whether computed at the old or the new rate. This is a behavioral effect—a matter of the adjustments which producers are induced to undertake by the change in the rate. Note that on the present assumption of strict complementarity of utility functions, the consequences of such substitutions on the production side, viewed from the consumption side, appear purely as wealth effects. If substitution effects on the consumption plan are "allowed," the effect of a fall in interest will be to shorten the average period of such plans. Thus, changes in the rate of interest tend to shift the average periods of production plans (receipt streams) and consumption plans (standard streams) in opposite directions. The implication of this is that it is not enough to consider the initial relation between the two average periods; if, for example, a consumer's receipt and standard streams initially have the same average period and not both have "frozen" time-profiles, a decline in the interest rate will still have a positive wealth effect.

The point just made could be utilized to provide a possible rationalization of the assumption that *reductions* in the rate of interest from an "historically customary" level will not have much of an effect on consumption "within a normal range." If the average period of the representative trader's standard stream exceeds that of his prospective receipt stream at the "customary" interest level, a fall in the interest rate would make him "poorer" and imply a negative wealth effect on his demand for current consumption. Independent households belonging to the younger age-groups would be affected in this manner. The effect on older households, with the head near retirement, would normally be in the opposite direction. The substitution effects would go in the direction of increased current consumption for all households. The net interest effect on aggregate current consumption might then be weak or nonexistent within a certain range. The lower the interest rate falls, however, the more general the incidence of positive wealth effects and the stronger such effects, reinforcing the substitution effect. It might then be argued that the point at which the total interest effect on aggregate consumption becomes strongly positive constitutes the lower bound to the "normal range" of interest variation. Such a lower bound should exist—Cassel's argument for the "Necessity of Interest" is an argument for its being at a positive level of long rates—since the increased demands for both investment and consumption which come into play at low rates, somewhere must run into the aggregative current resource constraint. But to my knowledge, the proposition that the consumption-income relation is interest-inelastic has not been advanced on grounds such as these. The above argument, while it implies such inelasticity for a certain range of interest, is also based on premises which affirm the position that, *in general,* interest rates significantly affect economic behavior.

The Hicksian concepts of "crescendo" and "diminuendo" should also be mentioned. If the total length of a transactor's receipt and standard streams are equal, the average period of one can only exceed that of the other if the former stream is rising through time relative to the latter.[15] The uses to which Hicks puts his analytical apparatus are by and large restricted to cases in which differences between the average periods of income and outgo are due to diminuendos or crescendos in this manner.[16] This restricted use of the apparatus implies that receipt streams and standard streams are assumed to be of the same over-all length. Hicks also concentrates on cases involving two *perpetual* streams, a procedure which must be linked to the income concept of *Value and Capital.*

Wealth effects and the "representative" transactor   Keynes postulated that his "windfall effect" would apply to the system as a whole. This Second Psychological Law states an assumed property of the *aggregate* consumption function. This means that individuals who experience a positive wealth effect from a fall in the rate of interest outweigh in the aggregate those who are made worse off by such an event. Is it possible to make a logically consistent case for the possibility of positive aggregative wealth effects? If such a case cannot be made, the attempt to find a rationalization of Keynes' windfall effect by the present route of inquiry must be abandoned.

---

15. It is always assumed that the present values of the two streams being compared are held equal. This is simply the assumption that traders always choose points *on* their perceived intertemporal budget-constraints.

16. Compare also his use of these tools in *Capital and Growth,* Oxford, 1965, esp. Chapters XX–XXII. The Average Period analysis has been one of the least widely recognized contributions of *Value and Capital,* and has seen little if any use even by Hicks himself in the more than two decades which separates these two works. Hicks' discussion of these concepts in *Value and Capital* tended, in fact, to minimize their usefulness. In the present context it is therefore of some interest that he has so recently chosen to resurrect this part of his early work in dealing with problems which are today much in fashion.

As with so many of the disputed issues in capital theory, the difficulty is that it cannot be settled within a framework which relies only on those very general assumptions which usually prove sufficient in "pure" statics. If one refuses to assume anything more than that the relevant production opportunities and utility functions have the usual convexity properties, no conclusions can be drawn with regard to the sign of the wealth effect. Some more restrictive assumptions are required. It is difficult to ascertain what Keynes' position was in this respect, for while he did assert that reductions in interest have a positive wealth effect, nowhere did he, as far as I know, attempt systematically to derive this proposition from explicitly stated capital-theoretic premises.[17] Any interpretation of his views must therefore be somewhat speculative—a fact which must be openly stated, although it is unlikely to be overlooked. Cassel's analysis of the issue is far more thorough than Keynes'. It seems warranted to rely to some extent on Cassel; we know that Keynes had studied Cassel's work and was influenced by it.

On the interpretation pursued so far, Keynes' aggregative wealth effect requires the assumption that, for a predominant group of households, the average period of anticipated receipts exceeds that of planned consumption. Put simplistically, the representative wealth-owner in the Cassel-Keynes world carries his wealth in the form of income-streams that are on the average "longer" than his preferred consumption stream (or standard stream). This seems a rather staggering generalization to make. Nonetheless, this must be the general import of the "stronger assumptions" which we have to look for. By inquiring into the possible rationale for such a position we will be able to obtain a more concrete picture of the kind of world that Keynes envisioned. In terms of standard "Keynesian" doctrine, it is a quite unfamiliar world.

---

17. Beginning in Chapter III, we have steadily emphasized Keynes' preoccupation with time-to-maturity or durability as the most significant "property" of assets. The importance Keynes attached to this dimension of asset structure is obviously significant here. Cf. also *General Theory*, Chapter 16, "Sundry Observations on the Nature of Capital." Keynes' discussion is too sketchy to be made the basis for a systematic interpretation of his (implicit) theory of capital. But it is significant that whereas Keynes (like Cassel) was quite critical of Böhm-Bawerk, his "observations" on capital stress the roundaboutness notion of the Austrians.

The considerations relevant to the issue fall neatly into two categories. We consider first those pertaining to the length of the standard stream, and second, those pertaining to the anticipated receipt stream.

The duration of the standard stream Having introduced Hicks' analysis it is incumbent on us to note that Hicks himself took the position that wealth effects ought to cancel in the aggregate and could therefore be ignored in the analysis of the system as a whole.[18] His position is, without doubt, the primary reason why his analysis of average periods has not excited much interest. The grounds on which he based this position are not entirely clear. The point which is relevant here concerns the income concept of *Value and Capital.*

Hicks' concept of income—of which he considered three slightly different varieties—was that of *net income.* It was by the same token a *permanent income* concept. The use of net income as the relevant measure of the individual's command over resources implies a utility function defined up to an infinitely distant horizon. If the standard streams are to be considered as net, permanent streams—meaning that consumption plans extend to Kingdom come—then positive wealth effects from reductions in interest cannot be attributed to receipt streams simply being "longer" than standard streams. An immortal trader does not benefit from a rise in the price of the consols he holds. The simplest, most straightforward rationalization of Keynes' wealth effect would then be ruled out.

This predilection for a net, permanent income concept one encounters almost everywhere in the capital-theoretic literature. The reason for this is of course that a gross receipts measure of income will not do—a transactor's gross receipts over an arbitrary period do not represent "what he can afford to spend" on

---

18. One should note that he proceeds in much the same manner to dismiss the income effects of price changes when going from the micro- to the macro-analysis of his static general equilibrium model. The assumption, then, is that someone's gain must be somebody else's loss and that while "redistributive effects" on the market excess demands for various commodities may result, these effects are entirely unpredictable and should therefore be ignored. We have previously noted a similar argument made by Hicks in yet another place, namely with regard to the effects of trading at "false prices." Cf. Chapter II:1.

consumption. From the obvious fact that gross receipts are generally an inappropriate indicator of the relevant budget-constraint, it does not follow, however, that net income is the right measure.[19] Net income is the rate of consumption that could be maintained *ad infinitum*. In a world where transactors do not live and consume forever, there is no obvious rationale for this income concept, and the value-theoretical concept of "wealth effect" should not be tied to it. It is unfortunate that the habit of using this variable has become so entrenched in the field.

Turning to Keynes, there is then one point on which we are on fairly firm ground as things go in this field: Man is mortal and Woman only slightly less so. There will be an end to the consumption stream. Inconvenient as this proposition is in meta-static welfare theory, it has its place here. One does not necessarily have to go along with the convenient assumption that households plan no bequests at all. Cassel reveals his firm faith in the strength of the "inverse" wealth effect of interest rate movements (once relatively low rates are reached) by permitting his representative transactor to take an interest in the consumption needs of his children. But he had to draw the line somewhere—his theory demanded that the consumption streams demanded by savers not be of infinite length:

More cannot reasonably be asked for. It would simply be absurd to consider and try to provide for the needs of our grandchildren or for still more distant generations.[20]

---

19. In general, it is not rational for a transactor to act as if he could afford to consume all of his gross receipts in any given short period, but *lifetime gross receipts* are surely a different matter. Rational behavior does not require that individuals leave all of their "capital" behind them untouched.

20. *The Nature and Necessity of Interest*, p. 142. Cassel concentrated on an objective which is of rather peripheral interest here—namely, that of proving the virtual impossibility of a zero level of long rate. To show that a zero rate would be incompatible with current resource-constraints, he hammered away at two points: (a) that substitution effects on production plans become very powerful at low long rates (the discussion here resembles the more recent exposition of Bailey in many particulars), and (b) that, even apart from readjustments on the production side, the inverse wealth effect will also be of great magnitude at low rates.

On the consumption-plan side of the problem, the net income concept must thus be rejected. Here the principal tenet of the Cassel-Keynes position must be that the utility function is truncated and the standard stream definitely of finite length.

The duration of receipt streams We will consider in turn (a) receipts from human capital, and (b) receipts from non-human capital.

(a) The time-profile of receipts from human capital constitutes the principal point *against* the simple interpretation of Keynes' idea sketched here. If people save principally for their own retirement, it must be recognized that at least one component of the total prospective receipt stream—labor earnings—has a total length shorter than the standard stream. The point has already been made that for the younger, economically active age-groups—whose wealth will consist principally of human capital—the wealth effect will be positively rather than inversely related to the interest rate. Also, for the system as a whole, the human capital of *active* generations will be a substantial component of the wealth of the nation.[21]

Cassel's early fame rested in fact to a substantial extent on his elegant demonstration of the latter point.

In arguing the Necessity of Interest, Cassel did not stack the cards in his own favor. He admitted, for example, various reasons why assets were likely to be demanded "for their own sake"—an admission which clearly introduces factors tending to raise the prices of income-streams and thus to lower rates of return relative to the levels implied by models in which such behavior is ruled out. He considers, for example (p. 143): ". . . a great capitalist . . . [who] simply accumulates for the sake of accumulation. There may be various reasons for doing this; pure vanity and a desire to rise in the estimate of what is called 'society'; the demand of the born leader of industry to direct, to govern, and to have a field of work large enough for his activity and energy . . ." etc. Compare A. C. Pigou, "Economic Progress in a Stable Environment," *Economica*, Aug. 1947, section III, in which Pigou builds his famous exposition of "Keynes' Day of Judgment" on postulates of this type.

21. We regard the aggregate consumption function as the sum of the consumption-expenditure functions of heads of households (or their wives). The "impoverishment" of dependent children due to a fall in long rates is thus irrelevant to the present issue. In view of the popularity of metastatic models with infinite time-horizons, it is perhaps still more urgent to point out that unborn generations have little opportunity to make their preferences effective in present spot and forward markets.

(b) With regard to the average period of the streams accruing to non-human capital, the first thing to consider is Keynes' insistence on the long-term nature of the "representative" physical assets. The great bulk of material wealth consists of very long-lived investments:

Much the greater part—probably not less than three-quarters—of the Fixed Capital of the modern world consists of Land, Buildings, Roads and Railways.[22]

And again:

Almost the whole [sic] of the fixed capital of the world is represented by buildings, transport and public utilities.[23]

Thus, the types of physical assets on which Keynes laid the greatest emphasis are classes of capital goods with an economic lifetime exceeding that of the average household. The effects of a reduction in the long rate are not due merely to the increased value in terms of standard streams of the inherited stock of capital. As has already been pointed out, the lengthening of production plans made profitable by the reduction in interest will also have wealth effects on consumption plans. Though not yet realized, such investment prospects are a relevant part of the transformation possibilities of the "representative" transactor. The budget-constraint is not just rotated around the point representing the endowment of streams inherited from the past—substitution possibilities in the production plan allow it to be shifted outward as well. Cassel relies heavily on this point.

As a counterweight to this argument, it may then be pointed out that the system's material wealth includes more than long-lived capital goods and rent sources. There are also inventories and equipment to consider—the "representative" types of capital goods of income-expenditure theory. On the one hand, then, we would have the long streams—land, structures, and the rest—and, on the other, prospective labor earnings, inventories, and equipment. We may perhaps assume that the former group of

22. *Treatise*, Vol. II, p. 98.
23. *Op. cit.*, p. 364.

assets has, on the average, a lower, and the latter a higher, rate of turnover than the average rate of turnover of the "stock of households." Since people do not generally work all of their adult lives, for example, it is clear that the labor force turns over faster than the population of households. And the turnover of stocks of consumer durables and producer durables are of course a good deal higher still. The average period of the gross streams from such assets is much shorter than that of the representative standard stream. If the issue were to be decided on the basis of such necessarily rough and very impressionistic comparisons of the duration structure of the system's human and material capital with the desired standard stream of its "representative household," Keynes' position on the wealth effect of interest movements would seem dubious to say the least.

Such a comparison is, however, not appropriate. One should recall Keynes' habit of referring to physical capital as "securities" when dealing with its store of value function. Much of the system's short-lived productive capital equipment is in fact financed through *equities*. The average period of the gross streams in prospect, given the collection of physical resources held by a corporation on a given date, may well be shorter than the average period of the representative standard stream. But this is not the relevant consideration if the claims on this part of the system's real resources, which households as the ultimate owners hold, are in the form of equity shares, which are to be regarded as perpetuities.[24]

It is, in fact, tempting to borrow an argument from Knight at this point. We cannot accept Knight's theory in its entirety. Two of the three positions for which Knight is so well known are quite alien to the whole structure of the present argument: (a)

---

24. Inventories are usually not equity-financed, but financed by loans through financial intermediaries. But it should be pointed out that the preferred portfolios of households will be "shorter" than the average period of consumption plans, i.e., shorter than would have been demanded under conditions of perfect information and foresight. In particular, households will demand a substantial volume of deposits of all kinds—Keynes' "money."

The present discussion is of relevance also to the Liquidity Preference theory of financial intermediation and the term structure of interest. This subject, however, is postponed to section IV:5.

his pure productivity theory of interest, and (b) his rejection of all turnover or roundaboutness concepts as irrelevant.[25] A third Knightian argument—which he used to bolster the rejection of "Austrian" approaches—is of interest, however. This is his thesis that receipt streams from non-human capital are to be regarded as *permanent net streams*. Knight "views saving . . . as being by its nature . . . the purchase of an infinite number of periodic income installments." [26]

Knight's position is that for analytical purposes all material capital should be regarded as permanent. Productive efficiency demands that, once an investment project has been undertaken and has proved justified in terms of the relative prices determined ultimately by the parameters of the general equilibrium system, the capital stock thus created must be maintained indefinitely:

It cannot now escape observation that "capital" is an integrated, organic conception, and the notion that the investment in a particular instrument comes back periodically in the form of product, giving the owner freedom to choose whether he will re-invest or not, is largely a fiction and a delusion.[27]

This states a condition for equilibrium to be maintained, for example, in a stationary system where technology, population (and its age structure), and labor force remain constant over time although individuals are born, age, and die. It does not imply that these mortal individuals are not free to *dissave* in the latter part of the life cycle. But it will generally be inefficient for individual dissaving to take the form of disinvestment:

---

25. These are connected. In Knight's Crusonia plant model, which is his chosen vehicle for the presentation of a pure productivity theory of interest, the average period of production is analytically quite meaningless. In this model, the prospective receipt streams are perpetual and have a compound rate crescendo equal to the rate of interest. Infinite streams have a finite average period only if their crescendo falls short of the interest rate.

26. R. E. Kuenne, *The Theory of General Economic Equilibrium*, p. 234. For Kuenne's resumé of Knight's position, cf. esp. pp. 233–37, 242–46.

27. F. H. Knight, "Professor Hayek and the Theory of Investment," *Economic Journal*, March 1935, p. 83. Quoted in Kuenne, *op. cit.*, p. 244. The same references are appropriate also in the second passage quoted.

[Consider] . . . the case of a part of a machine. The part cannot be liquidated without liquidating the machine. And the machine as a unit is in a similar sense a "part" of an integrated productive organization which is not bounded by the scope of "plant" or firm, but extends outward indefinitely to indeterminate limits.

A *priori*, we could conceive of a stationary system—to take the simplest illustration—in which households in the later part of their life cycles do not replace the capital goods they own as these wear out, but consume the gross receipts, while younger generations accumulate wealth by continuously undertaking the corresponding gross investments. If such an arrangement was viable, the duration structure of the physical capital stock would be directly relevant to the appraisal of Keynes' wealth effect.

Knight, however, denies this conception—it is "largely a delusion." In general, liquidation through consumption of gross income means that a loss is incurred. Most short-lived physical assets are, in fact, complementary in production to Keynes' Fixed Capital.[28] In this view, therefore, optimal inventories and short-lived machinery, etc., are to be regarded as "perpetual" capital just as much as the rent-earning "eternal soil" of the Classics. On this view, then, we would have, on the one hand, finite standard streams and, on the other, net, permanent receipt streams.

Summary   The discussion could be continued in this vein almost interminably. But little would be gained and nothing proved by doing so. The Hicksian apparatus can serve as a heuristic device in the interpretation of Keynes' conception—up to a point. But that point has been reached (and, some would say, passed). The nature of the problem is such that one's credulity is soon strained by the neglect of uncertainty. Yet, when uncertainty is brought in, "the sharp dichotomy between tastes and opportunities . . . is shattered," as Friedman put it; our neat and simple definition of "wealth" and "wealth effect" dissolves.

---

28. The social requirement of continuity in operations, which is the essence of Knight's argument, is thus one reason why individual shares in corporations take the form of "perpetuities." The corporate form is superior to the partnership, among other things, because of the cost involved in "disentangling" the equity of a retired or deceased partner.

"The act of saving," Keynes postulated, "implies . . . a desire for wealth as such, that is for the potentiality of consuming an unspecified article at an unspecified time." [29] Savers, consequently, do not evaluate their "wealth" simply in terms of the number of fixed standard stream units that they command, but are also concerned with the "liquidity" of their portfolios. The relevant utility functions are less simple than we have assumed. To satisfy their demand for "liquidity," Keynesian transactors will demand portfolios with an average period shorter than that of their life cycle consumption plans, i.e., portfolios containing assets that will have to be reinvested, perhaps several times, before they are cashed in to finance consumption in the dissaving stage of the life cycle.

Once we relinquish the treatment of saving as simply the purchase of bundles of differently dated amounts of "the" consumer good and admit a demand for "wealth as such," the door is open to Keynes' "Precaution, Foresight, Calculation, Improvement, Independence, Enterprise, Pride, and Avarice" and sundry other "spirits" of a more or less "animal" description.

Despite all this, however, the exercise has left us with a residue of insight into Keynes' "Vision" that is valid. Schematically, the system that he assumed—as revealed by the wealth effect and, as we shall see in section IV:5, by his theory of finance— can be described as follows. It is a system wherein the social function of production is eternal and the individual households, in comparison, ephemeral. "In the Long Run we are all dead," but production goes on and the capital stock is maintained and handed down from generation to generation. Ownership is divorced from the function of management of productive resources. Households in the early part of their life cycles consume less than the value of services which they contribute. Their resulting claims on the system's resources they accumulate in the form of "shares" in society's ongoing productive concern. Households in later stages of the life cycle consume more than the value of their concurrent productive contribution and are therefore "impoverishing themselves." This dissaving is to a substan-

---

29. *General Theory*, p. 211.

tial extent financed through the sale of income sources. Since the ultimate owners of the system's productive resources do not hold their claims on these resources "to maturity," their welfare depends upon the consumption value at which these assets can be resold. The higher the "real value" of these long-term assets the better off is the owner. A fall in the rate of interest means that this value increases and therefore has a positive wealth effect.

This "view of what the world is like" also implies that in the management of his portfolio, the representative transactor will be vitally concerned with the risk of capital loss and that, on balance, he will try to shed "capital uncertainty" rather than (net) "income uncertainty." This observation is pertinent to the debate which has sprung up around Keynes' theory of "normal backwardation" and the Liquidity Preference hypothesis of the term structure of interest rates. Before we turn to this subject, however, we must consider certain arguments that challenge the possibility of wealth effects and/or their relevance to aggregative analysis.

IV:4   Short-Run Wealth Effects in Aggregative Analysis; Information Failures in the Coordination of Intertemporal Production and Consumption Decisions

In modern "Keynesian" macrotheory, private-sector "wealth" is generally treated as a constant in the short run. The concept of "wealth" employed is usually that of consolidated "real" net worth. In the standard one-commodity models, the consumption good value of the capital stock does not vary with the interest rate or with changes in the marginal efficiency of capital; in addition, it is characteristic of this model that "the" price level is treated as approximately constant in the short run. The wealth-saving relation is therefore regarded as a topic belonging in the realm of long-run theory. The rule in such analysis is that wealth effects arise only through changes in aggregate stock quantities over time, and never through changes in prices in the present.

In general equilibrium theory the situation is similar. Under the conditions of a given technology and given resource endowments, wealth effects are assumed to be zero in the aggregate—with a small proviso: "except for the possibility of net distribution effects." It is recognized, in other words, that the income or wealth effects impinging on individual transaction plans may not cancel *exactly* in the aggregate. But it is also maintained that the impact of such net distribution effects on excess demand conditions in any particular market would be unpredictable even as to sign and that such effects should therefore be disregarded as a matter of principle.

In Neoclassical monetary theory, finally, we find an exception in the real balance effect. This effect has been the object of a tremendous amount of theoretical effort. But even in these models, wealth effects are most prominent by their virtual absence, for the real balance effect stands out in eminent isolation [1] —no other short-run wealth effects due to price changes are recognized. The wealth effect interpretation of the real balance effect has, in fact, also been challenged. Implicitly, it is argued, this interpretation rests on an arbitrarily assymetrical treatment of what is properly a distribution effect.[2] If this modern critique of the real balance effect were accepted we would thus end up with no aggregative wealth effects of any kind in short-run theory.

The appropriate role to be assigned to wealth effects of price changes is a complex problem involving a mixture of purely analytical and methodological issues. It is also in a murky state, for professional convention in macroeconomics strongly favors the use of models of a structure such that the possible relevance of wealth or income effects is a question that will in general not even be raised. According to one school of thought, to which we will come presently, there is no problem—there can be no aggregative wealth effect, only distribution effects. I do not believe it is as simple as that. The issue has not received all the attention it

---

1. Patinkin distinguishes between the real balance effect and a closely analogous "real financial effect" due to the rise in the real value of "outside" non-money claims consequent upon a fall in "the" price level. Readers who insist on the distinction may consider the statement in the text amended to *two* "lonely" wealth effects.

2. Cf. H. G. Johnson, "Monetary Theory . . . ," *op. cit.*, pp. 342–43.

deserves. I do believe that the aggregative wealth effects of changes in relative values is a topic which must be thoroughly investigated if we are to arrive at a clear understanding of the relationship between general price theory and "Keynesian" macroeconomics. If we are to hope for an eventual synthesis of value theory and short-run monetary theory, the uncertainty surrounding this issue—illustrated, for example, by the currently ambiguous status of the real balance effect—must be dispelled. That tall order cannot be filled here, but some of the questions involved need to be discussed.

Although Keynes' postulated wealth effect of interest changes has come to the forefront of our discussion, it is hardly a subject of such intrinsic importance as to provide much support for the sweeping statements just made. Another such issue, which has been referred to more than once, may again be mentioned. It provides an illustration of greater general significance since it does not involve the "special" assumptions apparently underlying Keynes' wealth effect and his theory of Liquidity Preference. The issue concerns the convention prevalent in modern "pure" monetary theory of assuming that the redistribution of "wealth" between creditors and debtors due to movements in "the" price level will have no predictable effects on aggregate demand, and that one may therefore disregard the financial structure of the private sector and deal only with its consolidated balance sheet. It is from this strange point of departure that so much effort has been directed into largely sterile investigations of models in which money is "neutral" or just *barely* non-neutral, i.e., into the investigation of "possible worlds" in which the occupation of monetary theorist would serve no useful social function. This type of theory rests on implicit assumptions that undercut the rationale of private-sector lending and borrowing and of the existence of specialized financial markets and institutions. It disregards the role played by such markets in establishing an efficient "division of labor" enabling wealth-owning widows and orphans to turn over the management of productive wealth to entrepreneurs with special skills. It refuses to attach any optimality conditions to the real value of outstanding intra-private-sector credit contracts that have been willingly entered into and, consequently, does not perceive that, e.g., a deflation doubling this value creates balance sheets that would never have been willingly chosen by either side of the market, and that such a deflation, therefore, must make traders worse off "on the average." But the trouble with a monetary theory of this sort lies much deeper and has its root in the failure to perceive the concept of *default* as fundamental to the understanding of the "Social Contrivance of Money." But a systematic critique of this "modern" brand of monetary theory cannot be attempted here.[3]

The following two closely related objections to the foregoing section's discussion of wealth effects experienced by the "representative" transactor need to be considered:

(1) Market experiments which ask for the effects of a shift in an endogenous variable are pure nonsense. All prices, including interest rates, are endogenous when the entire closed system is considered. Prices can only be treated as parameters in the context of individual experiments. The question whether a change in interest rates has a positive or negative wealth effect on transactors in general is meaningless, since it is based on a strictly illegitimate conceptual experiment.

(2) If technology and the system's resource stocks are assumed given, aggregate "wealth" has thereby been fixed by definition. Any analysis that leads to the conclusion that a positive wealth effect may occur must implicitly violate the constraint imposed by the given production possibilities frontier.

Both objections assert that an analysis including aggregative wealth effects of price changes must involve a *fallacy of composition*. Although the two reduce at bottom to one, it is appropriate here to deal with them separately.

---

3. "Modern" monetary theorists have lost sight of the ancient wisdom expressed in a pamphlet by Thomas Manley: "This were very true, admitting all men were of equal brains and education, to traffick in one sort or another. . . . 'Tis much better for the publick that experienced Traders hire money, and employ it, than sit still, whilst commerce is manag'd by the unskillfull. . . ." (cited by Cassel, *op. cit.*, p. 11). In the United States, Gurley and Shaw represent the exceptions on this issue. By all accounts one of the strangest of the many curious incidences in post-Keynesian theoretical development is the failure of their attacks on the "Net Money (and Net Worth) Doctrine" to force a general re-evaluation of the conventional approach.

The causes of system-state transformations   In the realm of long-run comparative macrostatics, the question of the "effects" of movements in a single price is meaningless (outside of stability analysis). Such comparative static exercises presume that two "full" equilibrium states are compared. The "cause" of a change from one such state to another cannot be attributed to endogenous variables, such as the interest rate; a transformation of system state must be ascribed to a shift in one of the system's parameters. In equilibrium economics, the parameters of a system are conventionally grouped into the classes of preferences, physical transformation possibilities, and resource endowments. Changes in aggregate wealth, if definable, are ultimately to be ascribed to changes in technology or resources when dealing with a closed system. (When preferences change there is normally no basis at all for comparing "total wealth before and after.")

In the analysis of dynamic processes, things are a little different because of the presence of *lagged* endogenous adjustments. A price may change "today" because of a change in technology or resources which took place in the past, etc. But the methodological imperative remains the same nonetheless and this is especially clear when the process-analysis borrows the long-run comparative static method and proceeds in terms of the type of period-analysis discussed in Chapter II. The only difference is that we have more "parameters" to consider, i.e., the values of those endogenous variables the adjustment speeds of which have been ranked "below the line." Changes in those variables which are treated as "truly" endogenous even in the short run must still be accounted for by referring to a shift of one or more of the parameters in this expanded list.

Violations of this methodological precept are not uncommon. Conceptual experiments investigating "the effects" of "disturbances" which turn out to be changes in the value of some purely endogenous variable are frequently encountered: "Suppose investment falls . . . etc." When, in short-period analysis, the ranking of adjustment speeds and the various lags assumed are not spelled out in systematic detail, it is sometimes not so obvious whether such suppositions make sense or not. The test, however, is simply whether the impact effects of the disturbance on excess demand conditions in the various markets satisfy Say's Principle or not. When it does not—as is frequently the case, for example, in textbook expositions of the effects of various fiscal policies—the "new equilibrium" deduced is simply not an admissible transformation of the initial state postulated.[4] It is also a good rule to keep an eye out for the term "autonomous." The financing of a "rise in autonomous expenditures" is often not accounted for. Thus, one may be treated to an "autonomous" increase in government expenditure (causing an excess demand for commodities) without anything being said about the corresponding excess supply of bonds and/or money, etc.[5]

So, we must account for the parameter shifts which may be responsible for the "fall in the rate of interest" considered in connection with Keynes' wealth effect. And, if the wealth effect on expenditures is assumed positive, we must account for where the financing of increased expenditures comes from. The long-run parameters are fixed. The following changes in the values of "short-run parameters" are relevant:

(a) A Central Bank injection of high-powered money (or lowering of Bank Rate). The expansion of the banking system as a whole is characterized by excess supply of money and a corresponding excess demand for bonds, etc.

(b) A change in the expectations of bear speculators. Repeated experience of continuing low short rates causes investors gradually to revise their opinions of the range of long-term secu-

---

4. Such exercises are especially insidious when presented as arithmetical examples. Looking at the initial and the supposed terminal simultaneous solution separately, each is a consistent (albeit incomplete) description of a possible state of an economic system. When we have descriptions of a seven year old boy and an eight year old girl and there is nothing "impossible" about either description, we still know that one cannot be a "later state" of the other. Unfortunately, it is a bit more troublesome to sort out the inadmissible transformations from the admissible ones in dealing with income-expenditure comparative statics.

5. A decrease in "autonomous" consumption (a decline in the intercept of the consumption-income relation) is the usual prelude to presenting the so-called "Paradox of Thrift." The implicit assumption, as pointed out earlier, is usually that all of the rise in "non-consumption" goes into an excess demand for money, i.e., constitutes simply an increase in *ex ante* hoarding.

rities prices that is "safe." Expansion of aggregate demand is in this case financed by the former bears dishoarding.

(c) An increase in real balances through a fall in "the" price level induced by an inherited excess supply of labor.[6]

Given production possibilities and changes in "wealth" For an explicit and closely reasoned case for treating price changes as having only substitution effects one must turn to those economists, usually regarded as belonging to the "Chicago school," who have advocated the use of income-adjusted demand curves as a general analytical principle.[7] The context which the Chicagoans have in mind in advocating the use of income-adjusted demand curves is usually that of analyzing the (long-run) consequences of various tax, subsidy, or tariff schemes, etc. What

---

6. Cf. the discussion of the "Keynes-effect" in Chapter V:1, below.

7. For a critical scrutiny of this methodological position which covers several aspects of the issue that cannot be taken up here, cf. the excellent paper by Professor Yeager, "*Methodenstreit* over Demand Curves," *Journal of Political Economy*, Feb. 1960. The arguments which Yeager examines are taken chiefly from papers by Friedman, Bailey, and Buchanan. This "Chicago tradition," if it may be called that, goes back at least to Frank Knight. But Knight's methodological strictures pertain to the realm of partial equilibrium analysis and explicitly *exclude* that of monetary dynamics: "All plane curves have severe limitations for representing a system with more than two commodities, and this is particularly true of the demand curve for a single commodity in terms of money. It is impossible to assume all 'other things equal'; in particular a choice must be made between assuming the constancy of all other prices and of the individual's real income. Contrary to the tendency in recent writing, I favour the latter alternative, *because it affects a sharp separation of the problem of money from that of relative prices.*" F. H. Knight, *Risk, Uncertainty, and Profit*, "Preface to the Reprint of 1948," p. xlvi, italics added.

The issues chosen by Friedman to illustrate the advantages of the income-adjusted demand curve also belong in the realm of *long-run* comparative statics, i.e., they are issues for the analysis of which it is proper to abstract from "the problem of money." Cf. his "The Marshallian Demand Curve," *Journal of Political Economy*, Dec. 1949, reprinted in *Essays in Positive Economics*, Chicago, 1953. One should recall that, with respect to *short-run* macrotheory, the "sharp separation" which Knight refers to was the main target of Keynes' critique of received doctrine.

Bailey has applied these methodological strictures to the case that is of immediate interest to us, namely that of "changes in the rate of interest . . . , while the real resource or wealth position of the economy is given and is unaffected by the supposed changes in the rate of interest." Cf. his *National Income and the Price Level, op. cit.*, Chapter VII.

they object to is a partial equilibrium analysis based on individual experiments which, when used in such contexts, often involves the danger of drawing conclusions that rest on a hypothetical "new" equilibrium situation which *violates the resource-constraints* applicable to the system as a whole. A partial equilibrium analysis based on the Hicksian individual demand curve is likely to lead to results of this kind. When this is the relevant context, the "Chicagoan" method has obvious merits since it guarantees that the analysis is restricted to *realizable* price and quantity vectors.

We have discussed Keynes' wealth effect while assuming given technology and given stocks of productive resources. These assumptions fix the intertemporal production possibilities frontier. But the conception of the "wealth of nations" with which we have to contend *defines* aggregate "wealth" as constant for any process in which the production possibilities frontier does not change. On this conception, changes in the rate of interest could have only substitution effects under the conditions assumed.[8] This concept of "wealth" differs from the one used in the preceding section, being linked to production possibilities rather than to utility levels.[9] But this is rather beside the point for Keynes, as we have seen, took note of this apparently paradoxical aspect of his windfall effect: "A country is no richer" when the general level of securities prices goes up without any change in objective transformation possibilities, "but the citizens, beyond doubt, *feel* richer."

The purposes for which the exclusive use of income-adjusted demand curves has been advocated have been those of comparative statics proper, i.e., not the "bastardized" comparative statics

---

8. Cf., e.g., Bailey, *op. cit.*, p. 181.

9. To make the distinction clear, assume that it is possible to define a community indifference map. Then, a bond tax *cum* lump-sum subsidy policy of the kind considered by Bailey (p. 183) will move the system to a point which, while on the production possibilities frontier, is on a lower community indifference curve. Since it makes people in general "worse off," the policy would have a "negative wealth effect" in the Hicksian sense of the term used here. By the same token, the assertion that such adjustments involve "only substitution effects" involves a usage obscurely different from that of Hicks—which is the more generally accepted one.

of Keynes' short-run period method, but the comparative analysis of full (long-run) equilibria. The methodological arguments
advanced apply whenever the problem to be analyzed makes this
approach appropriate. They should not be uncritically applied to
the analysis of disequilibrium problems even if the approach to
these problems borrows heavily from the toolbox of "true" comparative statics. If transactors have full information, we must
certainly assume that each separately and all together make a
correct appraisal of their "wealth." In the comparative analysis
of full equilibria, both the initial and the terminal state are such
full information states. When only such states are considered,
"wealth effects" can only arise through changes in production
possibilities.

Suppose, however, that we want to make statements about the
stability of the terminal equilibrium state or about the movement of the system from initial to terminal state? Then the
methodological strictures are no longer relevant, as Yeager points
out:

. . . there are several uses of supply-and-demand analysis other than
to make comparative-static predictions. There can be good reason for
studying disequilibrium situations—for studying what demanders and
suppliers would be wanting to do at a price at which their plans cannot in fact mesh. Precisely one of the characteristics of a disequilibrium situation, and one of the reasons why it cannot endure, is that
*real incomes appear different to people from what they can actually
be.* We conceive of disequilibrium situations precisely in order to
show that they are *not* genuinely attainable in the sense that the plans
of various persons can be carried out and can mesh.[10]

"The citizens," in other words, may "feel richer" (or poorer)
than is consistent with the system's actual over-all production
possibilities.

Perceived versus potential wealth   Bailey's conclusion is that

As long as people are aware of their true long-run wealth-positions
both before and after the change in the rate of interest, the effect of

---

10. Yeager, *op. cit.,* p. 58, italics added.

the change upon their behavior (apart from any redistribution among individuals of wealth in the relevant sense) will consist of a pure substitution effect.[11]

This statement acknowledges that the variable relevant to the plans that transactors will try to put into effect is that of their "wealth positions" as perceived by themselves. Bailey does not seriously consider the question of whether perceived wealth might differ, in the aggregate, from potential wealth as defined by the system's production possibilities frontier. (Nor need he, as long as the analysis is kept in the realm of pure long-run comparative statics.) But the justification given for equating perceived and potential wealth is too categorical:

This argument . . . depends solely on the *assumptions of rationality* and of continuity of variation in . . . subjective marginal rates of substitution.[12]

This hints at a quasi-methodological argument which, though never stated in explicit detail and therefore difficult to appraise, is becoming so ubiquitous that it should be considered. Thus one finds frequent suggestions to the effect that an analysis which invokes wealth effects *at the impact* of a disturbance (which does not change the system's physical production possibilities) implicitly assumes "irrational behavior," or "assymetric distribution effects," or an "illusion" of one description or another. Whatever the wording, the assertion is that the appearance of wealth effects in the analysis of the adjustment process reveals the use of some "arbitrary" assumption which, once recognized, could not be reasonably defended.

This type of criticism does not have the firm methodological foundation of the two arguments previously considered. Consider how it might be applied to Keynes' wealth effect. If we base this wealth effect upon the type of rationale developed in the previous section, it may be interpreted in a special sense as a

---

11. Bailey, *op. cit.*, p. 180, italics added.

12. *Op. cit.*, p. 182, italics added. To avoid misunderstanding, it should be noted that the *dis*continuity of variation in subjective marginal rates of substitution assumed in the preceding section has nothing to do with our objection to the statement quoted above. The assumption was used merely for convenience.

distribution effect. The vision of a system exhibiting Keynesian wealth effects was one of an economy in which the present generation of wealth-owners held a stock of capital that would survive them. A rise in the value of this stock would make them better off by raising their consumption potential over the remaining part of their life cycle. This presumes, one might argue, a redistribution in favor of the old and middle-aged, who are in command of the system's real resources, at the expense of younger active and currently inactive generations: dependent children and the unborn.[13] Thus, the wealth gain for the present owners of society's capital stock is seen to rest on the presumption that, all of a sudden, the next generation will be willing to pay a higher price in terms of consumer goods to take over at the helm. This presupposition may be attacked in various ways, e.g.: (a) the wealth effect is based on the implicit assumption of a "change in the preferences of unborn generations"—which seems rather strange—whereas "tastes" should be held constant in an appropriate formulation of the problem; or (b) if no such change in preferences is assumed, the wealth effect is "illusory" and has been generated in a purely *ad hoc* manner by injecting the assumption that the current generation is overoptimistic about the price that they will be able to extort when the time comes to relinquish the system's productive resources to the next generation. This would be an objectionable procedure, because it is always possible to generate all sorts of strange "effects" if the theorist is allowed to assume transactors to be "irrational" or "illusioned" in one way or another as it suits his purposes.

It has become quite fashionable to argue along such lines that

---

13. As long as one adheres closely to the sketch of the Cassel-Keynes world given in IV:3, this is in fact the line of argument that must be taken to controvert the presumption that wealth effects *must* cancel: The individual experiment used to establish the possibility of a positive wealth effect due to a fall in the interest rate assumed that the individual trader in question holds title to a prospective stream of receipts, the average period of which exceeds that of his planned stream of payments. This may be true for some individuals, but—the objection would be—it cannot be true for the "representative individual," since *one person's receipt must be someone else's payment* (of which more below). But, if the payment is to be made by today's dependent children (and the unborn), there will be no current effective offset to the positive wealth effect on the consumption demand of currently active and retired generations . . . etc.

it is "bad economics" to assume, for example, that increases in the "real" current value of the government debt held by the private sector would *ceteris paribus* have a positive wealth effect on consumption demand.[14] The appropriate formulation, it is insisted—again with at least a hint that anything else must involve an arbitrary assumption of consumer "irrationality"—requires the assumption that the wealth represented by scheduled government payments to bond-holders be offset against the implied tax liabilities which the public has incurred by allowing the government to issue the bonds in the first place.[15]

The *General Theory* has also been the subject of such critical exercises. Current "real" income, in Keynes' theory, varies while current production possibilities remain constant. Thus it has been argued that the "anti-Classical" features of Keynes' system result from hidden "special" assumptions of "irrational" or "money-illusioned" behavior, particularly on the part of workers.[16]

In this kind of "pure" monetary theory, one regularly encounters the preoccupation with the notion that states characterized by perfect and costless information represent the Natural Order of Economic Systems to which the economist "ought to" confine his attention—an idea which we have already commented upon in Chapter II. It is somewhat surprising that the real balance effect, alone among possible income effects, withstood for so long this self-liquidating trend of monetary economics.[17] But, as already mentioned, the wealth effect interpre-

---

14. The reference is to Professor Metzler's famous and, for a long period, highly influential paper, "Wealth, Saving, and the Rate of Interest," *Journal of Political Economy*, April 1951.

15. This also leads into questions of intergenerational redistributions of wealth of the kind sketched above, particularly in connection with the old problem of the "Burden of the National Debt."

16. This diagnosis of Keynes' contribution was considered briefly in II:3 and will be discussed somewhat further in V:3, below.

17. Professor Eisner's gibe, made well in advance of the more seriously intended criticisms of the real balance effect, was to the point: "It is interesting to note that the Pigou-effect, which we are here admitting, implies a curious type of money-illusion to which illusion-hostile neo-classicists might wish to take exception. For an increase in the real value of cash-balances makes society no wealthier

tation of the real balance effect is now also in dispute. Modern "pure" monetary theory hovers uneasily on the verge of the theory of the perfectly and costlessly integrated system, a theory which represents a thoroughly "anti-Keynesian" (not to say "super-Classical") paradigm and therefore an inappropriate frame of reference for the evaluation of Keynes' theory, including his wealth effect.

Clearly, the postulate that perceived and potential wealth are the same involves more than just the assumption of individual "rationality." It assumes *full information* and (by all means) "rational" appraisal of that information. To assume that the "wealth positions" of individuals as determined by their subjectively perceived opportunities "add up to" the potential wealth of the system as a whole, in or out of equilibrium, is to presuppose a consistency of individual views that *under certain conditions* may be brought about by the interaction of individuals in markets.[18] "Absence of illusions" arguments merely fudge the question of whether these conditions will be fulfilled for the problem under study. The "Fallacy of Decomposition" inherent in the use of such Crusoe-assumptions is a far more insidious danger in macroeconomic analysis than the more obvious and familiar fallacy of composition.

The coordination of individual activities over time   Yeager's quoted observation that, in disequilibrium, "real incomes appear different . . . from what they can actually be" states, in effect, the characteristic that distinguishes Keynesian from "Classical" economic theory. His statement may perhaps direct attention particularly to "apparent real incomes" which imply that the population of transactors acts on the collective "illusion" that the aggregate resource-constraint can be violated. But it is in fact just as applicable to a Keynesian depression, where transactors act as if they "could not afford" to purchase the full employment rate

---

in 'real' terms, that is in goods . . . etc." Cf. R. Eisner, "On Growth Models and the Neo-Classical Resurgence," *Economic Journal*, Dec. 1958, p. 718 n.

18. Cf. F. A. Hayek, "The Meaning of Competition," in *Individualism and Economic Order*, Chicago, 1948.

of output. In a depression, obviously, the system is inside the production possibilities frontier so that any event that improves the coordination of current activities and moves it towards the frontier will have a positive "income effect."

In Chapter II, involuntary unemployment was seen as the result of a communication failure: information sufficient to ensure the efficient coordination of activities was not generated and disseminated in time. Our lengthy discussion of the aggregative structures of the *General Theory* and of the standard Keynesian model has now brought us back to the information problem. But the context is somewhat different. In Chapter II, the discussion concerned exclusively the current spot markets for commodities and labor and the income-constrained process emerging through trading at "false prices" (and wages). The analysis made no reference to intertemporal relative prices, whereas the present issue concerns the adequacy of existing price mechanisms for the coordination of activities *over time*.

In Chapter II, Keynes' model was contrasted to the atemporal Walrasian general equilibrium model. The Walrasian model keeps to the production possibilities frontier, whereas in the Keynesian, real income and employment are variable. Here it is similarly convenient to contrast Keynes' theory with the metastatic model. The metastatic model keeps the system on the production possibilities frontier—and "no mistake about it"—whereas in the Keynesian model "wealth" is variable. The correspondence goes further, because the role of money is crucial in both contexts. In Chapter II, the use of money as *the* means of payment was an essential link in Keynes' explanation of the failure to coordinate decisions to demand and to supply labor. The use of money as a store of value plays an equally essential role in his explanation of why the interest rate does not "equalize" saving and investment.

Professor Malinvaud, who has done much to improve our understanding of the conditions defining the efficient intertemporal production programme in the context of the metastatic model, has also considered the question of to what extent existing market institutions would allow this time-path to be approximated:

[The metastatic model] is supposed to prove the efficiency of a decentralized organization of production and consumption in which the same prices and the same interest rates would be imposed on everyone. . . . The model is based on the assumption that, for each commodity and at each point in time, there is a market where the supplies and demands implied by the present plans for this commodity and this time manifest themselves already now. Future markets provide a good concrete example of this abstract notion. . . . [But] these markets affect only some major agricultural products and raw materials, and they are bound to a short-term future.

It seems obvious that, when producers are contemplating their big decisions on investment, they cannot refer to any market through which they could know the future prices of the products they will have to use or manufacture. Similarly, the existing markets do not perform any check on the consistency of the long-term production and consumption plans of the various agents for the various commodities.[19]

This statement can be read as an admirably concise summary of Keynes' somewhat rambling analysis of the problem which is found scattered through the *General Theory*. We are dealing with a system in which "there exist only markets for present commodities and a financial market." This means that present plans for future demands and supplies of different commodities and physical assets will not "manifest themselves already now" in markets where competitive forces would assure that they are made consistent:

It is often claimed, however, that the financial market ensures some coherence by achieving a balance between the aggregate value of investments and the aggregate value of savings. On the financial market, the long-term interest rates would fulfill the part played by prices on commodity markets.[20]

This claim needs to be carefully considered, especially since securities markets are normally regarded as the most rapidly adjusting markets. Rather than jumping directly to a Keynesian

---

19. E. Malinvaud, "Interest Rates in the Allocation of Resources," in Hahn and Brechling, eds., *The Theory of Interest Rates, op. cit.*, pp. 217–18.
20. Malinvaud, *loc. cit.*

system, we may first consider the question in a context midway between the metastatic model and Keynes' model, namely the "Temporary Equilibrium" construction used by Hicks as well as by a distinguished array of pre-Keynesian monetary theorists. In models of this type, not only the bond market but all spot markets, including the labor market, are assumed to clear in the short run. This is also the context of Hicks' argument that individual wealth effects of interest rate changes tend to cancel in the aggregate:

If an individual's average period of expenditure is greater than his average period of receipts, this means that he plans to spend less than he receives in the present and near future, to "spend" more than he receives in the remoter future. . . . He may therefore be described as "planning to be a lender." Such persons are made better off by a rise in the rate of interest.[21]

Similarly, persons who would be made better off by a *fall* in the interest rate are described as planning to be borrowers. Thus, borrowers and lenders experience wealth effects of opposite signs when the rate of interest changes. Hicks continues:

In our investigations into static theory, we have been accustomed to find that income effects, even when they are important on one side of a market, always have something to offset them (more or less) on the other side. . . . Are the income effects [of interest changes] likely to cancel out? . . . The broad reason why they should tend to cancel out is that, for equilibrium on the market for securities, it is necessary that current borrowing and current lending should be equal.[22]

Note that differences in the average periods of an individual's prospective receipts and planned payments are identified with *ex ante* borrowing or lending. It may be conceded that, as long as we consider only the bond markets, it is appropriate to focus on loanable funds flows and to ignore the existing stock of bonds, since it is certainly unreasonable to suppose that traders have inconsistent anticipations of receipts and payments that are al-

---

21. J. R. Hicks, *Value and Capital,* p. 233.

22. *Op. cit.,* p. 234–35.

ready fixed in financial contracts. But this cannot be the whole story. *The consolidation of balance sheets does not remove the system's net worth.* The stocks of durable physical assets remain to be considered. An individual with an average period of receipts exceeding that of his consumption plan need *not* "plan to be a borrower"—he may plan to be a future seller of durable capital goods or equities. Similarly, the individual, whom Hicks places "on the other side of the market," may not plan to be a lender at all. He has the option of storing his wealth in the form of equities or physical capital, rather than in the form of claims on other transactors. There is nothing in Hicks' argument to show that, in the absence of a complete complement of forward markets for such assets, the system will nonetheless function in such a way that future receipts and payments arising from transactions on capital account will be even approximately matched "already now." Asset values will be based on quite incomplete information; the citizens may well "feel richer"—or poorer—although the "country is no richer." If households hold a large proportion of their non-human net worth in the form of "perpetual" equity, it is neither impossible nor "irrational" (considering the information available) that the representative household may be made to feel better off by a rise in the general level of asset prices.[23]

In Hicks' Temporary Equilibrium analysis, not only bond markets, but all markets will clear in the short run. The processes investigated are assumed to show continuous full resource utilization. This is the kind of system presumed by Wicksell, Lindahl, Myrdal, Hayek, and several other economists writing on problems of monetary dynamics in the interwar period. It is clear from the works of these theorists that, even if the discussion is confined to such full employment economics, one cannot rule

---

23. It is interesting to note that the first edition of *Value and Capital* did not take the real balance effect into account. In the second edition, Hicks responded to the criticisms of Lange and Mosak on that issue by admitting: "I was too much in love with the simplification which comes from assuming that income-effects cancel out when they appear on both sides of the market" (p. 334). While this did not lead him to reconsider also the assumption that the wealth effects of interest changes cancel, it may well be that the same remark applies also to this problem.

out the possibility of systematic tendencies among the majority of transactors to alternatively undervalue or overvalue their "real wealth." Wicksell's inflation process, for example, starts from a situation in which it is explicitly assumed that the non-banking sector is misled by actually established market prices—market rate is below natural rate. The emergence of an inappropriate market rate may be due to either sins of commission or of omission on part of the Central Bank. For the kind of world envisaged by Cassel and Keynes, the explanation of the ensuing inflation would rely in part upon the wealth effect of the rise in securities prices.

Keynes on the coordination of long-term production and consumption plans   If, in inflations, society is in the grips of the "illusion" that citizens can command more real resources than are available or forthcoming, in the depressed state which is more typically the Keynesian concern, the illusion is that they are insufficiently wealthy to purchase the full employment rate of output. In the Keynesian world, financial markets are manifestly incapable of providing for the consistency of long-term production and consumption plans. The condition that the excess demand for "bonds" be zero does not insure a "correct" value for the interest rate. The inconsistencies of plans that the price system leaves unreconciled pertain not only to "future dated" goods, in which little or no current trading takes place, but to spot markets as well. But it was nonetheless Keynes' position that it is the failure of the incomplete market mechanism to reconcile the implied values of forward demands and supplies—particularly in the fairly distant future—that is the source of the trouble. Unemployment of labor and other resources is a derivative phenomenon, albeit the depressed level of current income is the most striking manifestation of the wealth effects of a disequilibrium vector of perceived intertemporal values.

It is the very essence of Keynes' argument that the interest rate cannot be relied upon to "equate" saving and investment (at full employment) and that bond markets may clear at a wide range of interest rate-employment combinations. A decline in the marginal efficiency of capital makes the perceived wealth of the owners of that capital decrease; a sufficient reduction in the interest rate would (more or less) offset this negative wealth effect and serve to keep the system on its production possibilities frontier. But speculation, Keynes postulated, will prevent market rate from keeping pace with natural rate. The significance of the wealth effects, particularly of interest rate movements, in Keynes' theory is somewhat obscured—in the same way as his position on the interest-elasticities discussed in III:3 and IV:1— because it is, so to speak, the wealth effects that do not take place (due to the inflexibility of long rates in speculative markets) which loom over the analysis of the income-constrained process.[24]

In appraising the course which the Keynesian Revolution has taken, it is highly significant to observe that we do not appear to have any subsequent analyses which at all improve upon Keynes' discussion of these information problems. Producers and consumers have to make their plans on the basis of information on (a) the spot prices for all goods, and (b) the yields on bonds of a more or less full spectrum of maturities. The information is incomplete in one major respect, namely with regard to the future prices of commodities which would clear the respective markets at future dates given the anticipated demands and supplies more or less vaguely implied in present plans. These prices are relevant to present activities of traders; yet, in their place, we must put a "State of Expectation" and there are no mechanisms to ensure that the expectations of different traders mesh.[25]

---

24. Recall the point made in the previous section: If the utility functions of ultimate wealth-owners show a high degree of intertemporal complementarity, the substitution effects on production plans of interest rate changes are reflected mainly as wealth effects in the adjustment of consumption plans.

25. Even this is oversimplified. As indicated in Chapter II, a more thoroughly Keynesian formulation would have to take into account not only price expectations but also quantity expectations, just as the Keynesian spot economy must be dealt with not only in terms of Walrasian price vectors but also in terms of realized quantities in the manner demonstrated by Clower. It is only in the context of the temporary equilibrium approach, which presumes that traders will always be able to realize the purchases and sales desired at the prices faced, that it is sufficient to confine attention only to price expectations. Currently unemployed workers are unlikely to base their plans on the assumption that labor markets will always clear in the future, although they do not do so now. The

Keynes divided the information problems of the system under the two headings of the "Marginal Efficiency of Capital" and "Liquidity Preference." The missing forward prices for commodities and services come under the first of these headings. For the system to approximate the hypothetical efficient path of the meta-static model over some time-span, both the marginal efficiency of capital and interest rates must correctly anticipate and reflect future demands and supplies in commodities and financial markets. Dividing the topic as Keynes did, we consider first the problems which arise due to the absence of forward markets operating to reconcile the supply of producers with the demand of households for future dated commodities. Second, we consider why the financial markets do not function in a manner which would make the first kind of information superfluous. On the former topic, then, we start with Keynes' observation that

All production is for the purpose of ultimately satisfying a consumer. Time usually elapses, however—and sometimes much time—between the incurring of costs by the producer . . . and the purchase of the output by the ultimate consumer. Meanwhile *the entrepreneur* (including both the producer and the investor in this description) *has to form the best expectations he can as to what the consumers will be prepared to pay* when he is ready to supply them . . . after the elapse of what may be a lengthy period; and *he has no choice* but to be guided by these expectations, if he is to produce at all by processes which occupy time.[26]

The main point here is that there is no available direct information on what "consumers will be prepared to pay" in the fu-

---

formal mathematical problems involved in the Clower type of model have not yet been solved, however, and the generalization of the approach to include not only spot but also (implied) forward markets is entirely beyond the capacity of the present author at least. The following discussion is not so ambitious, however, that our neglect of quantity expectations will matter much.

26. *General Theory*, p. 46, italics added. When we come to the second problem noted in the text, we must take account of the fact that, in the later parts of the book Keynes does separate the roles of "the producer" and "the investor"—the distinction is, if anything, overdrawn. On this Classical tactic of identifying certain important classes of transactions with transactor stereotypes which are discussed as if they never engaged in other classes of transactions, cf. Chapter V:3, below.

ture. The producers "have no choice" but to form their own estimates and there is no mechanism to ensure that incorrect estimates will quickly be discovered:

> . . . it is of the nature of long-term expectations that they cannot be checked at short intervals in the light of realized results.[27]

In order to be able to command consumer goods in the future, households must acquire some store of value. Saving implies an increase in the demand for consumer goods *sometime* in the future. But with existing institutions the emergence of notional excess demands for future dated commodities cannot be effectively communicated to producers:

> An act of individual saving means—so to speak—a decision not to have dinner to-day. But it does *not* necessitate a decision . . . to consume any specified thing at any specified date. Thus it depresses the business of preparing to-day's dinner without stimulating the business of making ready for some future act of consumption. . . . If saving consisted not merely in abstaining from present consumption but in placing simultaneously a specific order for future consumption, the effect might indeed be different. For in that case the expectation of some future yield from investment would be improved, and the resources released from preparing for present consumption could be turned over to preparing for the future consumption. . . . The trouble arises, therefore, because the act of saving implies, not a substitution for present consumption of some specific additional consumption . . . but a desire for "wealth" as such, that is for a potentiality of consuming an unspecified article at an unspecified time. The absurd, though almost universal, idea that an act of individual saving is just as good for effective demand as an act of individual consumption . . . etc.[28]

The analysis is excellent. But if the passages in which Keynes hammers away at this point are read with a "Classical" perfect information model in mind, they may easily give a first impression of pure nonsense, e.g., as asserting that we may have one excess demand schedule (here for present consumption) shift downward without any corresponding upward shifts of excess

---

27. *Op. cit.*, p. 51.

28. *General Theory*, pp. 210–11. This is the much-maligned Chapter 16. See also Chapters 5, 7, 9, and 12.

demand schedules anywhere else in the system. The difficulties met by a "Classical"-minded reader are the same as those he encounters in reading Keynes' attack on Say's Law (or, rather, on the analytical abuses of Say's Law to which Keynes regarded everybody but himself as addicted). Critical readers of this attack read it as a denial of Say's Principle and find it to be a confirmation of Keynes' haughty neglect to "spend twenty minutes" learning price theory. Sympathetic readers consider it an embarrassment from which Keynes must be rescued by drawing a novel distinction between Say's Law and Walras' Law, making of the former an analytically most vulnerable target. But these matters have already been discussed in Chapter II, and it is unnecessary to rephrase the argument of that chapter in every particular to fit the present intertemporal context. Once more the crux is Clower's distinction between "notional" and "effective" excess demand functions.[29] Say's Principle tells us that notional excess demands do not evaporate into thin air. In this sense, a "general glut" is impossible and "supply does create its own demand." Keynes' point is simply that *effective* demand may decline in the aggregate, effective demands being desired purchases that are communicated directly to producers. The actual information mechanism composed of existing markets lacks certain "circuits," in effect. Thus, "a fresh act of saving" does not produce a signal telling producers directly to re-evaluate their opinions of the prospective yield on capital.

The second part of the problem is whether existing "circuits" will in any case transmit information that will induce producers to undertake the appropriate volume of investment. Keynes was quite aware that this *can* happen—if "the" interest rate falls (securities prices rise) without siphoning off saving, through bear speculation, into hoarding. He argued that this will not often be the case. He took the position that, whatever level of

---

29. Clower, "The Keynesian Counter-Revolution . . . ," *op. cit.* Say's Principle, Say's Law, and Walras' Law are used above in the sense of Clower. Say's Principle, to repeat, is simply the condition (or assumption) that individuals choose points on their effective budget-constraints in the formulation that the summed *ex ante* values of a trader's net demands and net supplies equal zero.

long rate was necessary to induce producers to keep investment at the full employment level given inherited money wages, this was the level financial markets "ought to" bring about.[30] From this he derived the proposition that, whenever endogenous market forces failed to drive the interest rate to this "optimal" level, the monetary authority "ought to" step in and provide whatever amount of high-powered money was necessary to neutralize the demand for "hoards" and thus bring securities prices to required levels.

What interests us here are the reasons Keynes gave for the failure of financial markets to function as they "should." Apart from numerous other passages, the entire twelfth chapter of the *General Theory* is devoted to this question. Keynes' mournful diatribe on the functioning of the organized securities exchanges is too lengthy and so well known that extensive quotations may be dispensed with. The inadequate information on which even the most knowledgeable traders must act is vividly described. "The social object of skilled investment should be to defeat the dark forces of time and ignorance which envelop our future." The modern exchanges Keynes deemed inadequate to the task, particularly since the "actual, private object of skilled investment today" does not correspond to the "proper" social task of these markets, namely that of "forecasting the prospective yield of assets *over their whole life*." The modern exchanges, in Keynes' view, have instead become the scene of a "battle of wits to anticipate the basis of conventional valuation a few months hence—a game of Snap, of Old Maid, of Musical Chairs." [31] One notes his

---

30. This involves some problems: If the future prices perceived by producers are below the levels implied in the consumption time-paths planned by households, the interest rates necessary to vanquish the pessimism of producers would be below the money rates consistent with an efficient time-path. For some discussion of these issues, cf. Chapter VI:2.

31. The colorful language tends to swamp the more sober counterpoints (pp. 158–59): "If I may be allowed to appropriate the term *speculation* for the activity of forecasting the psychology of the market, and the term *enterprise* for the activity of forecasting the prospective yield of assets over their whole life, it is by no means always the case that speculation predominates over enterprise . . ." etc. Also, p. 162: "We should not conclude from this that everything depends upon waves of irrational psychology. . . ."

insistence that transactors pay more attention to capital value than to "permanent income."

This picture is the background for Keynes' analysis of how, when a reduction in the marginal efficiency of capital requires a considerable reduction in long rate, bear speculation will prevent a sufficient rise in bond prices. The crucial role that he assigned to the "speculative demand for money" has been criticized in recent years. We will deal with this issue in Chapter V:3, below.

IV:5   The Duration Structure of Physical Capital and the Term Structure of Interest Rates

Meiselman's work, which we discussed briefly in Chapter III:1, reawakened theoretical interest in the dormant subject of the term structure of interest rates. In recent years, the debate has been lively and the theoretical and empirical contributions numerous.[1] The various approaches to the problem which have been propounded, criticized, and defended in this debate are usually grouped according to how much they emphasize, tone down, or dispute the relevance of the following three elements of term structure theory.

(1) *Expectations* with regard to the future course of short rates. If future short rates were perfectly foreseen, current long rates would be geometric averages of the short rates which are relevant, given the term to maturity of the long asset. Meiselman's Pure Expectations hypothesis assumes that traders who take account only of expected values of future short rates are sufficiently well financed to dominate the market, so that observed long yields do, in effect, reveal the consensus of these traders with respect to future short rates.

(2) *Liquidity Preference* in this context denotes the hypothe-

---

1. In addition to the works by Meiselman, Kessel, and Wood previously cited, the following may be mentioned: J. M. Culbertson, "The Term Structure of Interest Rates," *Quarterly Journal of Economics*, Nov. 1957; B. G. Malkiel, "Expectations, Bond Prices, and the Term Structure of Interest Rates," *Quarterly Journal of Economics*, May 1962, and "The Term Structure of Interest Rates," *American Economic Review*, May 1964, with a "Comment" by M. J. Bailey; and J. van Horne, "Interest-Rate Risk and the Term Structure of Interest Rates," *Journal of Political Economy*, Aug. 1965.

sis that the market, on balance, prefers shorter assets and longer liabilities, so that short assets will normally command a "liquidity premium." This means that, in a state of "normal expectations"—when expected short rates are all equal to the current short rate—the yield curve will be upward-sloping (with the second derivative of term negative).

(3) *Market Segmentation.* A pure Market Segmentation hypothesis would assert that hedging propensities—the desire of traders to match the maturity structure of the two sides of their balance sheets—are exceedingly strong so that cross-elasticities of both demand and supply between maturity segments of the market are practically negligible. In the United States, Professor Culbertson is generally regarded as the theorist laying the greatest stress on the low value of cross-elasticities, particularly in the short run.

What concerns us here is the Liquidity Preference hypothesis as it applies to term structure theory. It is particularly connected with the names of Keynes and Hicks. Despite the historical fact that observed yield curves have often been downward-sloping, this hypothesis was widely accepted until Meiselman challenged it. The value of Meiselman's contribution lies most of all in the operational method, based on Cagan's work on hyperinflations,[2] which he developed to estimate the expectations element. The Liquidity Preference element had previously been accepted basically on faith, since no such systematic method had been available. Meiselman found no evidence for the Liquidity Preference hypothesis, and he attacked it as founded on an *a priori* presumption for which convincing *a priori* reasons were lacking. The widespread belief in the validity of the hypothesis remained, however, and a number of subsequent contributions have attempted both to strengthen the theoretical foundations of the hypothesis and to provide empirical support for it. Kessel's empirical work has done the most to put Meiselman's *Pure* Expectations hypothesis in doubt and to reassert the Keynes-Hicks hypothesis.

The objective of the present section is to relate the *a priori*

---

2. P. Cagan, "The Monetary Dynamics of Hyperinflation," in M. Friedman, ed., *Studies in the Quantity Theory of Money,* Chicago, 1956.

discussion of the Liquidity Preference hypothesis to our previous discussion of the basis for Keynes' wealth-saving relation. Before proceeding with the Liquidity Preference element of Keynes' theory of the term structure, however, we must first clear the ground by noting his position on the role of expectations and on market segmentation.

Keynes on the role of expectations   The role Keynes assigned to expectations can be most readily perceived in his analysis of economic developments in the decade following World War I.[3] This interpretation forms the background for his diagnosis of the causes behind the Great Depression, which was gathering momentum at the time he was finishing the *Treatise*. Keynes attributed the prosperity of the twenties to a Schumpeterian innovation-induced boom. During most of the decade, short rates were above long rates, a phenomenon which a "pure" liquidity preference hypothesis could not have accounted for. Keynes discussed the relationship between the two sets of rates at some length. Since, as we will note below, the tendency in the more recent debate on the subject has been to confine the discussion of the yield curve to a partial equilibrium analysis of financial markets only, it is of particular interest to note that Keynes, here as always, insists upon considering physical and financial investment opportunities together: The downward-sloping yield curve of the early twenties he regarded as the result of a typically Schumpeterian "clumping" of innovations having the effect of raising the prospective profitability of less relative to more "roundabout" investment projects.

Keynes' inference that the forces underlying the boom had played themselves out already in the mid-twenties is of some interest. This diagnosis was based partly on the observation that at that time short rates "crossed over" long rates (from above). Whether the inference is justified or not, this mode of reasoning is certainly evidence enough of his awareness of the role of expectations. One should also note that, until the appearance of Meiselman's work, few if any economists attached the same significance as Keynes did to the yield curve as a diagnostic

---

3. Cf. *Treatise*, esp. Vol. II, Chapter 37.

instrument for those responsible for monetary policy. Keynes particularly stressed the "crossing of rates" as a highly significant indicator of the way the economy was going.

In the later twenties, U.S. short rates were again above long rates, a fact Keynes attributed to an inappropriate monetary policy. Since, according to his diagnosis, the postwar boom had run its course, a return of long rate—which had remained at historically very high levels in the first half of the decade—to "normal" (prewar) levels was indicated, were severe deflationary pressures to be avoided. Such a drop in long rate, Keynes noted, must be accompanied by a very considerable upward revaluation of equities, in particular those of "public utilities and similar semi-monopolistic industries." Federal Reserve policy directed towards dampening the stock market boom prevented this necessary adjustment of market rate. While Keynes did not dispute the widespread opinion that the speculative fever on the exchanges had led or was leading the market to overshoot the new "natural" level of stock prices,[4] he was severely critical of the objective pursued by the Federal Reserve for the same reasons that he had been adamantly opposed to the British return to the prewar gold-parity of the pound. A restrictive monetary policy aimed at security market speculators, he pointed out, would have but a marginal effect on the "Financial Circulation" but would impinge heavily on the "Industrial Circulation," thus making a contraction of output and income inevitable. He regarded it as imperative that Central Banks refrain from letting stock market events divert them from their proper task of attempting to keep long rates in correspondence with the "natural rate."

Thus Keynes would have concurred with Friedman and

---

4. Compare his views on the functioning of the organized exchanges, discussed in the previous section, esp. his emphasis on the failure of traders to concentrate on the proper evaluation of the present value of investments "over their whole lives" and on the "games" Keynesian investors play where the winners are those who make the best guess on the conventional appraisal of capital values "a few months hence." The game to play when, as in the Keynesian view of the late twenties situation, "real" forces are operating to raise the value of equities will be that of speculating "on the trend"—behavior that can be expected to lead to overshooting.

Schwartz [5] in all essentials of their critique of Federal Reserve policy in this period and in attributing the onset of the Great Depression to the period of tight money preceding the actual downturn in activity, although he would, as usual, have conducted the analysis in terms of interest rates and "credit conditions," rather than in terms of the stock of money.[6] As a contrast to the explanations of the Great Depression offered by later Keynesians—and, in particular by the "Keynesian" Stagnationists —the *Treatise*'s analysis of the late twenties period is highly interesting.

Keynes on market segmentation   The assumption that hedging behavior is more or less universal is a crucial element not only of the Market Segmentation hypothesis, but also of the Liquidity Preference hypothesis. In this respect, the difference between the two types of explanations of the term structure is one of degree. All theories of portfolio management deal with balance-sheet choices in terms of trade-offs between expected income and the avoidance of variously specified "risks." In the "pure" market segmentation case, the maximization of income is assumed entirely subordinated to the desire to hedge against risks by matching the maturities of assets and liabilities. In the pure case, therefore, there would be no switching between maturities in response to changes in relative prospective yields, implying that short and long rates will respond virtually independently of each other to changes in the stock of contracts oustanding in the respective maturities. No one holds this theory in its pure form, but the theorists who come closest to this view will attribute a very significant role to relative stock supplies.

The most detailed account of Keynes' views on the cross-elasticities between maturity segments of the market is found in connection with his discussion of the yield curves during the 1920's just referred to. His position is far removed from the Market Segmentation theory; the object of his discussion is to

---

5. M. Friedman and Anna J. Schwartz, *A Monetary History of the United States 1867–1960*, Princeton, 1963, Chapter 7.

6. "Too high long rate" was his general explanation of the basic cause of depressions. For a discussion of this diagnosis, cf. V:2, below.

show that long rates can be controlled through the manipulation of Bank Rate. Consequently, he stresses the trade-off between "safety" and income and the switching between maturities that will take place in response to changes in the relation between short and long yields:

> If the running yield on bonds is greater than the rate payable on short-term loans, a profit is obtainable by borrowing short in order to carry long-term securities, so long as the latter do not actually fall in value during the currency of the loan. . . .
>
> There are a number of financial institutions—amongst which the banks themselves are the most important, but also including Insurance Offices, Investment Trusts, Finance Houses, etc.—which vary from time to time the proportionate division of their assets between long-term and short-term securities respectively. Where short-term yields are high, the safety and liquidity of short-term securities appear extremely attractive. But when short-term yields are very low, not only does this attraction disappear, but another motive enters in, namely, a fear lest the institution may be unable to maintain its established level of income, any serious falling off in which would be injurious to its reputation. . . .
>
> Now banks above all prefer short-term assets, if they can afford to hold them. But when their yield falls below a certain point, they cannot afford to hold them.[7]

Keynes made one important reservation: it would normally take considerable time before the ripples of substitutions induced by changes in short rates reached long rates. Only changes in long rate would have substantial effects on investment and aggregate demand. A monetary policy pursued only by open market operations in bills and changes in Bank Rate would, therefore, be subject to considerable lags, creating a commensurate danger of the Central Bank contributing to the instability of the system. Keynes' discussion of the term structure is also the occasion for his famous exposition of the "Bismuth-Castor Oil Cycle."

---

7. *Treatise*, Vol. II, pp. 357–58. A discussion of speculation on the organized exchange follows which, while less colorful, in all essentials adumbrates Chapter 12 of the *General Theory*.

The Keynes-Hicks theory of Liquidity Preference　We come then to the Liquidity Preference element of Keynes' theory. Most of the recent discussion of the hypothesis has concentrated on the explanation of bond yields. We should recall, therefore, that Keynes relied on the same assumption of aversion to risks of changes in asset values, which is the idea basic to his discussion of the term structure of interest rates, in his "normal backwardation" theory of price determination for stock-flow commodities. The implication in that context is that the observed "future" price represents a downward-biased estimate of the future expected price, just as in the Liquidity Preference theory of term structure, the forward short rates are taken to be similarly biased estimates of expected future short rates. The "normal price" to which the *Treatise*'s analysis of the pricing of Liquid Capital refers is the price which will equate rates of supply and demand over the longer run.

The Liquidity Preference hypothesis, as it applies to the term structure of bond rates, has been criticized by Meiselman, Bailey, Johnson and others, basically on "pure" choice-theoretical grounds. The proper framework for a discussion of this criticism and an attempt to clarify Keynes' position with regard to it is, therefore, a static one. A static context gives time for all adjustments to take place and in such a context we may consequently judge Keynes to be clearly opposed to the market segmentation idea. Similarly, he gives full play to the role of expectations, so that in what follows we may safely assume the simplest case of "normal expectations."

Given a state of "normal expectations," the Liquidity Preference theory postulates that the yield curve will be upward-sloping. Normally no reservation is made in connection with this postulate about the quantities of short-term and long-term government (or foreign) bonds outstanding. Hicks, who more frequently than Keynes has been the indicated target of the criticisms that concern us here, put the matter thus:

it . . . appears that the forward market for loans (like the forward market for commodities) may be expected to have a constitutional weakness on one side, a weakness which offers an opportunity for speculation. If no extra return is offered for long lending, most people (and institutions) would prefer to lend short. . . . But this situation would leave a large excess demand to borrow long. . . . Borrowers would thus tend to offer better terms in order to persuade lenders to switch over into the long market. . . . A lender who did this would be in a position exactly analogous to that of a speculator in a commodity market. He would only come into the long market because he expected to gain by so doing, and to gain sufficiently to offset the risk incurred.

The forward rate of interest for any particular future week. . . . will have to be higher than the short rate expected by these speculators to rule in that week, since otherwise they would get no compensation for the risk they are incurring; . . . [this] risk-premium . . . corresponds exactly to the "normal backwardation" of the commodity markets.[8]

The crux of this "constitutional weakness" of the long end of the market is the risk presumed generally to be involved in long lending and the related assumption that lenders are risk-averters so that their speculative services can be obtained only at a price. Hicks also considers the role of transactions costs in this connection. Several of the more recent contributions devote rather lengthy and complicated arguments to the influence on the term structure of brokerage and other transactions costs under various conditions. For our purposes, at least, a detailed discussion of these costs is superfluous. Both the risk issue and the transaction cost issue may be illustrated with a simple example.

Suppose we have a transactor who wants to invest a given sum with the desired encashment date ten years into the future. If the yield curve is horizontal, he will prefer a ten-year bond. (We may assume that the securities considered do not pay coupons at regular intervals, but pay back principal and accumulated compound interest in one installment at maturity.) If he buys a shorter term bond, say of five years' term, it is uncertain at what rate of interest he can reinvest the proceeds in five years' time, although the mean expectation is that of the same rate as today. He thus runs the risk of earning less income over the whole ten-year span. If he is a risk-averter he will assume this *income*

---

8. *Value and Capital*, pp. 146–47.

uncertainty only if the shorter bond is offered to him at a higher
yield (lower price) than the ten-year bond. His revealed preference for the ten-year bond will be stronger the higher the
anticipated transactions cost of reinvesting in the interim. If he
buys a twenty-year bond, it is uncertain what its present value
will be ten years from now, although the mean expectation is
that it will then trade at a price equal to the originally invested
sum capitalized forward at the current rate. But he runs the risk
of the future ten-year rate being higher than today's, in which
case encashment after ten years will mean a capital loss. If he is
a risk-averter, he will assume this *capital uncertainty* only if the
longer bond stands at a discount relative to the ten-year bond.
His revealed preference for the latter will be stronger the higher
the anticipated transaction cost of selling off the longer bond.

The question here is purely qualitative: *A priori,* should we
expect the yield curve to be horizontal, to slope downward, or to
slope upward? Transactions costs will only accentuate the downward or upward slope determined by risk considerations and
may, therefore, be ignored. The basic question concerns the
predominance of capital-uncertainty presumed by Keynes and
Hicks.

The critics of Keynes and Hicks tend to argue that there are
no good *a priori* grounds for assuming that, in the system as a
whole, capital-uncertainty will be predominant and that, consequently, it is the theorist's responsibility to await the outcome of
empirical tests before proceeding on the assumption that the
Liquidity Preference hypothesis is warranted. Thus Bailey, for
example, concedes that "It is true that the evidence, e.g., that
presented by Kessel, . . . overwhelmingly supports the proposition that short-term securities tend to have a lower yield than
long-term ones," but he argues, in effect, that as a matter of
"pure" theory the appropriate position is one of equal ignorance:

We should realize . . . that it is also possible for an asset to have a
shorter maturity than its holder would desire at a flat yield curve. If
the expected time at which he wants his capital in cash is later than
the maturity of the asset, he gains no additional capital security but
suffers some income uncertainty compared to that corresponding [to]
an asset of the appropriately longer maturity. The premium he re-

quires to induce him to hold the short-term asset we might call a "solidity premium." [9]

One should note that, although Keynes assumed "normal backwardation" to be characteristic of securities markets in general, he did bring in the desire for "income solidity" to explain why the slope of the yield curve could not be arbitrarily steep, thus warding off a market segmentation interpretation of the hedging arguments contained in the Liquidity Preference theory.

In a vein similar to Bailey, Johnson warns that the modern general equilibrium literature on asset prices and yields

has some implicit biases which are apt to mislead the unwary, especially in its application to the analysis of the term structure of interest rates. . . . there is a tendency to follow too closely Hicks' original sketch of the approach in identifying the typical asset-holder with a bank, borrowing for a shorter term than it lends and therefore preferring the shorter-term assets.[10]

This line of argument goes back to Meiselman. But there were really two prongs to Meiselman's attack on the Liquidity Preference convention. One was the argument used as an assumption in the development of his own model (and not refuted by his tests) that there exists a group of "sufficiently well-financed" speculators who regard all maturities as perfect substitutes at a yield curve which reflects expected future short rates without bias. The existence of hedger groups is acknowledged, but whatever the type of risks faced by these groups would be in a given situation and whether they reveal "solidity preference" or "liquidity preference," the services of maturity-indifferent speculators would be available to society at no cost. This in itself is enough to yield the pure expectations hypothesis—the argument implies that the yield curve will be flat in a situation of normal expectations.

But Meiselman was also concerned to argue that the Pure Expectations hypothesis would be validated even if "transactors with risk aversion dominate the market." His contention in this

9. Bailey, "Comment," *op. cit.*, p. 554.
10. H. G. Johnson, "Monetary Theory and Policy," *op. cit.*, pp. 347–48.

case is that Hicks' more or less implicit assumption that *the system as a whole* will face the "basis risk" [11] of capital uncertainty is not warranted:

Hicks' analytical conclusions do not follow from his assumption of risk aversion. Lenders face the same uncertainty as borrowers and can, if they so prefer, also hedge against the consequences of interest rate fluctuations. The hedging mechanism for borrowers and lenders is identical and involves matching the expected payments streams of assets and liabilities. Contrary to Hicks' assertion, there are many institutions which appear to be hedgers in some degree and which have strong preferences for holding long-term assets. Among them are life insurance companies, and pension, endowment, and trust funds. . . . [If transactors of this type dominate the market] "normal backwardation" will be negative. *If a constitutional weakness does exist, it is not at all clear which side of the market is, or ought to be, the weak one.* The *net* hedging position is the relevant variable, and net hedging can be either short or long.[12]

Thus, there would be no presumption of a basis risk for the system as a whole. Whether the representative trader is a risk-averter or not is then simply irrelevant—there is no risk to avoid. Again, the point made is that the situation as far as "pure" theory goes is one of equal ignorance:

If . . . transactors with risk aversion dominate the market, it again is an empirical matter whether the short-hedgers or the long-hedgers will typically be the ones selling or buying the implied "insurance", and similarly it is also an empirical matter which class of hedgers typically sells "gambles" if transactors with risk preference dominate.[13]

An analogy: the sign of "the" interest rate and the slope of the yield curve Keynes is admittedly a fair target for this sort of thing—he was not averse to engaging in the same kind of polemics on occasion: "A correct theory, therefore, must be

---

11. Meiselman's concept of "basis risk" is useful, particularly if applied to the system as a whole (cf. our discussion of assumptions with regard to risk as determining the choice of asset aggregates, Chapter III:2). His definition is: "A basis risk occurs when a transactor wishing to hedge cannot arrange to have perfectly offsetting items on both sides of his balance sheet. . . ." Meiselman, *op. cit.*, p. 8 n.

12. Meiselman, *op. cit.*, pp. 14–15, italics added.

13. *Op. cit.*, p. 16.

reversible so as to be able to cover the cases of the marginal efficiency of capital corresponding either to a positive or to a negative rate of interest." This point, which has been made innumerable times both before and after Keynes, is directed towards the formulation of "the problem of interest" commonly used by an older generation of theorists: "Why do present goods stand at an *agio* relative to future goods?" Keynes' little barb is addressed in particular to Böhm-Bawerk with whom he, like Cassel, had little patience:

Some, probably most, lengthy processes would be physically very inefficient, for there are such things as spoiling or wasting with time. . . . Only if the desire to postpone consumption were strong enough to produce a situation in which full employment required a volume of investment so great as to involve a negative marginal efficiency of capital, would a process become advantageous merely because it was lengthy; in which event we should employ physically *inefficient* processes, provided they were sufficiently lengthy for the gain from postponement to outweigh their inefficiency. We should in fact have a situation in which *short* processes would have to be kept sufficiently scarce for their physical efficiency to outweigh the disadvantage of the early delivery of their product.[14]

Actually, of course, Keynes goes on assuming a world in which the "real" marginal efficiency of capital is always, and has always been, positive—although he does speculate on the possibility of bringing it to zero in the not too distant future. The negative (real) rate possibility plays no part whatsoever in his theory. What is interesting about his reflections on this hypothetical case

---

14. *General Theory*, p. 214. Two notes: (a) This again illustrates the importance of the distinction between consumer goods and capital goods in Keynes' thought. The last sentence obviously does not make sense if the "early delivered product" is a schmoo which can be physically reinvested in another short high-yield process. Keynes' discussion, here as elsewhere, treats his consumer good as a perishable final product which, when held as a stock of "Liquid Capital," will incur positive carrying charges. (b) The passage must be interpreted as a piece of "static" (though not "stationary") theory, in the sense that a given technology is assumed with "no hangover from previous technologies." We have already seen that Keynes, in a more dynamic context, granted that yields would often decrease with term to maturity, and that he explained this case with reference to the "scarcity" of newly innovated processes with a short pay-back period.

is the way in which he links it to the possibility of a downward-sloping yield curve.

We have two questions: Why do present goods stand at a premium over future goods? Why do t-year securities stand at a premium over $(t + \sigma)$-year securities? Both formulations may be criticized for tending to obscure the analogous nature of spot and intertemporal relative prices and also as potentially misleading in presuming "constitutional weaknesses" that may not always obtain. But, granting the point of these objections, one should note that the formulations at least have the virtue of suggesting that the two problems are not unconnected.

In recent years, the two issues have in the main been "farmed out" to two different groups of theoretical specialists. Since there is little overlap between the two groups, this is not an altogether happy arrangement. The theory of the determination of *the* rate of interest (the "general level" of the yield curve) has been largely left to specialists in capital theory, where the problem has traditionally belonged. The theory of the term structure of rates (the shape of the yield curve) has become a branch of monetary theory. A few things should be noted with regard to this division of labor:

The determination of the level of "the" interest rate is a general equilibrium problem. In the "pure" theory of interest, the basic determinants are the system's intertemporal physical transformation possibilities and intertemporal consumption preferences. Normally, specialists in capital theory will work with a barter system, where borrowing and lending are assumed to take the form of forward contracts for commodities (or, possibly, labor services). The term structure problem, on the other hand, is usually treated in partial equilibrium terms and the excess demand relations studied pertain to monetary contracts. Reference is seldom made to the underlying intertemporal production possibilities and consumption preferences, which are the capital theorist's stock-in-trade. In the first approximation to the theory of "the" interest rate, perfect foresight is conventionally assumed —the existence of uncertainty is not fundamental to the problem. The entire issue between "marginal liquidity preference" and "marginal solidity preference" revolves around the type of *basis risk* which the system as a whole will want to hedge against. Thus the presence of "risk" is fundamental to the term structure problem and cannot be disregarded even in a "first approximation."

The capital theorists will often favor a basic model of the Fisherian two-period, or similar, type. The only temporal distinction made is between "the present" and the indefinite "future." The choice facing households is between alternative combinations of "present consumption" and "consumption postponed." The interest rate is determined by the conditions that the system be on its production possibilities frontier and that excess demand for present consumption be zero. The excess demand for future consumption will then also be zero. This "future consumption" is then regarded vaguely as "consumption postponed beyond today"—and the question *how long* households desire to postpone consumption is not raised.[15] In this way, the term structure problem disappears from view.

Once again, we may compare this with the approach favored by Cassel, who recommended dealing with the determination of the interest rate in terms of the demand for and supply of "waiting." He defined this variable as "measured by the product of such a sum of value [i.e., the value of consumption postponed] and the time of waiting." [16] As is so often the case with the older capital-theoretic approaches, this is an easy target for criticisms emphasizing Cassel's "cheating" with the index number problem. "The" interest rate will obviously be overburdened if it is to serve two functions at once—i.e., to coordinate decisions both with respect to the amount of resources carried over into the future and with respect to the length of time for which the consumption of final product is postponed. Cassel's assumption

---

15. Usually it is necessary to regard period 2 as *"all* the future," implying that consumers want to spread the consumption of current saving over an infinite time-period, i.e., that saving constitutes demand for *permanent net streams*. Implicitly or explicitly, the measure of "wealth" is that of the permanent income concept discussed in Chapter IV:3.

16. Cassel, *op. cit.*, p. 42. This is the definition of the "supply of waiting"; for the demand for waiting (identified with the demand for the use of "capital") cf., e.g., p. 48.

that this problem can be taken care of by collapsing it into a single dimension by means of his particular definition of "waiting" is a bit optimistic. But his usage at least has the considerable advantage of drawing attention to Wicksell's "longitudinal dimension" of the allocation problem—to the "temporal depth-perspective" so conspicuously absent from many modern models, but which we have found to be a central conception in Keynes' thought. It is not self-evident that the presently fashionable approach is to be preferred—it can be freed from index number objections, but only by assuming that households desire to accumulate permanent consumption streams. For historical reasons, probably connected in particular with the amount of theoretical energy fruitlessly "wasted" on attempts to keep the Austrian approach alive, capital theorists seem to exhibit more stringent scruples with respect to index numbers than economists generally display in other areas. Considering the problems involved, for example, in the "real income" and "aggregate output" variables which macroeconomists are resigned to swallow, the implicit immortality assumption is not necessarily a cheap price to pay for avoiding the Cassel concept of waiting.

Keynes' position on the term structure issue should, as previously hinted, be tied in with his use of the wealth effect. In Chapter IV:3, we sketched a system in which households ultimately have to carry "longer" assets than (assuming risk aversion) they would want to at a flat yield curve. Hence the basis risk is that of capital-uncertainty. Rates of interest are generally positive and the yield curve upward-sloping. The only model one can offer as a contrast is a construction of Samuelson's which embodies the opposite "pure" extreme. In Samuelson's "consumption-loan" model,[17] it is postulated that no possibilities exist of transforming present into future goods, while at the same time transactors earn no income during the last third of their life cycles. With no "natural" stores of value, and in the absence of a storable money or similar institutionalized "Social Contrivance,"

---

17. P. A. Samuelson, "An Exact Consumption-Loan Model with or without the Social Contrivance of Money," *Journal of Political Economy*, Dec. 1958. Cf., also, Samuelson's exchange with W. H. Meckling in the same journal, Feb. 1960.

free competition among traders desiring to save in the face of the impossibility of doing so would bring the interest rate to minus infinity. This is indeed the ultimate negative rate case. In order to deal in a meaningful fashion with the term structure of rates, the model would have to be modified, but as it stands it will serve as a contrast to the kind of world envisaged by Keynes: in Samuelson's model, households are constrained from carrying receipt streams as "long" as the streams they would desire to hold. The "constitutional weakness," therefore, will lie on the supply side of forward markets.

It should be noted that Hicks bases his "constitutional weakness" case on the hedging-propensities of producers who:

. . . are already committed to needing loan capital over extensive future periods. They may be embarking on operations which take a considerable time to come to fruition; or they may merely be laying down plans for continuous production, in the form of a long series of planned inputs and outputs, which it will not be easy to break off at any particular point. . . . On the other side of the market there does not seem to be any similar propensity . . . etc.[18]

This just barely hints at the appropriate role of the system's physical assets and investment opportunities in the analysis of the term structure problem. It is not so strange that Meiselman (who quotes it) and other critics of Hicks pass it by merely with comments to the effect that there is no obvious reason why an offsetting propensity should be lacking on the other side of the market. (Hicks, moreover, is inconsistent according to the present interpretation, for the arguments used in recent years to throw doubt on the liquidity preference proposition of the predominance of long hedgers are based on the same kind of analysis of bond markets *in vacuo* as Hicks employed in dismissing the wealth effect.)

Keynes' position is, however, indeed based on (largely implicit) assumptions about the nature of the system's physical transformation possibilities and the resulting duration structure of its stocks of "real" capital. It is implied that, in equilibrium

---

18. Hicks, *loc. cit.*

with a given technology having been thoroughly assimilated, "roundabout" processes will be physically more efficient on the margin than the hypothetical shorter processes which would have allowed the representative household to hedge its consumption plans perfectly. If all traders were to subordinate income prospects entirely to risk-avoidance and to attempt to hedge their future purchase plans perfectly in order to avoid "gambling" on the value at which assets can be resold, yields on short production processes and corresponding assets would be driven very low—perhaps below zero. At the same time, many unutilized "roundabout" processes would promise a very high yield indeed. *The Keynesian picture is one of a system "tempted" by the profitability of long processes to carry an asset stock which turns over more slowly than households would otherwise want.*

To illustrate, consider again the criticism of the Keynes-Hicks hypothesis that it "identifies the typical asset-holder with a bank." The characterization is apt, for it is now apparent that Keynes did indeed assume the "typical" trader to be in a situation somewhat analogous to that of a bank. A transactor "representative" of a closed system (where amounts lent and borrowed are necessarily equal) does not, of course, lend long and borrow short as a bank does. The average asset-holder would instead be an individual at the midpoint of his life cycle, owning a *per capita* share of the system's physical capital. From some future date onward, he plans to consume in excess of concurrent gross income, the amounts and dates of these "encashments" being presently uncertain. The maturity structure of his representative share in the system's physical asset stock is presumed "too long" to match this encashment schedule. Assets may have to be sold at a loss to meet planned encashments. In Keynes' kind of world, therefore, the representative transactor—who is assumed to be a risk-averter—must be offered some compensation for the risk that this speculative position entails, just as the bank must be offered a yield-differential between deposits and earning assets in order to borrow short and lend long.[19]

---

19. The analogy can be stretched further: The end of an "over-investment" boom, as described by some pre-Keynesian writers, might be likened to a "run on

Unfamiliar as this whole conception may be, it is the key to Keynes' entire theory of finance. To Keynes, it is *the* function of securities markets and of financial intermediaries to enable individual households to hold short assets (or long assets without being committed to long holding periods) while, at the same time, the system as a whole freezes a vast portion of its material wealth in long-lived assets in order to secure the benefits of roundabout processes.

The organized securities markets in Keynes' theory   In Chapter IV:3, it was necessary to stick to a rather mechanical picture of the Keynesian "Vision" in order to avoid entangling the discussion of the two Average Periods in problems of uncertainty. For the wealth effect of interest rate changes to be inversely related to the direction in which the rate moves, it is then necessary to postulate that receipt streams from non-human capital are in general "much longer" than planned consumption streams. The assumption of virtual certainty does not provide an analytical framework in which Keynes' wealth effect can be seen in the most plausible light. To make it seem at all worthy of consideration, one is constrained to blow up the Hicksian notion of production plans "which it will not be easy to break off at any particular point" to Knightian proportions and paint a picture of a system of mortal consumers constrained to maintaining the existing capital stock in perpetuity.

This we are now in a position to modify. Our discussion in the previous section of the information problems characteristic of the Keynesian system raised a number of points which deserve further scrutiny. Two aspects of the information problem involved in the "saving-investment process" were emphasized. The first of these was the fact that saving consists in abstaining from

---

the Bank" for example. If the desired dissaving by the older generation would begin substantially to exceed the planned saving by younger generations, the price of assets in terms of consumer goods must drop and the dissavers will find themselves "defrauded" of the affluent retirement they had counted on. Cf., e.g., *Treatise*, Vol. II, pp. 99–101. One may note that attempts by income-expenditure theorists to make sense of older "over-investment," "under-consumption," and "over-saving" theories (and the distinctions between them) in terms of the standard one-commodity model have often proved quite futile.

present consumption without *"placing simultaneously a specific order for future consumption."* In explanation of this, we merely noted the absence of future markets which could accommodate savers wishing to place such orders. In the context of Keynes' discussion, however, it is quite clear that this is not the root of the matter—the problem is that savers do not want to commit themselves, that they want to stay "liquid," that they "desire 'wealth' as such"—"a potentiality of consuming an unspecified article at an unspecified time." If, in fact, savers were invariably willing, or even eager, to freeze their future consumption paths in the present, the system would presumably be more richly endowed with forward markets of this kind than is actually the case. But even so, one should note that savers in a Cassel-Keynes world would not be able to place forward orders corresponding to the total value of their presently postponed consumption *without incurring risks.* If, for the future periods corresponding to the dissaving period of the life cycle, they place forward orders to a value exceeding that of the anticipated gross income on their portfolios, they would in general not be able to cover these forward purchases by corresponding forward sales of assets—they are depending upon currently inactive generations to "come along" as the future purchasers of these assets.

This, perhaps, is the ultimate source of the problem. But, in any case, the fact that households are unwilling to commit themselves to placing future orders means that we have a picture significantly different from that of section IV:3. In that previous discussion uncertainty was more or less ignored, and the comparison of the average periods of prospective receipts and consumption outlays provided little rationale for households to prefer a portfolio with an average period shorter than that corresponding to the expected life cycle consumption path of the representative household. Keynes' reasoning in the passages cited demonstrates that he assumed that households will prefer a considerably more "liquid" portfolio.

The second information aspect of the saving-investment problem had to do with the failure of financial markets to produce "substitute information" leading to the same full employment result envisaged for a system with a full complement of forward markets. This information failure arises because speculators on the organized exchanges always have "an alternative to the ownership of real capital-assets, namely the ownership of money and debts," and bear speculation can therefore set in motion a train of events which will prevent savings plans from leading to the appropriate level of production of new capital assets.

The interesting thing about Keynes' discussion of this second aspect of the problem is his stress on its being historically derivative to the first. Ideally, households would desire to accumulate their wealth not only in a form "short enough" so that dissaving in the later part of the life cycle can be done by consuming gross income without necessitating the resale of income sources—they also prefer to hold portfolios with an even higher turnover. Portfolios with a high rate of gross income to capital value will be preferable to portfolios of the same value and equal net, but lower gross, income in many contingencies. Thus they provide insurance against unexpected or unplanned outlays—from which we may derive the hypothesis of a "precautionary demand" for short—"liquid"—portfolios, etc.[20] If, on the production side, entrepreneurs were to be constrained from investing in any physical assets with a value turnover longer than the average portfolio turnover preferred by the representative household (at a flat yield curve at least), growth would be stymied at a pre-industrial level of real *per capita* wealth:

In former times . . . enterprises were mainly owned by those who undertook them or by their friends and associates. . . . Decisions to invest in private business of the old-fashioned type were . . . *largely irrevocable, not only for the community as a whole, but also for the individual.* With the *separation between ownership and management* which prevails to-day and with the *development of organised invest-*

---

20. We may have such a "precautionary demand" also for one of the reasons adduced in support of the assumption that households are unwilling to commit themselves by placing orders for specific consumption goods for specific future dates—i.e., as a precaution against changes in the household's consumption "tastes" which surely are not fixed, or perfectly foreseen, over the life cycle. High gross income portfolios also provide "reinvestment options." It should be pointed out, for example, that one basis risk facing the system as a whole is that of capital losses due to obsolescence of real capital assets, as when equipment of superior efficiency is innovated.

ment markets, a new factor of great importance has entered in, which sometimes facilitates investment but sometimes adds greatly to the instability of the system.[21]

Keynes thus views the development of institutionalized arrangements making possible the separation of ownership and management, and the development of organized securities markets and of firms specializing in various forms of financial intermediation, as a prerequisite for a highly industrialized society based on private enterprise. The general notion is common enough. What is not so common is the stress on the contrast between the great duration of the receipt streams generated by the productive sectors of a modern system, in which "almost the whole of the fixed capital is represented by buildings, transport, and public utilities," and the liquidity preferences of ultimate wealth-owners. In Keynes' grand conception, the basic function of "Finance" in modern systems is to reconcile the desire of households to be "liquid" with the technological necessity for the system as a whole to carry vast stocks of "physically illiquid" capital goods: *"there is no such thing as liquidity of investment for the community as a whole."* [22]

The development of modern organized investment markets and financial intermediaries has meant that:

Investments which are "fixed" for the community are . . . made "liquid" for the individual.

With a ready market for the resale of assets:

each individual investor flatters himself that his commitment is "liquid" (though this cannot be true for all investors collectively) . . .

Individuals are rendered "liquid" in the sense that they need *not* commit themselves to holding assets *to maturity.* This, to Keynes, is where the second aspect of the information problem

---

21. *General Theory,* pp. 150–51, italics added. The separation of ownership and management we already stressed in IV:3 as basic to the Keynesian vision of the world.

22. *General Theory,* p. 155, italics added.

causing the failure to coordinate intertemporal plans comes in, for he assumes that traders with no commitment to hold to maturity will show little concern to forecast the yield of investment prospects "over their whole life." The sorry spectacle of "the games that people play" on the Exchanges, that he painted, is to be expected:

These tendencies are a scarcely avoidable outcome of our having successfully organized "liquid" investment markets.[23]

Now, this does not seem right: Whether people hold assets to maturity or not, there is surely a strong incentive to try to evaluate the yield of assets over their whole life. Those investors who do a good job of it should regularly gain at the expense of the others, including those who just gamble on the market opinion of next week.

Keynes' analysis makes sense only on one assumption. It is important that we be clear on what this assumption is, for it expresses a fundamental *a priori* conviction of his which, although highly debatable as a general proposition, underlies virtually his whole life-work on problems of economic stabilization. It is this: *Whenever money income, output, and employment decline, too high long rates are ipso facto to blame.* This is quite clear in the *Treatise*—a contraction is caused by a market rate above natural rate—but it has not been so obvious that the same assumption permeates the *General Theory* also.[24]

When income declines, it is because entrepreneurs do not create real assets to the same value that savers try to accumulate. Coordination of the two types of decisions breaks down because bear speculators step in and supply savers with assets from their portfolios and "hoard" the proceeds. By so doing they prevent the interest rate from declining to a level sufficiently low to

---

23. The above quotations are taken from the *General Theory*, pp. 153, 160, and 159, respectively.

24. The *General Theory*'s preference for the use of fiscal rather than monetary policy measures in certain types of situations is not entirely consistent with the diagnosis that too high interest rates are *always* at the root of unemployment problems. But Keynes' diatribe against speculation on the Exchanges makes no allowance for this. Cf. V:2 and VI:2, below.

induce entrepreneurs to undertake the full employment amount of investment. In the passages quoted above, Keynes asserts, in effect, that whenever investors do not passively acquiesce in a rise in bond prices but counteract the decline in long rates by bearish sales, they are always "in the wrong." If they did not gamble on transitory fluctuations in asset prices, but seriously tried to evaluate the lifetime yield prospects, they would come to realize that higher securities prices are indeed warranted.

This may be true in some situations, but it certainly is not true in all situations of low or declining income. As an across-the-board generalization, it will not stand up to scrutiny. But to this matter we will return in sections V:2 and VI:2.

If the bears were constrained to hold their portfolios to maturity, they could not step in between savers and entrepreneurs in this way. Keynes toyed with several ideas to "force the investor to direct his mind to the long-term prospects and to those only" but rejected each in turn—his own analysis of the function of the financial markets indicated that, were the "liquidity" of investments to be drastically reduced and the individual trader forced to commit himself over the long term, this would "seriously impede new investment." The analysis implies in fact that sufficiently drastic action in this direction would force the system ultimately to contract by letting the stock of non-human capital run down without replacement or maintenance.

Financial intermediaries: Keynes and the "New View" in banking theory The predominance in modern monetary theory of consolidated balance-sheet models have been referred to several times in our discussion. In the standard model, the only capital account variables explicitly considered are the stocks of money, of "outside" bonds, and of physical capital. Preoccupation with the comparative static analysis of short-run solution states most often precludes a systematic analysis of the intersectoral fund-flows implied in the processes studied. The assumption that aggregate demand, and the short-run solution state generally, is invariant to the stocks of outstanding intra-private-sector debts and claims also implicitly asserts the irrelevance of such fund-flow analysis. The apparent conventional satisfaction with this approach seems a survival of the early "Keynesian" conviction of the "unimportance of money and finance."

Economists dissatisfied with this conception of the passive adaptation of financial to "real" variables have repeatedly mounted attacks on the conventional macroapproach.[25] But the task of transforming intuitive dissatisfaction into convincing analytic criticism has proved quite difficult, and the task of constructing new macrotheories which incorporate "Finance" in a systematic and significant way, even more so. The result of such efforts often becomes, as in the Radcliffe Report, only a repetitive insistence on the vital importance of "liquidity"—a variable which resists scalar measurement and remains "slippery and ill-defined." [26]

In the present study, these issues have been avoided as far as possible. Without pursuing the subject in detail, we may, however, note that many of the ideas which in recent years have come to the forefront in the discussion of the role of financial intermediaries were anticipated by Keynes. This is not to claim great credit for him, since recent writings in this area have to a great extent been devoted to rehashing theoretical issues made familiar in the Bullionist controversies and the controversy between the Banking and the Currency schools.[27] A few compara-

---

25. The Radcliffe Report and the work of Gurley and Shaw have previously been mentioned. Cf., also, the earlier paper by R. N. McKean, "Liquidity and a National Balance Sheet," *Journal of Politicial Economy*, Dec. 1949, reprinted in *Readings in Monetary Theory.*

26. Johnson, "Monetary Theory . . . ," *op. cit.,* p. 352.

27. Monetary theorists seem doomed to repeat doctrinal history, for example, on the eternal question of the "proper" definition of "money." At the time of the Bullionist controversy, the question was whether bank notes were to be considered as part of the money supply or as a coin substitute tending to "increase the velocity of 'money.' " In the latter half of the century, notes were well established as part of the money supply proper, and the question was whether demand deposits were to be considered as part of the money supply or as a currency substitute tending to "increase the velocity of 'money.' " In recent years, we have debated whether time deposits, etc., can properly be included in the money supply or whether they should be treated as money substitutes the availability of which will increase the velocity of the money stock proper. The theoretical conundrums that will be produced before long by computerization of the payments mechanism one can only view with apprehension.

tive notes on Keynes and Gurley and Shaw are of interest here.

Let us start by noting an important difference in emphasis in the analytical treatment of financial intermediation. The conception around which Gurley and Shaw organize their analysis of intermediation is that of the distinction between primary or *direct securities* and *indirect securities*. Other distinctions between types of assets are subordinate. Primary securities are a heterogeneous lot, and the information needed to appraise their "quality" will often be expensive for the individual investor to obtain. The imperfect homogeniety of such assets will also mean that the investor will find them "illiquid" if he wants to resell them short of the maturity date. The acquisition of information about primary securities is subject to returns to scale; expertise in investment in certain types of such assets enable intermediaries to appraise their "quality" at lower cost. The Law of Large Numbers normally insures the well-run intermediary against large cumulative net deposit drains; for a large portion of its portfolio, therefore, the imperfections of the markets in which heterogeneous primary securities can be resold are of less consequence. Financial intermediaries are thus able to acquire "illiquid" primary securities while issuing "liquid" indirect securities to the non-financial sectors. The superior qualities of the latter will mean that the public is willing to acquire them at a lower expected yield than the public would demand in order to absorb the same volume of primary securities. In the works of Gurley and Shaw this is stressed as the basic function of intermediaries—they substitute indirect for direct claims on producers in the portfolios of the public and derive their income, as firms, basically from the rate-differential between primary and indirect securities.

In Keynes' work, of course, all other distinctions between assets are subordinated to that of the distinction between long-term and short-term assets. We have already seen how, on subject after subject, the dimension of duration or term to maturity was central to his thought. It is not surprising that it dominates here also. To Keynes, therefore, financial intermediaries are basically in the business of lending long and borrowing short and derive their income, as firms, from the rate-differential between the two asset types. The typical Keynesian financial institution is, indeed, the Hicksian bank, whereas the mutual fund is in many respects as good a prototype as any of the Gurley and Shaw intermediary.

This distinction between the two approaches captures much of their "flavor" but, in substance, the difference remains one of emphasis. A "general theory" of intermediation would build on both ideas and no purpose is gained by asking which one is the more fundamental. As noted at the outset of Chapter II, the "competitive" general equilibrium model implies that traders face perfectly elastic demand and supply schedules for all goods, so that all goods are perfectly "liquid." The social contrivance of "money" is superfluous in perfect information models, and so is intermediation of the Gurley-Shaw kind.[28] Keynes rejected this conception while stressing the fundamental differences between a money economy and a barter system. His definition of "money" covered also the deposit-liabilities of intermediaries, and his analysis of the role of "money" in income-constrained processes can just as well be developed on the basis of the Gurley-Shaw direct-indirect idea as on the basis of his own favored long-short distinction. In the shortest end of the asset-spectrum, the two conceptions tend, in fact, to become analytically indistinguishable. The "liquid" qualities of the liabilities of banks, mutual savings banks, savings and loan associations, etc., may be "explained" at first hand by reference either to their "indirectness" or to their "shortness"—but their concrete advantages to the public remain the same under the cover of either label.

Keynes was quite modern indeed in his treatment of the role of financial intermediaries in the saving-investment process. The two-asset model of the *General Theory* gives little scope to such analysis, and one must turn to the *Treatise*. Some of the problems with the *General Theory* model may be noted. An objection often made is, for example, that the inelastic expectations Keynes

---

28. In their major work, *Money in a Theory of Finance*, Gurley and Shaw attempted to present their ideas while sticking as close as possible to the traditional perfect information framework. In the event, it appears they came too close—the strategy has served to minimize the impact of their contributions.

attributes to investors would not explain a speculative demand for "money" but, at best, for short governments and interest-bearing deposits.[29] This sort of criticism could well be amplified. One reason why the emergence of an excess demand for "money" will spell contraction of real output and employment, on which Keynes laid great emphasis, was that the "elasticity of production" of money was near zero: the trouble arises when "people want the moon . . . the object of desire (*i.e.*, money) is something which cannot be produced."[30] This ultimate external constraint, which prevents the private sector from adjusting to an "excess demand for the moon" in any other way than by reducing aggregate money expenditures, can only be taken to refer to the stock of high-powered money—to the exogenously determined stock of ultimate (nominal) liquidity. "Money" in this context, then, does not correspond to the inclusive definition used in the rest of the book. And it is, indeed, a long way from the development of an excess flow-supply of long-lived assets at initial levels of asset prices and income to the emergence of an excess demand for high-powered money.

The reconciliation is to be found in the *Treatise*. Keynes' analysis of the financial side of the contraction process once again reveals the time-to-maturity dimension of asset structure to be the key to his analytical conception of the dynamic problem. (It also reveals this one-dimensional view of financial structure to be somewhat too simplified and "neat" for comfort. Characteristics of assets other than term to maturity are reduced to footnote material.) Keynes views the system of financial markets simply as neatly "staggered" from the shortest end (high-powered money) to the longest (consols and equities), with various specialized investors and institutions overlapping maturity segments "along the way" to ensure that excess demand pressures in

---

29. Cf., e.g., Johnson, "The *General Theory* . . . ," pp. 8–9, who objects that Keynes' method of "aggregation undoubtedly tends to exaggerate the importance of the speculative . . . demand for money, since it overlooks the likelihood that . . . speculation will take the form of movements between securities of different types rather than between securities and cash." Cf. also the criticism of the Speculative Demand discussed in Chapter V:2, below.

30. *General Theory*, p. 235.

one end of the continuum will ultimately—through a chain of "belated and imperfect reactions"—be transmitted to the other end.

The conception may be likened to an accordion—the term "concertina" having been pre-empted—which may be compressed (or extended) from either end. Actions by the monetary authority will operate on the "short end," changes in the marginal efficiency of capital or in the propensity to save will impinge first on the "long" end. In short-run equilibrium, excess demands should be zero in all financial markets. In Keynes' conception of the financial system, it is sufficient to study the excess demand conditions in just one of the markets—and it does not matter much which one. The fulfillment of the equilibrium conditions may be checked at any of several points on the accordion. The emergence of an excess demand for high-powered money, or for cash, or for interest-bearing deposits has the same implication—contraction. It is sufficient to keep track of one of these, but the analytical context may—as in the *General Theory* —make it more convenient to focus now on one, then on the other.

In the *Treatise,* Keynes favored focusing on the "demand and supply of savings deposits." Assume that, in a given initial situation, the marginal efficiency of capital declines, implying a reduction in the natural rate. If there is no bear speculation on the exchanges, the market rate would decline to the point where the demand price for investment goods would be maintained and *ex ante* saving and investment "equated" at the initial income level. But normally, Keynes assumed, bears will start to supply long assets from their portfolios to savers, preventing the price of long bonds from rising sufficiently and the price of equities from being maintained. The bears will move towards the short, "liquid" end, switching the funds obtained from savers into saving deposits:

If, however, the banking system operates in the opposite direction to that of the public and meets the preference of the latter for savings-deposits by buying the securities which the public is *less* anxious to hold and creating against them the additional savings-deposits which the public is *more* anxious to hold, then there is no need for the price-

level of investments to fall at all. . . . A fall in the price-level of
securities is therefore an indication that the "bearishness" of the
public . . . has been insufficiently offset by the creation of savings-
deposits by the banking system. . . .

The price-level of investments as a whole, and hence of new investments, is that price-level at which the desire of the public to hold
savings-deposits is equal to the amount of savings-deposits which the
banking system is willing and able to create.[31]

To Keynes, the organized exchanges are the markets for long-
term securities. To Gurley and Shaw, they are above all the
markets for direct securities. But the substantive differences in
analysis should not be exaggerated. In both cases the point is
that if the volume of new long-term direct securities absorbed by
the non-banking public declines, maintenance of the income
level requires that the rate of expansion of financial intermediaries is correspondingly stepped up.[32]

Keynes went on to use the above argument in abbreviated
form. His repeated references to the "equality of demand and
supply of savings-deposits" as the condition determining "the
price-level" were not well received by the critics of the *Treatise*.
Occasionally, the objection was raised that Keynes did not make
it clear whether it was the equality of savings and investment *or*
of the demand and supply of savings deposits that was the
"basic" equilibrium condition of his analysis. Since, in the given
context, one implies the other,[33] Keynes' habit of switching from

---

31. *Treatise*, Vol. I, pp. 142–43. Keynes appends the footnote that "I am ignoring
here the complications . . . arising out of the possibility of transferences between
the savings-deposits and the cash-deposits." One might add that the "accordion
conception" also ignores a number of other "complications" arising from flow-of-
funds alternatives other than the alternative brought to the forefront. Modern
Quantity theorists would also desire some consideration, for example, of the possibility of "transferences" between cash deposits and currency.

32. Cf., e.g., J. G. Gurley and E. S. Shaw. "Financial Intermediaries and the
Saving-Investment Process," *Journal of Finance,* March 1956, reprinted (in part)
in W. L. Smith and R. L. Teigen, *Readings in Money, National Income and
Stabilization Policy,* Homewood, Ill., 1965.

33. In the same way an elementary fund-flow analysis will show that the saving-
investment equality of the *General Theory* model implies a net effective flow-
demand for "money" of zero.

one to the other according to whether the immediate analytical problem concerned "real" or financial markets need not concern us here. Another point, often raised, is of some interest in connection with the recent literature on financial intermediaries. This objection was that the assumption that banks and financial intermediaries could control the volume of saving deposits supplied did not seem very reasonable.[34]

Keynes, as we have seen, did not regard the distinction between cash deposits and interest-bearing deposits as crucial in macrodynamic analysis. Nor did he draw a sharp line between commercial banks and non-bank financial intermediaries. Since commercial banks were by far the dominant deposit-issuing intermediaries in the British system at the time, the fudging of this distinction was quite natural, whereas in the recent literature the intellectual effort required to dispense with it is quite noticeable. Like the more recent monetary theorists who concern us here, he laid great stress on the intermediary functions performed by commercial banks: "[T]he modern banker performs two distinct sets of services. He supplies a substitute for State Money . . . [and] is also acting as a middleman in respect of a particular type of lending."[35] But in postulating that the banking system had control of the supply of saving deposits, Keynes actually went quite a bit farther in obliterating the distinction between "commercial banking" and "financial intermediation" than modern writers on the subject have been willing to.

The old-fashioned conception, towards which the recent reaction has been directed, was that a sharp distinction could be drawn between banks and financial intermediaries, basically on

---

34. Cf., e.g., the two previously cited papers by Hayek, "Reflections on the Pure Theory of Money by Mr. J. M. Keynes," Parts I and II; and Klein, The Keynesian Revolution, p. 25.

35. Treatise, Vol. II, p. 213. Cf. also p. 214–15: "This duality of function is the clue to many difficulties in the modern Theory of Money and Credit and the source of some serious confusions of thought. . . . Now a partial selection of some amongst these truths and blind eye to others of them have led to the opposed points of view which are characteristic . . . of the vast bulk of non-academic monetary literature." All this echoes D. H. Robertson's Banking Policy and the Price Level. The "dual role of banks" was not Keynes' own idea. Cf. Harrod's Life, p. 372.

the grounds that the respective volumes of liabilities were determined for the banks "by supply" and for intermediaries "by demand." The modern critiques of this distinction tone it down by stressing that the volume of demand deposits will depend also on money-demand factors and that banks, therefore, are in that respect not in such a dissimilar position from that of financial intermediaries. Historically, monetary theorists, particularly in the United States, have for decades fought on a united front against the "real bills doctrine." At long last, the heretic forces of bankers, economists, and politicians believing in the sufficiency of conditions of demand for the regulation of the money supply have been reduced under steady fire to insignificance. Hence, it has in recent years become possible to relax the vigil against *laissez-faire* banking ideas. The profession has thus become ready for the rediscovery, announced with some fanfare, that there *was* an element of truth in the "Principle of Reflux" of the Banking school.[36] Banks, then, are now considered somewhat similar to intermediaries in that, for both kinds of institutions, demand will affect the volume of liabilities. Less attention has been given to the corresponding argument, which one finds in the *Treatise*, that intermediaries are somewhat similar to banks in that they are not completely passive suppliers in the determination of their liabilities.

Summary   In this chapter we have tried to bring to the surface the "Vision" of the structure of modern economic systems that is the unifying conception underlying Keynes' wealth-saving relation, the scattered rudiments of a capital theory he presented, his diagnosis of the fundamental information problems in modern private enterprise economies, and his Liquidity Preference theory with its many appendages. The extent to which this "Vision" is valid and useful cannot be decided on the basis of the kind of "casual" and generally hard-to-interpret observations on the comparative duration of production plans and consumption

---

36. Cf., e.g., Gurley and Shaw, *op. cit.*; J. Tobin, "Commercial Banks as Creators of 'Money,'" in D. Carson, ed., *Banking and Monetary Studies*, Homewood, Ill., 1963; L. E. Gramley and S. B. Chase, "Time Deposits in Monetary Analysis," *Federal Reserve Bulletin*, Oct. 1965.

plans to which part of section IV:3 was devoted. Such arguments can, at best, serve to acquaint one with some of the more unfamiliar analytical features of the Grand Design. The design, of course, can never be the ultimate framework for a fully developed theory of Capital, Money, and Finance. There are many problems in the analysis of the capital accounts which will not fall conveniently into place when framed in this Keynesian perspective.

It would appear then that one has to rely primarily on the study of financial markets and financial intermediaries to produce evidence in support for—or evidence invalidating—this basic conception of Keynes'. A few observations seem relevant:

(1) One aspect of Keynes' Liquidity Preference theory was the Speculative Demand for "Money." His explanation of this speculative demand rested upon the assumption of inelastic expectations with regard to the future course of long rates. In the course of the modern reaction towards the Keynesian Liquidity Preference theory, a number of *a priori* objections to this assumption have been raised. These we consider in Chapter V:3. Here we will note only that time-series data on the term structure of rates indicate that the amplitude of cyclical fluctuations in short rates greatly exceeds that of long rates. This indicates that expected future short rates are generally less than unit-elastic with regard to changes in the current short rate and, therefore, supports Keynes' assumption of inelastic expectations.

(2) The empirical findings of Kessel *et al.* similarly tend to support the Keynesian hypothesis that "normal backwardation" is characteristic of bond markets in general. Such backwardation implies (a) that risk-averters dominate the market and (b) that the predominant risk which the market seeks to shed is that of uncertainty of capital value. This, in turn, means that the system as a whole is carrying longer term assets than the representative ultimate wealth-owner would prefer if faced with a flat yield curve.

(3) In the course of the debate initiated by Meiselman, a tremendous amount of ingenuity and empirical effort has gone into investigating the question of whether forward short rates, implied in current long rates, are biased estimates of currently

expected future short rates. The Liquidity Preference hypothesis asserts that such forward rates should have an upward bias. The Pure Expectations hypothesis denies any bias. A "solidity preference" hypothesis would imply a downward bias.

There is room, however, also for cruder test questions, particularly in connection with the suggestions that, on grounds of equal ignorance, the solidity preference notion should have a claim on the attentions of "pure" theorists commensurate with the Liquidity Preference hypothesis. One particular "mental experiment" is pertinent here: In a world of solidity preference, short rates generally exceed long rates. Intermediaries that borrowed short and lent long would have to pay for the privilege.[37] Can one conceive of a system with a financial structure reasonably resembling that evolved by the major Western countries, surviving in the hypothetical setting of a solidity preference world? [38]

---

37. Cf. R. A. Kessel, *The Cyclical Behavior of the Term Structure of Interest Rates,* p. 53: (italics added): "A number of financial institutions (in particular, commercial banks, the Federal Reserve System, savings banks, investment banks, savings and loan associations, life insurance companies, government, municipal, and corporate bond dealers, and the Federal National Mortgage Association), although conventionally regarded as being extremely conservative, are speculators in the money and capital markets. The average maturity of their assets is greater than the average maturity of their nonequity liabilities. Hence, they are speculators in the sense that they are long on long-term money and short on short-term money *and, by and large, live on the carry. Their economic viability is a function of the spread in yields between their assets and their liabilities.*"

38. One can (with some effort) conceive of a situation, à la Keynes, with a downward-sloping yield curve wholly in the *negative* range. This would be the decaying world portrayed by several earlier authors in which households have to pay entrepreneurs to "take care of their capital." It does not preclude an intermediary function, but intermediaries would borrow long and lend short, profiting "on the carry" from having their equity decaying at a slower rate than that of households. "Pure" as such theoretical ingenuity is, it is also tiresome.

V·KEYNES AND POST-KEYNESIAN MONETARY THEORY

V:1 The "Keynes-effect" and the "Pigou-effect"

In the Keynes and the Classics debate, the "Pigou-effect" became over a number of years the subject of a surprising amount of theoretical attention. Though the Pigou-effect in itself is of subsidiary importance in the context of the present work, it is still of some interest to see to what extent the present interpretation of the *General Theory* may add something to this debate.

The relevant literature is well known and it is superfluous, at this late date, to review the many contributions to this topic in any detail. Many famous economists have participated: among the first to discuss the topic were Haberler, Kalecki, Pigou, and Scitovsky. Somewhat later came the first articles by Patinkin on the subject: the "real balance effect" has consistently been the cornerstone of Patinkin's subsequent theoretical work. This work in turn has stimulated an enormous literature to which almost all monetary theorists of note have contributed at one time or another. (The exceptions, it seems, are all to be found among the Neo-Quantity theorists.) We will confine our attention to the works of Patinkin and Kuenne as representative of the Neoclassical interpretation of Keynes' position on some—not all—of the relevant issues.

The conventional statement of the issue One should first recall the context in which the debate began and the objectives of those authors who first called attention to the Pigou-effect. Both the "Keynesians" and the "anti-Keynesians" took for granted the prevailing income-expenditure interpretation of the *General Theory*—i.e., that Keynes' book in almost all respects made a "clean break" with the past, that it represented a "revolutionary" departure from everything that had gone before, that it advanced a new kind of macroeconomics which attached no significance to relative prices, and so forth. In particular, the contributions first elaborating the Pigou-effect should be seen against the background of the "Stagnationist Keynesianism" of the time—against the insistence of the "Revolutionary" income-expenditure theorists that their model proved the possibility of an *unemployment equilibrium,* from which endogenous market forces were powerless to relieve the system. This was the then-current thumbnail definition of the Keynesian Revolution's significance.[1]

This has remained the perspective from which the Neoclassicists view Keynes' contribution. Kuenne's recent re-evaluation of Keynes, for example, starts from the following point of departure:

Form the restricted viewpoint of the pure theory of general economic systems . . . Keynes' fundamental challenge to neoclassical theory is quite clear: it lies in his construction of a model from which flexibility of the money wage rate cannot eliminate an excess supply of labor.[2]

---

1. It was sometimes noted, with some contempt, that the Great Instigator himself was missing in the assault launched on the barricades of the "Classical" Establishment. The question of whether unemployment could exist without the "assumption of various frictions, imperfections, and rigidities of the real world" is the occasion for Klein's previously noted comment: "Unfortunately, Keynes has practically admitted that he . . . would answer *no*. Again, as in the *Treatise,* Keynes did not really understand what he had written. . . ." Cf. Chapter I, p. 35, above.

2. R. E. Kuenne, *The Theory of General Economic Equilibrium, op. cit.,* p. 347. One may gain some perspective on Kuenne's discussion of Keynes by considering how his statements would apply to Wicksell. Consider Wicksell's "cumulative process": Can it be said to represent a model from which rising (falling) prices and wages cannot eliminate an excess demand (supply) of commodities and labor? If so, does it not also pose a "fundamental challenge" to Neoclassical theory?

Later, Kuenne re-emphasizes that to evaluate Keynes' theory properly it must be regarded as "a system which yielded an excess supply of labor with *no tendency towards self-correction.*" [3] This states the Neoclassicists' concern with the Keynesian system quite precisely: Did Keynes *prove* that the "automatic forces" of the system could not possibly eliminate an "unemployment equilibrium" such as he posited? In order to investigate the question, thus formulated, one must obviously give all the automatic equilibrating tendencies the time to do their work. Consequently, the question becomes whether Keynes proved the non-existence of a stable full employment equilibrium. Correspondingly, the Neoclassicists take it as their objective to demonstrate (a) that there must exist at least one potential vector of non-negative prices conducive to full employment, and (b) that this hypothetical full employment situation would be attained by a sufficient all-around deflation.

With the answers to the questions posed by the Neoclassicists we have no quarrel. But it is otherwise with the questions themselves. Pertinent as they are in relation to the standard income-expenditure model, they have no relevance at all to Keynes' theory. The answers may be briefly reviewed.

In the solution state of the income-expenditure model we have unemployment of labor at the going money wage rate. It may be assumed here that *effective* excess demands are zero in other markets. The defenders of "Classical" doctrine were then concerned to show that a sufficient reduction in money wages, allowing also a substantial decline of money output prices ("the" price level), would restore real output to the full employment level. The argument hinged on the adjustments to increases in the real purchasing power of the money supply brought about by a fall in money prices. At *some* level of money prices an excess supply of money must develop which spills over into increased demand for output. There must, then, also be one level of money prices low enough for real demand for output to correspond to full employment.

This was the Pigou-effect. Its proponents were cautious not to

---

claim too much for it. The process itself might create expectations of further price declines increasing the demand for real balances. Ultimately, however, the process would do the trick, even in this case—at some low level of prices the increase in real balances must swamp even the effect of such elastic expectations. (Keynes had been wary of relying on this process partly for this reason—in the case of elastic expectations, it would raise the "liquidity yield" of a given volume of real balances, and a central problem of depressions, in the rather tortuous formulation of Chapter 17, was that the elasticity of this liquidity yield with respect to real balances was rather slight; the Pigou-effect proponents recognized that there he had a point.)

The significance of the effect was even further circumscribed, however. Deflation causes redistribution of real wealth from debtors to creditors. If the distribution effects on aggregate real demand were adverse, the decline in the price level must proceed even further, to extremely low levels, for the real balance effect to swamp the effect of bankruptcies, etc. Even so there would exist a hypothetical price level restoring real aggregate demand to full employment levels. On the other hand one could, for the sake of the argument, assume that distribution effects were neutral. In that case, Kalecki pointed out, the fulcrum on which the Pigou-effect could exert expansionary leverage appears to be very narrow indeed: the increase in the real value of the banking system's demand liabilities will have to be offset against the increase in the real value of their holdings of private-sector debts. Thus, "money" was defined as the volume of high-powered money for the analysis of this effect. A slender reed to lean on! Matters could be made to look a little better, however, if the "real financial effect" of the increases in the real value of the private sector's holdings of outside debt was also recognized. The significance of this modification hinges upon the magnitude of government bond liabilities and on the extent to which they can be regarded as properly "outside" in nature.

Contemplating this adjustment process, even the adherents concluded that a passive government policy relying on the Pigou-effect was definitely not to be recommended. The claim made for the argument was restricted to a reassertion of the "logical consistency" of Classical theory, the more extravagant claims of "Keynesians" to the contrary. The latter group of economists, naturally, were not impressed. For all practical purposes, the revolutionary onslaught had carried every important bastion of the "Classic" citadel. That a few die-hards of the garrison refused to switch sides, and could not forcibly be dislodged from the Ivory tower to which they had of free will retreated, could be taken with equanimity in view of the point's lack of strategic significance.

What makes this battle so incongruous in retrospect is that it was fought on the wrong ground, for the wrong reasons and also, certainly, at the wrong time.[4] Keynes did not live to comment on the spectacle. What, then, did he have to say, in the *General Theory*, on the possibility of restoring full employment by money wage adjustment?

Keynes on "changes in money wages"   There are, in fact, a great number of relevant passages and a comprehensive text-critical review would carry us too far. The statement most pertinent to the Pigou-effect debate follows a number of pages in which Keynes has considered a long list of possibilities: the feedback effect on aggregate money demand of a fall in money wage rates, the distributive effects, the effects through short-run price expectations on the imputed holding yield on money, and the effects on the marginal efficiency of investment in the case of inelastic long-run money price expectations:

It is, therefore, on the effect of a falling wage- and price-level on the demand for money that those who believe in the self-adjusting quality of the economic system must rest the weight of their argument; though I am not aware that they have done so. If the quantity of money is itself a function of the wage- and price-level, there is indeed, nothing to hope in this direction.[5]

---

4. The victory of the income-expenditure economists was completed during the period of post-World War II inflation when the Treasury-Federal Reserve agreement fixed market rate at an extremely low level and all the "horses" (which, supposedly, had refused to drink "when led to water" all through the thirties) were found not only to drink copiously, but to wallow in liquidity with the most indecent zest.

5. *General Theory*, p. 266.

The latter sentence is especially noteworthy. Characteristically, Keynes' period-analysis assumes that quantity adjustments will, at least, keep pace with price adjustments. If banks, following for example, an old-fashioned "real bills" policy, adjust their private-sector credit to the money value of output, the money supply, conventionally defined, will indeed decline almost *pari passu* with the wage and price level. Though quite significantly different in analytical approach from the latter debate's assumption of virtually constant money supply, but "absence of distribution effects," Keynes' implied conclusion is much the same as Kalecki's: the relevant fulcrum is at best a most narrow one, namely the quantity of high-powered money in the system.[6] Since the volume of "outside" assets, of fixed nominal par-value, is small, a truly tremendous deflation would be required for the real balance effect to become significant *as long as the money prices of consumer goods, capital goods, and labor services fall roughly in the same proportion.*

The nominal volume of "outside" money is very small. In several passages, Keynes in fact ignores it, implicitly assuming, it seems, a purely "inside" money. For example:

If, indeed, some attempt were made to stabilise real wages by fixing wages in terms of wage-goods, the effect could only be to cause a violent oscillation of money-prices. For every small fluctuation in the propensity to consume and the inducement to invest would cause money-prices to *rush violently between zero and infinity.*[7]

It is, of course, the recurrence of phrases such as the one italicized that so disturbs the Neoclassicists. That "there might be no position of stable equilibrium," or that

. . . prices would be in unstable equilibrium . . . racing to zero whenever investment was below [the critical level], and to infinity whenever it was above it . . .[8]

---

6. The pressure on banks to undertake a "real expansion" of their deposit liabilities, which arises from deflation, will also be less the larger the proportion of initial nominal high-powered money consisting of borrowed reserves. The Central Bank may be faced with a "reflux" of these reserves.

7. *Op. cit.*, p. 239, italics added.

8. *Op. cit.*, pp. 269–70. Compare, e.g., p. 253.

certainly suggests, *particularly when read as referring to the standard one-commodity model,* a direct attack on the prime article of "Classical" faith, to wit, that there should be *some* adjustment of prices possible such that full employment of resources will be attained.

Keynes' argument could have been elaborated with more care. But to him the point was not novel—it was *almost* pure Wicksell. Almost, but not quite, for Wicksell's cumulative process was played out under full employment conditions, whereas Keynes' (deflationary) process assumed that some unemployment had already emerged before the general collapse of reservation prices set prices "racing to zero." [9] Keynes could not very well have foreseen the furor that was to center around this point. Least of all could he have foreseen that a later generation would "grade" his theoretical contribution almost entirely on his discussion of it. His departure from Wicksell in allowing for output as well as price-level adjustments had been part and parcel of the message of the *Treatise* and had not received such an outpouring of adverse comment as to make him hesitate to repeat it:

---

9. According to the present interpretation of the structure of Keynes' model, we could translate the quoted arguments into the terminology favored in the *Treatise:* "If money wages and output prices were perfectly flexible, any event which causes a departure of the natural rate from the market rate would cause money prices to rush violently towards either zero or infinity."

An attempt to restate Wicksell's discussion in terms of a "period model" would reveal a different dynamic structure lacking this dramatic instability. Take, for example, Wicksell's analysis of the inflationary case—market rate below the normal rate. This model would assume that money prices adjust "infinitely fast" in the markets for commodities and labor so that these clear at any moment. The short-run solution of this period model would not show effective excess demand for these goods implying prices rushing on their way to infinity; disequilibrium would be revealed rather by the existence of excess demand for bank credit (and conversely excess supply of "bank notes" offered by the banks)—"notional" magnitudes not made "effective" in the short run, but implying a larger money supply and higher prices in the next unit period.

Wicksell's discussion is, on the other hand, similar in that he also first describes the disequilibrium process and only later points out that the bank's willingness to continue to feed the inflation at rates below the normal rate will ultimately be limited by their available reserves—the "outside" money of the system. While Wicksell prefers to illustrate his analysis with inflationary cases, it is perfectly obvious that his model, if turned to a deflationary situation will yield the Pigou-effect—albeit of the anemic Kalecki variety. Cf. K. Wicksell, *Lectures on Political Economy,* London, 1934, Vol. II, pp. 189–201.

[The position will not improve] since the spending power of the public will be reduced by just as much as the aggregate costs of production. By however much entrepreneurs reduce wages and however many of their employees they throw out of work, they will continue to make losses so long as the community continues to save in excess of new investment. Thus there will be *no position of equilibrium* until . . . etc.[10]

The *Treatise,* however, was recognized as a variation on the Wicksellian theme. The corresponding passages of the *General Theory,* Chapter 19, have not been so recognized—and therein lies most of what is amiss with the Neoclassical appraisal of Keynes, as we shall see.

The extreme wording of the passages quoted suggests that the closest parallel to Keynes' argument is Wicksell's "pure credit-money" case, i.e., the case in which there is no ultimate "outside" check on how far the credit-expansion (contraction) and inflation (deflation) can go. A pure credit-money is also a pure "inside" money. Professor Johnson has suggested that Keynes may be defended on this basis:

. . . Keynes' theory of employment . . . is guiltless of the charges brought against it by Pigou and elaborated by Patinkin and others if interpreted as applying to an inside-money world.[11]

Numerous passages consistent with such an interpretation could be quoted. The *pros* and *cons* on this matter alone could be made the subject of a lengthy text-critical review.[12] This we will

---

10. *Treatise,* Vol. I, pp. 177–78, italics added.

11. H. G. Johnson, "Monetary Theory and Policy," *op. cit.,* p. 343.

12. Partly because, whereas a pure credit-money system is a pure inside-money system and *vice versa,* some semantic questions with which considerable care would have to be taken would still remain. Thus, when a "modern" theorist refers to a pure inside-money case, he is apt to think of it as one in which price-level movements have no "real balance effect" and may therefore proceed with little or no relation to what the nominal stock of inside money happens to be. In the older literature, on the other hand, the pure credit-money case was usually dealt with as a special case of the Quantity Theory so that, whereas price-level movements could in principle proceed indefinitely without being reversed, their proximate cause was generally assumed to lie in an antecedent change in the (inside) money stock.

avoid, for were such a defense of Keynes to be successful, it would only serve to bury the old quarrel with the major issue still unresolved. In any case, I do not believe that a strict interpretation on Johnson's lines can be maintained. It is not likely that Keynes would have conceded that the applicability of this theory was restricted to "the worst of all conceivable systems" characterized (as he put it) by "the abuses of a *fiat* money which has lost all its anchors." [13] We must allow at least for a residue, however slim, of outside money "anchoring" the financial sector of the system to which Keynes' discussion refers.

Keynes, I believe, must be read as admitting the real balance effect and thereby the "logical possibility" on which the Neoclassicists have laid so much stress:

But if the quantity of money is virtually fixed, it is evident that its quantity in terms of wage-units *can be indefinitely increased* by a sufficient reduction in money-wages; and that its quantity in proportion to incomes generally can be largely increased . . .[14]

The trouble (as far as his critics are concerned) is that Keynes insists that the "only hope" from the real balance effect must lie in the effect *on the interest rate* of the increase in real balances, for example,

. . . if competition between unemployed workers always led to a very great reduction of the money-wage, there would be a violent instability in the price-level. Moreover, there might be no position of stable equilibrium except in conditions consistent with full employment; since the wage-unit might have to fall without limit until it reached a point where the effect of the abundance of money in terms of the wage-unit *on the rate of interest* was sufficient to restore a level of full employment. *At no other point could there be a resting-place.*[15]

Variations on this statement are scattered all through the book; there can be no doubt that Keynes meant that an increase in real

---

13. *Treatise,* Vol. I, p. 170.

14. *General Theory,* p. 266, italics added.

15. *General Theory,* p. 253, italics added. Note the careless formulation ". . . fall *without limit until* . . . ."—the passages in which the price level is said to rush between "zero and infinity" should perhaps also be read in this manner.

balances, whether by injection or deflation, would have a significant effect on employment *only* by lowering the rate of interest
and *thereby* affecting aggregate demand. This adjustment possibility is known as the "Keynes-effect" in the literature.

With the "Keynes-effect" Keynes conceded that, *as a matter of
logic, deflation could work*. From that point on, he restricts
himself to arguing against a policy of relying on deflation on the
twin grounds (not unrelated) of "social justice and social expediency." His Neoclassical critics agree that such a policy
would be impracticable and insist that their only objective is to
show that a return to full employment through wage-deflation is
logically possible. So why are they not satisfied? The answer, as
we shall see, is twofold: because they labor under a misconception of what Keynes tried to demonstrate, and because they
entirely misunderstand the structure of the model to which his
argument refers.

An inventory of sundry "effects"   Before we proceed to the
Neoclassical critique of Keynes, however, we had better take
stock of the many diverse "effects" with which we are by now
encumbered.

   The Pigou-effect is an effect *on* real consumption expenditures.
   It is *due to* an increase in real balances which, in turn,
   has been *brought about* by a proportional fall in all
   money prices (except of "bonds").

   The "real financial effect" is also an effect *on* consumption. It
   is *due to* an increase in the real value of all nominally
   fixed "outside" non-money claims held by the private
   sector which in turn, has been *brought about* by a proportional fall in all money prices (except of "bonds").

   Keynes' "windfall effect" should be recalled as an effect *on* consumption (again) *due to* a rise in the value of private-
   sector net worth in terms of current consumer goods. It
   is *brought about* either (a) by an improvement in expectations about the future earnings to accrue to "capital," or (b) by a fall in the interest rate. The ultimate

cause of (a) or (b) moreover, can be "anything" (that makes theoretical sense).

The "Keynes-effect" is an effect *on* aggregate demand (i.e., on *both* consumption *and* investment) *due to* a fall in the rate of interest which, in turn, has been *brought about* specifically by an increase in real balances—*and* the increase in real balances, finally, should be due to all-around deflation.

This is the usage. When spelled out in this way, it is quite obvious that there is ample room for differentiating quite a number of other "effects" distinguished either by the component of expenditures ultimately affected or by one or another link in the chain of causation that brings this about. And, indeed, a "Lerner-effect" and a "Tobin-effect," for example, have gained a certain currency. But these as well as others we will endeavor not to bring into the discussion.

The Neoclassical critique We may then consider Patinkin's critique of Keynes' position on the subject of the economic system's capacity for self-adjustment through deflation. Patinkin first insists that Keynes' system does contain some "outside" money and, in addition, government bonds which are to be regarded as "outside." [16] This, presumably, Keynes would willingly have conceded. A fall in the money prices of commodities should therefore have both a "real balance effect" and a "real financial effect." Patinkin proceeds to "speculate on the train of reasoning which caused Keynes to ignore" these effects:

It seems likely that he did recognize the influence of wealth on consumption . . . , but thought of this influence only in terms of [physical] assets. Correspondingly in his main discussion of the short-run consumption function—where, by assumption, the stock of [physical] assets is fixed—he did not even consider the possible influence of wealth. On the other hand—and this is precisely what our interpretation leads us to expect—as soon as Keynes discussed a period long enough for noticeable capital growth, he immediately recognized that

16. D. Patinkin, *Money, Interest, and Prices,* 2nd edn., New York, 1965, p. 635. This is in response to the suggestion by H. G. Johnson discussed above.

the resulting increase in wealth causes a decrease in the propensity to save. But this, unfortunately, did not bring him to realize that an analogous influence could exist even in the short run, provided one took account of . . . assets [the nominal quantity of which is fixed] as well as [physical] ones.[17]

Let us first consider the "real financial effect" apart from the "real balance effect." It can hardly be denied that Keynes ignored any explicit analysis of the increase in the real value of "outside" bonds due to deflation. In our discussion of the choice of alternative aggregative structures for the capital accounts, in section III:2 above, we noted that Tobin's distinction between "physical" and "financial" assets is the one more relevant to make when the analytical problem concerns rapid movements of the price level. The fact that Keynes apparently did not bother with this distinction between "physical" and "financial" long assets, but implicitly continued to regard his non-money assets as a homogeneous aggregate, may simply indicate that for various reasons he had but little interest in the possibility of automatic adjustment through deflation. It is also possible, however, that he made a mistake and thought that the matter was taken care of, however cursorily, by the assumptions he had adopted in order to make all non-money assets homogeneous in terms of anticipated holding yield at a point in time.[18]

---

17. *Op. cit.,* p. 636 (Supplementary Note *K*). We have changed the quote to avoid Patinkin's usage of "monetary" versus "non-monetary assets," since his definition of the latter is different from the similar-sounding term used previously in this thesis. We have used "non-money assets" as a convenient label for all assets which are not "money" (according to some definition of the latter). Patinkin uses "non-monetary" to denote assets which do not have a par-value fixed in nominal terms. The above use of "physical" instead of "non-monetary" follows Patinkin's Note *K* of the 1st edn., and also his discussion of the same topic in "Price Flexibility and Full Employment," *Readings in Monetary Theory,* pp. 269–70.

It is somewhat startling to find that in all these three versions of his critique of Keynes on this matter, Patinkin "documents" his assertion that Keynes' short-run consumption function disregards asset variables entirely, by reference to the *General Theory* pp. 91–95—*the very pages which we have quoted extensively in documenting the "windfall effect"!* Cf. Chapter IV:1.

18. *General Theory,* pp. 227–28. It will be recalled that Keynes' aggregation of the capital accounts made use of "risk" and "liquidity premia" to "adjust" the anticipated yields on different kinds of non-money assets. He also made an adjust-

That the "real financial effect" is ignored should, in my opinion, be conceded. Patinkin's critique of Keynes, however, really centers upon another point, namely that Keynes implicitly assumes "that the real-balance effect does not directly influence the commodity market [19] . . . [Keynes'] model . . . has both inside and outside money and should accordingly have provided for a . . . real-balance effect *in all markets*." [20]

Patinkin's critique is entirely to the point in relation to the "standard" income-expenditure model. It is also the more relevant because his model is of the same aggregative structure as the income-expenditure model and his discussion, therefore, concerns the logical consistency of this model on its own terms. But with regard to the *General Theory*, his critique is misconceived. Keynes was not a "Keynesian." Patinkin's theory deals with a four-good world containing commodities, labor services, bonds, and money. He discussed the *General Theory* with reference to this model. Having just considered Keynes' probable error with regard to the "real financial effect," we can presently ignore the bonds of Keynes' model. The Keynes model relevant to Patinkin's criticism is then one which contains: consumer goods, capital goods, labor services, and money.

Consider now Keynes' repeated insistence that an increased supply of money in terms of wage units works through lowering the rate of interest. From our previous discussion we know what this means (on the present interpretation of the *General Theory*): the effects on commodity markets are as "direct" as can be desired. Given the State of Long Term Expectation, a decline in the rate of interest implies *a rise in the price of capital goods in terms of wage units*. The demand price of augmentable capital

---

ment for the *expected* "percentage appreciation or depreciation" of one asset in terms of another. This does not help in the present context, where the appreciation of money is *realized* within the unit period. Keynes' analytical habit of lumping together "bonds" and physical assets was well ingrained—it goes back at least to the very first pages of the *Tract*.

19. Patinkin, 2nd edn., p. 634. Cf. also, e.g., pp. 21 n., 180, 188, 241, 264–65, Note *K*:1, etc. That this is the point considered by Patinkin the central one is indicated on p. 636: "For this reason our criticism of Keynesian economics on this score has concentrated exclusively on the commodity market."

20. *Op. cit.*, p. 635, italics added.

goods rises relative to their cost of production at the output rate of the moment. Investment will increase with further "multiplier effects" on aggregate demand, given the initial marginal propensity to consume. But the propensity to consume will also be directly affected—it will increase through the wealth effect of the rise in "real net worth." Thus in *both* commodity markets—and there are two, not just one as in Patinkin's system—excess demand appears (if zero to begin with) immediately as the rate of interest declines. The consumer goods market does not have to "await the workings of the multiplier"—the wealth effect is direct. General deflation, then, will help—*if, at some point, the decline in money asset prices starts to lag significantly behind the fall in money wages and consumer goods prices.* What Keynes denied was that a *proportional* fall of all money prices could be of significant help.

Patinkin uses the word "directly" in a different sense, however, and his critique implies a question not yet considered. It may be put in the following manner: Does Keynes' discussion imply that, in his system, the partial derivative of commodities markets demand functions with respect to real balances (the rate of interest, in particular, held constant) is zero? There are three considerations relevant to this question:

(a) Keynes' judgment about the relative quantitative significance of the two effects. A change in the rate of interest will increase the price in terms of wage units of all long-lived assets in the system; the Pigou-effect proper works on the narrow fulcrum of "outside" money only—"there is, indeed, nothing to hope in this direction." [21] It is probable that Keynes simply

---

21. Cf. *Treatise*, Vol. II, the previously cited pp. 98 and 364.

The volume of "outside" money normally constitutes but an insignificant fraction of the total consolidated net worth of the private sector. One must note, however, that judging the "strength" of wealth effects by the change in the "real" value of some component of net worth is a questionable practice. (If the real balance effect were indeed "very weak," the price level would presumably be in near-neutral equilibrium—at least upwards, in which direction no rigidities are claimed. This does not seem consonant with observation.) Pesek and Saving, *op. cit.*, have initiated the attack on this practice in connection with their treatment of ("inside") money as net wealth.

The usual measure of the "gap" between actual and equilibrium "real" magni-

ignored the real balance effect, to the extent that it did not work through the interest rate, as a "secondary magnitude"—the kind of assumption so common in all comparative static analysis.[22]

(b) The wealth effect and the real balance effect are otherwise not "different in nature." A proportional decline in all money prices increases the real value of that part of net worth held in the form of money. If money is defined to include only non-interest-earning assets, the real balance effect does not, by itself, increase the real value of the permanent income-streams over which the transactor at that moment has command. The same can be said for Keynes' "windfall effect": the individual holds the same permanent real streams as initially but the current "real value" of his net worth is increased. (As previously noted, Keynes regards intertemporal substitution effects as of "secondary magnitude.") Thus, "if a man is enjoying a windfall increment in the value of his capital, it is natural that his motives towards current spending should be strengthened, even though in terms of income his capital is worth no more than before."

Presumably, Keynes would have said exactly the same thing if pressed on the issue of the "pure" real balance effect.

(c) Adjustments in "securities" markets are assumed to proceed faster than in other markets. As previously mentioned, Keynes treated titles to physical capital goods as "securities" in the *Treatise*. The assumption is of the kind characterizing "period-model" analysis of dynamic adjustment processes generally. Stock market prices adjust on the "market day"—to a level consistent with current expectations which are in turn inelastic on the "market day" and are, indeed, only revised in the "long run;" effective excess demands in commodities markets become zero only in the "short run." There is ample evidence for the assumption of this ranking of the relative adjustment speeds in Keynes' work. Patinkin works with the same assumption him-

---

tudes may not give a good indication of the strength of equilibrating tendencies, nor—in particular—of the pressure on aggregate demand to be expected, given such a gap of known magnitude. The issues raised by Pesek and Saving will presumably be a major concern of monetary theorists for some time to come.

22. Cf., e.g., P. A. Samuelson, *Foundations of Economic Analysis*, pp. 26–27.

self.[23] There is no reason to believe that Keynes' way of invariably tracing the effects of increases in the real money supply through the securities markets reflects anything other than this kind of, quite conventional, period-model assumption.[24]

No participant in the debate has argued that the Pigou-effect proper is of major magnitude "within the normal range" of price-level variation. Still, Keynes' critics insist that his theory is *fatally* flawed by his lack of concern for this effect. Clearly, it appears fatal only because the Neoclassicists refuse to take the Keynes-effect seriously. When Keynes tenders this effect in recognition of the possible benefits of deflation, he is received as a Greek bearing gifts. This suspicious attitude, of course, is based on the belief that Keynes shared with the income-expenditure school the assumption that both consumption and investment expenditures are virtually completely interest-inelastic. If that were true, the Keynes-effect would indeed be a sham. But we know this belief to be unfounded.

The tangled misconceptions underlying the Neoclassical appraisal of Keynes stand out most clearly in Kuenne's discussion. His basic preconception, as we have seen, concerns the *intent* behind Keynes' argument—Keynes, he postulates, intended to prove that wage-deflation provides no possible way out of an unemployment situation. Thus, when Keynes argues that a reduction in money wages (the marginal efficiency of capital constant) will not help *if* it does not serve to reduce the rate of interest, Kuenne regards the proviso merely as a "hedge" obscuring Keynes' basic contention—that money wage reductions do not help *period:*

Common sense obstructs logical consistency at crucial points. Keynes's hedge concerning the constant rate of interest in his conclusion above is one such example.[25]

---

23. Patinkin, 2nd edn., e.g., p. 80.

24. Cf. *General Theory*, p. 205: ". . . broadly speaking, the banking system and the monetary authority are dealers in money and debts and not in assets or consumables."

25. Kuenne, *op. cit.*, pp. 355–56. This is much like criticizing Wicksell for straying from "logical consistency" by "hedging" his analysis of the cumulative process

Kuenne goes on to remove all such "obstructions" by constructing a model with a "complete dichotomy," not between money and all other goods as in the case of "Say's Identity," but between "paper and real sectors." This construction he labels "Keynes's Identity"! It involves the postulate that the effect of an increase in real balances due to deflation "is confined to the securities markets or is absent. . . . all potential effects . . . on the real goods sector must be effectively nullified to preserve Keynes's Identity." [26] This last requirement can be fulfilled only in the familiar ways: either by assuming the Liquidity Trap or by assuming complete interest-inelasticity of both consumption and investment demand.[27]

Clearly, "Keynes's Identity" is grotesquely mislabeled. Nothing could be more foreign to Keynes' theory than this dichotomy between "real goods" and "paper." If his analytical procedure is to be criticized, it is—as previously conceded—because he does *not* take care to distinguish clearly between physical and financial non-money assets even when the problem at hand so requires.

V:2   Keynes' Diagnosis of the "Causes of Unemployment"

The previous section dealt with the immediate issues raised by the Neoclassical critique of Keynes. We should now leave these problems aside in order to consider the deeper questions related to Keynes' diagnosis of the maladjustments which lead to depressions. Keynes, as we have seen in our discussion of the "real financial effect," treated the analysis of deflation in a somewhat cursory manner. Though he returns to the topic at intervals

---

with the proviso that it would come to a halt were the market rate to be brought into line with natural rate.

26. *Op. cit.,* p. 358.

27. This being so, Kuenne can only end up with the same old "terms of the truce," i.e.: "To the extent that Keynes focussed attention upon the slowness, or weakness, of . . . adjustments, his analysis contributes fruitful insights. But in the field of static general equilibrium theory . . . his performance was essentially a failure." (*Op. cit.,* pp. 360–61.)

throughout the book, it is often handled with apparent impatience. In our view, his thoughts on this matter have been misinterpreted—in itself evidence that the analysis was less than thorough. How is this to be explained? Three different interpretations may be considered.

First, the most common interpretation is perhaps that, once having adopted the assumption of "wage-rigidity" and built his model on this assumption, Keynes had little further interest in questions relating to money price flexibility. That this is a superficial explanation is apparent both from our discussion in Chapter II and from the fact that Keynes devoted a large portion of the latter half of the *General Theory* to these problems.[1]

A second, more weighty, interpretation is the one repeatedly emphasized by Lerner in opposition to the conventional one: Keynes correctly feared the disintegrative effects on the system of relying on, or forcing, drastic price-level adjustments. This point should always be made in this context; there can be no doubt about its relevance or validity.[2] There is no need, however, to pursue it further here than has already been done in Chapter II:4.

The following, third interpretation, in my opinion, goes fur-

---

1. Here we fully agree with Patinkin. In the revised version of "Price Flexibility and Full Employment" (*Readings in Monetary Theory*, p. 283 n.), he comments: ". . . in the light of Chapter 19 of the *General Theory* . . . it is difficult to understand how wage rigidities can be considered a basic assumption of the Keynesian theory of unemployment. From this chapter it is quite clear that wage rigidities are *not* an *assumption* of Keynes' analysis, but rather a policy conclusion that follows from his investigation of the probable effects of *wage flexibility*. . . ." Etc.

Patinkin's discussion is cast in the terminology of period-analysis. This is somewhat unfortunate here, since it means a tendency to refer to wage-rigidity and, what he calls, "a regime of flexible prices" as *mutually exclusive* possibilities. It is a principal tenet of the present work that a deeper understanding of Keynes' contribution must grow from a consideration of the case of *imperfectly flexible* prices and the information problems characterizing such a "regime."

2. Once again, Keynes' convictions stand out much more clearly and forcefully, unobstructed by the intricate scaffolding of "professional" economic analysis, in several of his more "popular" writings. Apart from the previously cited "Social Consequences of Changes in the Value of Money," Parts II and III of his *Essays in Persuasion* contain a number of relevant papers, the most well known being "The Economic Consequences of Mr. Churchill." For the two contributions of A. P. Lerner, cf. p. 108 n.9 above.

ther towards the core of Keynes' thinking on macroeconomic problems.

The general equilibrium model used as a diagnostic tool   We have consistently viewed Keynes' contributions to economic theory as part of a great over-all effort to *extend* the use of the (largely received) tools of general value theory beyond the area represented by problems of general equilibrium and into the area of macrodisequilibrium. His contribution, in other words, has been viewed as an attempt to carry on from the points where an older generation left off, *not* as an attempt to sweep the boards clean of traditional theory. This venture forward from the theory of economic equilibrium into the area of disequilibrium problems—which, despite Wicksell, Lindahl, Myrdal, and others, presented large expanses of virgin territory—also meant, as we have emphasized, that he turned his attention away from the traditional preoccupation with long-run tendencies towards the problems of macroeconomic adjustment processes in the short run.

What is the logical point of departure for someone approaching the problem of disequilibrium armed with the tools of general equilibrium analysis? The problem may be put in the following manner: In general equilibrium, the plans of all transactors are *consistent* at the ruling vector of prices. All plans, therefore, can be simultaneously carried out in trading. The realized results of exchange do not then, in themselves, force a change of plans upon the transactors. With all economic activities progressing in this consistent manner, the system can be analyzed much as a Crusoe-economy (with a Robinson possessed of rather unusual qualities of foresight and steadfastness of purpose).

Contemplation of a situation of macrodisequilibrium yields a different picture. Only a bout of acute schizophrenia in Robinson could possibly throw the Crusoe-economy into the straits of depression. Perhaps the stark irrationality of disequilibrium when viewed in this artificial context accounts somewhat for the vehemence with which the possibility of a "general glut" was at one time so often denied. There is, indeed, something of a schizophrenic quality to economic disequilibrium processes—particularly recognizable, of course, in violent deflations and inflations, when not only the economic, but also the political and social integration of the system breaks down. Just as a scientist concerned with mental health will turn to the study of mental illness, Keynes turned his abundant energies to the study of disequilibrium.[3]

In disequilibrium, then, the "notional" excess demands of individual traders are *not* consistent in the aggregate. Nonetheless, general equilibrium theory tells us that potentially there does exist a vector of prices that would allow all plans to be realized. Disequilibrium, therefore, implies a ruling price vector in one or more respects different from the appropriate one.[4] The diagnostic task facing the economist may then be conceived to be that of specifying the fundamental discrepancy between the equilibrium price vector and the initial disequilibrium vector. But the task is complicated by the fact that, once ill, the patient rapidly develops a number of additional complaints of a quite alarming nature. During the larger part of his career, Keynes apparently took much the same attitude towards the latter problems as that of a psychoanalyst who trusts that, if the fundamental trauma can only be found and relieved, all the subsidiary behavior disorders are likely to disappear by themselves in short order. He was not without some faith in the self-recuperative powers of the market system. But the desperate plight of the thirties shook his faith in the possibility of being successful with such basic therapy before the patient was beyond all help; in an emergency it was necessary to prescribe drastic measures to relieve directly the most painful of the symptoms of disease.

In deflationary disequilibrium, the economy develops symp-

---

3. In the United States, his motives have often been construed in a less benevolent light by the more violent opponents to the federal policies pursued in his name. "Evidence" for Keynes' subversive ulterior motives are found in his sins of omission—his lifetime output contains, perhaps, a lower than average number of pages extolling the "invisible hand" and the inestimable benefits of mental health.

4. Cf. J. R. Hicks, "Methods of Dynamic Analysis," *op. cit.*, esp. Hicks' comments on Lindahl's work in the field of macrodynamics. More recently Hicks has expanded on his discussion of alternative dynamic approaches in *Capital and Growth*, Oxford, 1965.

toms of unemployment very rapidly. The "Classical" diagnosis of such disequilibrium was "too high money wages," and the "Classical" prescription "deflation." [5] Diagnosis and prescription alike were the subject of Keynes' vehement malpractice charges: to him the "Classical" cure smacked of leeches and bloodletting—primitive and disreputable methods which were likely, as often as not, so to weaken the patient as to kill him. As often happens, modern research has led to a somewhat milder judgment of certain ancient medical practices than the "Age of Reason" was willing to accord them; this has seldom if ever led to their revival. Keynes would no doubt have given evidence of his generally lively antiquarian interest in the result of the Pigou-effect debate: that, in certain unlikely circumstances, involuntary unemployment could indeed be cured by balanced deflation. It is not likely that it would have influenced his recommendations on the economic policy to be pursued.

Ironically, the income-expenditure theorists are often, though not always, in accord with the "Classical" diagnosis: unemployment shows that wages are too high and it would be well if they were lower. But they generally agree that nothing can be done about it and turn, therefore, to Keynesian prescriptions.[6]

Spot prices: wages versus asset prices Though widespread unemployment is the most drastic *symptom* of deflationary disequilibria, Keynes maintained that the *cause* of depressions should be sought in other markets. In a situation of actual or threatening contraction, the ruling price vector differs from the appropriate vector. *The essence of Keynes' diagnosis of depressions is this: the actual disequilibrium price vector initiating the*

---

5. It must be remembered, however, that Keynes' "Classical economist" was largely a strawman: the label simply will not stick on the majority of the influential economists of the thirties. Cf. Section II:4 and Schlesinger, *op. cit.*

6. Lack of concern with the diagnosis, unfortunately, has often meant that Keynes' fiscal emergency treatment is prescribed indiscriminately. At one time it was even the doctrine that the emergency medicine had better be administered in ever-increasing doses to economies having reached the feeble old age of "economic maturity." Economists concerned with "institutional arteriosclerosis" as another danger to mature economies have understandably been much concerned with the side-effects of such treatment.

contraction differs from the appropriate, hypothetical equilib-rium vector in one major respect—the general level of long-term asset prices is lower than warranted.

Thus the "Classical" and the Keynesian diagnoses are jux-taposed. Observing unemployment, the "Classical" economist —and, again, let us not forget that this unworthy fellow is a stereotype constructed by Keynes to represent a contemporary school of thought that he opposed—draws the conclusion that wages are too high and "ought" to be reduced. In Keynes' theory, the maintenance of full employment depends upon the mainte-nance of a "right" relation between the general level of asset prices and the wage unit. High asset prices imply high levels of demand for both new investment and consumption. At high asset prices, the anomaly of traders in the aggregate not feeling "wealthy" enough to absorb the full employment rate of output will not occur. Keynes' point is that when the appropriate price relation does *not* obtain, *it is in general not wages but asset demand prices that are out of line.*

From this diagnosis stems what I take to be Keynes' funda-mental objection to the "Classical" medicine of deflation: *al-though the most eye-catching symptom of maladjustment is that of great excess supply in labor markets, money wage rates may very well be "correct,"* i.e., roughly equal to the money wages that the system would have in equilibrium. Once demand prices for augmentable assets have moved to "too low" a level, the pressure of excess supply in the productive sectors of the econ-omy will rapidly be transferred back to the labor market over the whole front. Although this has been allowed to occur, *the burden of adjustment should not be thrown on this market.*[7] Asset prices are "wrong" and it is to asset markets that the cure should, if possible, be applied.

Several times we have referred to Keynes' reputation for ignor-

---

7. Note that this adds another argument to the Keynesian case for recommending the pursuit of a policy aimed at stabilizing wages. Patinkin considered this policy conclusion to follow from Keynes' investigation of the "probable *effects* of wage flexibility" and this is, as we have stressed, part of Keynes' case. The other part, which we are now emphasizing, is perhaps even more important and rests on the "probable causes" of an excess supply of labor.

ing the application of the lessons of general price theory, sins of omission that are variously explained by emphasizing either his personality traits—his iconoclastic streak or his abundant self-confidence—or his supposedly limited mastery of the subject. To the extent that the interpretation offered above is accepted, this view of Keynes stands in need of drastic revision. The traditional diagnosis of depressions which lays the "blame" of unemployment on the obstinate behavior of labor is based on a *partial* equilibrium analysis inappropriate to the problem at hand (which concerns the malfunctioning of the system as a whole). Keynes' diagnosis conceals a number of difficult issues on which positions at variance with his may well be taken, but the diagnosis is not based on the naive presumption that the causes of macrodisequilibria are to be found in the markets which at any time exhibit the most dramatic symptoms of maladjustment. He approached the ("general *dis*equilibrium") problem from a *general equilibrium* perspective.

This observation is particularly pertinent to the appraisal of Keynes' analysis of the hypothetical consequences of a "regime" of flexible money prices and wages. Keynes' statements to the effect that money wages would "rush violently between zero and infinity," etc., *can* be read as a denial of the *existence* of a full employment price vector. It appears that in the course of the Keynes and the Classics debate they have often been interpreted in this manner as indicative of the careless lightheartedness with which Keynes was supposedly inclined to shove traditional price theory aside. But to read them in this way is to ignore the Keynesian diagnosis of how deflationary pressure comes to emerge. They should not be so read. It may well be the case that Keynes' *obiter dicta* on the subject of a regime of price-flexibility hide some questionable premises but the naive contention that no hypothetical price vector exists which would bring about full employment is not involved. Keynes' position is consistent with the existence of a whole class of price vectors capable of bringing about full utilization of resources in the current period. His assertions rest on a conception of a "quite Classical" nature—i.e., that could the set of all full employment price vectors be known and studied, it would be found that for each relative price there is a more or less restricted range of values consistent with full resource utilization. He concentrated specifically on the case where, given the history of the system up to the period in question and the resultant State of Entrepreneurial Expectation, there is a definite upper bound to the range of long rates of interest consistent with full employment. His discussion of money wage flexibility proceeds on the assumption that the State of Liquidity Preference is such that "the" interest rate lies above this range. The question to which he addresses himself is whether, given the resulting inappropriately low value of non-money assets in terms of wage units, a fall in money wages will help to restore full employment.

Intertemporal transformation opportunities: entrepreneurial expectations versus market rate   We have regarded Keynes' diagnosis as based on a comparison of the actual vector of observed prices ruling at the onset of a contraction with the hypothetical vector which would pertain in a system characterized by perfect information. We may consider first a case which is even more restrictive than the one made by Keynes. The comparison should not be just a matter of spot prices; the two vectors to be considered contain both spot and forward prices. The hypothetical "perfect" vector contains a full set of forward prices; the actually observed vector contains only bond rates of interest for various maturities and current money prices for other assets from which unique inferences about forward values cannot be made. According to Keynes' diagnosis, it is fundamentally the *intertemporal relative values* observed or implicit in the actual vector which are "wrong." The statements previously quoted presume that intertemporal prices are inappropriate. The more restrictive case starts from the assumption that current full utilization of resources requires the establishment of a *unique* intertemporal price vector. This would mean that the set of equations representing the intertemporal general equilibrium system has only one solution. That the *efficient* time-path is unique is, indeed, commonly assumed in work on the so-called "metastatic" models. The assumption here—suggested for illustrative purposes only—is stronger, since it asserts that if one, or some, of the intertemporal relative values is "wrong," no suboptimal solution having the property of clearing all spot markets for factor services would exist. It denies, in other words, the existence of Hicksian "temporary equilibria"—i.e., short-run solutions which, though off the equilibrium time-path, clear all *existing* markets [8] in the present.

If, then, in a system such as the one posited, we consider a situation in which some of the endogenous variables have "got stuck" at values incompatible with the "global" solution, we get a first approximation to Keynes' argument. The assumptions made imply that, *as long as the interest rate stays "too high,"* there are no possible adjustments of current money output prices and money wages which could wipe out excess supplies in spot markets. In a regime of extremely high money price velocities, such excess supplies would, indeed, send money values "rushing violently towards zero."

Now this is a stronger position than one would care to take. But then Keynes did not argue this extreme case. Thus, he was not categorical—if intertemporal relative values are out of line, there is nothing to *guarantee* that there exist values for the other unknowns of the problem (current money prices and wages) such that clearance of factor services markets will nonetheless be ensured: "there *might be no* position of stable equilibrium except in conditions consistent with full employment."

Furthermore—and more significantly—the "conditions consistent with full employment" that he envisaged are not as restrictive as those just discussed. Existing market institutions do not register a full complement of forward price quotations. The condition that Keynes regarded as necessary for full employment in the present is that "real" asset values be maintained at a specific level. This does not require that both entrepreneurial expectations and "the" interest rate be such as to keep the system on its hypothetical equilibrium time-path. There is room for offsetting errors with respect to intertemporal relative values. The condition may be fulfilled with a too low, "pessimistic"

---

8. It is *not* assumed that this hypothetical system is more richly endowed with forward markets than the systems which we actually observe.

MEC-schedule if the interest rate is correspondingly low or, conversely, one might observe a boom "in which over-optimism triumphs over a rate of interest which, in a cooler light, would be seen to be excessive." [9] But if these factors combine to make "real" asset values too low, Keynes could see no hope in a *balanced deflation* in which money asset prices and money wages fall *pari passu*.

Since in Keynes' analysis entrepreneurial expectations and Liquidity Preference are treated as (almost) independent co-determinants of asset values, there are *two* routes through which a fall in money wages might turn the deflation "unbalanced" in such a way as to restore full resource utilization. One possibility is that current money prices fall faster than future expected prices. This change in some of the unobservable intertemporal price relations would "increase the marginal efficiency of capital; whilst for the same reason it may be favourable to consumption." [10] The other possibility is the "Keynes-effect" proper—that the rise in the value of the money stock in terms of wage units will bring about a fall in "the" interest rate.

Moreover, of the two factors which combine to make asset demand prices too low, Keynes generally blamed too high long rates rather than too pessimistic entrepreneurial expectations for the *onset* of depressions. Once the income-constrained process had been allowed to gather momentum, of course, expectations would no longer be such as to sustain full employment even in conjunction with a "metastatically right" interest rate. [11] But this

---

9. *General Theory*, p. 322. The distinction between entrepreneurial expectations and Liquidity Preference as the two factors determining asset demand prices will be considered further in connection with our discussion of Keynes' views on the issue of fiscal versus monetary policy in Chapter VI:2.

10. *General Theory*, p. 263. The statement in the text is somewhat more general than the one made by Keynes, who stressed the cost side, i.e., the case of a "reduction of money-wages [which] is expected to be a *reduction relatively to money-wages in the future* . . ."

11. The longer the system wallows in depression, one must also surmise, the farther would the dry rot eat into the all-important long-term end of expectations making the demand price schedules for durable capital assets more elastic with respect to the rate of investment and, therefore, the rate of investment in Fixed Capital less and less susceptible to control through the rate of interest. The longer a depression has lasted, the less safe is Keynes' habit of simply identifying present asset values with the asset demand price. Cf. Chapter III:3.

is a derivative phenomenon. *To Keynes, too high a long rate was the "fundamental trauma"* and its correction an all but necessary condition for recovery. Over many years, this conception formed the basis for his pronouncements on matters of public policy.[12]

This, of course, is (at long last) the whole point of the Keynes-effect. Keynes' Neoclassical critics have brushed it aside because they have not understood his diagnosis. The Keynes-effect will work because it relieves the fundamental "cause" of the type of disequilibrium that Keynes postulated.[13]

Thus, Keynes' diagnosis of the conditions leading to a downturn in activity focused on the relation between the money prices of non-money assets and the money wage rate. If this relation was out of line, moreover, he put the "blame" on too low asset values as a rule, not on too high wages.[14] The conclu-

---

12. Cf. Harrod's *Life*, p. 399: "Most important of his contributions during this year (1930) was his article in the September issue of the *Svenska Handelsbanken Index* on the future of the rate of interest. He had become convinced that the time was ripe for a large and permanent reduction throughout the world. This was to be the basis of all his future thinking on economic policy; it also determined his investment policy on his own behalf and that of the institutions which he advised." Since Keynes put his money where his mouth was, one cannot very well regard his Keynes-effect just as a "hedge" of a merely academic argument.

13. It is instructive to note, for example, the disturbance considered by Kuenne in his appraisal of Keynes' contribution to "pure" theory (*op. cit.*, p. 349): "From a position of general equilibrium we suppose the economy to be jarred by an increase in the excess demand for money to a positive level. . . ." Also, p. 356: "Now, let us start with a full general equilibrium and assume that the public suddenly desires increased real balances, obtaining them by reducing excess demands for consumption and investment goods. Let all markets but those for labor and money be reequilibrated . . ." etc.

While this is the premise from which Kuenne departs, it is also the conclusion Modigliani, among others, arrives at: "It is true that a reduced level of employment and a reduced level of investment go together, but this is not, in general, the result of [a] causal relationship. It is true instead that *the low level of investment and employment are both the effect of the same cause, namely a basic maladjustment between the quantity of money and the wage rate.*" F. Modigliani, "Liquidity Preference and the Theory of Interest and Money," *Econometrica*, Jan. 1944; cf. the reprint in *Readings in Monetary Theory*, pp. 224–25, italics added.

14. This part of the diagnosis raises some questions to which we will turn shortly.

Harrod (*op. cit.*, p. 454) puts the matter succinctly: "He did not think that the high wage was the cause of unemployment or that lowering the wage would—subject to [the Keynes effect, etc.]—increase employment." Note that *two* "be-

sion is that deflation will help *only if* it changes this relative price in the appropriate direction, i.e., *only if it cures the malady that underlies the emergence of excess supply of commodities in the first place:* "we must base any hopes of favorable results to employment from a reduction in money-wages" on an increase in the value of non-money assets in terms of the wage unit. Such a favorable result might occur through one or the other of the possibilities outlined above. Of the two, however, Keynes stressed the possibility of a reduction in the rate of interest—that of a favorable shift of the marginal efficiency of capital was generally held imprisoned in the *ceteris paribus* assumptions of his short-run analysis. Directly, the stimulating effects will fall "mainly on investment"; the wealth effect on consumption demand is regarded as definitely subsidiary.

To this analysis, the enormous subsequent debate has added the footnote that the Pigou-effect shows the "logical possibility" of a favorable result produced by a mechanism which (a) does not operate through investment demand at all, and (b) depends upon neither of the two possibilities which Keynes regarded as the only relevant ones. In retrospect, it is hard to see that this point deserved much more ink than Keynes spilt on it (in dismissing it), though a veritable torrent has been forthcoming. The explanation must be that, working with the one-commodity model,[15] these critics of Keynes have not understood that his

---

liefs" are involved—Keynes' Neoclassical critics have concentrated on the second to the exclusion of the first.

15. It is the present author's belief that this misinterpretation of Keynes has arisen and gained currency mainly because of the predominance of the one-commodity model in this area. This does not mean, however, that it is not possible to capture much of the essence of Keynes' argument concerning the information problems involved in the so-called "saving-investment process" in the context of a model which makes no distinction between consumer goods and capital goods. But in order to do so, most of the analysis, which Keynes preferred to conduct in terms of relative "spot" values, must be translated into an analysis dealing, on the one hand, with the expected price of "the" future commodity in terms of the present commodity and, on the other hand, with the money rate of interest. Since such a model circumvents many of the index number problems that "perplexed" Keynes, it is actually simpler to handle than Keynes' own system. Despite this relative simplicity, it seems to have been presumed that such an analysis would be price-theoretically much "too sophisticated" to conform to Keynes' intentions.

whole discussion proceeds from the premise that we have to deal with a situation in which relative values have gotten out of line. The motivation for the whole debate must lie in the presumption that Keynes had rejected the fundamental premise of traditional theory—namely that there must be *some* readjustment of relative values possible such that full employment would result—and, perhaps, also in a disturbing feeling that he had come very close to justifying this rejection. If these are not the premises motivating this debate, how is it to be explained? But these exegetical premises are, according to our interpretation, false.

Keynes and the Wicksellian heritage As indicated earlier, there are certain questionable aspects to what we have called "Keynes' diagnosis." Keynes blithely side-stepped a number of difficult issues which had come to the forefront of the debate on Monetary Dynamics during the early thirties. On the purely technical aspects of these issues at least, the great post-Wicksellians often showed more sophistication than did Keynes. Several of his contemporaries provided a more systematic and, in several respects, more penetrating analysis of "what goes wrong with relative values" in macroeconomic fluctuations.[16] But in acknowledging this, we must also reiterate a point stressed in Chapter II, namely that none of these authors provided a systematic analysis of the income-constrained process, the idea which is the hallmark of the *General Theory*.[17]

We cannot go into a detailed discussion of these problems. Such a discussion would involve delving into the extensive and

---

16. Cf. esp. E. Lindahl, *Studies in the Theory of Money and Capital*, New York, 1939 (the main part of which is based on work published in Swedish in 1929 and 1930); G. Myrdal, *Monetary Equilibrium*, London, 1939 (Swedish original, 1931); F. A. Hayek, *Prices and Production*, London, 1931, also, *Profits, Interest and Investment*, London, 1939. Although D. H. Robertson cannot be classified as a follower of Wicksell, he should also be mentioned here; in particular, his *Banking Policy and the Price Level*.

17. The processes investigated by Lindahl, for example, generally consisted of a succession of "temporary equilibria," i.e., states characterized by clearance of all spot markets and the general realization of immediate trading plans, although not by the fulfillment over time of the expectations on which these plans are at any time largely based. The "multiplier" idea came into the Swedish discussion with E. Lundberg, *Studies in the Theory of Economic Expansion*, Stockholm, 1937.

difficult interwar literature on the criteria for a "neutral monetary policy," on the issue of "forced saving," on what has been termed Hayek's Concertina- and Ricardo-effects, on the difficulties connected with Wicksell's concept of the Natural Rate—and so forth.[18] The relationship between Keynes and the later "Keynesians" must remain our main concern.

It seems clear that Keynes consciously did his best to dodge the issues raised in the post-Wicksellian debate. In retrospect it is amazing how successful he was, for following the appearance of the *General Theory* they were in short order forgotten. But this "success" came at a price; in part at least, Keynes avoided controversy by not stressing the (at the time) controversial aspects of his diagnosis. In so doing, he in effect invited subsequent misinterpretation.

We have tended so far to draw a line between Keynes' diagnosis and the policy implications derived from it. This has served our analytical convenience but it involves an oversimplification that must now be corrected. Actually, a clear line of this sort cannot be drawn. His diagnosis is not just based on "positive" economic analysis free of normative ingredients. Policy judgments enter in from the very start. In particular, Keynes tends to take for granted the universal appropriateness of his own criterion for the conduct of monetary policy and implicitly to inject this criterion in his discussion of the maladjustments leading to contraction. Put somewhat roughly, this criterion is that the monetary authority in any given period "ought to" maintain the general level of asset prices (in terms of money) which has been reached in the preceding period, *if* that period was one of full employment. This would mean that the rate of output of augmentable assets would be maintained, in turn implying maintenance of the previous level of employment at the old money wage rate. If unemployment has already developed, the Central Bank should force asset prices back up to a level at which investment would be sufficient for full employment at going

---

18. Most of these issues, moreover, were never resolved but, like the contemporary controversies in capital theory, were simply swept aside by the Keynesian Revolution. This being the case, it is impossible to deal with them adequately within a reasonably brief compass.

money wages. In neither case would a reduction in money wages be needed.[19]

Had Keynes retained the terminology of the *Treatise*, in which the diagnosis of the maladjustment leading to contraction of aggregate money demand was a market rate higher than the natural rate, both his position on the interest-elasticity of investment and his discussion of a regime of flexible money wages would have been much clearer to his readers. But in the *General Theory*, Keynes discarded these concepts:

I am now no longer of the opinion that the concept of a "natural" rate of interest, . . . has anything very useful or significant to contribute to our analysis. It is merely the rate of interest which will preserve the *status quo*; and, in general, we have no predominant interest in the *status quo* as such.[20]

The reason for this change of mind is clear. The concept of "natural rate" which Keynes employed in the *Treatise* was that rate which would serve to maintain the demand prices of assets of the preceding short period. Changes in the marginal efficiency of capital would imply changes in this hypothetical rate such that the present value of some representative augmentable asset

---

19. Note the sharp contrast, e.g., to Hayek. In Hayek's theory the boom was caused by a market rate held below natural rate and consequently involved over-investment. The crisis would arrive when it is no longer possible to maintain the low ratio (in value terms) of consumer goods to investment goods output. When consumption demand "breaks through," asset demand prices fall as market rate *rises* to the level of natural rate, whereas Keynes' crisis arrives when market rate starts to lag behind the *decline* of natural rate. In Keynes' eyes there is no "real" reason why asset values should fall. In Hayek's case the decline of investment is a required and "salutary" adjustment. To Keynes, asset values fall for "monetary" reasons (speculation on the Exchanges) and a low interest Central Bank policy is obviously called for. To Hayek, a Central Bank rule of maintaining asset demand prices relative to money wages would be the more disastrous the longer it was pursued. And, at the downturn, wages are right to Keynes, inflated to Hayek, etc. For a beginning to a much needed reappraisal of Hayek's contribution to Monetary Dynamics, cf. J. R. Hicks, "The Hayek Story," in *Critical Essays in Monetary Theory*.

20. *General Theory*, p. 243. For earlier critical examinations of Wicksell's concept of the "normal rate," cf. Lindahl, *op. cit.*, Part Two, Chapter VI, and Myrdal, *op. cit., passim*.

was maintained.[21] The *Treatise* set the natural rate as the shifting target for monetary policy (without too much concern for the difficulties which the Central Bank might encounter in trying to keep track of this unobservable magnitude). But the *Treatise* also presumed that the situation preceding the short period, on which the analysis focused, was one of full employment. If, instead, it was one of depressed activity, the policy criterion is not relevant even if it could be made operational—we have no interest in preserving such a *status quo*.

Keynes went on to suggest that:

> If there is any such rate of interest, which is unique and significant, it must be the rate which we might term the *neutral* rate of interest, namely, the natural rate in the above sense which is consistent with *full* employment, given the other parameters of the system.[22]

This suggestion would seem, at first, to open the door to a restatement of the *Treatise*'s diagnosis in these redefined terms. But Keynes refrains from making explicit use of this notion of a uniquely definable "neutral rate." The general idea of defining some "neutral state" to serve as a standard by which to define the existing maladjustments, and thus to arrive at "objective" policy proposals about what should be done, is very tempting. But, as the interwar debates between the many distinguished economists who were attracted to it showed, the idea is fraught with difficulties. Quite a number of different such standards were suggested, leading to a technically very complicated and, in the end, largely inconclusive discussion. It is curious to observe how, in the *General Theory*, Keynes again and again approaches this notion from different angles only to refuse, at the last moment, to commit himself explicitly:

---

21. In terms of the simplified illustration used previously, a reduction in the marginal efficiency of capital means a reduction in the number of "unit streams" perceived to accrue to a specific type of capital good. To preserve the demand price of this good, an offsetting rise in the value of "unit streams"—a fall in the market rate—is required.

22. *Loc. cit.* Keynes goes on to argue that the "tacit assumption . . . required to make sense of the classical theory. . . . [is] that the actual rate of interest is always equal to the neutral rate . . . ," etc.

But at this point we are in deep water. "The wild duck has dived down to the bottom—as deep as she can get—and bitten fast hold of the weed and tangle and all the rubbish that is down there, and it would need an extraordinarily clever dog to dive after and fish her up again." [23]

If Keynes refused to venture out in deep water in public, there are still many passages to show that he nevertheless had a "private" position on the issue. His arguments on monetary policy, in particular, repeatedly indicate that when asset values are too low, the long rate of interest is *ipso facto* to be regarded as "too high." Fiscal policies and the acceptance of the government of "an ever greater responsibility for directly organizing investment" are measures advocated,

since it seems likely that the fluctuations in the market estimation of the marginal efficiency of different types of capital . . . will be too great to be offset by any *practicable* changes in the rate of interest.[24]

The main reasons given for the suggested innovations in employment policy are that the State of Liquidity Preference may make it quite difficult for the monetary authority to bring about a sufficient reduction in long rate and that it is also quite difficult to persuade it to try very hard. The question is never seriously considered whether it would not be best to leave the long rate alone.

The following statement may be taken as a brief sketch of a hypothetical "neutral state":

In optimum conditions . . . production should be so organised as to produce in the most efficient manner compatible with delivery at the dates at which consumers' demand is expected to become effective.[25]

Schematically, we may regard the realization of an optimum production programme as requiring, at one and the same time,

---

23. The famous Ibsen quotation is given on p. 183, but would have been equally appropriate in several other places.

24. *General Theory*, p. 164, italics added. Cf. also p. 309.

25. *General Theory*, p. 215.

both an "optimum" interest rate, or term structure of interest rates, *and* an "appropriate" State of Entrepreneurial Expectation. Suppose that a situation arises in which the State of Expectation happens to be "appropriate"—we will not attempt to probe beneath this vague term at this point—but that the long rate is higher than "optimal," so that asset demand prices are too low for full employment at going money wages. Then it seems quite reasonable to demand that the Central Bank should go to great lengths in trying to reduce the interest rate, even to engage in a monetary policy *à outrance*. If, however, the actual interest rate equals the "optimal" rate consistent with the suggested "neutral state," while asset prices are too low due to a State of Expectation which is "inappropriately pessimistic"—what then?

Consider what would happen if, in this situation, the long bond rate were forced down to whatever level was necessary to equate *ex ante* rates of saving and investment at full employment. This would mean that prices of bonds—assets with *contractually fixed* long receipt streams—would shoot up while equity prices remained approximately constant instead of declining. Through a succession of short periods, with aggregate money expenditures at the full employment level, initial opinions about the future yield on capital would be revealed as too pessimistic. Anticipated returns to capital go up. The contractually fixed return streams on bonds remain the same, and it now becomes inevitable that bond-holders take a capital loss (in real terms).

The Central Bank now has two options. (a) It may elect to stand by doing nothing, in which case present values of capital goods and equities rise with a concomitant increase in both *ex ante* investment and consumption. Since the situation is one of full employment, inflation must result and the "real value" of nominally fixed contracts decline. (b) It may choose to act along Keynesian lines so as to increase market rate sufficiently to prevent any rise in capital goods values. Bond-holders lose again, since this means a reduction in the money value of bonds.

This illustration is highly relevant to our discussion in the following section of the assumptions underlying Keynes' Speculative Demand for Money. In this case, where the long bond rate was "optimal" to begin with, inelastic expectations with regard to the future course of bond prices would be quite appropriate. The speculator who sells off his long bonds when prices are still rising and buys them back when prices have fallen back is better off than the rentier who is not an active trader but who keeps a substantial portion of his net worth in bonds. The incentive to bear speculation is consequently strong. If the bears are right to begin with, and if the bear army swells rapidly when prices rise, the Central Bank, following Keynes' principles, will have to engage in quite large operations, buying high and selling low, in order to vanquish first the bears and then the bulls. Consequently, it will take large losses. For the type of eventuality just considered, a good case can be made for using fiscal consumption-stimulating policies instead. This would gradually rectify entrepreneurial expectations even while the interest rate was maintained at the initial ("optimal") level. The government, instead of the Central Bank, would be running the required deficit. I am not aware, however, that Keynes argued the case for fiscal policies in this more positive vein. He tended to recommend them on the negative grounds of adequate monetary measures being impracticable.[26]

Thus, although Keynes relinquished the natural rate terminology of the *Treatise*, his position underwent no fundamental change. He managed in this way to avoid getting entangled in the defense of a concept which the theoretical debate in the interval between his two books had shown to involve great difficulties. The difficulties remain, however—they have only "ducked" below the surface of his discussion. The notion of a "neutral" monetary policy or other aggregative policy which the economist would be able to recommend with a good conscience as based on only "objective" grounds or "positive" analysis, is a chimera. The case just considered is only an illustration. If the State of Expectation is such that, if it were combined with an "optimal" interest rate, the system will proceed on an equilibrium time-path with unfolding events continuously verifying these expectations—then one can have few reservations about

26. Cf. Chapter VI:2.

recommending Keynes' policy of establishing this "optimal" rate on "technical grounds" only. But this case is of little interest—it is the one case where the "technical" economic adviser is not likely to be needed. It is basically a case of the State of Expectations being one of perfect foresight and will be revealed as such if the actual interest rate is "optimal." The interest rate, furthermore, is not likely to diverge much from this standard; if the information available to entrepreneurs is all that accurate, the information available to investors could hardly be much worse. If expectations are in this way consistent with following an equilibrium-path from the period in question onward, this will in most cases imply that the system is already on such a path and has been on it, or close to it, for quite some time. This would mean also that the system would already have a history of "optimal" stabilization policies or, probably, a history in which stabilizing intervention was found to be unnecessary.

In any actual situation, macrodynamic policy problems have to be considered in a context of, as Keynes would put it, "hangovers from past states of expectation." Guides to policy cannot then be based on purely "positive" economic theory of a static or metastatic nature, because the "bygones are bygones" postulate, characteristic of such models, is simply not applicable. Keynes refused to become embroiled in the controversies surrounding alternative attempts to define "neutral policies" and did not attempt to defend his proposals in such terms. His discussion of policy questions frankly mixes the positive analysis with considerations of political expediency and with value judgments, e.g., in favor of labor and against the rentier. Analysis and personal judgment blend in his position that it is more important to have asset prices high enough for full employment at the going money wage than to maintain interest rates at levels which will be warranted in the longer run. If full employment can be achieved through bringing interest rates down, this is *always* worth doing. In part, it is quite a personal blend, different from later majority Keynesianism, for example, in the attitude shown to balance of payment problems—the government and the monetary authority should above all act so as to provide for full employment at the inherited general level of money wages and

"the same conclusion will hold good for an open system, provided that equilibrium with the rest of the world can be secured
by means of fluctuating exchanges." [27]

Thus it was Keynes' position that the "treatment" of recessions
should proceed on the understanding that, *as a rule*, asset prices
are too low and not wages too high. There is a positive element
to this diagnosis that should be recognized. The representative
non-money asset which Keynes had in mind is a long-lived asset.
Labor services and also "liquid" commodities are short-term.
Keynes' discussion involves the judgment that prices are much
more likely to be grossly "mistaken" for the former class of goods
than for the latter classes. This judgment is supported by a
comparison of the adequacy of the information on which prices
will be based in the two ends of the "maturity"-spectrum and of
the speed and reliability of the feedback mechanisms on which
different markets can depend to reveal mistakes before prices
and stock supplies have deviated very far from the respective
warranted time-paths.[28] In Keynes' opinion, therefore, markets
for "liquid" commodities and labor services will not be important
as *sources* of major fluctuations and he tends to regard, for
example, changes in the rate of inventory accumulation as an
amplifying rather than initiating factor in such fluctuations.[29]

---

27. *General Theory*, p. 270. This preference for resorting to a flexible exchange
rate whenever domestic full employment threatened to come into conflict with
external constraints, was a position never relinquished by the architect of the
IMF. Note that he advocated freeing the system from balance of payments constraints *so that a low interest policy could be pursued with impunity at home.* It
is easily imagined what he would have said of the 1967 British policy of (a)
devaluing (i.e., stepping down to a lower "*peg*"), while (b) raising Bank Rate to
an unprecedented level.

28. Cf. esp. *General Theory*, Chapters 5, 12, and 16:1. On the adequacy of
information on which to base the valuation of long-lived assets, the picture
painted in Chapter 12 of the "dark forces of time and ignorance which envelop
our future" is well known. On the adequacy of feedback mechanisms we have,
e.g., the observation in Chapter 5 that "it is of the nature of long-term expectations that they cannot be checked at short intervals in the light of realised
results." Observations on these information problems are scattered all through the
book. Only a rereading of the work with this particular issue in mind will give an
adequate appreciation of the extraordinary extent to which Keynes was preoccupied with it.

29. In the section to follow we return briefly to this issue.

This, however, is not quite the whole story. There was, as Wright has noted, "another Mr. Keynes . . . though admittedly a junior partner. *He* is the man who points out that money wages can be too high." [30] In his two major works, however, the possibility is not given much attention. The *Treatise* recognizes that the monetary authority may have to deal with a disequilibrium caused by a "spontaneous" wage-push or a *"coup de main on the part of Trade Unions."* [31] But this is more the exception that proves the rule, for the topic is passed over very quickly. In the *General Theory* it does not appear at all—as one would expect from the historical context of the work.

Another possibility is more illustrative of how Keynes' personal judgments are intertwined with positive analysis in his position that the burden of adjustment should not be thrown on the labor market. If the Central Bank through a prolonged period permits a market rate below the "neutral" rate, money prices and money wages will be inflated. Keynes, however, would still have the Central Bank proceed *as if* money wages were "right"—if necessary by resorting to a flexible exchange rate, as previously noted.

There are many differences, theoretical as well as sociopolitical, between Wicksell and Keynes, although we have previously emphasized the similarities. On no other single point were they as diametrically opposed as on the policy to be practised after a period of inflation. Both agreed that the monetary authority was to be blamed for any serious, prolonged inflation (or deflation).[32] Wicksell was adamant that social justice demanded that

---

30. D. McC. Wright, "Comment" (on H. G. Johnson, "The General Theory . . .) *American Economic Review,* May 1961, p. 19.

31. *Treatise,* Vol. I, pp. 166 ff and 157.

32. The Central Bank has it coming both ways. Keynes is very much like Professor Friedman—which is to say that he differs radically from the "Keynesians"—in one notable respect: The first step towards an understanding of past business fluctuations consists in noting the sins of the monetary authority. The fact that Keynes' view of the world implied that these would most often be sins of omission, rather than commission, did not mean that he was at all less harsh in his criticisms of central bankers. In the standard income-expenditure theory, the monetary authority has little power to influence anything and is thus absolved from responsibility.

such an inflation be reversed by deflationary policies, and he spent the last decade or more of his life trying to get the Swedish authorities to "undo" the World War I inflation. Keynes, certainly, took the social injustices of inflation seriously, but was as adamant in opposing the British deflationary postwar policies designed to restore the old parity of the pound. To him deflation was always the more serious danger. As a general rule, he advocated steering a course somewhat closer to the Scylla of inflation. If an incompetent helmsman forced you to suffer the monster, he would not advocate a subsequent visit to the cumulative whirlpool of Charybdis.

Keynes' differences from Wicksell on this point are due to his beliefs about the dynamics of the system. We have discussed the diagnosis of disequilibria in relation to the hypothetical solution vector of prices of an atemporal, static general equilibrium model or a metastatic model. In terms of such comparisons, prescription may seem to follow directly from diagnosis—if the interest rate is too high, bring it down; if wages are too high, wait for them to fall. But the mode of analysis utilized in this section is too infested with comparative static reasoning to be a fully reliable guide to Keynes' views. Waiting for wages to fall means to let the income-constrained process go unchecked. The income-constraint feedback on sales expectations means that producers will not demand the full employment quantity of labor services at the point when wages, on their painful downward course, reach the level indicated as required by the initial diagnosis. In Keynes' theory, they must first dip far below this level (so that the Keynes-effect or Pigou-effect takes hold) and then rise back to the sustainable equilibrium level in pace with reviving entrepreneurial sales expectations. Keynes' objections against relying on this "automatic" process we know: (a) If it is slow, its social consequences are too costly and too dangerous to be contemplated; (b) if it were to be rapid, the extreme instability of money values would shake the monetary system apart. Thus, Keynes' conclusion: If a misguided monetary policy had once permitted wage-inflation, the best policy would be to attempt a stabilization of money wages and prices as rapidly as possible.

V:3   Liquidity Preference and the Speculative Demand for Money

Chapter IV dealt with the value-theoretical basis for Keynes' Liquidity Preference hypothesis. The role which this hypothesis plays in Keynes' explanation of how unemployment comes to emerge we have emphasized throughout: the demand for money depends upon the anticipated money volume of transactions and (inversely) on the rate of interest. If the system is exposed to a disturbance which lowers the prospective rate of yield on physical assets computed at initial asset values, a net excess demand for money ("hoarding") will emerge; demand prices of augmentable assets will fall and money expenditures for the production of such assets will decline; the "multiplier" will amplify this initial reduction in expenditures . . . etc. In this section, we will concentrate on one aspect of the Liquidity Preference theory, namely the relationship between yields on non-money assets and the demand for money. On this subject also, there has been a gradual shift away from Keynes' original position. The changes that "Keynesian Economics" has undergone in this area are as significant as any of the developments previously discussed. Yet many of the aspects in which the "modern" treatment of Liquidity Preference departs from that of Keynes will appear more or less as corollaries of these previously considered developments.

Notes on the evolution of Liquidity Preference doctrine   The speculative demand for money played a crucial role in Keynes' theory. In modern "Keynesian" theory, this is no longer so. To understand this development, it must be put in the context of the evolution which the Liquidity Preference doctrine as a whole has undergone. Some of the following notes repeat observations already made and may be made brief; others we will want to discuss at somewhat greater length.

(a) In the later macroeconomic literature, "Liquidity Preference" has become a term practically synonymous with "Demand for Money," [1]—"money" being defined as means of payment. In Keynes' own usage the term has a much broader connotation: "Liquidity Preference" is not just a colorful term for "money demand." In the two-asset model, with which most of the *General Theory* deals, "demand for money" could indeed have been substituted for "liquidity preference" in most contexts. Keynes' choice of the more fanciful term must be regarded as another attempt to condense a large part of his analysis in the *Treatise*. The *Treatise* discusses in detail a number of private-sector credit markets through which the induced adjustments to disequilibrating disturbances are transmitted from the long end to the short (in the case of a decline in the prospective return to physical assets), or from the short end to the long (in the case of action by the monetary authority). In the *General Theory*, the term "liquidity preference" is often the only reminder that the relevant short-run adjustment processes involve also these markets in debts and claims.

(b) Similarly, Keynes' definition of "money" is much broader than that used by later Keynesians. Not only are all kinds of deposits generally included, but Keynes is also willing to draw the line between "money" and "non-money assets" more or less wherever analytical convenience dictates in dealing with a specific problem. This flexibility with regard to the definition of "money" is a natural concomitant of the attempt to compress the essentials of the Liquidity Preference theory within the simplified framework of a two-asset system.

(c) In the more recent "Keynesian" literature, the microtheory of money demand is usually developed in terms of individual transactor choices between means of payment and the nearest money substitute. The short rate appears as "the" interest rate in

---

1. There are naturally several exceptions among individual authors. The more prominent British Keynesians constitute a "collective exception" which should be noted. Cf. esp. N. Kaldor, "Speculation and Economic Stability," *Review of Economic Studies*, Oct. 1939, reprinted (with minor revisions) in his *Essays in Economic Stability and Growth*, London, 1960; J. Robinson, "The Rate of Interest," *op. cit.*; and R. F. Kahn, "Some Notes on Liquidity Preference," *Manchester School of Economic and Social Studies*, Sept. 1954.

this theory, the long rate being determined by the current short rate and market expectations about the course of future short rates. This is in contrast to Keynes' consistent focus upon the long rate as "the" pivotal rate in the structure of rates, with short-run movements in Bank Rate or other short rates regarded as significant only in so far as, through a chain of substitution effects, the long rate is also affected.[2] There is no necessary reason why one approach should not yield the same result as the other—the analysis of the determination of the *level* of rates could presumably focus either on the long or on the short end of the term structure. The shift of focus is, however, indicative of the general change of perspective. In the income-expenditure version of the "Keynesian system," the perspective is "foreshortened"—instead of "money" and a very long-lived asset, the structure is represented by two assets very close to the short end.

(d) "Modern" micromodels of the demand for money concentrate on the transactions demand for means of payment.[3] The flow of funds of the transactor unit over the short term are regarded as uncertain to a degree. Inability to make prompt payment out of cash holdings entails some penalty cost. Transactors can insure themselves against this penalty by holding larger average cash balances—the larger average balances, the better the "coverage" obtained. The price for such insurance is the opportunity cost of the earnings sacrificed on an alternative investment; the alternative investment considered may, for example, be Treasury bills. The transactions cost of moving out of bills into cash makes investment for very short periods in such bills uneconomical. The higher the bill rate, however, the higher the marginal cost of a given amount of "insurance" or, viewed from the other side, the greater the number of potential encash-

---

2. Cf., e.g., *General Theory*, p. 206: "The monetary authority often tends in practice to concentrate upon short-term debts and to leave the price of long-term debts to be influenced by *belated* and *imperfect* reactions from the price of short-term debts;" etc. (italics added). For the same emphasis on the significance of the lags involved, cf. *Treatise*, Vol. II, Chapter 37, e.g., p. 351.

3. Two articles have been most influential: W. J. Baumol, "The Transactions Demand for Cash: An Inventory Theoretic Approach," *Quarterly Journal of Economics*, Nov. 1952, and J. Tobin, "The Interest-Elasticity of Transactions Demand for Cash," *Review of Economics and Statistics*, Aug. 1956.

ments of bill holdings that will be covered by earnings from a given investment in bills. The transactions demand for cash therefore is seen to depend inversely on "the" rate of interest.

The money demand of this model corresponds to Keynes' demand for transactions and, to some extent, precautionary balances. Precautionary balances are held for purposes of "insurance" of this kind. Keynes recognized the interest-elasticity of the demand for cash on both counts but judged that it was "likely to be a minor factor except where large changes in the cost of holding cash are in question." [4] He did not assume away this interest-elasticity entirely—a less aggregative liquidity preference analysis of the financial side of the contraction process than that found in the *General Theory* would give a more detailed picture of adjustments in the short end. A lowering of rates on close cash substitutes would be seen to induce substitution of means of payment for such assets by the non-banking sector; at the same time, lower rates on, or just lower demand for, short-term bank credit would serve to increase the banking system's demand for excess reserves, thus lowering the volume of demand-deposits supplied on a given monetary base. But the interest-elasticity of transaction balances plays virtually no part in the cause-and-effect scheme outlined in the *General Theory*. Keynes regarded the interest-elasticity of all kinds of "inventories"—whether of cash or of goods—as a "secondary mag-

---

4. Cf. *General Theory*, pp. 171, 196, also p. 168: ". . . we can usefully employ the ancient distinction between the use of money for the transaction of current business and its use as a store of wealth. As regards the first of these two uses, it is obvious that up to a point it is worth while to sacrifice a certain amount of interest for the convenience of liquidity. But, given that the rate of interest is never negative, why should anyone prefer to hold his wealth in a form which yields little or no interest to holding it in a form which yields interest . . . ?"

The last query should be noted, since in recent criticisms of Keynes' money demand theory it is often argued or implied (cf. below) that he was insufficiently impressed with the arguments underlying the "Classical" view that there is something basically "irrational" in hoarding behavior, and that this is the reason why he (supposedly) did not go to the trouble of providing a satisfactory rationale for storing value "in a form which yields little or no interest." Actually, it is hardly possible to state this "Classical" view in more forceful terms than Keynes did: "Why should anyone outside a lunatic asylum wish to use money as a store of wealth?" ("The General Theory of Employment," in S. E. Harris, ed., *op. cit.*, p. 187).

nitude." Modern macromodels also assume the interest-elasticity of goods inventories to be virtually zero, but regard that of cash inventories as sufficiently high to explain contractions of any magnitude without dragging in the "doubtful" speculative demand.

The Baumol-Tobin-type model may well give an exaggerated impression of the interest-elasticity of the demand for transactions balances, particularly in the context of British financial institutions. In the discussion above, it was assumed that the relevant "penalty cost" of running out of cash was constant and did not vary with the bill rate. The penalty cost, however, may be that of utilizing stand-by credit or overdraft facilities at the cost of an interest charge which does vary in rough proportion to the bill rate. Even in the Baumol-Tobin model, only fairly "large" transactors will find it advantageous to manage their cash balances with an eye to the bill rate; these are also the transactors most likely to have arranged such stand-by facilities. In a partial equilibrium analysis involving these three alternatives, and with the two rates assumed closely correlated, it is not evident that the interest-elasticity of the demand for cash balances will be as quantitatively significant as it appears in the Baumol-Tobin framework.[5]

The point to stress, in comparing Keynes and later theorists on this issue, is, however, slightly different. Once we start adding another alternative to the two considered by Baumol and Tobin, still others press for attention. What about the opportunity cost in terms of higher yielding investments of holding wealth in the form of bills? What about the banks' desired supply of money when the yield on eligible bank assets changes? One is thus forced step by step to consider the entire financial structure and, ultimately, to link up the financial yield structure with the

---

5. I am indebted to Professor A. A. Walters for this point. Walters has in an unpublished paper investigated a number of alternative possibilities of this kind and found that the implied theoretical interest-elasticity is in many cases quite small.

In order to see the alternatives which Keynes considered the most important in the inventory management of cash balances, the *Treatise*, Chapter 3, should be consulted.

prospective yield on *physical capital.* Though there is nothing necessarily wrong about focusing on the choice between money and near-money, and thus on the short rate, in analyzing the determination of the general level of the rate structure, there is a definite heuristic risk in adopting this myopic perspective: the yield on the system's stock of physical capital and the "real forces" of productivity and thrift recede so far into the background that they may be forgotten. That an economist of Hicks' caliber seemingly fell into this trap is warning enough.[6]

When, as the macrodynamic context demands, these questions are brought up, the narrow focus on the demand for cash, characteristic of modern models, becomes inappropriate. The broader perspective of Keynes' Liquidity Preference theory—for want of a still more general approach—is needed.

(e) In the more recent monetary discussion, the money-

---

6. In *Value and Capital,* Chapter XIII, Hicks argued that interest arose from the imperfect "moneyness" or illiquidity of non-money assets, seemingly implying— without actually considering such a hypothetical case—that "the" interest rate would have to be zero in a world of certainty and no transaction frictions.

Hicks' interest theory was severely criticized by Modigliani in his famous "Liquidity Preference and the Theory of Interest and Money," *Econometrica,* Jan. 1944, and by Samuelson in the *Foundations . . . ,* pp. 123–24. Samuelson pointed out that "in such a world securities themselves would circulate as money and be acceptable in transactions"; either the yield on "money" would be equal to that of other securities or money "would pass out of use, wither away and die, become a free good." (Actually, the hypothetical construction of "the certain world" leaves very little room for monetary instruments, interest-bearing or not. Equity titles might change hands on occasion. Whether they could be said to "circulate" is a semantic conundrum—the teleological vision of the metastatic world allows no genuine "transactions" to take place as the clockwork goes through its paces. All economic choices have been made once and for all with the Watchmaker Himself presiding over the initial *tâtonnement.*)

In fact, it is not entirely clear what Hicks' position on this issue was at the time, although Chapter XIII contains quite a number of seemingly uncompromising formulations of a "pure liquidity preference theory of interest." In his preceding chapter (esp. pp. 159–60), Hicks had drawn a very sharp—but not very clear—distinction between "the true rate of interest, which . . . is a money rate" and the own rate on the "auxiliary standard commodity," a numeraire which can be chosen at random among the "real" commodities of the system. With respect to these two rates, he had then pointed out that ". . . there is no reason why this 'natural rate' should be the same as the true *money* rate of interest." In particular, he never specifically argued that this real rate would be zero under certainty conditions.

demand function is usually conceived as a *stable* relationship between the demand for cash balances and "the" (observed) rate of interest. Most of the voluminous empirical work on the demand for money that has appeared in recent years also represents a search for such a stable long-run function.[7] This is in radical contrast to the implications of Keynes' theory. Keynes very definitely predicts that this relationship will be *unstable* in the longer run: the demand for money at a given income level

will not have a definite quantitative relation to a given rate of interest of r;—what matters is not the *absolute* level of r but the degree of its divergence from what is considered a fairly *safe* level of r . . .[8]

Over time, opinions of this "fairly safe" level will be revised in the light of experience. In Keynes' theory such revisions imply shifts of the money-demand function commonly used in "Keynesian" macromodels. This also means that in a situation of unemployment, the interest rate—like the wage rate—will continue to "crumble" merely with the passage of time and even in the absence of additional "exogenous" disturbances impinging on the system. In this sense, therefore, Keynes' short-run analysis can be said to assume two "rigid" price relations and not just one. In the income-expenditure model, in contrast, the interest rate is "perfectly flexible" in the sense that it continuously keeps to a level consistent with the long-run liquidity preference function. To Keynes, who attached minimal significance to the interest-

---

7. The various authors differ both in their definition of "money" and in their choice of the "representative" interest rate and other independent variables entering into the budget-constraint. We confine our discussion here to the partial relationship between money demand and "the" interest rate.

A recent exception to the prevailing preoccupation with estimates of the money-demand function based on "yearly data covering more than half a century" is H. R. Heller, "The Demand for Money: The Evidence from the Short-Run Data," *Quarterly Journal of Economics*, May 1965. The paper contains a number of observations relevant to the present issue. Most interesting, in relation to Keynes' theory, is Heller's *tentative* finding of short-run "ratchet-effects" around the estimated long-run function, suggesting that in long-run estimates "the short-run elasticities, which are relevant for policy considerations, are submerged" (p. 299).

8. *General Theory*, p. 201. Compare p. 203: ". . . its actual level is largely governed by the prevailing view as to what its value is expected to be." Etc. Cf. also p. 168.

elasticity of the demand for transaction balances under conditions approximating those of certainty, the "Classical" theory —the Quantity Theory of Money—would come into its own if it could be assumed that the liquidity preference function was devoid of any "hangovers from past states of expectation."

In Keynes' theory, short-run variations in the interest rate are thus constrained by the prevailing market opinion of the "normal" level of long rate,[9] much as money wages rates in atomistic labor markets are tied down by "memories" of past wages earned. It is necessary to insist that this conception has nothing to do with the "Liquidity Trap." The relative inflexibility of long rate is of crucial importance in Keynes' theory. But it must not be confused with what is commonly known (inaccurately) as "Keynes' special case."

(f) A largely semantic observation may also be noted. Keynesian models emphasize three crucial decisions: (1) how much to consume out of current income, (2) how much to "invest" and how much to hoard out of the amount not spent on consumption, and (3) how much capital goods to produce in a given period. In common with most theorists of his own generation, Keynes found it convenient to identify these choices with different transactor stereotypes, namely the Consumer, the Investor (Bull or Bear), and the Entrepreneur, etc. This anthropomorphic verbiage is at best a haphazard way of dealing with transaction-structure problems. It can be confusing and it would perhaps be preferable to dispense with it, particularly in models in which it is assumed that no aggregate excess demand functions are affected by "distribution effects." But in the case of such an ingrained usage it is, perhaps, idle to cry for "reform."

As an illustration of the semantic traps, one may consider an argument which has frequently been expounded as a diagnosis of the fundamental element in Keynes' contribution. A "sophisti-

---

9. We have chosen to call this the "normal rate" in accordance with Keynes' usage in his analysis of speculation in "Liquid Capital," where the long-run equilibrium price which traders *expect* to obtain once, for example, "abnormal" inventories have been worked off, is referred to as the "normal" price. Cf. *Treatise*, Chapter 29. Remember, however, that Wicksell frequently used the term "normal rate" for the "natural rate."

cated" interpretation of the argument yields a diagnosis in accord with that implied in our present interpretation of Keynes. But the way in which the argument is often stated in the text-book literature is likely to leave the unwary student with a superficial understanding of the issues. The following paraphrase is concocted in an unfair way so as to make this sorry result probable:

Keynes, in contrast to the Classics, emphasized that saving decisions and investment decisions are typically made *by different people*. Although the Classics were aware of the fact, they did not perceive its significance. Keynes realized that it had an extremely important implication, namely that it is not at all certain that planned saving and planned investment will be equal at a full employment level of income. Thus, in this neglected fact lay the key to the Keynesian Revolution . . . etc.

To be rightly understood, this exegetical argument should be supplied with a number of provisos. Thus, one might consider a hypothetical economy entirely devoid of intra-private-sector credit markets so that saving and investment *must* be undertaken by the same people, and then ask whether Keynes' analysis of the income-constrained process would be entirely irrelevant to such a system. The answer is that such a process is quite possible, since a situation of aggregate *ex ante* hoarding may still emerge with planned saving exceeding investment. As for the "Classics," *the* problem which was their constant concern was defined exactly in the above manner—i.e., in a market system, decisions to produce and decisions to consume (or to hold) any good whatsoever are made by "different people" and will not be consistent purely by chance.

Thus the peculiarity of the saving-investment process does not lie in the fact that the decisions are made by different groups of people. That Keynesian processes are extremely unlikely to occur in a Crusoe-economy is after all a trivial point. In order to justify the emphasis which Keynes put on the saving-investment process, one must take into account the arguments he adduced in support of the contention that existing market institutions are *especially* inadequate when it comes to the task of coordinating these decisions. In arguing this case, he stressed, as we know, the "dark forces of time and ignorance" enveloping the future, the fact that there are few forward markets through which saving decisions can be communicated to entrepreneurs as effective demand for produced commodities at specified future dates, etc. And on this level of analysis, the presence of intra-private-sector credit markets does play a vital role in his analysis: in Keynes' view, the sorry fact that the organized exchanges become the scene of "a game of Snap, of Old Maid, of Musical Chairs" explains why these markets do not adequately substitute for the hypothetical, full complement of forward markets of metastatic theory.[10]

Thus it is, after all, implied in Keynes' considered position that if saving and investment decisions were in fact always undertaken by the same people, a *closed system* would be quite unlikely to fall into a serious recession, because of a decline of the marginal efficiency of capital (or a decline in the propensity to consume). He would have acknowledged that in a system where credit markets are rudimentary and of marginal significance only, it is still *possible* that an *ex ante* excess of saving over investment would emerge. A war scare might cause hoarding, for example. But apart from such "non-economic" causes, an excess demand for money with the consequent reduction in money expenditures could only come about as a consequence of a reduction in the money stock—an event which under the given conditions of a closed system, etc., would require postulating a truly monumental incompetence on part of the monetary authority.

---

10. Consider, for example, the wishful speculation on possible remedies, *General Theory*, p. 160: "The spectacle of modern investment markets has sometimes moved me towards the conclusion that to make the purchase of an investment permanent and indissoluble, like marriage, except by reason of death or other grave cause, might be a useful remedy for our contemporary evils. For this would force the investor to direct his mind to the long-term prospects and to those only. . . ." (But he goes on to point out the costly consequences of measures designed to reduce "liquidity" in this manner.) The proposal would "marry" the saver and the entrepreneur by eliminating the "resale market" for claims on firms—but saving decisions and investment decisions would still be made "by different people."

The theory which Keynes constructed was specifically designed to deal with movements in aggregate demand initiated by changes in entrepreneurial opinions about prospective yields on capital. His theory did not deny that a serious contraction would ensue if the monetary base and the money supply were reduced, and Keynes would have been the last to share the congenital reluctance of so many later "Keynesians" to interest themselves seriously in the findings of the Neo-Quantity theorists on this point. He regarded this possibility as of the very greatest relevance. The "Classical" macroeconomics on which he had been brought up—a body of policy-analysis for practical purposes coextensive with nineteenth-century English Central Banking doctrine—revolved almost entirely around the problem of coping with monetary disturbances impinging upon the domestic economy by way of the balance of payment. Amidst the ashes and ruins of the nineteenth-century international economic order, however, these problems were not uppermost in Keynes' mind and he was in any case resolved that they must not be allowed to compound further the disastrous situation of the mid-thirties. Arguing that a policy of flexible exchange rates be adopted to enable the monetary authority to neutralize any tendency to an external drain on bank reserves, he concentrated on the analysis of fluctuations connected with changes in velocity rather than in the stock of money.

This is the context in which his views on the saving-investment process should be put. The distinction between households doing the saving and entrepreneurs ordering capital goods to be produced is important because, in modern systems, the coordination of these two activities is entrusted to credit markets in which *speculative activity* plays, in Keynes' opinion, an inordinately large and frequently dysfunctional role.

Thus, by this route, we come back once again to the same point—*the crucial role which Keynes assigns to the speculative demand for money* and its interest-elasticity. It is due to the *inelastic expectations* of investors and their consequent speculative behavior that disturbances which have the effect of lowering the "neutral rate" will siphon off money income into demand for additional money balances. He indicates clearly enough that, if such markets were absent or if institutional arrangements could be devised which reduced to a minimum the incentive to speculate on the short-run movements of capital values, the interest-elasticity of money demand based purely on the "transaction and precautionary motives" would not be significant enough to cause him fears of substantial *ex ante* hoarding in the event of a decline in prospective yields.

The important point in Keynes' analysis is simply the predominance in the system as a whole of these inelastic expectations. There is consequently no need to insist on his particular gallery of transactor stereotypes, each with his assigned decision to make. It is particularly inopportune to do so if the reader's "intuition" is likely to be offended by the crucial role apparently assigned to the "speculators" of the organized exchanges. Later Keynesians have generally been loath to believe that Wall Street plays a significant role in "wagging the whole dog." The crucial variable, in any case, is *ex ante* hoarding, and Keynes was in the habit of having his speculator stereotype—the Bear—perform this hoarding. But the inelastic expectations which explain attempts to hoard can just as well be assigned to the Consumer, or the Entrepreneur (or the Banker, or the Central Bank, etc.).

Thus, Professor Eisner's emphasis on the inflexibility of the prospective rate of return required by Entrepreneurs as *the* distinguishing feature of (truly) Keynesian models seems in all essentials consistent with the interpretation of Keynes advanced here. The Entrepreneur may "himself" be a bearish speculator.[11] But Keynes' theory of Liquidity Preference is already extremely condensed in the *General Theory* as compared to the *Treatise;* it seems better not to use such a further shortcut, lest the central role of money and financial markets in Keynes' thought be entirely lost from view.

(g) Our last note repeats an earlier conjecture concerning the source of the widespread misinterpretations of the *General*

---

11. Cf. R. Eisner, "On Growth Models and the Neo-Classical Resurgence," *Economic Journal*, Dec. 1958, and for pertinent evidence consistent with the cyclical flow-of-funds implications of this view, W. F. Payne, *Industrial Demands Upon the Money Market, 1919–57: A Study in Fund-Flow Analysis* (NBER, Technical Paper 14), New York, 1961.

Theory model that we have outlined. Enough has been said about the significance of the interest-elasticities of Keynes' aggregate demand components. These specifications of the model's qualitative properties have been ignored by later income-expenditure theorists, as we have seen. It is suggested that a major reason for this neglect of what Keynes has to say on the interest-elasticities of investment and saving is that, in his analysis of the contraction process, he himself proceeded to ignore them *because the very process being investigated presumed that interest rates be inflexible in the short run.*[12] Since movements of the interest rate were constrained, the effects of changes in the interest rate on the money value of demand for commodities could be lumped among the "secondary magnitudes." Subsequent "Keynesians," however, "let loose" the interest rate again (in the range above the "trap" level, that is). But by then, as we have seen, the conventional "Keynesian model" had evolved an aggregative structure quite different from that of the *General Theory*—a model-structure within which variations in "the" interest rate presented no significant incentive for traders to alter their spending behavior. That such a flexible rate was inconsistent with the original Keynesian model was therefore not recognized.

The modern criticism of Keynes' speculative demand The preceding discussion points to one issue as the central one: Keynes' *speculative* demand for money has been all but relinquished by modern theorists as an element of "general" macrotheory. Keynes regarded this concept as a cornerstone of his theoretical structure. In the current view, Keynes' theory of speculative behavior is seen as an unsightly crutch which the

---

12. Cf. our discussion above of his procedure with regard to the transactions demand for cash, the interest-elasticity of which he recognized for "large changes" in the interest rate. Compare also the previously discussed passage in which Keynes—after having rather carefully recorded changes in asset prices as one of the "major factors *capable of* causing short-period changes in the propensity to consume"—argues that the analysis can be carried forward in terms of the simple consumption-income relation because "the *short-period* influence of changes in the rate of interest . . . is *often* of secondary importance." (italics added)

"Keynesian" macromodel would do better without. To Keynes, uncertainty about future interest rate movements is "the *sole intelligible explanation*" of the emergence of an *ex ante* rate of hoarding substantial enough to bring about a major contractionary movement. A recent authoritative pronouncement on his theory, in contrast, takes "the chief limitation of his analysis to be his concentration on expectations of future changes in interest rates as the determinant of the asset-demand for money." [13] The "speculative motive" is regarded as an *ad hoc* explanation of the interest-elasticity of the money-demand function—in current discussions of the topic one sometimes perceives the implied hint that, if Keynes had only had the ingenuity to find a more "intellectually satisfactory" explanation of the dependence of money demand on interest rates, he would not have chosen to lean on such a slender reed. Since subsequent models have provided a choice-theoretical rationale for the interest-elasticity of transactions and precautionary money demand, we no longer need to rely on this contrivance of Keynes'. Keynes' monetary theory

has been refined and elaborated by subsequent writers in the Keynesian tradition. In the process, Keynes' most extreme departure from previous analysis—his emphasis on the speculative demand for money at the expense of the precautionary—has been gradually abandoned . . .[14]

It is important that we consider this in some detail.

The allegedly *ad hoc* element of Keynes' theory is his *postulate of inelastic expectations* about the future course of long-term rates of interest. This view of Keynes' theory has been summed up by labeling it a "bootstrap" theory of interest.[15] In the *General Theory*, Keynes had little to say about how the market's view of the normal rate is determined at any time. (Neither did

---

13. *General Theory*, p. 201 (italics added), and H. G. Johnson, "The *General Theory* . . . ," *op. cit.*, p. 10.

14. H. G. Johnson, "Monetary Theory and Monetary Policy," *op. cit.*, p. 344.

15. Although intended as a gibe, the "bootstrap" label is, in a way, a useful one—it is less misleading than the "indeterminacy" label often affixed to Keynes' interest theory and might serve to stave off the sort of "repairs" to the model which presume that Keynes lost sight of the interdependencies of his system.

he present an explanation of the initial level of money wage rates, the amount of capital in existence, the size of the population and labor force, the state of technology, or any of the other variables treated as "parameters" in his short-run analysis.) Viewed in purely static terms, or from a longer run perspective, any short-run model which postulates a number of historically given parameters leaves a large number of things "unexplained." But it is reasonable to require that the theory be judged either for logical consistency *on its own terms* or on empirical grounds.

Keynes' theory has not been judged on its own terms. On the interpretation advanced in this study, it is—in terms of Professor Samuelson's classification [16]—a "dynamic and historical" theory. Keynes' critics all too often have cast it in the mold of a "static and non-historical" system. In the framework of such atemporal constructions, "inelastic expectations," reservation prices, etc., appear entirely unmotivated. This has been our complaint already in Chapter II. But the present issue presents perhaps the best illustration of the development of post-Keynesian monetary theory into a theory of a genus entirely different from that of Keynes' own.

Inelastic versus unit-elastic expectations   As in Chapter II, we may posit two extreme possibilities: (a) a short-run model which assumes that expectations about the long-run normal level of long rate are *absolutely inelastic* in the current unit period, and (b) a short-run model which assumes that expectations in this regard are *unit-elastic*. The former would be a *General Theory* model, the latter a "modern" model. The question is of the same type as the one posed in Chapter II: Does the economic system function more in resemblance with the "Classical" pure price-adjustment model or with the Keynesian income-adjustment model? The answer is a matter of judgment at this juncture. Both models are extreme; which one constitutes the better approximation to reality is a question that will ultimately have to be settled empirically. Here we can only consider the *a priori* criticisms leveled against Keynes' theory.

---

16. Cf. P. A. Samuelson, *Foundations of Economic Analysis*, pp. 315 ff.

Tobin's reinterpretation of liquidity preference as an attitude towards risk [17] has been as influential in shaping the development we are now concerned with as his and Baumol's papers on transactions demand. The article applies the Markowitz portfolio-selection approach to the positive problem of the demand for "money." A risk-averting transactor facing a decline in the expected yield of risky assets will, Tobin demonstrates, increase the ratio of money to such assets in his portfolio. This is the point, of course: this substitution of money for earning assets will take place at the margin *even if yield expectations are unit-elastic.* Thus, again, it is not *necessary* to postulate inelastic expectations in order to derive an interest-elastic money-demand function.[18]

That this approach is useful is not at issue. Keynes' sketchy "risk-premium" discussion of these problems has been replaced by a systematic analysis of a model for which the underlying assumptions are made carefully explicit.[19] The Mean-Variability approach has one considerable disadvantage in the present context in that the choice problem is defined in terms of alternative probability-distributions of holding yields over a unit period that is usually left undefined. This formulation consequently conceals

---

17. J. Tobin, "Liquidity Preference as Behavior Towards Risk," *Review of Economic Studies*, Feb. 1958.

18. One difficulty, noted by Tobin, should perhaps be pointed out: if the relevant alternative asset is a capital good with a real yield variance *less* than that of money while the expected real holding yield on money is zero, then money is simply "inferior" as a store of wealth; in such a case of very uncertain expectations about future money price levels, the "precautionary demand" for money is zero, independent of the (positive) expected yield on capital goods. Tobin, however, assumes the alternative asset to be a "bond." Nonetheless, the problem should perhaps be kept in mind in view of Tobin's emphasis on the physical-financial over the long-short distinction.

19. Keynes' best effort is the presentation of the theory of "normal backwardation" in the *Treatise*. The "normal backwardation" case presumes that the current price of a stock-flow commodity is equal to the "representative expectation" of the "normal" future spot price. If the representative mathematical expectation of the future spot price is not held with "absolute confidence"—i.e., expectations not single-valued—the current futures price will be below the spot price by an amount in excess of the interest rate corresponding to the "risk-premium." Even here, however, Kaldor's presentation (*op. cit.*) is superior to Keynes'.

the distinction between capital-value uncertainty and income-uncertainty which we know to be basic to Keynes' theory of portfolio management. Tobin, however, demonstrates elegantly that the modern model can be taken through its paces both under the "speculative assumption" of inelastic expectations and under the "precautionary assumption" of unit-elastic expectations: "the stickier the investor's expectations, the more sensitive his demand for cash will be to changes in the rate of interest." [20] Some of Tobin's conclusions are of particular interest to us here:

> The theory of risk-avoiding behavior. . . . does not depend on inelasticity of expectations of future interest rates, but *can proceed* from the assumption that the expected value of capital gain or loss from holding interest-bearing assets is *always* zero. In this respect, it is a *logically more satisfactory* foundation *for liquidity preference* than the Keynesian theory described. . . . The risk aversion theory of liquidity preference mitigates the *major logical objection* to which, according to the [previous argument] . . . , the Keynesian theory is vulnerable.[21]

---

20. Tobin, *op. cit.*, p. 86.

21. *Op. cit.*, p. 85 (italics added). Tobin furthermore notes that his model has "the empirical advantage of explaining diversification—the same individual holds both cash and 'consols'—while the Keynesian theory implies that each investor holds only one asset."

It is true that Keynes presented no micromodel explaining diversification. His casual approach to this whole range of questions may legitimately be the object of criticism—readers certainly have had to pay a high price for his characteristic impatience with analytical detail when bent upon economic-political persuasion. But Keynesian traders do hold "both cash and consols"—this degree of diversification being "explained" by the postulate that the "liquidity yield" on money declines with the amount of real balances held—and Tobin's critique is to that extent, at least, overdrawn. The sketchy analysis of Keynes' Chapter 17 has the objective of stressing the "inelasticity of substitution of money" and tends to exaggerate the elasticities of substitution between different non-money assets for that purpose. The fact that Keynes fails to extend the proposition of liquidity premia declining with "quantity" held to other assets is very noticeable in his handling of these aggregation procedures. It should not be denied that Keynes' discussion of these problems usually appears to presume that individual traders hold a quite limited number of assets at any one time and that changes in relative market values will most often cause them to go from one "corner solution" to another—a change in the long rate "will persuade some Bull to join the Bear brigade," etc. But there are also numerous passages, both in the *Treatise* and in the *General Theory*, in which it is quite evident that individual transactors are not assumed to attempt taking "infinite positions." One gets less than full value

There is here, certainly, a strong suggestion that Keynes' assumption of inelastic expectations is an undesirably "special" element in a model aspiring to the status of a "general theory." The assumption is a "logically unsatisfactory foundation" on which to build. In order to evaluate this contention we should consider, first, the assumptions forming the context of Tobin's analysis of liquidity preference. For "the major logical objection" to Keynes' theory, Tobin refers to Leontief and Fellner. Their case against Keynes must then be the second item on our agenda. Our frame of reference is the Keynesian short run— there is no need to cite Keynes' reminders that the speculative demand is nonexistent in full equilibrium states and that, in the comparative analysis of such states, the quantity theory comes into its own.

The context of Tobin's analysis is indicated in these introductory remarks to his paper:

The alternatives to cash considered, both in this paper and in prior discussions of the subject, in examining the speculative motive for holding cash are assets that differ from cash only in having a variable market yield. . . . They are, like cash, subject to changes in real value due to fluctuations in the price level. . . . all these assets, including cash, are merely minor variants of the same species, a species we may call monetary assets—marketable, fixed in money value, free of default risk. The differences of members of this species from each other are negligible compared to their differences from the vast variety of other assets in which wealth may be invested: corporate stock, real estate, unincorporated business and professional practice, etc. The theory of liquidity preference does not concern the choices investors make between the whole species of monetary assets, on the one hand, and other broad classes of assets, on the other. . . . Liquidity preference theory takes as given the choices determining how much wealth is to be invested in monetary assets and concerns itself with the allocation of these amounts among cash and alternative monetary assets.[22]

This narrow conception of the subject of liquidity preference is indeed, as Tobin implies, characteristic of the post-Keynesian

for one's (considerable) trouble in reading Keynes, if one insists on a literal interpretation of the "single-valued" terminology and does not allow for his "implicit theorizing" on the diversification issue.

22. Tobin, op. cit., p. 66.

approach. The whole setting of the discussion differs drastically from the context intended by Keynes: (a) in the "prior discussion of the subject" found in the *General Theory*, the alternatives to cash which Tobin specifies are *included* in "money"— specifically *because* they are but "minor variants of the same species" differing "from cash only in having a variable market yield" but not a variable present money value; (b) the *alternatives to "money"* considered by Keynes comprise all non-money assets, including in particular physical assets; these assets differ from "money" in being *long-lived* and having a potentially highly variable present money value; (c) Keynes' Liquidity Preference theory *does* concern the choice between "money" and such assets as corporate equities and real estate, i.e., the choice between holding "money" or titles to *augmentable* physical assets; (d) Keynes' liquidity preference analysis is not confined to dealing with the allocation of a given value sum among alternative assets on the individual experiment level. It deals as well with the determination of the "real price" of existing non-money assets and, consequently, treats aggregate net worth as a variable; it is also basically an exercise in *stock-flow analysis*, for the all-important end to which Keynes designed the apparatus is the determination of how much of the current rate of household saving is channeled off into bear hoards rather than into the financing of investment. If Keynes dealt cursorily with the stock-flow dimensional aspects, the modern treatment ignores them entirely.

The two perspectives on liquidity preference could hardly be more different! With the exception of the British Keynesians cited earlier, it is a general weakness in the later "Keynesian" literature that it deals with liquidity preference in a context of choice among *financial* assets only. This tends to obscure the vital stock-flow relation involved: the ultimate rationale for viewing a general rise in the price of income-streams with "inelastic suspicion" lies in the simple fact that it will, *ceteris paribus*, cause a rise in the rate at which augmentable sources of such streams are produced. This is easily forgotten when the analysis directly concerns only financial assets—it is not necessarily the case that the rate of change in the stock of "outside" financial assets depends closely or uniquely (or even positively) upon the current price which emerges in the market; the Central Bank, for example, is not normally a profit-maximizing enterprise. Suppose for the sake of argument that the monetary authority can be ignored and the stock of high-powered money taken as given; we confine our attention to a closed system with no other "outside" assets than the stock of physical capital.

The question to be asked is whether inelastic expectations are generally "illogical" (or even "irrational" perhaps) within a system where long-lived augmentable capital goods comprise the dominant store of value. Far from being a special case, inelastic expectations must in this context be the general case. Unit-elastic expectations are the "special case" for which a number of restrictive assumptions must be made. At the close of the previous section, a disequilibrium illustration of the argument was given that involved a situation in which entrepreneurial expectations were unduly "pessimistic," so that investment would be insufficient for full employment at the "optimal" rate of interest. It was shown that bond-holders would be better off if they resisted attempts by the monetary authority to reduce the interest rate to the level required for instantaneous full employment. In the following illustration, Keynes' wealth-saving relation is used to impose an upper limit on the warranted rate of growth of the stock of physical capital. It is assumed that it is not possible to sustain a rate of growth higher than the warranted, particularly since we assume that no Central Bank is present which could operate so as to produce an adequate amount of "forced saving" for a prolonged period.

The non-money store of value is augmentable. The higher its current price, the higher the flow-rate of net output. The "real" price at which the private sector will be willing to hold the existing stock of capital depends upon the size of the stock in relation to "income." [23] The faster the rate growth of the capital stock, therefore, the faster the rate at which the "real price" per unit

---

23. A given state of technology is assumed *and* a declining marginal productivity of capital stock. In the case of a Knightian "Crusonia plant" model, the relevant prices are "technologically fixed"—and, presumably, subject of inelastic expectations.

will decline—i.e., the lower the realized holding yield.[24] Thus, there exist *"real forces"* in the system which, if allowed to operate, determine the price of capital goods "in the long run."

Recall Keynes' analysis of pricing in the market for a good of which considerable stocks are held, though carrying costs are relatively high. His discussion presumes the existence of a hypothetical "normal price" determined by real forces—namely, the price which equates flow-demand and flow-supply in the longer run when "liquid stocks" of the good are "normal" (and, hence, excess stock demand zero). The market must form *some* opinion of this level of the normal price:

> if we assume that through a miscalculation of supply and demand redundant stocks have accumulated . . . , the price must fall sufficiently far below the anticipated normal price to provide the carrying charges through the period which is expected to elapse before the redundant stocks are completely absorbed.[25]

Note that the price at which the market is willing to carry "redundant stocks" is the price relevant to the entrepreneurs of the industry in deciding upon the volume of employment to be offered at going money wage rates. Futures markets and the pricing of liquid stocks are of course problems falling within Keynes' definition of "speculative behavior."

Also in the case of the aggregate stock of Fixed Capital there exists such a hypothetical "normal price" consistent in the long run with the basic real determinants of Productivity and Thrift. At any one time, therefore, there exists some range of asset prices so high that, if a price in this range were momentarily to emerge, excessive investment would before long cause holding yields to be negative. If we assume perfect certainty for the moment, it is clear that some asset price levels could not emerge because *purely endogenous forces*—accurately foreseen in this case— would make the investor suffer capital losses not offset by current returns. Admittedly, the "dark forces of time and ignorance" are of the essence when dealing with long-lived capital goods.

---

24. Cf., e.g., J. R. Hicks, "Methods of Dynamic Analysis," *op. cit.*, p. 149.
25. Cf. *Treatise*, Vol. II, p. 136.

But since, in the case of perfect certainty, there are prices so high as to be incapable of being maintained, it is anything but unreasonable to assume that, in any actual situation, there exist some potential prices so high that their emergence would not be regarded by investors with an attitude of "bland unit-elasticity."

Consider, again, the case of "Liquid Capital." If, "through some miscalculation of supply and demand" a price exceeding normal price has emerged in this market, the flow-rate of supply exceeds that of demand. "Unit-elastic price expectations" in such a case are "irrational": if price is maintained, stocks will go on accumulating without end. Unjustified prices cannot be maintained for very considerable periods, however, because (a) carrying costs are substantial in relation to the anticipated normal price, and (b) the market is capable of anticipating the correct "normal price" within a fairly reasonable margin of error—since, due to (a), it does not have to take the very far future into account.[26]

Thus there is nothing "illogical" about inelastic expectations *per se*. The steady-state conception of traditional statics does not pose a methodological imperative in the construction of "dynamic and historical" systems. Quite the contrary. We must conceive of transactors generally acting on the common sense principles affirmed by Field Marshall Slim's adage: "Things are seldom as good or as bad as they are first reported."

It is indeed the case of generally unit-elastic expectations that emerges as an "academic possibility" of little, if any, interest. To put the issue in extreme fashion: Can we even conceive of purposive human activity in a context where all events are

---

26. For these reasons, among others, Keynes regarded "redundant Liquid stocks" as an "accentuating factor" in depressions rather than as an initiating factor. In his partial equilibrium analysis of this market he did not stress the distinction between the long-run equilibrium price and the subjectively estimated "normal price." (His reasons for ignoring this distinction may be inferred from the discussion in Chapter 5 of the *General Theory*.) He argued this case (against Hawtrey) repeatedly. This lack of interest in the endogenous inventory cycle—and short cycles generally—is characteristic of Keynes: his interest in "recessions" and temporary setbacks of that order was but mild; his motivation was the urgency of finding a cure for the major catastrophes which he regarded as threatening the international capitalistic system.

deemed equi-probable—which is to say, where prior experience is judged to be no guide at all? Used in the dynamic, historical, short-run context that was Keynes', the familiar analytical tools that are so reliable in "pure" long-run statics create a Beyond the Looking-Glass world full of strange paradoxes: individuals act without the benefit of prior knowledge, yet collectively as if possessed of perfect information. Or (viewed from the perspective of Chapter II): individual A bases his choices on the knowledge of the relevant aspects of what everyone else will do, yet A's decisions are part of the information utilized by everyone else.[27]

That memories of past prices do not affect present trading *cannot* be made the general assumption for all markets. If traders were to wake up one morning with general amnesia about past prices, the resulting chaos cannot even be imagined. It is only in the hypothetical world of Walras that all the information required to coordinate the economic activities of myriad individuals is produced *de novo* on each market day. Ninety-nine percent of the information on which traders act in the short run is stored, not newly "produced." In any actual system, this "stock of knowledge" is undoubtedly subject to "radioactive depreciation," but is is only in constructions of the Walrasian type that bygones become bygones with the close of each market day, and it is only in contexts of such a long-run nature that the depreciation of memories has reduced the "hangover" of past events to insignificance, that the static apparatus of unit-elastic expectations, reversible asset demand schedules, *et hoc genus omne* is really applicable. Even the most "casual empiricism" indicates that the assumption of markets for durable assets entirely devoid of "speculative" activity is extremely implausible, if not nonsensical.

If "inelastic expectations" would be appropriate under conditions of perfect foresight, it is certainly reasonable to assume their existence in the case of uncertainty. In the case of perfect foresight, however, the market forms an entirely accurate prediction of the long run "normal price" of the capital stock. In the

---

27. Once more the reference is to Hayek. Cf. his "The Meaning of Competition," in *Individualism and Economic Order*.

terminology of the *Treatise,* it will know what the natural rate *is.* Perfect information implies continuous equilibrium of the entire system. To get to the core of Keynesian theory, one need only add the (perfectly reasonable) assumption that the actual market is not always able to forecast the natural rate accurately. Its estimate—the "normal rate"—will often diverge from the justified or natural rate. In particular, the market may be slow to adjust to changes in the natural rate—changes which may be induced by any of a large number of "real factors." For "to diagnose the position precisely at every stage . . . may sometimes be . . . beyond the wits of man." [28]

The criticisms of Fellner and Leontief   For the "major logical objection" to Keynes' Liquidity Preference theory, Tobin cited the prior works of Leontief and Fellner. Fellner's argument is the one which concerns us most directly.[29]

Fellner argues that there is a curious *asymmetry* in Keynes' assumptions about behavior in different markets. The inelasticity of expectations seems to be of vital importance in the bond market but in no other market in the system:

It is not convincing that at low interest rates a rise in these rates is expected and that these expectations are responsible for the increase in hoarding at low rates and for the incompleteness of the downward adjustment of the interest structure. . . . If the expectation of a return to normalcy is strong enough to produce significant phenomena it is likely to produce a recovery to previous levels of the main economic variables, including the [investment] function and thereby of the interest structure.[30]

28. *Treatise,* Vol. I, p. 255.

29. W. Fellner, *Monetary Policies and Full Employment,* Berkeley and Los Angeles, 1946, Chapter V, esp. pp. 145–51. In the context of this study, Fellner's argument is the more interesting because its analysis of unemployment is more sophisticated than that most often met in the later income-expenditure literature. Fellner's short-run analysis pays scrupulous attention to the problems of "period models," for example, and his understanding of the logic of "income-constrained processes" is indicated (e.g., p. 140): "In the 'perfectly competitive equilibrium,' full employment is produced not merely by the complete fluidity of prices but also by the absence of uncertainty," etc. Cf. also Fellner's emphasis on "hoarding" as a crucial variable, below.

30. Fellner, *op. cit.,* pp. 148–49. Compare p. 150: "It seems . . . unconvincing to argue that a cyclical decline in net rates produces the expectation of a cyclical

The comparative static formulation of this argument is somewhat misleading since it tends to direct one's attention away from the line of causation and temporal sequence of events with which Keynes' original analysis was concerned. This stands out more clearly in Tobin's paraphrase of Fellner:

> Why . . . are interest rates the only variables to which inelastic expectations attach? Why don't wealth owners and others regard pre-depression price-levels as "normal" levels to which prices will return? If they did, consumption and investment demand would respond to reductions in money wages and prices, no matter how strong and how elastic the liquidity preference of investors.[31]

The Keynesian answers to these queries are, of course, that inelastic expectations *do* attach to other prices as well; that producers and wage-earners *do* regard pre-depression price levels as "normal" *to begin with*—that is exactly what triggers the income-constrained process. In the Keynesian *process-analysis* of output-contraction and deflation, the interjection of the second query is out of place because the analysis implies that money prices and wages will not fall *until* faith in the "normalcy" of previously prevailing prices has been thoroughly undermined. As long as sellers believe that it will in short order be possible again to obtain pre-depression prices, reservation prices will hold up. Keynes, as we have seen, gave adequate recognition to the point in any case: "If the reduction of money-wages is expected to be a *reduction relatively to money wages* in the future, the change will be favourable . . ." etc.[32]

Fellner elaborates on the argument in the following way:

> This set of assumptions, underlying the speculative theory of hoarding, is highly artificial. The assumptions are not logically inconsistent but they lack plausibility because they imply that the public is consis-

---

rise and thereby produces cyclical depression hoarding, whereas analogous expectations of a return to normalcy fail to materialize for other markets and therefore fail to bring about an actual return to normalcy."

31. Tobin, *op. cit.*, p. 70.

32. Cf. V:2 above.

tently and obstinately wrong and that a certain type of "incorrect" behavior is limited to one market.[33]

But, one must insist, *in macrodisequilibrium the public is "wrong"*—and if the disequilibrium is persistent, this is because the public is, indeed, "obstinately wrong," refusing to adopt a price vector consistent with over-all equilibrium.

The *General Theory* does not postulate different basic behavior patterns for different markets. The argument that its inelastic expectations are "limited to one market" we have already controverted above: markets for current output and factor services would indeed clear continuously if sellers were always willing to accept whatever price is acceptable to the buyers with whom they happen to be in contact at the moment. If the unemployed laborer, considered in Chapter II, had "completely unit-elastic expectations," he would perceive no reason to engage in a more or less lengthy search for the best obtainable wage, but would accept any wage, however low, at which his services could be sold on the spot. Thus, this criticism, curiously enough, is more relevant to the *Treatise* than to the *General Theory*, since the *Treatise* does treat markets "asymetrically"—a decline in the natural rate below market rate (maintained due to the inelastic expectations of "speculators") is portrayed as leading to a fall in the price level rather than to a contraction of employment and output.

The discussion of Keynes' "diagnosis" of unemployment disequilibrium may also be recalled. In a partial equilibrium analysis of the labor market, unemployment may seem due to the "obstinately incorrect" behavior of workers. But the "normal wage" on which workers (unsuccessfully) insist *may* be (close to) the "natural wage"—i.e., to the money wage which would permit full employment if all other prices were "correct." Thus it is true, in a sense, that Keynes still tends to "limit" incorrect behavior to one market—but it is true in a sense quite different from that conveyed by Fellner and Tobin.

Fellner's argument that if inelastic expectations ruled in all markets, this would "produce a recovery to previous levels of the

---

33. Fellner, *op. cit.*, pp. 150–51.

main economic variables, including the investment function"
seemingly presumes that there is no underlying "real disturbance" causing the contraction. If we assume, in truly Keynesian
fashion, that the initial disturbance is due to a "decline in the
marginal efficiency of capital"—i.e., a downward re-evaluation
by entrepreneurs of the prospective return to capital—*and* that
this re-evaluation is indeed warranted, then a return of the investment function to the "previous level" would not be justified.
Now such a re-evaluation may in itself seem to indicate an
elasticity of expectations on the part of entrepreneurs which does
not characterize investors. Keynes, however, did not attribute a
complete fluidity of expectations to entrepreneurs either. Instead, he postulated that their forecasts of prospective returns to
capital would be revised rather infrequently. This, in fact, was
one of the major problems. Investment could proceed for long
periods, under conditions of basically unchanged technology, at
a pace faster than the growth in population and labor force, and
and at a roughly constant level of long rate, before the slowly
accumulating evidence of an exhaustion of warranted investment
opportunities at this level of long rate caused entrepreneurs to
revise their views of the marginal efficiency of capital. In Keynes'
view, therefore, these revisions took place in discontinuous steps
—this being a major reason why the market rate would lag
behind. Such revisions of entrepreneurial expectations, when
they finally occur, may overshoot the mark, the new view being
unduly pessimistic. Even if we assume, however, that the revised
expectations are entirely accurate in themselves, it is clear that a
restoration of equilibrium does not imply a return to "previous
levels" of the main economic variables. Instead, a new and lower
equilibrium growth-path is indicated, with a higher rate of consumption, a lower long-term rate of interest, *and* a lower rate of
investment.

Keynes' view appears eminently reasonable—the "errors"
which are capable of causing a major maladjustment are most
likely to come about in those markets where the maintenance of
equilibrium over time requires the consistency of forecasts and
plans into the far future. It is here that the available information
will be most inadequate.

There remains, then, Fellner's point about the different degrees of "obstinacy" with which people persist, in various markets of the Keynesian model, in engaging in behavior that prevents the equilibrating adjustment of the system. We have repeatedly stressed the possibility that, from a general equilibrium perspective, the attempts, e.g., of workers to maintain money wage rates, may be "justified"—or, at least, not very far off the mark—while the state of entrepreneurial expectations or the insistence of investors on a market rate in line with outdated views of normal rate, are unjustified. Nonetheless there are perfectly good reasons why workers and producers should be less obstinate in their behavior, however "nearly justified," than investors in theirs. The costs of carrying redundant Liquid Capital are substantial and will force price reductions before very long. A fall in the short-term interest rate of one or two percent, as Keynes pointed out, makes very little difference. Similarly, the costs of going unemployed—of "carrying labor services"—are high indeed, compelling a fairly rapid revision of the worker's reservation price. Here too, even the existence of a "perfect credit market" in personal credit—i.e., credit against security in future labor earnings—would make but a marginal difference. In these markets, therefore, the "costs of being obstinate" fall to a very substantial extent directly upon the obstinate transactor himself—and he cannot but perceive this.

In the market for long-term assets the situation is quite different. In the first place, the *ex ante* opportunity cost of holding highly liquid securities, rather than long-term securities, may not appear very substantial. Second, once the bears prevail, and the system enters an income-constrained process, the fall in capital values which is likely to ensue will convince them *ex post* that they did the "right thing"—they did avoid (some of) these capital losses. And the tremendous social costs of their "obstinacy" are of course borne for the most part by producers and workers; but this cost does not enter into the speculators' calculations. The connection is far from obvious:

. . . the failure of employment to attain an optimum level being in no way associated, in the minds either of the public or of authority, with the prevalence of an inappropriate range of rates of interest.[34]

---

34. *General Theory*, p. 204.

Thus, while the economist is wont to console himself with the thought that, in any given *single* market, destabilizing speculation is bound to cost speculators dearly, at least in the long run, a macroeconomic perspective is less reassuring. The Pavlovian mechanism usually assumed to teach speculators to perform in a "system-functional" manner is not adequate to the task in this context. Speculation in securities markets, which stabilizes the *price* of long streams, will impose *quantity* adjustments—real income oscillations—on a system exposed to shocks whose absorption requires changes in market rate. The bears of 1929–30 made fortunes, despite the fact that, had a monetary policy *à outrance* been followed, they would have lost heavily. The actual course of events did not teach them a lesson. But then the bears had a most powerful ally in the monetary authority—itself bent upon breaking the bulls.

The comments by Leontief, referred to by Tobin, appear more as clarifications than as objections, from the standpoint of the present interpretation of Keynes' theory.[35] Leontief stressed the "short-run" character of Keynes' theory, noting that in the long run of Classical theory the demand for speculative balances must be zero. The paper is in part very critical in tone, but the criticism of Keynes concerns more the appropriateness of the Cantabrigian "period-analysis" as a tool of dynamic analysis (and of the admittedly loose use of the term "equilibrium" characteristic of the Cambridge School) than the substantive issues presently under discussion.[36] There is perhaps more than a hint in Leon-

---

35. W. Leontief, "Postulates: Keynes' *General Theory* and the Classicists," in Harris, ed., *op. cit.* Cf. esp. section 6 of this paper.

36. In part Leontief's comments read almost as a paraphrase of one of Keynes' own efforts to restate the issues separating him from "orthodox theorists" on the theory of interest. Cf. his "The Theory of The Rate of Interest," in *The Lessons of Monetary Experience; Essays in Honor of Irving Fisher,* 1937, reprinted in W. Fellner and B. H. Haley, eds., *Readings in The Theory of Income Distribution,* Philadelphia, 1946, esp. pp. 423–24. E.g.: "I do not see, however, how [the amount of inactive balances can be independent of the rate of interest], *except in conditions of long-period equilibrium,* by which I mean a state of expectation which is both definite and constant and has lasted long enough for there to be no hangover from a previous state of expectation. . . . [This] the orthodox theory requires. . . . If I am right, the orthodox theory is wholly inapplicable to such problems as those of unemployment and the trade cycle, or, indeed, to any of the

tief's paper of a disagreement with Keynes on a basically empirical issue—namely on the approximate "calendar time counterpart" of the "short run" in Keynes' formulation of interest theory. While Leontief is not explicit on this point, it seems probable that he would disagree with Keynes on the speed with which existing feedback mechanisms would force a revision of inappropriate expectations.[37]

The "money illusion" issue once more   Finally, the charge should be mentioned that Keynes committed the "heinous crime of building money illusion into the assets demand for money."[38] Patinkin, in particular, elaborates at length on this charge and considers this alleged treatment of the speculative demand for money as a "vital oversight" which "is all too unconsciously exploited" in the *General Theory*.[39] The truth of this matter is by now so deeply embedded beneath a thick crust of doctrinal exegesis that an almost interminable discussion would be required to support the contention that Keynes' speculative demand was *not* based on an implicit assumption of "money illusion," in any useful sense of the term. A systematic critique of the "evidence" cited by Patinkin and of his supporting argumentation would also have to carry us back over much of the ground already covered: the dynamic specification of Patinkin's own theory is different from that of the *General Theory* model—the "Patinkin week" does not correspond to Keynes' "short run"; the

---

day-to-day problems of ordinary life. . . . The orthodox theory is . . . particularly applicable to the stationary state." (italics added)

37. Cf. Keynes, *General Theory*, p. 204: "[The rate of interest] may fluctuate for decades about a level which is chronically too high for full employment," and the statement quoted above, according to which the consequences of such a state of affairs are "in no way associated, in the minds either of the public or of authority" with this cause. In reading Keynes' statements on this issue it is very important to keep in mind that he is not talking about the speed of a purely endogenous adjustment process involving only the private sector. The "obstinate maintenance of misguided monetary policies" is his explanation of the maintenance of inappropriately high long rates over such protracted periods of time. Cf., e.g., *Treatise*, Vol. II, pp. 384 ff, and Chapter IV:1, above.

38. H. G. Johnson, "The *General Theory* . . . ," *op. cit.*, p. 9.

39. Patinkin, 2nd edn., pp. 373–75. Cf. also Note K:2 and its references to many other places in the book where the point is re-emphasized.

aggregative structures of the two models are quite different—and Patinkin, as we have seen, is not clearly aware of these differences; thus he overlooks the "windfall effect" and pays insufficient attention to the fact that, in Keynes' model, changes in the interest rate imply changes in the relative price of the system's *two* commodities, with implications for the "real value of money," in Patinkin's sense, that are far from clear-cut. And so on. We will leave the purely exegetical aspects of this question aside.

It remains a fact that the "real" solution state of Keynes' model is not invariant to changes in the nominal supply of money. The question then is to what extent, if any, it is "useful" to ascribe the distinctive differences between the Keynesian short-run model and the long-run general equilibrium model to assumptions of "money illusion" built into the former. Thus, in addition to Keynes' speculative demand, his labor-supply function has also been regarded from this standpoint, i.e., as ascribing "money illusion" to workers.[40]

This approach may have its value in defending the logical consistency of "Classical" doctrine against the attacks of Stagnationist "Keynesian" zealots. But the "money illusion" labels can be quite misleading when it comes to appraising the positive contributions attempted by Keynes. The type of behavior associated with "money illusion" is the economist's prototype of irrational behavior. It is fairly clear what the assumption of "absence of money illusion" means when the reference is to the theory of individual choice. The conventional theory of choice presumes full information on the part of the choosing agent, however, and the extension of the same basic paradigm to problems of choice under conditions of Knightian risk still assumes that the transactor has full information on the probability distributions of relevant outcomes.

---

40. Compare, Chapter II:2 and II:3, above. Cf. the earlier paper by Leontief where this approach was first taken: "The Fundamental Assumption of Mr. Keynes' Monetary Theory of Unemployment," *Quarterly Journal of Economics,* Nov. 1936. As already indicated above, Leontief in his later essay on Keynes chose to emphasize the short run-long run distinction instead. It should similarly be noted that Patinkin in evaluating Keynes' contribution also takes the same tack in the end. Cf. *op. cit.,* Note K:3.

On the macrolevel the application of the concept of "money illusion" is less straightforward. Disequilibrium, as we have emphasized throughout, means that individuals have to act on "imperfect information." It also means that the vector of ruling market prices is, in one or more respects, "inappropriate." Indeed, disequilibrium in a Crusoe-economy would be evidence of "irrationality" (though even here "money illusion" may not be the most helpful diagnosis of Robinson's malady). But even though the emergence of a "general glut" may rightfully be regarded as evidence of the sickness of the socioeconomic system, it should not be inferred that this is due to "irrationality" on part of the individuals and groups composing the system. The point has already been discussed in Chapter II—rational, "optimizing," behavior by individual transactors will not lead to a rapid re-establishment of exchange equilibrium when "false prices" constitute an important part of the information on which individual choices are based.

Disequilibrium macroeconomics need not be based on "special assumptions" postulating the irrationality of certain transactor groups or of all transactors. Attempts to pinpoint the reasons for the disequilibrium implications of various short-run macromodels by searching for "implicit assumptions" of "money-illusioned behavior" seem, therefore, to constitute a particularly unfruitful type of semantic exercise.

VI·TWO POSTSCRIPTS

VI:1 Keynes' Pure Theory: Communication and Control in Dynamic Systems

A prospective summary has been given in Chapter I and a retrospective summary will not be necessary. Numerous issues have been discussed in more or less detail. Some of these would be recognized as significant *per se;* others normally belong in the footnote underbrush of the macroeconomic literature. In the present study, more space has been given to the latter than to the former in several instances. The topic of the interest-elasticity of saving is an example.

On each of these issues, the objective has been to compare Keynes' position with that of later theorists who have been influential in the development of the type of macrotheory which dominates the teaching of the subject today. This majority school macrotheory is not a homogeneous or uniform doctrine, but it has been impossible to chart individual differences on all the issues and to avoid dealing in generalizations.

In the choice of analytical issues and of later theoretical arguments to be juxtaposed against those of Keynes' the author has had to exercise his personal judgment. Unavoidably, these judgments are in varying degree subjective. Some acquaintance with the history of economic doctrines will indicate the futility of trying to force others to concur in such personal judgments by constructing elaborate rationalizations of them. I have attempted to be frank about my preconceptions, although undoubtedly some important preconceptions remain implicit, and it must be left to the reader to form his own opinions. There is also another, rather obvious, way in which subjective judgment has been exercised, namely the exclusion of topics. There are a number of issues which loom large in the "Keynesian" literature which we have hardly touched upon at all. Similarly, the coverage of Keynes' ideas has been less than complete.

Thus, the study does not meet exegetical standards of objectivity and comprehensiveness. As the title warns, it is tendentious —but not, I believe, arbitrarily so. It is clear that one cannot establish the suggested distinction between the Economics of Keynes and Keynesian Economics as analytically useful, or even convenient, by mere accumulation of instances in which Keynes' ideas can be shown to differ from those expressed in subsequent works in which the "Keynesian" lineage is dominant or at least prominent. The general opinion seems to be that subsequent developments have retained and improved upon what was worthwhile, while discarding only what was ill-conceived. It is not necessarily the case that a clearer understanding of Keynes' thought, which is what we have tried to provide, would give cause to revise this opinion.

In large degree, the previous chapters have been concerned with the "accumulation of instances." To give some coherence to the numerous observations made, we have tried to organize them in terms of a few key concepts—"dynamic structure" in Chapter II, "aggregative structure" in Chapter III, and the "dimension" of term to maturity or "duration of use or consumption" in Chapter IV. But, though these concepts may be useful for structuring the discussion, they hardly "prove" that the Keynesian Revolution got off on the wrong track and continued on it.

It is sufficiently obvious by now that this is the author's opinion. Clearly, this is the thesis of the present work in which largely subjective elements figure most prominently. It is also clear why this must be so. Scientific "revolutions" are never consummated in the works which initiate them. The seminal works will be prompted by dissatisfaction with existing doctrine, a dissatisfaction voiced in the form of more or less cogent criticism; this criticism, in turn, is made the basis for indicating novel directions of departure. The seminal thinker will himself press on with more or less success in some of these directions while other ideas will be left merely as suggested "pointers," and so on.[1] Keynes fits this pattern. Some of his criticisms of "Classical" doctrine were ill-conceived, others were unhappily formulated. Some of his ideas were pursued in depth and their implications chartered in some detail; in other areas we are shown only the tip of the iceberg and the subsurface mass remains a matter of speculation. This being the case, the question of whether subsequent work has developed the most "worthwhile" elements of his contribution unavoidably becomes one to which a completely objective answer cannot be given. The answer given will depend on what the individual economist finds in the book.

The reader of a study of the present sort may well have the right to request that, in conclusion, the author should surmount the "accumulation of instances" and at least attempt a sweeping generalization or two. In the present instance, the required generalization should indicate the theoretical direction in which I feel the *General Theory* pointed and the promise which the Keynesian tradition has not fulfilled. Before going out on the limb, however, a few brief reminders are in order.

In Chapter II, we suggested that the "Keynes and the Classics" issues are better approached from a dynamic than a comparative static perspective. This was at first given a rather mechanical formulation. Keynes, we argued, reversed the ranking of price and quantity velocities underlying Marshall's distinction between the "market day" and the "short run." It was

---

1. The relevant reference is again to T. S. Kuhn, *op. cit.* The theses regarding the "Structure of Scientific Revolutions," which Kuhn develops on the basis of historical studies of developments in the natural sciences, generally fit the Keynesian Revolution most admirably. But we cannot elaborate on this here.

emphasized that the income-constrained process could be explained without invoking the strong assumption of rigid wages by simply relinquishing the strong assumption of infinite wage velocity. We then discussed the implications of removing from the system of atomistic markets the *deus ex machina* of traditional general equilibrium theory—the Walrasian auctioneer. Next, we paraphrased Alchian's analysis of adjustments in an isolated market by traders who do not know what the market-clearing price would be. This uncertainty about equilibrium price is the main implication that follows from removing Walras' auctioneer. Extending the analysis to a system of several markets, the feedback effects on other markets of the emergence of unemployed resources in one market are seen to imply a dynamic behavior of the system of the type investigated by Clower. Keynes' multiplier-process is a simplistic version of the income-constrained process. The significance of Clower's analysis lies in the general equilibrium approach—the multiplier is explained without removing relative prices from the model.

This chapter already adumbrates the "sweeping generalization" to be made. The main points are that in the system lacking the *tâtonnement* mechanism (1) *individuals still "maximize utility"* and are neither constrained from bargaining on their own nor are they "money-illusioned" or otherwise assumed irrational; (2) *price incentives remain as before*—the absence of the auctioneer does not mean that relative prices are less effective in controlling the behavior of individual traders; (3) *the "right" price information* required for the perfect coordination of the economic activities of innumerable traders *is not guaranteed* in the short run. It is from the last point that the analysis of Keynesian processes starts.

Chapter III compared the aggregative structures of the standard income-expenditure model and the *General Theory* model. Keynes' method of lumping together bonds and capital goods and the presence of two distinct produced commodities in his model were documented. The distinctions between non-money assets and consumer goods and between non-money assets and "money" were shown to be based on the "location" on the maturity continuum of the respective aggregates. In both cases the line is drawn between "high" and "low" interest-elasticities of present value. The chapter also considered the old questions of the importance of money and of "the" interest rate in Keynesian economics. The last section sought to confirm Harrod's thesis of the "importance of interest" in Keynes' thought: Keynes never wavered from the position that movements in long rate create incentives which are highly effective in inducing adjustments of individual production and trading plans.

Chapter IV is the most speculative. It represents an attempt to reconstruct the "*Gestalt*" of Keynes' ideas on capital theory. It sufficiently documents, I believe, that he was not blind to the "influence of capital and wealth on behavior," and also that the key to his thought in this area is the assumed great longevity of "almost all the capital in the World." Beyond that, one is left to fill in as best one can the outlines of a theory to which Keynes' left only sketchy clues. This I have tried to do, but I am conscious that the scholarly status of parts of Chapter IV must remain somewhat that of the "Artist's conception of Ninive in the year 2000 B.C." which one sometimes finds in archaeological books for the lay public—however grand the panorama, it may all have to be changed the next time another scholar puts the spade to the ground.

The income-constrained process may be developed perfectly well within the framework of a one-commodity model. To anyone taking the position that the multiplier-analysis of the *General Theory* comprises "the essence" of Keynesianism, Chapter III and IV are, by that definition, of "academic" interest at most. To this one must respond that when the multiplier takes hold there is already "something wrong" with the system. What generally goes wrong first is the coordination of production, trading, and consumption plans in the future. Keynes conceived his task to be that of "analyzing the economic behavior of the present under the influence of changing ideas about the future." And "it is by reason of the existence of durable equipment that the economic future is linked to the present." It may still be argued that the basic conception can be realized within the one-commodity framework simply by postulating that the commodity will partake of the nature of a *Gebrauchsgut* when used as a source of factor services and of a *Verbrauchsgut* in consumption. As before, the present value of capital stocks in terms of consumer goods will then be independent of both expectations and interest rate, although the propensity to invest will not. But in Keynes' conception the "dark forces of time and ignorance" wreak their havoc on the present by impinging on current capital values. The confusion of the future is transmitted to the present through this particular channel. The ramifications of this point we discussed both in Chapters IV and V. It cannot be doubted that Keynes attached crucial significance to it, but that does not mean that it poses an analytical imperative to the modern theorist.[2]

What one must insist upon with regard to these later chapters turns out to be essentially the same three points by which we summarized Chapter II. In that chapter the point of reference was the static atemporal general equilibrium model. What has been added to the picture of Keynes' theory in later chapters is the "temporal depth" dimension. In Keynes' theory: (1) *traders do maximize utility and profit* in the manner assumed in Classical analyses of saving and investment; (2) *intertemporal price incentives are effective*—changes in interest rates or expected future spot prices will significantly affect present behavior; (3) *the information requirements* for keeping the system on an equilibrium path are fulfilled only by purest luck.

We have repeatedly referred to the need to discover a basis on which a synthesis of "Keynesian" economics and "Classical" value theory can be achieved. For a non-economist, one may note, it would not seem obvious that a synthesis of pre- and post-revolutionary thought is necessary. One does not, after all, berate Einstein for failing to elucidate how a synthesis of the General Theory of Relativity and Ptolemaic astronomy should be

---

2. My own "intuitions" on this matter doubtlessly shine through in the body of the text: I believe it would be best to chuck out the GNP-deflator once and for all and to tackle the difficulties which arise when the simplifications afforded by working with "real" income, "real" output, "real" balances, in the conventional sense, are openly recognized as treacherous. I am particularly skeptical about the value of trying to extend monetary theory into a general Theory of Finance by multiplying the number of financial markets tacked onto the old one-commodity model.

achieved. For several reasons, which we need not elaborate further, the situation is quite different in economics. Neither the Keynesian Revolution nor the Counterrevolution has carried the day, and modern macroeconomic theory hovers uneasily between Keynesian thesis and the anti-thesis of resurgent Neoclassicism.[3] At one extreme we have "Keynesian" models manifesting a universal "elasticity-pessimism" and assigning virtually no meaningful role to relative prices. At the other extreme we have the burgeoning monetary general equilibrium literature of Pigovian parentage and the still more "general" metastatic growth models.

To come, then, to the sweeping generalization: The main conclusion, I believe, is that the long debate has failed to achieve a viable synthesis of the worthwhile elements of Classical theory and Keynes' theory basically because one elemental but vital distinction has not been made clear.[4] The distinction pertains to the dual role of the price mechanism in a large system where economic decision-making is decentralized. The "automatic" functioning of the system in Classical theory depends on the efficient performance of both roles—*prices should disseminate the information* necessary to coordinate the economic activities and plans of independent transaction units, and *prices should provide the incentives* for transaction units to adjust their activities in such manner that they become consistent in the aggregate. The Classical economists proper constructed a theory of the coordination of the private enterprise system which was essentially a long-run theory. Keynes recognized the merit of traditional theory as a theory of long-run tendencies. It was mainly the great Neoclassical system-builders who began to apply their apparatus to the short run and the "market day." In the aftermath of the successful solution of

---

3. One might pose two anti-theses, the second being the Neo-Quantity theory. I believe, however, that the main issues between income-expenditure theorists and Neo-Quantity theorists could be settled (assuming a will to negotiate) without any substantial progress with regard to the problems between Keynesianism and the traditional Theory of Markets.

4. The distinction is, of course, drawn every day of the year in such fields as Soviet Economics, and is also otherwise exceedingly familiar—except, it seems, in this important context.

several long-standing problems in value theory, which the Marginalist Revolution had achieved, this ebullient optimism with regard to the uses of contemporary economic analysis was perhaps natural.

Keynes rejected the Neoclassical notion that the price mechanism would efficiently perform the information function in the short run. He did not take a position substantially different from the traditional one on the effectiveness of price incentives in controlling the behavior of individual transaction units.

The majority of both Keynesians and anti-Keynesians seem convinced that the baby went out with the bath water; they differ mainly on whether the brat would ever have amounted to anything and whether the departure, therefore, should be lamented or not. How else is one to explain the "Keynesian" preoccupation with wage-rigidities, interest-inelasticities, constant capital-output ratios, liquidity traps, and the like? How else can one explain the movement which Clower aptly names the "Keynesian Counterrevolution"? The main thesis of the counterrevolution is widely accepted; to wit: "The model which Keynes called his 'General Theory' is but a special case of the Classical theory, obtained by imposing certain restrictive assumptions on the latter." In other words, models which do not assume perfect information are "special cases" of the perfect information model! The counterrevolutionary thesis is not made less nonsensical by the frequently appended reservation that the Keynesian "special case" is nonetheless interesting because, as it happens, it is more relevant to the real world than is the "general" (equilibrium) theory.

Walras' general equilibrium theory was a most remarkable achievement. Keynes dashed off freehand sketches where Walras, in his time, supplied workmanlike blueprints. What one should note is that the inspiration to Walras' blueprint derived from Newtonian mechanics [5]—the scientific paradigm most universally admired in his day. The Walrasian model is admirably

---

5. I have this on the best authority: In his seminar in doctrine-history at Northwestern, Professor Jaffé told of the tremendous impression which a treatise in "Celestial Mechanics" made on the young Walras and of his determination to demonstrate the "Harmony of the Spheres" prevailing in the free enterprise system.

suited to the study of the *incentive* function of prices, the performance of which is a necessary but not sufficient condition for the coordination of a decentralized system. But from the standpoint of dynamic theory, it remains what cyberneticians term a Clockwork model—a strictly deterministic, Newtonian mechanism in which prices perform the functions of levers and pulleys.

This kind of Newtonian conception of what the economic system is like works very well in equilibrium economics. In the study of economic fluctuations, unemployment, and money, however, it tends to bias one's perception of the nature of the problem in a particular direction. When the huge machine does not work as it is supposed to (one tends to infer) it *must be* either because someone has thrown a spanner in the works— "monopolists and unions fix prices"—or because the cogs are slipping someplace—"savers and investors do not respond to interest incentives." Sometimes the suspicion unavoidably sneaks in that the machine is a Rube Goldberg contraption in the first place—"there may not exist a market-clearing vector of nonnegative prices." We are almost buried under the evidence that any variety of mathematically consistent models exhibiting unemployment and/or fluctuations can be built on this philosophical basis. Yet, might it not be time to consider whether the direction in which the Newtonian conception leads us is really the most fruitful one for "purely" theoretical inquiry to pursue?

There have always been warning signals even in the realm of "Classical" statics: the return to entrepreneurs, for example, has resisted satisfactory incorporation in the marginal productivity theory of distribution. The reason is clear: the analysis of the distribution of income to other factors is built upon assumptions of perfect information with regard to production functions and exchange opportunities. Returns to the knowledge possessed by entrepreneurs can only be plastered onto this underlying conception in a most *ad hoc* manner, particularly if one insists on trying to deal with information as a good or factor service analogous to any other. This same difficulty is also apparent in comparative static treatments of innovation.[6] The treatment of

---

6. Schumpeter was intensely bothered by the deterministic nature of the Walrasian model and wrestled interminably with the question: "How can changes

knowledge-information as just another stock-flow commodity is a feature of modern research on problems of human capital and education with which one must be uncomfortable—as one must be generally with respect to the persistence of an economic analysis based on the Neoclassical theory of production applied to a society where human agents are more and more exclusively engaged in the generation, transmission, reception, and processing of information and not in the Smithian pin-making tasks which represent the prototype labor activity of traditional theory.

One definition of cybernetics is "the study of communication and control in dynamic systems." Communication and control, of course, correspond to the price information and price incentives referred to above. As we have seen, however, it is only in Walrasian systems with continuously clearing markets that prices alone carry all the information on which individual decisions will be based. Clower's analysis of systems exhibiting Keynesian dynamic behavior reveals the immense formal complexity of the analysis required in dealing with models in which both ruling and expected prices and realized and anticipated quantities influence transactor behavior. It also reveals the economic theorist's almost complete lack of acquaintance with a problem which has for so long been avoided by various expedient assumptions.

In retrospect, I feel that this was the direction in which Keynes' work pointed. Cybernetics as a formal theory, of course, began to develop only during the war and it was only with the appearance of Professor Wiener's book in 1948 that the first results of serious work on a general theory of dynamic systems —and the term itself—reached a wider public. Even then, research in this field seemed remote from economic problems, and it is thus not surprising that the first decade or more of the Keynesian debate did not go in this direction. But it is surprising that so few monetary economists have caught on to develop-

---

occur in the 'Circular Flow' of economic activity?" (The intertemporal generalization of the general equilibrium model had not been achieved in his time, but Schumpeter perceived, rather vaguely, what it would be like and dismissed it as an approach irrelevant to the question of development.) His solution to the question was, of course, to treat innovations as purely "emergent properties."

ments in this field in the last ten or twelve years, and that the work of those who have has not triggered a more dramatic chain reaction.[7] This, I believe, is the Keynesian Revolution which did not come off.

In conveying the essential departure of cybernetics from traditional physics, Wiener once noted:

> Here there emerges a very interesting distinction between the physics of our grandfathers and that of the present day. *In nineteenth century physics, it seemed to cost nothing to get information.*[8]

In context, the reference was to Maxwell's Demon. In its economic reincarnation as Walras' auctioneer, the demon has not yet been exorcised. But this certainly must be what Keynes tried to do. If a single distinction is to be drawn between the Economics of Keynes and the economics of our grandfathers, this is it. It is only on this basis that Keynes' claim to having essayed a more "general theory" can be maintained. If this distinction is not recognized as both valid and important, I believe we must conclude that Keynes' contribution to pure theory was nil.[9]

That is the generalization I would make. To forestall misinterpretations, it calls for some concluding notes.

(1) On the "generality" of the *General Theory*. There is, of course, a different sense of the term in which traditional general equilibrium theory is the more "general" construction, namely that often equated with "empty." It is an almost completely

---

7. I am told that Professor A. W. Phillips, who is probably the best-known proponent of a cybernetic approach to macrodynamics, was initially an engineer. A. Tustin (*The Mechanism of Economic Systems*, London, 1953) was and remained an engineer.

8. Norbert Wiener, *The Human Use of Human Beings*, 2nd edn., 1953, p. 29, italics added.

9. If that were the conclusion, we are obliged to ask: What has all the furor been about? Even as it is, the history of the development of Keynesian economics gives ample reason for increased self-consciousness on the part of economists about the forces that guide their enterprise. If Keynes did not pose a theoretically *fundamental* challenge to accepted thought, but still managed to upset the apple-cart so completely, the Sociology of Economic Knowledge would seem to acquire a priority on the efforts of economists that one would be loath to accord it.

"featureless" model in the sense that we know very little about the economy it is supposed to portray except that it has n goods and m transactors.[10]

The characteristic implications of Keynesian theory, on the other hand, do not derive simply from the realization that transactors do not possess "perfect information." Keynes, as we have seen, gets beyond this platitude by specifying a transactions structure composed of a large number of assumed "features," e.g.: (a) goods can only be bought with "money" and only sold for "money"; (b) the means of payment is not a commodity producible through the employment of labor by the private sector—at least not at constant cost; (c) the only cost of storing money is the interest foregone; (d) labor is wage labor in manufacturing, not self-employed in the production of commodities; nor are labor services saleable directly to households; (e) saving decisions and investment decisions are vested in largely non-overlapping groups of people; (f) transactions costs, including costs of acquiring price information, are relatively low in securities markets, making it inexpensive for individual transactors to move in or out of such assets; (g) savers are generally not willing to enter into contracts for the future delivery of specific consumption goods, so that no markets exist for forward trading in such goods; (h) the efficient utilization of available technology dictates that the great bulk of the system's physical capital is very durable—there is no such thing as "liquidity" for the community as a whole; (i) people are mortal, short on foresight, but long on memory; etc.

These are the features that impart to the theory its characteristic Keynesian content. By the same token, the implications dependent upon these assumptions are (healthily) falsifiable. Obviously, the assumptions do not pertain to "all possible worlds"—or even to the great variety of economic systems to the analysis of whose *equilibrium states* the general equilibrium theory is perfectly applicable. Similarly, some of Keynes' favorite assumptions may not apply to the United States today or even to the United Kingdom of his own day, e.g., his views on the role of

---

10. As an illustration, compare Patinkin, 2nd edn., pp. 76–77.

short-sighted "gambling" on the Exchanges, on the well-nigh inexorable inflexibility of long rate, or—by all means—on the interest-elasticity of investment. But such questions on these and similar empirical matters I do not see as relevant to the appraisal of his contribution to pure theory.

(2) Nor has it been my intention, in arguing that Keynes' theory is more "general" than he has been given credit for, to suggest that it embraces all types of malfunctions to which systems with a Keynesian transactions structure may be subject. In particular, the persistent emphasis on the fact that he did not build on the assumption of "rigid wages" is not meant to deny that institutional "rigidities" exist in the real world and pose serious problems.

But the arteriosclerosis of a social system caught in a stalemate of vested interests is a different illness from the subtle neurological dysfunction described in Keynes' theory of unemployment. For reasons that should be obvious, it is important that the distinction be clearly drawn. The two maladies are simply distinct and by no means mutually exclusive. Nor do the two together exclude other possibilities, e.g., that the system may be racked by recurrent attacks of Central Bank perversity. (Casual inspection would seem to indicate that it is a rash man who insists that there is but one thing wrong with the world.)

(3) The contention that there was more to Keynes than has been preserved in present teaching does not carry with it the prescription that we go back to GO and rehash all the old controversies from the perspective of this study. (The prospect, in fact, is almost too horrible to contemplate.) It has become conventional to temper the severity of modern criticisms of Keynes' theoretical ideas with generous praise for the proven usefulness of his basic analytical apparatus. In regard to pure theory, as opposed to national income accounting, my own views are just the reverse. His basic theoretical conception I find intensely interesting, but I doubt that his analytical apparatus can ever be the vehicle for its development and the realization of its promise.

It is the standard income-expenditure model and its use in national income analysis that those who praise Keynes' apparatus have in mind. This tradition, I have argued, has not built further on, or even preserved, all the worthwhile elements of Keynes' thought. (Nor has it discarded only his analytical errors and most ill-considered empirical hunches.) This in itself is sufficient proof that Keynes' apparatus did not serve to communicate his ideas accurately. I do not believe, moreover, that the main arguments stressed in this study will appear novel to Keynes' colleagues and students or even, perhaps, to the students of his students.[11] If more of Keynes is preserved in the British than in the American tradition (as is my impression) this again indicates that his analysis is not altogether adequate for the communication of his theoretical conception—or personal association with Keynes and oral tradition would make no difference.

Keynes, as we have repeatedly remarked, tried to bend the tools of traditional statics to the analysis of a conception of a basically "dynamic and historical" nature. In a way, the degree to which he succeeded is remarkable. Had his method indeed been entirely sound, however, it is hard to imagine that Keynesianism would have succumbed so meekly to the Neoclassical synthesis. This, I think, is true, although his concentration on the involuntary unemployment *state*, in which the income-constrained *process* ensues, also contributed to mislead later economists into giving his system a purely static and ahistorical interpretation.

The unclear mix of statics and dynamics would seem to be the main reason for later muddles. One cannot assume that what went wrong was simply that Keynes slipped up here and there in his adaptation of standard tools, and that consequently, if we go back and tinker a little more with the Marshallian toolbox his purposes will be realized.[12] What is required, I believe, is a

---

11. To those who still have a fresh memory of "the early days" of the Keynesian debate and of the issues which then stirred much interest, it will be apparent (I hope) that I have much less of a quarrel with, say, Harrod and Mrs. Robinson or even (on "involuntary unemployment," for example) with A. H. Hansen than with latter-day textbook Keynesianism and the results of the Neoclassical synthesis.

12. I cannot see that much would be achieved, for example, by the construction of another simultaneous equation model which correctly reflects the aggregative structure, price-elasticity assumptions, and so forth, of Keynes' theory but is

systematic investigation, from the standpoint of the information problems stressed in this study, of what elements of the static theory of resource allocation can without further ado be utilized in the analysis of dynamic and historical systems. This, of course, would be merely a first step: the gap yawns very wide between the systematic and rigorous modern analysis of the stability of simple, "featureless," pure exchange systems and Keynes' inspired sketch of the income-constrained process in a monetary exchange-*cum*-production system. But even for such a first step, the prescription cannot be to "go back to Keynes." If one must retrace some steps of past developments in order to get on the right track—and that is probably advisable—my own preference is to go back to Hayek. Hayek's Gestalt-conception of what happens during business cycles, it has been generally agreed, was much less sound than Keynes'. As an unhappy consequence, his far superior work on the fundamentals of the problem has not received the attention it deserves.[13]

VI:2 Keynes' Applied Theory: The Effectiveness of Monetary Policy

This study has concentrated on Keynes' contribution to theoretical economics. We have been interested in his views on economic policy only at one remove. But a number of scattered observations have nonetheless been made on this subject in order to support and document arguments relating to his "Pure Theory." It seems appropriate, finally, to collect notes.

---

otherwise a pendant to the standard model. (Although it would be helpful for some doctrine-historical purposes.) Nor is it simply a matter of then tinkering with recursive versions of such a construction in the way that the standard model has been adopted to growth and cycle problems. Modern cybernetics, as Wiener would tell us, is not simply Newtonian mechanics "jazzed up" with leads and lags.

13. Cf., esp., "Economics and Knowledge," "The Use of Knowledge in Society," and "The Meaning of Competition," all in *Individualism and Economic Order*. Professor Hicks' "The Hayek Story," in the *Critical Essays*, does not deal with these three masterpieces and, therefore, goes only part way to a full reappraisal of Hayek's contribution.

Because we do not want to launch into another lengthy investigation, we will stick to a single theme: The Keynesian tradition, particularly in the United States, has been associated with a decided preference for fiscal over monetary stabilization policies. Historically, this preference has been bolstered by certain arguments to the effect that monetary policy is generally "ineffective." Since abounding faith in fiscal measures and a withering away of interest in monetary policy was one of the most dramatic aspects of the "Revolution," there is, I believe, a tendency to impute to Keynes himself the policy views characteristic of the New Economics in its early stages. The question is to what extent it is warranted to do so.

Historical perspective on this question has been difficult to maintain. There are a number of reasons why accounts of his views commonly tend to oversimplify his position, to dramatize unduly the divergences between the policy ideas advocated in the *General Theory* and his previously published views, and in particular, to exaggerate his stand in favor of fiscal stabilization policies and the extent to which he downgraded the usefulness of monetary policy. We should begin, therefore, by considering these reasons.

Today the *General Theory* is remembered chiefly as a policy tract that signaled a revolution in professional thinking and popular attitudes on stabilization policy. That it is so remembered is due in part to the establishment of the Neoclassical synthesis, i.e., to the acceptance of a doctrine which denies the *General Theory* any fundamental contribution to pure theory. In part, it is due simply to a confusion of intent and content with actual results. For the first ten or fifteen years at least, the actual "Economic Consequences of Mr. Keynes" were the combined doctrines of the general ineffectiveness of monetary policy and of the general effectiveness of fiscal policies. In fact, of course, the *General Theory* gave less space to systematic discussion of policy issues than any other book by Keynes. While the *Tract on Monetary Reform* was principally concerned with economic policy, and the *Treatise on Money* was equally divided between one volume on "Pure Theory" and one on "Applied Theory," Keynes' *magnum opus* was almost exclusively devoted to pure theory. Its sundry reflections on policy matters are scattered, in parenthetical fashion, as the progression of the theoretical argument dictates. There are no separate chapters on stabilization policy corresponding to the systematic treatment of the subject given by today's "Keynesian" textbooks.

One must recall, therefore, that the case *for* fiscal policy was in the main constructed by later Keynesians. Almost the entire corpus of fiscal policy theory identified with the "New Economics" has been a post-Keynes development. One does not find Lerner's "Functional Finance" concept explicitly elaborated in the *General Theory*.[1] The concept of the "deflationary (or inflationary) gap" and the associated array of algebraic exercises on the income-expenditure model, such as the balanced budget multiplier theorems, belong to a later period. The once-popular idea that the maintenance of full employment requires ever-increasing government expenditures came into fashion first with the incorporation of the accelerator in Keynesian models.

The case *against* monetary policy that was current in the forties, and of which one still hears occasional echoes, similarly was not due to Keynes. Yet the doctrine of the ineffectiveness of monetary policy has become firmly associated with his name. Although Keynes sometimes took delight in the role of the iconoclast, an interpretation which reads this later doctrine into his work is lacking not only in textual support but in simple psychological plausibility. One would no more expect the Heir Apparent to the great tradition of British monetary thought to write a Tract on the Uselessness of Monetary Policy than one would expect a British admiral to publish a Treatise on the Uselessness of Sea Power. A Lord of the Admiralty might well expound on the limitations of sea power in relation to strategic objectives better pursued by other means, or exhort the public on the uselessness of a navy with too few or outdated ships; or

---

1. If Keynes' direct contributions to fiscal policy theory are often exaggerated in retrospect, the contributions of his contemporaries are also correspondingly overlooked. Viner, in particular, had preached the essentials of functional finance as early as 1931. Cf. J. Viner, "Comment on My 1936 Review," in R. Lekachman, ed., *Keynes' General Theory: Reports of Three Decades*, New York, 1964, pp. 263–64.

naval officers of distinguished experience might burst into print warning against relying on a navy that has not adapted its tactics to modern developments or is riddled with incompetents in high command. Such controversies are bound to surface from time to time—but one cannot expect from such quarters to meet the thesis that Naval Might is Useless.

Nor did Keynes become a renegade from that other time-honored British tradition. He did pose a case against reliance on monetary policy for the pursuit of certain objectives under certain conditions, i.e., for the reversal of a "cumulative" process triggered by a disequilibrium diagnosed as being of a particular type.[2] He did argue that new instruments needed to be added to the traditional armory of Central Banks, i.e., open market operations in long-term and "risky" securities.[3] He did argue that the "tactics" of Central Banks needed revision to cope with the problems of the time and in the light of (his) new theory of the *modus operandi* of monetary policy. And he was an acerbic critic of the performance of central bankers in the late twenties and early thirties.[4] But one does not find the sweeping thesis that monetary policy in general and by its very nature is ineffective.

The later "Keynesian" dogma on this issue was argued in terms of the properties of a static simultaneous equation system. The standard argument makes no reference to past states of the system, nor to a specific historical and political real world context. Thus the conclusions tend to emerge as if they were universally valid: "The interest-elasticity of investment is for various reasons quite low. Hence, monetary policy is not a very useful stabilization instrument." This familiar type of argument does not rely on specific conditions obtaining at a particular time and place. In contrast, when Keynes in 1936 expressed himself "now somewhat sceptical of the success of a merely monetary policy,"[5] he drew on his personal diagnosis of the nature of the

2. Cf. Chapter V:2 and below.

3. Cf. *Treatise*, Chapter 37; *General Theory*, pp. 197, 202–8.

4. Cf., e.g., pp. 285–86, 352n.

5. *General Theory*, p. 164. Compared with the often categorical formulations of later detractors of monetary policy this is weakly worded indeed! Note especially

problems facing Britain in the interwar period and also on his judgments of the kinds of policy that were politically feasible in that context. These time- and place-bound considerations naturally cannot without further ado be invoked in judging the prospective success of monetary measures, say, in the United States of the sixties.

The interest-inelasticity of investment became the pivotal argument in the New Economics position on the issue. As we have repeatedly emphasized, this postulate did not enter into Keynes' analysis at all.[6] The dogma of the interest-inelasticity of expenditures as the bane of monetary policy did not originate in Cambridge but in Oxford.[7]

In Keynes' theory, control over long rate means control over investment and, thereby, money income and employment. From a purely technical standpoint, the potential effectiveness of monetary policy hinges upon how quickly it will be possible to bring long rate to the required level. In Keynes' view, entrepreneurial expectations were exceedingly volatile and subject to sudden, exaggerated shifts, whereas the long rate was "the most stable, and the least easily shifted element in our contemporary economy."[8] In practice, the prospects for a successful monetary policy would depend, in addition, on the Central Bank's ability to diagnose situations quickly and correctly and on its determination in pursuing the requisite policy. This sketches the main considerations discussed by Keynes in both the *Treatise* and the *General Theory*.

Between the *Treatise* and the *General Theory*, Keynes did grow more pessimistic about monetary policy and more insistent on the need for direct governmental measures. But this shift of opinion was very subtle and far from drastic. Two factors com-

---

that Keynes' scepticism concerns an *exclusive* ("merely") reliance on monetary policy.

6. Cf. Chapter III:3.

7. With Keynes, Lavington, Pigou, and Robertson dominating the scene between the wars, it is tempting to say that it "could not have" originated in Cambridge. Stretching our previous analogy, the famous Oxford Surveys appear in retrospect somewhat as "Sandhurst Essays on the Uselessness of Sea Power."

8. *General Theory*, p. 309.

bined in making it seem more dramatic than it really was to his readers.

First, there was the eye-catching change from the modified Quantity Theory framework of the *Treatise* to the multiplier-analysis of the *General Theory*. This switch of the immediate focus of attention from the excess demand for money to the excess supply of commodities (or labor) undoubtedly reinforced the impression that, in the later work, Keynes suddenly scuttled monetary policy. But this, we have argued, did not reflect any basic change in Keynes' views of the processes generating changes in money income and of the role of financial markets in such processes. The Fundamental Equations of the *Treatise* had to be given up because they simply did not serve their original purpose, i.e., to explain the role of changes in relative prices in the monetary transmission mechanism and in income movements generally. Thus, we link Keynes' relinquishing of a monetary approach to income determination to the development of his ideas between the *Tract* and the *Treatise;* it was not related to the main message of the *General Theory* and does not reflect a new-found conviction on Keynes' part that "money is unimportant." [9]

Second, Keynes' reputation outside Britain rested on the *Tract* and the *Treatise*,[10] both works that had dealt almost exclusively with monetary issues. The *Treatise*'s most controversial feature, in fact, had been the thesis that income disequilibria generally had monetary "causes" [11]—for which, consequently, monetary remedies were appropriate. And the *Treatise* had next to nothing to say about fiscal policy. Against this background, therefore, the *General Theory*'s doubts about the prospective efficacy of banking policy and its pleas for public works programs and a "somewhat comprehensive socialization of investment" [12] must have

---

9. Cf. Chapter I:2, pp. 21–23.

10. No doubt *The Economic Consequences of the Peace* was still his most well known book at this time. But we are speaking here of his fame as an economist.

11. "Monetary cause" in the sense that attention was focused on the factors preventing a continous adjustment of market rate to natural rate rather than on the factors responsible for the movements of natural rate.

12. *General Theory*, p. 378.

struck many readers as a dramatic departure on Keynes' part.

In his efforts as a financial journalist in Britain, Keynes had, however, consistently argued for public works ever since 1924.[13] There were two parts to this advocacy. On the one hand, the government was urged to subsidize or directly to undertake investment in certain sectors as a matter of longer-run growth policy. Underlying this recommendation were Keynes' worries about Britain's capital outflow and its implications for domestic long-term investment. In the *Treatise,* this theme received but brief mention—it is significant that it was put under the heading of "International Complications." [14] Following Britain's return to gold at the old parity, maintenance of employment under conditions of an overvalued currency (rather than maintenance of domestic capital-formation for its own sake) became Keynes' chief argument for this policy. On the other hand, he also argued for public works as a supplement to monetary policy in combatting the shorter-run "Credit Cycle." In this context, he saw public works as a "pump-priming" device[15]—i.e., as a means of jolting a temporarily disorganized economy back towards full employment equilibrium, not as a continuing measure needed to close an otherwise inexorable "deflationary gap." Neither of these two cases, therefore, has much in common with the standard textbook "Keynesian" policy prescriptions based on closed-system, comparative static models.

The *General Theory* added very little to this. If Keynes' position in that book appears more radical, this is mainly because the "socialization of investment" was there argued with little explicit reference to the International Complications that had initially prompted him to advance this recommendation. It is hard to judge to what extent this represents anything more than merely the omission of part of the supporting argument.

When dealing with Keynes' views, one must not divorce the

---

13. R. Harrod, *The Life of John Maynard Keynes, op. cit.,* esp. pp. 345–51 and 411–24. Harrod's *Life* is indispensable to anyone seeking to obtain a balanced view of the evolution of Keynes' economic-political views.

14. *Treatise,* Vol. II, p. 376.

15. Cf. his testimony before the Macmillan Committee, as reported in Harrod, *op. cit.,* esp. p. 417.

question of the appropriateness and efficacy of monetary measures from the perceived problem which they are designed to correct. In Chapter V, Keynes' diagnosis of the social malady, for which monetary policy was one of the cures to be considered, was discussed in terms of the relationship between the actual and a hypothetical "equilibrium" price vector. This theme deserves some further consideration.

In general, we have argued, Keynes either assumed that wages were "right" or else recommended that the monetary authority should act "as if" they were. The *Treatise* recognized the possibility that the system might be disequilibrated through "spontaneous" wage-push but really had nothing to say on how to deal with this eventuality.[16] There was, however, one period during which Keynes had to grapple with a situation in which "too high wages" were the crux of the problem, namely the years following Britain's ill-starred relapse to gold at the old parity.[17] In this case, however, "too high wages" translate simply into "overvaluation of currency" and it is therefore of limited relevance in the standard context of the debate over the efficacy of monetary policies which has been that of the closed system. Keynes' first preference was for dealing with the situation by going to a flexible exchange rate. His second, third, etc., preferences are even more revealing, however. When forced to realize that the prospects for flexible rates were nil, Keynes pleaded energetically for the partial socialization of long-term investment and for a protectionist trade policy (although he knew this to be anathema to all his economist friends)—in short for *virtually any scheme that would permit Britain to avoid resort to a policy of high interest rates* [18] and thus, hopefully, to escape the pains of wage-deflation.

---

16. Thus economists who diagnose wage-push or administered price inflation as the chronic problem in the postwar world tend to regard the *General Theory* as an inadequate, if not positively dangerous, guide to the design of present-day policies. Cf. D. McC. Wright, *The Keynesian System,* New York, 1961, Chapter 5, esp. pp. 83–85.

17. Harrod, *op. cit.,* esp. p. 411.

18. The present U.S. interest-equalization scheme would have been just the thing!

The general problem, consequently, was "too low" demand prices for augmentable assets. We have distinguished two possible reasons for such a state of affairs: the long rate of interest may be too high, or entrepreneurial demand forecasts may be unduly pessimistic. It is helpful at this point to consider separately the problem of maintaining a high level of activity and forestalling a downturn and the problem of engineering a recovery from a depressed situation.[19]

Keynes saw the problem of preventing a downturn essentially as one of ensuring that the "right" rate of interest will prevail. This is the problem which should be the normal task of the monetary authorities and the problem to which the *Treatise* was primarily devoted—as previously noted, the bulk of that book presumes that entrepreneurial expectations are roughly right. The normative force of the main prescription of the *Treatise* derives from this assumption.[20] If expectations are not approximately right, there is nothing "natural" about the natural rate. The recommendation that the monetary authority cause market rate to move in such a manner as to maintain the demand prices for augmentable assets inherited from last period, presumes that this long rate will generally be an "equilibrium" rate. Whenever, in a high employment situation, investment starts to rise or fall, thereby threatening inflation or deflation, the *Treatise* treats this as evidence of an inappropriate level of market rate.

Consequently, the appropriate cure consists of a monetary policy designed to correct market rate. It was this presumption that Hayek attacked in criticizing the *Treatise*'s neglect of "real" causes of business fluctuations. Keynes' hypothesis about the cause of downturns rules out the possibility that the equilibra-

---

19. By the time Keynes was writing the *General Theory*, Britain was again off gold, and the constraints due to "International Complications" discussed at length in the *Treatise* were no longer relevant. Nor, therefore, are they relevant to the question of why Keynes became more pessimistic about the prospects for successful monetary policies and so we will be concerned, in what follows, solely with the closed-system arguments.

20. And this assumption is also the chief limitation of the book's policy program —the problem posed is simply too easy for its solution to be very helpful. Cf. Chapter V:2, pp. 349–50.

tion of the system might require transition to a rate of investment substantially lower than that prevailing in the boom. His views, therefore, flew in the face of the widespread contemporary opinion that the causes of depression were normally to be found in the "excesses" of the preceding boom. It is significant that the *Treatise*'s outright rejection of the entire class of "overinvestment" theories was not at all tempered in the *General Theory* [21] for the American school of "Keynesian Stagnationists" was later on to popularize the view that the investment levels of the 1920's could not possibly have been sustained.[22] Naturally, this doctrine had to deny that investment could have been maintained simply by "monetary" machinations. And it was in the intellectual atmosphere of stagnationism that the dogma of the inefficacy of monetary policy first emerged and came to prosper.

The stagnationists, of course, claimed Keynes among their intellectual forebears. The *General Theory* did indeed give considerable space to speculations on the problem of maintaining full employment in a system approaching a state of capital saturation. These referred, however, to a hypothetical and far distant future—to the environment that might (in the absence of substantial technological progress) result from a generation or two of continuously high rates of investment. In such a state, the marginal efficiency of capital would also have crept below the margin necessary to cover lender's risk and the cost of financial intermediation. Thus, Keynes' concession that the Liquidity Trap "might become important in the future." [23]

Keynes himself never advanced this not altogether respectable piece of science-fiction as a diagnosis of the 1930's. The interpretation of the contemporary situation as one characterized by lack of "outlets for saving" and as an illustration of the static Liquidity Trap came into Keynesian economics with Alvin Hansen and

---

21. Cf., esp., *General Theory*, pp. 320–24, 326–29.

22. Compare *General Theory*, p. 323: "It would be *absurd* to assert of the United States in 1929 the existence of over-investment in the strict sense." (italics added)

23. *General Theory*, p. 207. In 1936, as previously noted, Keynes still knew "no example of it hitherto."

others. This is not to deny that Keynes looked forward to an indefinite period of, at best, unrelenting deflationary pressure and that he painted it in colors not many shades brighter than the gloomy hues of the stagnationist picture. But these stagnationist fears were based on propositions that must be stated in terms of time-derivatives. Modern economies, he believed, were such that, at a full employment rate of investment, the marginal efficiency of capital would always tend to fall *more rapidly* [24] than the long rate of interest. Put forward as an inherent tendency of capitalistic civilization, this chronic disparity between the two time-derivatives seems a doubtful proposition. But it sums up a considerable proportion of the passages in which Keynes vented his later doubts on the efficacy of monetary policy.

As we have repeatedly emphasized, Keynes held very strong views on the inflexibility of long rate. When he states that the long rate "may fluctuate *for decades* about a level which is chronically too high" [25] one should no doubt see this in the historical context of the "obstinate maintenance of misguided monetary policies" [26] of which he steadily complained. Still, the conviction shines through everywhere in his writings that the long rate will only come down at a most excruciatingly slow pace even in the absence of perverse monetary policies. This assumes a general wrong-headedness, obstinacy, and power on part of an ever-present "Bear army" that is, at least, implausible. To Keynes, apparently, every decline in the demand price for, and in the rate of output of, augmentable capital goods that had ever occurred represented evidence in favor of this view. But it cannot be accepted as such for there is nothing to warrant the underlying theoretical presumption that the "true" equilibrium rate of interest always is whatever rate it would take to bring about a full employment rate of investment.[27]

According to Keynes' diagnosis of the situation between the

---

24. *General Theory*, e.g., pp. 219, 228.
25. *General Theory*, p. 204, italics added.
26. *Treatise*, Vol. II, p. 384.
27. We return to this point once more below, p. 415.

wars, a continuous decline in the marginal efficiency of capital should be the natural course of events. The postulated tendency for market rate to lag behind meant an ever-present threat to full employment. Over the longer term, consequently, the task facing policy-makers was to ensure that market rate kept pace with the downward trend of natural rate so that a serious downturn could be avoided.

In the *Treatise*, there is no question but that the monetary authority can do it—if it only keeps at it continuously. A steady chastisement of bearish speculators might be needed but, in pure principle, the banking system "can by the terms of credit influence *to any required extent* the volume of investment." [28] This does not mean that the technical execution of the required policy will be an easy task: "we have *not* claimed that the banking system can produce any of these effects instantaneously; or that it can be expected always to foresee the operation of non-monetary factors in time . . ." [29] Whereas Keynes had no doubts of the interest-elasticity of investment, he did recognize "an appreciable time-lag" [30] between changes in long rates and changes in the rate of output of capital goods. Little can be done about this lag, however, and the one that mainly concerned him, therefore, was that inherent in the traditional Bank rate *cum* Bills Only mode of Central Bank operation. One of the reforms most emphatically urged in the *Treatise* was thus that the monetary authority should operate directly in the long end of the market —a recommendation echoed in the *General Theory's* complaint that Central Banks were wont to "leave the price of long-term debts to be influenced by belated and imperfect reactions from the price of short-term debts." [31]

The argument of the *Treatise* taken as a whole definitely leads to the conclusion that a "merely monetary" stabilization policy is theoretically *feasible*—if not practically advisable, for we know that its author during the same period publicly argued for various

---

28. *Treatise*, Vol. II, p. 346, italics added.
29. *Loc. cit.*
30. *Treatise*, Vol. I, p. 364.
31. *General Theory*, p. 206.

measures to supplement monetary policy. Keynes' precondition for success, naturally, was a Central Bank accepting his unconventional views of what could be done, of what should be done, and of how to go about doing it in concrete instances. This precondition was, of course, not fulfilled. By the time of the *General Theory*, Keynes had every reason to be less sanguine about the prospects for a successful monetary policy. His membership on the Macmillan Committee had given him the best possible platform from which to press his reforms on the authorities—but he had found them unwilling to listen.[32] This, perhaps, was not unnatural. Keynes' ideas were unconventional in an area of endeavor where men in authority are chosen on solid reputations for conventional wisdom. And acceptance of Keynes' views of a Central Bank's potential power to control events would have meant the acceptance of a frightful psychological burden of responsibility for the actual course of events.

If the *General Theory*, therefore, was pessimistic on monetary policy and seemed to urge "socialization of investment" as wellnigh the only salvation from depression, this reflected Keynes' mid-thirties views not only of what a Central Bank can do but also of what the Bank of England could be made to do [33]—in what proportions, we will perhaps never know. It should be remembered, however, that the *General Theory* castigated as *"dangerously and unnecessarily defeatist"* the notion that even "the *most enlightened* monetary control might find itself in difficulties . . . [such that] none of the alternatives within its power might make much difference to the result." [34]

The question of the effectiveness of monetary policy in depression remains to be considered. Here, asset demand prices are too low because entrepreneurial demand forecasts are attuned to a

---

32. Harrod, *op. cit.*, pp. 413 ff.

33. Critical as Keynes was of Central Bankers, he was also temperamentally loth to admit that Reason might not triumph in the end and his fundamental optimism breaks through also in the *General Theory*: "Recently, practical bankers in London have learnt much, and one can almost hope that in Great Britain the technique of bank rate will never be used again to protect the foreign balance . . ." (*op. cit.*, p. 339)—on which it is superfluous to comment.

34. *General Theory*, p. 327, italics added.

continuing slump. To restore a full employment rate of investment by "merely" monetary policy, market rate has then to be
brought down much further than would be needed if entrepreneurial expectations had not already been adversely affected. In
the *Treatise,* the problem of engineering a recovery is treated as
different in degree, but not in kind, from that of preventing a
downturn. Thus the prescription was not so much a different
policy as more of the same—a "saturation" dosage of open
market purchases.

Keynes' emergency proposal for a "monetary policy *à outrance,*" as we have seen,[35] obliges the Central Bank to pursue a
course which will generate losses both for itself and for speculators naive enough to take their cues from the authorities. The
clearest illustration involves the special case where the under-
valuation of assets is due entirely to the pessimism of entrepreneurs whereas the actually prevailing long rate is exactly the one
which would enter into a hypothetical full information state
information vector. The holders of securities are right and entrepreneurs wrong—so the policy recommended is one of dragging
the righteous through purgatory for the salvation of the un-
believer.

Surely, the case for relying on monetary policy in such circumstances is not a strong one. The longer-run consequences of
following the *Treatise's* suggestion make it even less so, for the
policy will be harder and harder to execute every time it is tried.
Keynes' bond-holders are notable for long memory and the learning experience afforded by a systematic Central Bank pattern of
buying high and selling low would not be lost on them: Those
who collaborate are rewarded with losses, those who operate
against the Bank make profits.

The alternative would be a policy of government deficit spending designed to "correct" entrepreneurial demand forecasts.
Direct expenditures on commodities will prevent the self-
fulfillment of pessimistic prophecies. By falsifying the forecasts,
a rise in asset values should be obtained without forcing down

---

35. Cf. Chapter V:2, pp. 348–49.

the market rate of interest.[36] This is the basic "pump-priming" case, for as full employment is approached the government spending program may be phased out without reopening a "deflationary gap" and throwing the system back into depression. Keynes' Macmillan Committee testimony was explicit on the transitory nature of the injections he deemed needed in order to cope with the "Credit Cycle":

Government investment will break the vicious circle. . . . I believe you have first of all to do something to restore profits and then rely on private enterprise to carry the thing along.[37]

Further reflection on the problem posed by a situation in which entrepreneurial expectations have been seriously eroded may well have contributed significantly to Keynes' new-found favor, in the *General Theory*, for fiscal pump-priming over the monetary policy *à outrance* advocated in the *Treatise*. But the *General Theory* does not carry the systematic analysis of the problem beyond the point reached at the end of the *Treatise*. The issues were left in an uncomfortably unresolved state. The diatribe on bear speculation in Chapter 12 of the *General Theory* would seem to indicate, in fact, that Keynes still regarded "too high" a rate of interest as the basic trouble in all depressed situations. His many comments on the inflexibility of long rate generally fail to distinguish between the two alternative problems of bringing the rate *down to* its "true" equilibrium level and of forcing it *below* the warranted level.

Unlike later Keynesians, Keynes never became "defeatist" on the potential efficacy of a monetary policy conducted according

---

36. In this particular instance, the government deficit need be financed through expansion of the money supply only to the extent required to prevent a rise in long rate.

37. Quoted by Harrod, *op. cit.*, p. 417.

Keynes' views on countercyclical pump-priming should be carefully distinguished from the other parts of his fiscal policy program. He recommended *continuing* government intervention to deal with the possible future threat of stagnation and, in particular, with the long-term consequences of being committed to maintaining an over-valued currency.

to his own prescriptions. If he appears optimistic in comparison with his followers, however, this is in part because he did not carry the analysis to its logical conclusions. In Keynes' world, "The real prospects do not suffer such large and quick changes as does the spirit of enterprise." [38] Holders of long-term securities are well advised to pay heed to the real prospects rather than to the evanescent spirits of enterprise (or to the pursuit of "Snap, Old Maid, and Musical Chairs"). When they do, the monetary authority will find Keynes' prescriptions hard to fill. These limitations on the usefulness of monetary measures Keynes never made clear. Thus, a more "pessimistic" appraisal of monetary policy can be made on terms that are entirely consistent with Keynes' own theory and without relying on the assumption of interest-inelasticity of expenditures which he did not accept.

Clearly, however, this could not amount to a rehabilitation of the early "revolutionary" view which denigrated the "importance" as much as the "effectiveness" of monetary policy. It is *not* a case for the general uselessness of monetary policy. On the contrary, the analysis makes clear the great power for good or evil that monetary policy must have within Keynes' theoretical framework. The main prescription of the *Treatise* is not affected by the finding that there are conditions to the correction of which fiscal measures are better fitted than monetary measures. It is still as vital as ever that the Central Bank act vigorously so as to hold market rate continuously in the near neighborhood of an appropriately defined "natural rate."

The upshot of all this is that the monetary authority ought itself to take the Long View and not use its powers in efforts to counter every temporary change in "business conditions" and employment.[39]

---

38. *Treatise*, Vol. II, p. 362.

39. We have previously cited this as the long-held position of Professor R. S. Sayers. In the United States, Professor Friedman is the most well-known proponent of this view. Cf., esp., his Presidential Address to the American Economic Association, "The Role of Monetary Policy," *American Economic Review*, March 1968. Friedman's analysis, of course, differs from that of Keynes in focusing upon the money stock, rather than the long rate, as the target of Central Bank action.

INDEX OF SUBJECTS

INDEX OF NAMES